18.99

The Suburb of Dissent

City and Islington Sixth Form College
Learning Centre
The Angel 283-309 Goswell Road
London EC1V 7LA
T: 020 7520 0652
E: sfclib@candi.ac.uk

CITY AND ISLINGTON
COLLEGE

This item is due for return on or before the date last stamped below. You may renew by telephone, email or online. Please quote your student ID if renewing by phone.

Fine: 5p per day

CPD6017

D1382105

New Americanists   A Series Edited by Donald E. Pease

THE SUBURB OF DISSENT

Cultural Politics in the United States and Canada during the 1930s

Caren Irr

Duke University Press   Durham and London   1998

© 1998 Duke University Press

All rights reserved

Printed in the United States of America on acid-free paper ⊗

Typeset in Stone Serif and Sans by Tseng Information Systems, Inc.

Library of Congress Cataloging-in-Publication Data appear on the last

printed page of this book.

... where should we find shelter

For joy or mere content

When little was left standing

But the suburb of dissent?

W. H. Auden, 1950

CONTENTS

ACKNOWLEDGMENTS

I have relied on the assistance and advice of many teachers, colleagues, and friends while writing this book. I would especially like to thank Cathy N. Davidson, who directed the dissertation on which this project is based. Her encouragement and savvy were invaluable. Many thanks also to Fredric Jameson, John H. Thompson, Arnold E. Davidson, Eve Kosofsky Sedgwick, and Larry Goodwyn. Paul Buhle, the anonymous reader, and Evan Watkins also generously read the entire manuscript and I appreciate their comments and queries.

I'd also like to thank the Canada-U.S. Fulbright Foundation, the Canadian Embassy, the Center for International Studies at Duke University, and the Research and Graduate Studies Office at the Pennsylvania State University for funding portions of my research. Staffs of the libraries at Duke University, the Pennsylvania State University, the University of Winnipeg, the University of Toronto, the University of Alberta, and McGill University were of immense assistance.

Other immensely helpful readers include members of the cultural studies reading group at Penn State, Mary Chapman and the American Studies reading group at the University of Alberta, and members of the Marxist reading group at Duke. Lise Favreau, Will Lowen, Olga Favreau, and James Everett made trips to Canada pleasurable as well as possible. David Richardson gave support for which I remain grateful. Ken Wissoker and Richard Morrison have patiently answered my questions about the publishing process. Finally, I would like to dedicate this book to my parents, Joe and Mickey.

INTRODUCTION

This study of the cultural politics of the 1930s begins explicitly where many others have begun implicitly—in the polarized climate of the Cold War. Several years ago, I came across the following anecdote from that conflict, and reading it clarified the complex situation of Depression-era writers. The formative features of 30s culture, I concluded, were not the automatic result of a dangerously un-American interest in Communist ideology, as so many have suggested; instead, it was in local attempts to address their peers that the 30s literary left adopted the gestures that now appear to be so habitual, so essential and necessary to their group identity.

At least, this is what Simone de Beauvoir suggests. In *America Day by Day,* a diary describing her travels through the United States during the late 1940s, Beauvoir reveals various sources of her transatlantic culture shock. She remarks on her surprise that everyone at American parties remains standing throughout the evening and notes her discomfort with the Hollywood-style facades of small-town storefronts. Although she had not expected café banter and picturesque villages, the sordid character of American life shocked her. Furthermore, she was surprised to find that the American writers who described that sordid character—writers admired in France at the time—were roundly condemned by the American intellectuals with whom she came into contact, and especially by those clustered around the influential journal *Partisan Review.* The names Steinbeck, Dahlberg, Caldwell, Dos Passos, and Wright brought invective to the lips of these New York intellectuals. The problem, she soon discovered, had partly to do with national culture and partly to do with political culture. U.S. intellectuals of the late 1940s staunchly defended their right to define American culture for themselves, and they refused to believe that French intellectuals' taste for hard-boiled naturalism had any more credibility than their later and equally suspicious enthusiasm for Jerry Lewis. At the same time, the *Partisan Review* group was especially eager to disavow the writers Beauvoir named, since many of these same critics had at one time loudly praised the naturalists' virtues; as Beauvoir puts it, "they had a violent hatred for Stalinism which made me realize that they had once been Stalinists."[1]

In other words, for Beauvoir, discovering American intellectual life meant discovering the paradoxes of anti-Communism. For her, national and political cultures were so intertwined that decoding one necessarily involved examining the other. Recognizing this entanglement, Beauvoir came to use sophisticated interpretive tools on the most casual of utterances. As an outsider to the closed system of American culture, she found that she needed to reconstruct the historical situation she was entering before making sense of the judgments offered to her during dinner-table conversation. She found she could understand the significance of statements being made to (and about) her only when she also understood the ways these statements negated other unstated and opposite statements. Once she began to attend to this chorus of inverted echoes, she could interpret the *Partisan Review* writers' curious hostility to naturalism as a response to that group's cultural and political situation.

For this study, Beauvoir's description of her revelation has been instructive. First of all, her anecdote highlights the cohesiveness of the literary left. Like other subcultures, the 30s left was unified by certain tricks of speech and ideologemes, and observing this culture from a distance—reading it, as it were, through Beauvoir's eyes—makes these characteristic phrases and intellectual habits all the more visible. At the same time, Beauvoir's anecdote makes it absolutely clear that hers is a postwar view of the 1930s; she does not allow her readers to forget that, in the mouths of the post–World War II intellectuals who have so strongly influenced our understanding of American literary history, "the 1930s" was not the name for a historical period also known as the Depression, but rather a political shorthand for Communism, socialism, or "Stalinism." Like Beauvoir, then, I have adopted the practice of equating a time period with an ideology because it introduces an interesting synecdoche. Although recognition of this practice was suppressed by persons such as Beauvoir's Cold War dining companions who habitually defined "America" as inherently and necessarily anti-Communist, at times they, too, allowed a dissenting part to stand for the whole. In the history of the 1930s and 1960s, left politics have been central to the definition of an "American" culture. The resulting tensions between center and periphery, America and communism have been crucial to the reputation and project of the writers of the 1930s.

Since the situation of the 1930s was itself complex, the method by which one approaches the period would also need to be sensitive to contradiction. For this reason, like Beauvoir, I have found it absolutely necessary to contextualize statements made about (and in) the 30s literary scene before drawing conclusions about their significance. Like Beauvoir, I have reconstructed debates surrounding famous statements frequently used to summarize what happened during the 1930s. Broadly speaking, this is a synthetic approach; I have chosen statements or texts and attempted to discover the persons or positions with whom they were in dialogue during the 1930s. I have asked whether they addressed other leftists or a more distant middlebrow audience, or whether the author was rallying intellectuals against journalists, or vice versa. In these contextualizations, however, my goal has not been to place particular texts ever more precisely in the endless internal schisms of the 30s left; rather, I have sought to identify and step back from these schismatic dialogues. My readings of texts from different locations in leftist culture emphasize the continuities of that culture across time and party factions. Throughout, this study suggests that dialogues within a text reformulate those taking place in the larger culture. Often at both levels these conversations reveal the contestable nature of categories that may appear fixed from a late-twentieth-century vantage point. For instance, as we've seen, in Beauvoir's companions' bald-faced rejection of "Stalinist" writers—a statement that could easily be read as simply anti-Communist—we can identify a dialogue with the speakers' youthful, "Stalinist" selves, and, more generally, a conversation with contemporaneous late 40s concepts of American culture.[2] In turn, this doubled use of "Stalinism" contributed to the sociopolitical process that helped the defensively anti-Communist American culture of the 1940s and 1950s define itself as a privileged site of ideological openness. This is the kind of interpretation this study seeks to produce; at both the textual and cultural levels, my goal is to render defensive monologues, like the rejection of "Stalinist" writers, multivocal.

The dialogue at the heart of *The Suburb of Dissent,* then, is between "America" and "Communism"; overall, this study maintains that America/Communism is one of the most powerful ideological oppositions of the twentieth century and that its components are irretrievably entangled with one another. Because such a wealth of discursive work has been aimed at rigidly distinguish-ing Americanness from Communist totalitarianism (and vice versa), these two positions are now most comprehensible in their opposition. Used together so often in contradiction, they accrue significance precisely because they are op-posed to one another. The way we use the terms "America" and "Communism" has contributed greatly to their meaning.

When examining the ways that patterns of usage have made these two terms mutually constitutive, it will be important for us to recognize that both "America" and "Communism" contain numerous tensions and contradictions. As so much recent work in American Studies and American literary criticism has demonstrated, the sign "America" names both a multicultural nation and a multinational culture; it is, at once, the flag flying over a composite of racial and ethnic cultures and the hemispheric label for a bloc of nations bound together by the processes of imperialism. Although these two referents are most definitely incongruent, each continues to make sense to a sizable audi-ence. We all understand that, at times, "America" means the United States and that, at other times, it describes the diasporic European cultural history shared by most New World nations. And, increasingly, this commonsensical differen-tiation of meanings on the basis of context is finding theoretical articulation. Increasingly often, cultural critics are investigating the ways that the character and extent of the U.S. nation differs from that of American culture, and often the sign "America" is used to label the thus far irresolvable stress between the categories of nation and culture. In the field of American Studies, in particu-lar, referring to the fictive national and cultural unity of "America" has become one way of setting its fractures.[3]

In this era of post-Communist triumphalism, however, it is less frequently acknowledged that, just as tensions strain the sign "America," the sign "Com-munism" also has multiple and conflicting referents. In various contexts, this sign refers to an ideology, a political practice, an intellectual method, a mid-twentieth-century multinational formation, and a set of subcultural social values.[4] Furthermore, within each of these usages, we can identify variations, conflicts, and disturbances. Of course, part of the success of "American" ide-ology in the United States has been to render the detailed history of such variation or schism-forming dull, even seemingly trivial in the face of the overwhelming foreignness of the whole Communist enterprise. But, without straining too hard against this deeply etched problem of attention span, we should be able to recognize that the significance of the "Communist" sign has been at least as thoroughly contested *from within* as the American one. In fact, I would argue that at certain historical moments it was exactly the stressful non-synchronicity of the various referents for "Communism" that made this sign so potent. Limiting ourselves to the 1930s, we find that converts to Communist political ideology often describe the powerful appeal of subcultural communalism, while, conversely, gaps between the principles of internationalism and the official Party's cynical geopolitical maneuvers often helped to disillusion persons who desired a holistic, unified Communism.[5] Like "America," then, the "Communist" ideologeme often operates because of (not in spite of) the lack of fit among its parts. Just as there are many Americanisms, there are many communisms.

Although it is important to point to the recurrent stresses within each ideological formation, in the pages that follow, I do not propose to examine either the Communist or American ideologeme in isolation. Instead, *The Suburb of Dissent* examines one site where the ideologemes of America and Communism overlapped and became mutually constitutive: the literary culture of the North American left during the 1930s. During this decade, several forms of Communism had their greatest appeal for American literary intellectuals—many of whom also became prominent spokespersons for a Communist Party–sponsored form of cultural nationalism. Early in the decade they wrote literary histories extolling an American tradition of revolutionary spirit, and later they ran Party candidates for office under the now-nonsensical slogan "Communism Is Twentieth-Century Americanism." In turn, this version of Communist Americanism was paralleled by an Americanization of Communism; although officially internationalist, the left cultural politics of this decade were strongly inflected by their national circumstances. A prominent concern with consumer culture and a tendency to conceptualize particular authors as pioneers or rugged individualists are only two of the many so-called American themes one might locate in U.S. Communist circles of the 1930s. I will be examining the ways in which these and other combinations ultimately resulted in important ideological and generic hybrids. The hybrids I look at most closely—literary histories, proletarian novels, and written documentaries—did not comb out all the ideological tangles of that decade, but they explored and made use of the oddities of their liminal position between American anti-Communism and Communist anti-Americanism.

In most cultural criticism concerned with the 1930s, these hybrid forms do not fare well. For two generations, critics have chastised the writers of the 1930s for supposedly obsessively sponsoring a doomed aesthetic and prohibiting experimentation, though more recently, post–Cold War scholarship has argued that the literary culture of the 1930s, while still less than ideal, was considerably less uniform, predictable, and coercive than earlier criticism of the period maintained.[6] Building on these revisionist studies of particular genres, figures, and subject positions, then, I will argue that the North American leftist culture of the 1930s was less foreign to contemporary concerns than we might imagine; specifically, 30s internationalism involved rethinking the internal and external boundaries of national culture. Its writers and writings crisscrossed national borders; they formed coalitions, established patterns of influence, and promoted forms of cultural distribution that altered and exceeded the categories of national culture. These activities suggest that, in W. H. Auden's phrase, the leftist attempts to use culture politically during the 1930s did not simply result in propaganda authored by the Soviet Comintern, but rather built a "suburb of dissent": the 30s literary left was a distinct community of its own, located on the margins of the larger culture of labor, but organized internally according to its own dynamics. In a territory somewhere between the mainstream urban intellectuals and a version of "the people" imagined as being rural, 30s left-wing writers occupied a liminal zone. They settled in the conceptual equivalent of the suburb, and this suburb became a unique cultural formation clearly marked by its inhabitants' continuing commitment to dissent.

To complete the metaphor, then, this study attempts an ethnography of "the suburb of dissent." I have assembled an account of the cultural practices of this suburb in an effort to identify its inhabitants' characteristic habits and gestures. I argue that these were developed in order to negotiate simultaneously Communist and American ideologies. Examining such practices will, I hope, reveal something about how a group of writers coped with the ongoing stresses of their opposition to dominant culture, as well as suggesting something more general about the role of subcultures in synecdochally setting goals for the culture at large.

Transnational Culture and American Studies, or Why Canada?

If academic publishing did not already have a well-established convention for using epigraphs that suggest, by their distance from the subject of the text, the supposed universality of one's themes, it might seem odd that I have taken the title of my contribution to American Studies from a poem by Auden, a self-exiled Englishman. In fact, I would be pleased if this choice seemed odd, since it is exactly this type of question about relations between national cultures that I hope to raise. One of the central themes of this study is the argument that the culture of the 1930s, that is, the "suburb of dissent," was transnational, and I intend this metaphor linking suburbs and transnationalism quite seriously. After all, like suburbs, transnational cultures are distinctively modern formations;[7] they are hybrids that increasingly occupy the spaces of the homogenous nation. They blur the boundaries between nations, much as suburban sprawl blurs and renders strictly formal the boundaries between urban centers such as Baltimore and Washington, D.C. Also, like suburbs, transnational cultures have often been considered bastard or devolutionary cultures. I am reminded of the film *The Gods Must Be Crazy,* in which a Kalahari bushman with no previous contact with European cultures finds a Coca-Cola bottle that was thrown from a plane. The narrative of the film, like many liberal and conservative critical responses to issues of cultural preservation, suggests that this contact between "traditional" societies and the modern, capitalist world-system produces a loss. For instance, in the film, the bushman's entry into the city, to return the bottle, is posited as a loss of innocence and cultural authenticity. The parallels between this mode of thought and Menckenesque urban intellectuals' ridicule of suburban Babbittry are very strong. To a certain kind of thinker, the suburbs have consistently represented the contamination of rural innocence by ignorant, debased imitations of big-city culture. This kind of scorn for the hybrids replacing authentic, local culture is an important common element in the way we have learned to talk about both the suburbs and transnational cultures.

Furthermore, it is no coincidence that one of the most vicious attacks on the middlebrow character of suburban intellectual life was voiced by the liberal anti-Stalinists associated with *Partisan Review* in the 1940s and 1950s. The cultural life of the suburbs had, to some New York noses, the same stench of monotonous conformity that totalitarianism did, and the only alternative was, to borrow the title of one of their famous symposia, "Our Country and Our Culture."[8] Although postmodern tastes find much of interest in the simulated world of suburbia and the smorgasbord of transnationalism, both of these formations seemed threatening to an earlier generation of intellectuals reared on literary traditions of a more strictly metropolitan, national character. The assumption that culture was local and coherent, like an island, rather than fluid and dynamic, like a body of water, strongly influenced modern, modernist taste.

Of course, the *Partisan Review*–ers were not alone in their dislike for hybrids. Their assumption that a unified and distinct national entity was the basis of cultural achievement also permeated the early postwar projects of American Studies. As a number of commentators have pointed out, most of the influential works of American Studies written during the 1940s and 1950s attempted to uncover what the authors saw as myths central to the American (read, U.S.) mind or the American social contract. They examined themes that commonly appeared in American cultural products, such as the virgin land, or the machine in the garden, or the American Adam. The underlying idea was that art, literature, and popular culture express archetypes that draw a disparate nation together into consensus, and the problem, as many have come to see it, with this consensus approach is that, although it was path-breaking in its interdisciplinary study and generative of important historicist readings of American culture, it tended to paper over conflicts within the consensus. Accounts like R. W. B. Lewis's *American Adam* described a mythic substructure of the culture and deemphasized the ways that myth was contested by particular regions, classes, races, etc. They emphasized the ideal unity of the culture and downplayed the actual strife within the nation.[9]

Following from this school of thought, and responding to varying degrees against it, has been what we might call the multiculturalist version of American Studies. Scholars of this persuasion concentrate on internal groupings within the United States as more or less representative of the divisions marking American culture as a whole. For instance, Jane Tompkins's important study of nineteenth-century sentimental fiction, *Sensational Designs,* argues that our current identification of a canon of major American writers was shaped by the gender relations of nineteenth-century literary culture; she concludes that contemporary projects might find so-called sentimental women writers at least as interesting as the canonical men. In work like Tompkins's, the *division* of power between men and women who write is the primary subject, with concern for unifying themes becoming secondary. Of course, this kind of work has been tremendously important in drawing attention to certain minority literatures (including working-class and left-wing writers), and the methods of reading against the grain of earlier criticism that scholars such as Tompkins demonstrate have had a salutary effect on cultural studies generally. Nonetheless, the multiculturalist project does produce some new questions. In particular, the emphasis on divisions within a culture introduces queries about the significance of the category of nation. We need only consider the vast popularity (in the United States) of the 1990–91 Persian Gulf military adventures to remember that nationalism, patriotism, and republicanism continue to play an important role in the experience of American culture, despite the presence of a quite advanced rhetoric about internal divisions within the nation. This observation has led some to ask whether national culture is always the work of dominant groups and whether it, too, displays traces of the cultural contests that underlie it. These questions have been central to the field of postcolonial studies.

In Americanist circles, however, postcolonialism has not meant what it does in British studies—the renewed consideration of the cultural history of imperialism, colonial rule, resistance movements, and their torturous efforts to forge independent cultures in a global context. Instead, Americanists have usually focused on immigration, ethnicity, and border cultures, with the emphasis falling on the ways that these formations reveal disruptions in the fictive unity of the nation.[10] This emphasis, of course, does not mean that the United States has not had formal and informal colonies—such as Puerto Rico, Guam, the Philippines, and parts of Samoa—whose postnational resistance movements can be examined, but rather that, for historical reasons, there has been greater interest in the colonies that lie within and across U.S. borders.

One of the most important concepts deriving from postcolonial studies of the Americas is the "contact zone." Forcefully articulated and applied in *Imperial Eyes,* Mary Louise Pratt's study of eighteenth-century travel writing, the concept of the contact zone names an arena in which two or more cultures meet and come into conflict such that each alters in response to the other; it is the site of a transvaluation of cultures. Like Nietzsche's transvaluation of values in *Beyond Good and Evil,* then, this concept offers a way of thinking about cultural contact as a process of mutual redefinition, rather than one-sided imposition or a strictly binary opposition. In the contact zone, both the imperializer and the imperialized arrive at a new self-definition as a result of the sight of one another.

An attractive feature of this concept is its emphasis on actually existing cultural formations. Pratt does not describe what should or should not have happened during the eighteenth century; she sets about finding categories to describe what did and does happen. Clearly, the early European exploration of the Americas changed European, as well as indigenous peoples, and postcolonialists' use of the term "contact" highlights the mutuality of this complex process, thereby enabling a new kind of cultural history to be written. An example might help clarify the difference made by this shift of attention. In *The Road from Coorain,* an engaging autobiography of growing up Australian, Jill Ker Conway explains the way one's immediate environment can be eclipsed in a postcolonial context. She describes how, as an Aussie schoolgirl, despite her geographical situation, imperial cartography dictated that she locate Turkey in the Near East, while nearby Indonesia belonged in the Far East category. Only as an adult did her study of American history help her to triangulate this colonial legacy; by way of some early American Studies texts she began to understand what was uniquely Australian about her surroundings. This description of learning how to unlearn, of learning how to reorient your map of culture toward your current site—this seems to me to be the most valuable aspect of the new American Studies. In the spirit of cultural materialism, it emphasizes the borders we experience continually and seeks concepts to describe them.

As noted above, though, most New Americanist studies of borderlands have focused on the southern border.[11] Fueled in part by Chicana/o pride movements of the 1960s and 1970s, many Americanists have made important strides toward theorizing and historicizing the development of Mexican/American cultural hybrids. However, perhaps because the large numbers of immigrants at the northern border of the United States are usually not distinguishable by language or skin color, relatively little attention has been paid in the United States to the U.S./Canadian border and the cultural conflicts characteristic of this zone.[12] In fact, as my research on this relationship progressed, I have become increasingly aware of the ways that, in the United States, we habitually disregard the Canadian border. For instance, U.S. meteorologists typically draw weather maps that outline only the United States, subdividing it into states and sketching its high and low pressure points. But above the forty-ninth parallel, nothing legible appears—just a blank Arctic desert from which ominous cold fronts occasionally descend. This practice suggests that, for all intents and purposes, Canada is just not present in the U.S. imagination. Unlike Mexico, which in the public culture of the United States at least has the questionable ap-

Figure 1 The borders of North American culture are regularly redrawn, as Douglas Coupland's map in the October 21, 1992 *New York Times* reminds us.

peal of exoticism, Canada does not have a label of marked difference attached to it; in the United States, Canada is a blank space, ideologically speaking.

This situation is especially apparent when you take up one of the favorite topics of Canadian commentators on Canada—the question of nationhood. In the United States, the only issue that brings the Canadian nation to the fore is the possibility of its disintegration; Quebecois separatism alone, with its faint twinges of Latin exoticism, spotlights Canadian national culture in the U.S. media. It is primarily as a sign under the threat of erasure that Canada makes sense as a nation in U.S. popular culture. I am reminded on this matter of a map published by Canadian novelist Douglas Coupland on the *New York Times* op-ed page on the eve of a 1992 referendum concerning Quebec's status as a distinct society (fig. 1).[13] Proposing to represent Canada and the United States in the year 2092, the map shows a North American continent divided into regions of cultural and corporate influence: The territory of the United States has been reduced to a United States of America extending north through the maritime provinces, west to the Rocky Mountains, and south to its border with the nations of Dixie and Texlahoma. Similarly, Canada has been divided into Cascadia (a western conglomerate of Alaska, British Columbia, Washington, and Oregon), a Canadian Loyalist Coalition of prairie provinces, a northern indigenous peoples' nation called Nunavat, an Ontario Republic, and, of course, Quebec—complete with a Bilingual Buffer Corridor. Undoubtedly, Coupland's point here is to parody the nationalist anxiety provoked by the specter of Quebec separatism—revealing it as (*a*) a sort of sci-fi horror story, and (*b*) operating in denial of the clearly marked regional differences already in existence. Now, one might expect that issues like those Coupland raises would appeal to those who oppose nationalism *a priori*.[14] One might think that the oddities of a nation like Canada, a nation always poised on the brink of postnationalism, would have a certain conceptual attraction for such thinkers. But to date this has rarely been the case in the United States. For the most part, the New Americanists' suspicion of nationalism has foreclosed the possibility of their examining the influence of nationalism and concepts of national culture at this site.

In my project, then, I have attempted to address the issues of nationalism and the U.S./Canadian border by drawing on the insights of postcolonial and New Americanist work. I have sought to question the implicit American exceptionalism of American Studies by including Canadian materials and discussion of the role of the U.S./Canadian border in my study, and I have paid attention to nationalism and tried not to subsume Canadian culture into a "North American" framework. After all, U.S. and Canadian political and literary cultures differ in important ways. They have different relationships to European culture; they operate on drastically different scales; and it is difficult to call the relationship between them anything other than cultural imperialism. Also, there is a dramatic trade imbalance in cultural exchange between the two countries, since the United States continually exports its popular culture to Canada while importing little in return. Furthermore, those Canadian products that are imported (such as the music of Albertan k. d. lang or Coupland's zeitgeist novel *Generation X*) are often imported without recognition of their Canadian origins. A silent "Americanization" of Canadian cultural artifacts seems to be a necessary part of their marketing in the United States. There is a strange similarity, I find, between this silencing (which usually also involves a muting of any social criticism of the United States) and the covering up of one-time Communist writers. Both necessitate a writer's speaking from within the national closet.

Within the parameters of the general problem of U.S./Canadian relations, the transnational character of leftist culture becomes particularly apparent. As I've already stated, the concept-metaphor I use to describe that character is the hybrid; throughout this study, I consider the 30s left as a contact zone between U.S. and Canadian culture in which a hybrid literary formation developed. The leftist subculture of the 1930s, I argue, was a cultural formation that exceeded the category of nation; it spilled out across national borders at the same time that it was marked by that border. As a subculture, it drew from its parent culture like a graft on a tree, but it was always to some degree at odds with that culture. Its fruits were hybrids of multiple parentage, and they could not always reproduce themselves. They were new strains—test strains—that bear witness to the techniques of interbreeding and scientific management of culture so characteristic of the early twentieth century. In other words, the tension-ridden hybrid product called leftist subculture offers a microcosmic view of the problem of transnational culture. Like a nation, the left is a fictive entity—or an imagined community—that, to some extent, repressed its actual heterogeneity in favor of an ideal citizen, the well-muscled and committed proletarian. Also, like a transnational culture, the left has been driven into awareness of its actual fractured state by struggles within and across its boundaries; its fictive homogeneity has, famously, disintegrated since the 1930s into the heterogeneous new social movements of the 1960s.

These issues arise most explicitly in chapter 1, in which, to complicate matters, I examine the ideas about national culture put forward within the fictional nation of the left. This chapter analyzes U.S. literary histories written during the 1930s and argues that the left codified the tautological narrative of national culture that literary scholars still struggle with today under the name "the canon." That is, leftist literary historians produced narratives that purported to describe the nation but were really descriptions and justifications of their own subculture. This argument is not meant as a condemnation of those or any other literary historians; rather, it seems to me that, for 30s leftists operating in a context in which the struggle to define the direction of a nation's cultural development was a struggle for immediate power, the concept of a coherent, distinct national culture was a radical one. Understanding the nation as a reflection of their own culture allowed leftists to see themselves as central to their historical moment, and it empowered them to act, as they saw it, as and for an idealized concept of the nation. This appreciation for the motivations for cultural nationalism, though, does not mean that the same strategies would be effective today. On the contrary, it is of more use to identify ways that this concept of the nation as a self-justifying centripetal force was transnational; it operated (as demonstrated in chapters 2 and 3) in both the United States and Canada during the 1930s. Thus, overall, I argue that 30s leftists put forward teleological ideas about cultural nationalism to underwrite their own fictive status as a nation and that this process worked variously but simultaneously in different nations. This situation ultimately reveals a transnational character of leftist culture rarely visible to its loudest and most nationalistic spokespersons.

Periodizing the 1930s, or Why Stop in 1941?

Clearly, if we take "the 1930s" as a slogan for "the left" in its cultural/intellectual form, then "the 1930s" did not cease to be central to North American culture in 1941. Quite the opposite. As Michael Denning, Maurice Isserman, and numerous historians of the 60s New Left have demonstrated, confronting the legacy of the 1930s had a formative influence on the intellectual and cultural hegemonies of the 1950s and 1960s.[15] As attention to the popular and middlebrow culture industries supplements scholarship on modernist art publishing, it is becoming increasingly clear to literary scholars that these influences have not always been simply negative. Woody Guthrie passing the folksinger baton to Bob Dylan might serve as an emblematic narrative here.

Nonetheless, it is not my goal here to extend the temporal framework in which we understand "the 1930s" so much as it is my goal to expand the spatial or geographical boundaries of that period. I am particularly interested in demonstrating that the concept of a period such as the 1930s is in part a factor of space or geography; I will illustrate below how standard histories of the 1930s differ in the United States and Canada. These are not *absolute* differences, since spatial parameters alone do not cause a temporal narrative to emerge. Yet we see when we examine national histories together that the pattern and significance of a 30s narrative vary noticeably with spatial differences. This variance influences the concept of "nation" employed across those spaces, the identification of resistant postnational forces, and relations to the public culture emerging from and protected by the nation.

Of the hundreds of histories touching on some aspect of the 1930s in the United States and Canada, relatively few attempt the kind of synthesis evident in Robert McElvaine's *The Great Depression, 1929–1941* and Michiel Horn's *The Dirty Thirties: Canadians in the Great Depression*. For this reason, I will use these texts for a brief comparison of the spatially inflected periodizations of the 1930s. McElvaine's 1984 history is a chronological narrative that identifies historical currents in Depression America and closes with a consideration of the continuing impact of the decade. The 1993 edition includes a retrospective introduction situating his work in relation to the corporate ethic of the 1980s and Reaganism. By contrast, Horn's volume is a collection of Depression-era documents arranged by subjects such as the economy, relief, and social reform. Published twelve years earlier, before any comprehensive synthesis of the Canadian 1930s was available, Horn's collection appeared as part of a wave of scholarship devoted to specifically Canadian issues. It was in the 1970s, for instance, that literary scholars began to turn their attention more regularly to Canadian subjects and to develop departments and academic programs focusing on Canadian national culture.

In light of these differences in format and timing, it is interesting to see how close the two volumes come in their timelines of the 1930s. Both McElvaine and Horn divide the decade into five phases of approximately two years each. Both mark the official beginning of the Depression with the crash of the Wall Street (and Toronto and Montreal) stock exchanges in 1929. Both identify the worst period of the Depression—defined by the highest unemployment, worst crisis of debt, and most punishing material conditions—with the trough of 1931–33. In both narratives, the relative recovery of 1934–35 is identified with a dramatic upswing of political activity—the Hunger March in Washington, D.C., the Popular Front, the On-to-Ottawa Trek. The so-called recession or second trough of the Depression appears in both narratives at the 1936–38 mark, in tandem with challenges to political initiatives such as the National Recovery Act. The final, fifth phase in both narratives arrives in 1939 when serious buildup for war begins, accompanied by an economic upswing or "recovery." Neither McElvaine nor Horn says much about the role of their respective nation-states in World War II, as this question introduces a range of issues requiring a broader scope. Insofar as their narratives discuss the rise and fall of the 30s left, both suggest that it changes formation and significance roughly around the time of the Hitler-Stalin pact of 1939.

What we see, then, is that both McElvaine and Horn take the economic developments of the 1930s as the "base," or at the very least as an element operating at a different register from other levels of their respective societies. They share a view of history as something that involves a sorting or distribution of effects across economics, politics, society, and culture. Despite this methodological constancy, however, we can identify differences at particular levels and differences in the relative weight each is assigned.

When dealing with politics, for instance, McElvaine's narrative of the U.S. 1930s is centralized, focusing on policy at the federal level. The rise and progress of the New Deal is an integral part of his account, and the topic has inspired a massive amount of scholarship on the part of historians of the period. One of the enduring legacies of the 1930s has of course been a sustained debate over the efficacy and desirability of the Keynesian welfare state. Like other commentators, McElvaine justifies discussions of non-federal and non-electoral politics with reference to their effect on the climate of reform associated with Roosevelt's programs. Protest movements acquire significance to the extent that their influence on the "center" can be demonstrated. By contrast, Horn's selection of documents from the Canadian side of the border emphasizes the variety of political responses to the Depression. Without assigning as much priority as McElvaine does to politics, Horn displays Social Gospel, social-democratic, Social Credit, Communist, liberal, and fascist rhetoric in his collection. This array is framed as the preface to a centralization achieved during the war—that is, as the stage for *later* political coherence. Various protest movements are not test cases for "influencing" the center so much as they are signs of an existing social fragmentation. The political level, then, has a different significance in the two narratives. In McElvaine's study, political developments actively check economic forces, balancing and restraining them, while in Horn's Canadian narrative, politics appears reactive with respect to the economy and, I should stress, with respect to U.S. politics. The punitive effects as far as Canadians were concerned of the Smoot-Hawley tariff limiting imports to the United States were only some of the most evident signs of the uneven distribution of political power on the North American continent during the 1930s.

Where social developments are concerned, McElvaine and Horn also describe differing patterns. McElvaine's history synthesizes a body of scholarship tracing large-scale demographic shifts that took place within the confines of the United States during the Depression; the great migration of African Americans from the rural South to the industrial cities of the Northeast and northern Midwest and the westward migration of poor white Southerners from the "dust bowl" are the two major narratives underlying McElvaine's history.[16] In addition, his history involves at various points descriptions of the relatively top-heavy class structure of U.S. society. Politics are in dialogue with an oligarchic social structure. This view is supported by oral histories of the New Dealers that underscore the social web linking them to one another and excluding less wealthy and educated outsiders.[17] While political power also followed the paths of class cronyism in Canada, Horn's narrative does less to stress this aspect of the social structure. Instead, he is more concerned with countering middle-class views of the Depression. Writing against a context that tended to emphasize the relative insecurity encountered by a petit bourgeoisie with something to lose, Horn makes special efforts to include the more disenfranchised voices of those who lost everything in the Depression. As a result, in comparison to McElvaine's history (which uses a similar resource—letters that panic-stricken citizens wrote to national leaders, begging for assistance), Horn's narrative paints a portrait of a society with somewhat narrower gaps between the very wealthy and the very poor. Furthermore, the sections of Horn's book devoted to the debate over dangerous single men and relief camps do not describe interregional migration as a solution to Depression-era social crises but rather as a problem. Within the Canadian context of a small, geographically dispersed population, demographic shifts like the great migration were both less feasible and less welcome than in the United States. As I illustrate in chapter 6, regional identities retained a strong significance for Canadians during the Depression. While social structures in the United States tended toward oligarchy, social structures in Canada—at least as outlined by Horn—followed a more decentralized, regionally distributed pattern.

Finally, with respect to cultural developments during the 1930s, McElvaine and Horn again take up different concerns. McElvaine's U.S. narrative places major focus on questions of "values" and popular culture—outlining the traces of a critique of capitalism in some of the most popular films, songs, and novels of the day. His central question is how Americans with a tradition of communal responsibility came to inhabit a commercial culture, and the overall shape of his narrative suggests a tragic answer. Ultimately the bureaucratic structures adopted as a transitional check on the encroachments of economics overtook their initial goals, ironically institutionalizing the commercial and alienated social experience they were meant to restrict. Horn's narrative, by contrast, does not have such a strong sense of closure. It is an unfinished narrative that asks how Canadians might continue to negotiate internal differences (mainly conceived of as differences of class, politics, and region) while also balancing cultural ties to Europe and the United States. Commercial and institutional cultures are concerns here, but not necessarily the main question. Writing in the face of the 60s revolutions, the final voices heard in Horn's collection defend their institutions; Hugh MacLennan, for instance, prophesizes that the victory of the New Left would mean the end of "western civilization."[18] A different kind of faith in the nation as a site of resistance—or at least activity— persists in the decentralized Canadian narrative of the 1930s than in the U.S. story of the rise and decline of the New Deal.

Overall, the weight in any given level of the Canadian narrative of the 1930s is always partially distributed outside the border of the nation, while in the U.S. narrative this is rarely the case. Thus, in the Canadian narrative, politics retains a measure of possibility; it is described as an arena where agency could be further developed in response to particular social and cultural formations and in reaction to an economy always at least partly out of national control. The U.S. narrative, by contrast, situates politics as a handmaiden of social divisions and downplays its capacity for acting in or on the economy. The slogan "cultural politics" thus identifies different configurations in the U.S. and Canadian contexts. Referring to a movement from politics to culture broadly conceived as including commercial productions in the United States and to a movement from culture conceived as interregional and international to politics on the national scale in Canada, "cultural politics" will prove a malleable term as we study its particular deployment by the literary left. To maintain our focus on these variations, then, I will retain the chronological parameters that, despite their differences, both Horn and McElvaine employ and limit my discussion of the suburb of dissent to the decade between 1930 and 1941.

The Scope of the Project

The chapters that follow examine the 30s literary left at three sites: national, proletarian, and mass culture. Each of these sites was crucial to the definition of the leftist subculture. The phantasm of national culture provided the ideological shell within which leftists located their origin; proletarian culture was their ideal, their projection into the future, while mass culture was one name for the circumstances of the present. In Raymond Williams's terms, these three sites defined residual, emergent, and dominant cultures for the left.[19]

At each of these sites of cultural contest and definition, I present readings of the development of that contest in a literary genre and in works by major authors. This doubled presentation introduces a secondary dialectic between author and genre. In other words, while leftist culture defined itself in mutually constitutive contact with adjacent cultural formations, such as national culture, within the left, another dialectic also developed between individual authors and the genres within and against which they wrote. Each individual author I examine was critical of major left genres, and the traction produced by that criticism helped each to produce an important work of left-wing literature.

Part I of *The Suburb of Dissent* considers national culture, beginning with literary histories written by leftist critics in the United States during the 1930s. These writers were among the early codifers of a coherent tradition of American literature, and I work to explain how and why that codification happened. Some of the conceptual and political difficulties with the literary historians' emphasis on national culture surface in chapter 2; here, I explore John Dos Passos's attempt in his *U.S.A.* trilogy to determine whether American culture has an overall pattern. The acceleration of technological development—specifically technologies relating to speed—interests Dos Passos greatly in *U.S.A.*, and he finally depicts a nation torn apart by the worship of acceleration. He describes different classes living at entirely different velocities and unable to communicate across that rapidly growing cultural divide. Chapter 3 examines a major Canadian author's retooling of the idea of national culture to fit the more recently colonial experience of a larger but less populous nation; Hugh MacLennan's early writings—up to and including *Two Solitudes*—present a unifying mythic geography as the basis of Canadian cultural nationalism. Although markedly different in literary result, this effort to redress the crisis of social stratification complements Dos Passos's project in *U.S.A.*

Part II turns toward the invention of what was called in the 1930s "proletarian" writing. In chapter 4, I argue that the central genre in which class issues were explored—the proletarian novel—was less formulaic and monologic than most readings would suggest; when read against contemporaneous discourses on class, the genre appears relatively flexible, relational, and influential. Nonetheless, pointed revisions of the proletarian genre were still central to the 30s left—especially around issues of race. Chapter 5 describes Richard Wright's efforts in *Native Son* to complement proletarian narratives with a psychologized understanding of African American urban life. Similarly, chapter 6 examines a range of alternatives to the proletarian novel written in Canada during the 1930s, many of which employ ethnicity and assimilation narratives as disruptions of class-based ideologies. This part, then, reveals the adaptations left-wing writers made to a supposedly rigid, teleological communist discourse.

Part III furthers this agenda by considering the relationship between the left and mass culture. Although the Marxist left is usually described as hostile to capitalist mass culture, I demonstrate that in practice it drew frequently from mass cultural forms and addressed the challenges of the surrounding media with reasonable and adequate innovations. In chapter 7, I categorize the types of short fiction most frequently found in U.S. and Canadian left-wing literary periodicals and illustrate the range of positions writers in each country adopted toward mass culture. In particular, the documentary form owes much to mainstream magazines of the period. Chapter 8 reads Nathanael West's quirky novel *A Cool Million* as an exploration of the structural similarities between an earlier form of mass culture—Horatio Alger stories—and the proletarian novel. Although not always understood as a leftist writer, West negotiates the territory between these two forms with a sureness and wit that reveal his comfort with the basic practices of leftist literary culture. Similarly, chapter 9 asserts that Canadian poet Dorothy Livesay's documentary poems of the late 1930s make innovative use of an emergent public culture. Her poems show her moving away from the equally bedeviled concepts of "the masses" and "the people" and toward "the public" as a literary category—a move that melded nicely into the concerns of the postwar literary scene. Thus, this part concludes by pointing to continuities between the 1930s and literary developments later in this century.

As the conclusion argues, it may well be that some of these continuities are particularly apparent because of the waning of the Cold War. In the mid-1990s, most people writing about the 1930s were neither participants in that decade nor Oedipal rejecters of it. Perhaps this is why it is now possible to admit how fully 30s writers and North American socialism in general set the scene for succeeding generations of authors and intellectuals. Also, from our post–Cold War vantage point it is now evident that the culture of the 1930s was not irredeemably soiled by this association with socialism; in fact, many late-twentieth-century concerns—with nationalism, race, gender, sexuality, and the marketing of culture, for instance—arose in the leftist culture of the 1930s and received careful, thoughtful treatment there.

Finally, it is important to rise to the challenge of comprehending the cultural politics of the 1930s, since this decade remains an important cultural reference point in debates over the significance of "America." The Depression continues to represent the kind of economic catastrophe possible in capitalist "America" as well as the fate of the few seriously revolutionary answers to such problems. It will be necessary to come to grips with the "redness" of the 1930s if we are finally, as a wealth of cultural commentary suggests, ready to reconceptualize "America" in a more open, less rigidly ideological manner.

PART I   NATIONAL CULTURE

Chapter 1

BEFORE F. O. MATTHIESSEN

30s Literary Histories and a Radical Concept of National Culture

If any single text can reasonably be called the foundational text of American Studies, F. O. Matthiessen's *American Renaissance* is probably the one.[1] In this erudite and imaginative study, Matthiessen locates a network of themes conjoining five major U.S. writers. These readings were so influential that they almost single-handedly established both a canon of American authors and the methodology with which those authors' works have been treated in subsequent criticism. Matthiessen's preference for a synchronic organization rather than a narrative one and his heavily overdetermined evasions (of Whitman's homosexuality, for instance) have been, until recently, adopted by most students of American culture. In short, Matthiessen's claim to fame has been providing American Studies with a sophisticated alternative to "the shallow mechanistic Marxism that prevailed during the 1930s."[2]

These days, however, Matthiessen is blamed for the sins of American Studies almost as often as he is credited with the field's foundation. On his shoulders falls responsibility for codifying the masculinist canon, solidifying the exclusivity of the great tradition, espousing nationalism, proselytizing humanism, and so on.[3] Almost all the bugaboos of late twentieth-century cultural criticism appear in his work and few have hesitated to point them out. In particular, postnational Americanists have struggled with Matthiessen, suggesting that he ignores the internal divide between the imaginary subject of national culture and various insurgent positions within that culture. Of course, this argument is primarily directed against the "consensus" theory of culture proposed by Cold War liberals such as Frederick Crews and Lionel Trilling, who argued that American public culture is a democratic unity forged out of disparate immigrant identities.[4] But, in the process of deconstructing consensus theory (by demonstrating its forcible exclusion and rearticulation of "minority" voices), postnationalists typically invent a certain consensus of their own. Antinationalism tends to collapse all forms of nationalism into a homogenous other, a practice which makes it almost impossible to distinguish someone like Matthiessen from the Cold War liberals. This critique of Matthiessen makes it very difficult to recognize that, before consensus theory became ubiquitous, another more radical thesis on national culture was available.

In the 1930s, well before the institutionalization of American Studies and in an era when the study of American literature was in its infancy, there was a concept of national culture based not on an opposition between national and insurgent subjects but on an alliance between the two; during the 1930s, left-wing cultural critics understood U.S. national culture as a radical—or revolutionary—tradition. I will argue that this view differed substantially from postwar consensus theories and was not necessarily "shallow" or "mechanistic." The pages that follow examine the 30s thesis in greater detail, but for now it is important to understand that someone like Matthiessen was positioned *between* 30s radicalism and the Cold War consensus. He was not simply articulating a repressive master-narrative. He was struggling to understand how a radical cultural politics could correspond to the nation transforming around him, and his study is as good a place as any to begin clearing our way through the morass of Cold War polemics to the quite different problematic that preceded them.

A Backward Glance at F. O. Matthiessen

In the "Method and Scope" section that introduces *American Renaissance,* F. O. Matthiessen both recognizes his debt to and differentiates himself from the preceding generation of socialist scholars. While Granville Hicks, Newton Arvin, V. L. Parrington, and other critics from the 1930s wrote biographies, intellectual histories, accounts of economic and social forces, and literary histories, Matthiessen asserts that he will discuss particular literary forms. While the previous generation surveyed the entire nineteenth century, Matthiessen limits himself to the five-year span he calls the Renaissance. While the others attempted to explain American literature, he explicates it. While they narrated suspiciously chronological literary histories, he allows recurrent themes to play across his text. In sum, while the critics of the 1930s demonstrated how "litera-ture reflects an age," Matthiessen shows how "it also illuminates" the age (x).

The word "reflects" is an important signal in Matthiessen's account, since it anticipates frequent postwar critique of the 30s writers, the critique that stresses the mechanistic, utilitarian side of their project. Charging that Hicks and the others reduced literature to a passive "reflection" of social forces, crit-ics of the literary histories of the 1930s often leap to the equally reductive conclusion that all leftist—and especially all Marxist—criticism of the arts must make such reductions; paradoxically, such critics charge that Marxist economic theory is the base from which a superstructure of faulty literary judgment must inevitably grow.[5] Matthiessen, however, does not adopt exactly this line of argument; in fact, he attributes the reflection thesis to Parrington, the most liberal and least "Marxist" of the 30s critics.[6] He chastises Parrington for using literature as a lens for viewing historical trends and for not paying enough attention to strictly aesthetic issues, but at no point does Matthiessen suggest that literature does not reflect social conditions.

Although written in 1941, this provisional acceptance of reflection theory does not differ substantially from the comments Matthiessen and many other cultural critics made at the height of the Depression. For instance, when re-viewing Granville Hicks's important study *The Great Tradition* seven years ear-lier in 1934, Matthiessen took a similar stance; he criticized Hicks's "method" while sympathizing with his politics and a number of his interpretations. Over-all, in this short review, Matthiessen argues that literature's role "is not only that of revolt, but the counterbalancing one of realization."[7] That is, Matthies-sen does not contradict Hicks's theory of literature; he supplements it. Mat-thiessen stresses a literary capacity for realizing contradiction in the present as well as a prophetic capacity for predicting "revolt." In essence, Matthies-sen aligns himself with what was known during the 1930s as the "anti-leftist" critique. Famously associated with *Partisan Review,* but also evident in a wide variety of left-wing literary commentary, the "anti-leftist" position modified the crude reflection theory attributed to so-called "leftist" extremists. Anti-leftists described literature as semi-autonomous in relation to social forces and placed great emphasis on appreciating, if not always emulating, new modernist writers, such as T. S. Eliot—a personal favorite of Matthiessen's. This position differed from the more aesthetically conservative line adopted by Hicks and a few others, but it was not by any means a heretical one among 30s radicals.[8] On the contrary, the "anti-leftist" critique that Matthiessen articulates was a recognizable and frequently heard voice in the debates over culture during the 1930s, and, despite the misleading label, it by no means signaled a critic's rejection of leftist politics in general.

Matthiessen's position as an "anti-leftist" who accepted reflection theory with some qualifications suggests that, although he differentiated his work from the historicist projects of the 1930s, his response to them was not nearly as hostile as subsequent literary historiography has implied. On the contrary, Matthiessen had a relatively friendly or, to use his own terminology, "organic" relation with the 30s writers. Furthermore, as William E. Cain has pointed out, the structure of *American Renaissance* "attests to his kinship" with other critics, scholars, and intellectuals of the 1930s.[9] In practice as well as theory, Matthiessen was a friendly, though critical, cousin of Hicks and friends.

To date, though, most efforts to describe the "kinship" relations of the 1930s seek to save a central figure, such as Matthiessen, from the contaminating influence of his or her peers. They focus on the ways that his work redeems itself from their influence. A responsible literary ethnography of the 1930s, however, will reevaluate the ground behind such figures. It will reevaluate the 1930s as a period and, in particular, as a movement in literary criticism. This task is made somewhat difficult by the fact that most histories of literary scholarship exclude leftist criticism from their purview or rely almost entirely on second-hand accounts of the left. Historiographies often apply separate standards of scholarship to the criticism from this decade on the grounds of its supposedly unusual ideological distortions.[10] Meanwhile, a second body of work on other aspects of the 1930s suggests that such judgments are usually not substantiated by first-hand examination of the sources.[11]

To counteract this overdetermined blind spot in the history of U.S. literary scholarship, then, this chapter examines the literary histories of the 1930s more closely—outlining the narrative of American culture which they rehearsed, pinpointing their formal problematic, and, finally, providing some historical context for these developments. The goal of my project is not to affirm the particular judgments the 30s critics made but rather to understand why their thoughts coalesced as they did in that moment of time; in particular, I am interested in demonstrating how, in contrast to the current climate in the United States, the concept of national culture was integrated with a radical cultural politics during the 1930s. Understanding this development alters the narrative against which we understand foundational figures such as Matthiessen.

Inventing the Great Tradition

Left-wing critics' most important efforts to describe a coherent tradition of American literature took place between 1927 and 1942. The group of writers engaged in this task was relatively small and produced more periodical articles than full-length studies during this period, but major works, such as V. L. Parrington's *Main Currents in American Thought* (1927–30), V. F. Calverton's *The Liberation of American Literature* (1932), Granville Hicks's *The Great Tradition* (1933), Van Wyck Brooks's *The Flowering of New England* (1937), and Bernard Smith's *Forces in American Criticism* (1939) did appear. These long studies were supplemented by the shorter criticism of Edmund Wilson, Malcolm Cowley, Mike Gold, and others.[12] Although one can locate significant disparities among these works—in the contest among Communist, Trotskyist, and liberal politics, and in the different standards exacted by writers who were journalists, academics, editors, and publishers by profession—they are nonetheless clearly of a piece. In Matthiessen's phrase, they share a commitment to a certain "method and scope." They all experiment with historical criticism, and they all organize the wide vistas of history into developmental narratives. Also, the parameters of this cluster of works are clarified by subsequent studies, such as Alfred Kazin's *On Native Grounds* (1942), Joseph Beach's *American Fiction, 1920–1940* (1941), and Matthiessen's *American Renaissance* (1941). Rather than sharing the project of the 30s literary histories, this second group of studies comments on the project as a phenomenon; the latter writers show the influence of an invention of American literature that was already in process.

The narrative of American culture that the 30s literary histories established is, by now, a familiar one. Concentrating on prose and especially the novel, Hicks and his contemporaries describe the broad trend of American literature as a flow, a flowering, a maturing, a current, a tradition, or a liberation. They chart a timeline that begins with a few lonely voices in the Puritan wilderness, struggles on to Cooper's robust frontier romances, peaks in the golden day of Whitman's epic poetry, strides bravely into Twain's honest Western humor and Dreiser's urban realism, and nearly peaks again in the naturalist muckraking era until it arrives at the glorious present. In short, theirs is a narrative of progress. Whether the critic considers the fetters on American literature to be Puritanism (Hicks) or gentility (Parrington) or the European cultural heritage (Calverton), he is primarily interested in documenting how the novel came to burst those fetters. These literary histories record a steady and irreversible tale of triumph.

Oddly enough, it is a distinctly national triumph. In a period in which defending American exceptionalist theses in political matters was a rightist heresy among Communists, the specificity and insularity of the nation were rarely, if ever, questioned in studies of culture.[13] On the contrary, the rise of a distinct national culture was identified with liberation, and considerable theoretical energy was expended in the defense of this thesis. Calverton, for example, outlines a four-part psychosocial schema to describe how national culture develops: First, a colonial culture adapts its mother country's literature to a new environment; then new conditions provoke changes in the old tradition and emphasize national or regional differences. Next, the struggle for political independence encourages the development of nationalist consciousness, until finally the colonial literature becomes a national one. In this schema, Calverton refers only to the literature of the United States, since this is the only English colonial culture he considers to have reached the fourth stage. Thus, in a paradox typical of American exceptionalist thinking, the 30s critics simultaneously narrate the supposedly unique maturation of American literature while also insisting that this maturation be the prototype for all other properly national literatures.[14] U.S. culture represents for exceptionalists an exemplary response to a postcolonial situation.

Less typical of American exceptionalism (which also often asks why the United States has proved singularly immune to socialism), however, is the tendency of the 30s literary historians to understand U.S. culture as essentially oppositional. Based on an analogy to a proposed alliance between radical intellectuals and the working class, this thesis asserted that American culture was already internally contradictory and that the national literary tradition reflected this self-opposition. This thesis appears most clearly in the literary histories' structure. In the group of studies under consideration, each author sets his analysis of the flow of American literature against the flow of other elements of the society with the express purpose of finding friction between the two. For example, Granville Hicks organizes his study this way: "On the material level the profit and loss account of that mad advance [of capitalistic enterprise]

is not easy to calculate. On the cultural level it can, *alas,* be more easily esti-
mated. In a society that regarded chaos as natural, that made greed a virtue,
that placed financial achievement before personal integrity, culture was not
likely to flourish" (3; emphasis added). I'll have more to say below about the
system of "levels" used here to describe social structure; for now it is important
to notice that "alas." This knowing sigh signifies that Hicks considers culture,
all culture, to be at odds with capitalism *a priori.* Since the sources, values, and
needs of culture oppose "material" ones, the poverty of culture indicates to
Hicks the extent of the sacrifice that capitalism had extorted from "society."

   In Hicks's analysis, the dominant class is so preoccupied with the greedy
"mad advance" that it abandons all culture to the noncapitalist classes, the residual and emergent classes. Lacking only Raymond Williams's terminology,
the critics of the thirties shared his basic model of social formation.[15] In
their cultural arrays, Tories and radical Republicans, decaying Southern aristo-
crats and rugged frontier individualists, wan expatriates and vigorous Socialist
muckrakers dominate the scene, and "bourgeois" or "petit-bourgeois" writers,
such as Hawthorne, must camouflage themselves in other class positions. As a
result, the literary historians attach even the figures in American literature who
have been most enthusiastically celebrated by procapitalists to oppositional
positions. A case in point: in their narrative, Emerson is an ethical anticapital-
ist saint, defending individual liberty in the last moment before it became an
excuse for unlimited capitalist expansion (Hicks, 9; Parrington, 272; Calverton,
chap. 5). In other words, since the 30s critics assume culture always presents a
radical critique of capitalism (whether from the left or the right), their critical
project is to decode that critique in works from which the passing of time may
have all but eradicated its markings.

   As noted above, such political judgments have helped the 30s critics acquire a reputation for being excessively reductive; Matthiessen, for instance,
objected to what he saw as a substitution of political for aesthetic judgment in
Parrington's work. Furthermore, it is often charged that this tendency in leftist
criticism led to a neglect of authors such as Twain and Poe and an exaggeration of the importance of politically agreeable minor writers such as Hamlin
Garland or some of the muckrakers. I would argue, however, that these politically motivated inclusions and exclusions are hardly more remarkable than the
inverse arrangements evident in contemporaneous studies by conservatives,
such as Constance Rourke. In her 1931 study of American humor, Rourke dis-

cusses Poe and Twain at length but makes no mention of the muckrakers or Garland. Yet, as the continuing significance of Rourke's work indicates, ideological choices do not preclude meaningful cultural criticism. In fact, the intersection between certain political judgments and aesthetic choices is common to both conservative and revolutionary criticism, and, in the long run, accounting for the history of such conjunctures is a more fruitful task than aligning oneself with one side or the other.

So, returning to aesthetic matters, it is significant that the 30s critics produced a literary-historical account that conformed closely to standards of nineteenth-century literary realism—as defined, for example, by Eric Auerbach. They described a sweep of history and paid especial attention to the role of the so-called common man in that sweep, and in so doing they quite consistently honored the European realists who were their own antecedents.[16] The content of their argument also insisted that the mainstream of American literature was saturated by the literary project of realism, and they assessed the trajectory of American literature in any particular period according to its proximity to realism. As a result, a realist version of Whitman was their ideal; they called Whitman "a great figure, the greatest assuredly in our literature," "the founder of the new American literature," and "the first genuine force in the creation of an American art" (Parrington, 3: 86; Hicks, 30; Calverton, 276). Whitman was applauded in part for his politics but much more fully for his literary method. His exuberant depiction of the everyday life of the working man and his generous attempts to synthesize history were considered the first, definitive steps toward a distinctively American literature. For the 30s critics, Whitman's realism could only culminate in the class-conscious realism of the proletarian novel.

The characteristics of proletarian realism remained much hazier in these literary histories than in the reviews and journalistic criticism devoted to the subject, but it was clear nonetheless that proletarian fiction would crown the American literary tradition. The literary historians fully expected that the proletarian novel would exemplify the political and aesthetic tendencies of American literature. It would exacerbate the contradictions between culture and capitalism, and it would discover new subjects for realist description among the working class—thereby bringing the American literary tradition to fruition.

The assumption underlying this emphasis on realism and especially proletarian realism was not that realism was the most interesting current of American literature, but that American literature was, by definition, realist. This assumption was crucial to the critical project of the 1930s, as evidenced by the literary historians' strenuous efforts to fit even an avowed modernist such as John Dos Passos into the realist mold. Most leftist critics emphasized the debt that a writer like Dos Passos had to Whitman and alluded only hastily to his "new style," or his "relatively unimportant" new devices (Calverton, 462; Hicks, 290). However, far from demonstrating a reduction of art to politics, this gesture demonstrates how important aesthetics were to the left. Leftist critics were more than willing to praise the writing of a Harvard graduate who referred to himself as a middle-class liberal throughout the ultra-radical Third Period of Communist Party policy (1928–35). They worked overtime to interpolate him into a tradition of realist writers in spite of anxiety about his aesthetic alignment—all on the strength of his gift as a writer. This eagerness demonstrates the 30s critics' reductiveness. They did not, however, reduce art to politics; in this instance, at least, they celebrated artistic merit over political correctness.

Overall, then, the 30s literary historians identified a national culture that was unified by a realist aesthetic and that emerged from a struggle between various regional tendencies. They narrated that culture's heroic battle against other "levels" of society and argued for the imminent triumph of oppositional literary values. Although they occasionally exaggerated the significance of personal favorites, for the most part they marked familiar high points in their narrative of cultural development in the United States. In their eagerness to found a political art suitable to the contemporary scene, the left literary historians of the 1930s mined the past for politically and aesthetically pleasing progenitors.

The Form of Literary History

As we've seen, the "shallow mechanistic Marxism" supposedly employed by the 30s critics drew fire from later commentators. The problems with this method have been attributed to sources as diverse as T. S. Eliot, nineteenth-century sentimental eschatology, and the base/superstructure model.[17] Although this metacritical approach has occasionally generated interesting contributions to the history of ideas, more often it conflates descriptions of the literary historians' critical method with summaries of the political positions they took—leading to the erroneous conclusion that the latter always determined the former. Attention to the formal practices organizing the literary histories of the 1930s, however, reveals that, although this form definitely has its structural weaknesses, in general, the literary historians of the 1930s employed a rather benign version of historicism. For this reason, to account fully for these narratives of national culture and to explain the fearsome reputation they acquired, one must finally turn away from their formal or methodological shortcomings and toward the discourses on nationalism that surrounded them.

The first significant formal feature of the leftist literary histories of the 1930s is the placement of the much heralded and dramatically new national realist literature written by, for, and/or about working people. Descriptions of this literature are typically placed at the end of a narrative of development—in the last chapter or at the end of a chapter. Whether damned or praised, this literature is credited with bringing the American literary scene into bloom. "It is the novel that reveals most completely the literary potentialities of the revolutionary movement," writes Hicks in the concluding "Trumpet Call" of *The Great Tradition,* while Calverton exclaims that the new authors "insist upon seeing America as it really is and not as they were taught to believe it is" at the end of his first section (Hicks, 298; Calverton, 40). This placement—even more than the overt claims that are made—suggests that the very project of writing American literary history was designed to provide an undergirding for proletarian literature. That is, the ends were, teleologically, presupposed from the beginning.

In order to complete their project and establish proletarian literature as the fulfillment of American literary history, the critics of the 1930s had to keep two projects afloat at once. These were the same two projects in which the proletarian novelists were engaged: they had to discover how to present a narrative of events familiar enough to satisfy the demands of realism, while simultaneously playing the prelude to a utopian conclusion.[18] They had to balance a narrative that accounts for freedom and indeterminacy with their sense of necessity and thesis. The basic problem that this dilemma poses in literary history is the relation of history to the intellectual.

If one cares to grant the intellectual some agency in effecting the overarching series of events called history, then a biographical approach might seem appropriate. At some point all the 30s literary historians (and the most influential, Brooks, employed this practice most consistently) took individual authors' careers as the organizational principle of the major subsections of their works. This practice also demonstrates that, far from suffering a "mechanical" reduction of a rich, complex human personality to a social force, these studies more often relied unreflectively on precisely the categories of individualism that they wished to explode. As a narrative strategy, selecting a theme, such as "Struggle and Flight" and exemplifying it with subsections entitled "1. Henry Adams 2. Edward Bellamy and the Utopians 3. Hamlin Garland . . ." obliges the critic to prove that the changes an author made in his or her life all refer back to the central theme (Hicks, ix). That is, rather than allowing the critic to elaborate the complexities of his own themes, the use of the individual as an instance of history confines his elaborative powers to explicating the way particular authors chose (or not) to think through his themes. As a result, a chapter like Calverton's "The Frontier Force" that relates several authors' writings to a central theme ends up rephrasing its historical narrative several times in order to highlight different portions of the theme; in chapter 5, Calverton rewrites his thesis about a distinctly American form of individualism developing on the frontier first to fit Emerson, then Alcott, Thoreau, Melville, Hawthorne, and finally Whitman. Each time the significance of the theme alters somewhat, until one doubts whether it has a focus at all. Thus, the purported constant that individual careers are supposed to instantiate — History — is in practice subordinated to the individual life span.

The alternative to using several authors to explicate an all-encompassing theme is to balance authors against one another in dyads or triads designed to express the fundamental contradictions of an era. In other words, one takes the career and works of an individual author to be emblematic of a movement, such as liberalism. Of the works under consideration, Parrington's ambitious three-volume *Main Currents in American Thought* employs this technique most thoroughly. For example, in his second volume, Parrington opposes the economic, political, and literary trends of the nineteenth-century South to those of the West, the Mideast, and New England in an elaborate eight-part structure that attempts to grant each component its due significance — no more and no less. The care which Parrington took to ensure that the structure of his study would reproduce the intellectual topography of the period is indicated by the chagrin with which he apologizes for his methodology: "the critic is reduced to patching together his account out of scanty odds and ends, or else settling down to do a series of full-length portraits, in which work, quite evidently, he will not get far. The inadequacies of the present study I am painfully conscious of: its omissions, its doubtful interpretations, its hasty generalizations, its downright guesses; but in the present lack of exact knowledge of the history of American letters, I do not see how such inadequacies can be avoided" (2: ix–x). What a shame-faced apology for a three-volume study that took at least four years to write and is quite far from being either "scanty" or "hasty"! This tone reveals the anxiety of a pioneer who finds himself on uncharted ground. With the ambition of a chronic overachiever, in the wilderness of the history of American letters, Parrington built a structure so abstract and so complex as to be uninhabitable. The disjuncture between the sheer mass of evidence one must absorb and the elegant simplicity of his overall structure finally dispels the dialectical tension necessary to the whole. In effect, the architectural form reifies the oppositions it establishes—sacrificing the actual complexity of the (usually political) distinctions it makes among different eras or regions to the aesthetics of balance, completion, and closure. Without a trustworthy frame-work, the extensive political and economic narratives that have been estab-lished (the conflicts between Puritanism and liberalism, agrarianism and capi-talism, and so on) devolve back into so much raw data, into an unapproachable complexity.

This lack of fit between the anarchy of the political and economic story and the teleology of the literary narrative characterizes Parrington's study and the other literary histories of the 1930s. To downplay this disjuncture between intellectuals and history, all of these critics employ, at one point or another, analogical structures of society. Hicks, as noted in the previous section, com-pared the "material level" of capitalist enterprise's "mad advance" to the "cul-tural level." Parrington asserted that he could choose between the economic and historical arena of investigation and the aesthetic: "I have been guided by what I conceived to be the historical significance of the several documents. With aesthetic judgment I have not been greatly concerned." Elsewhere he described his desire "to translate dogma into political terms." Similarly, Calver-ton wrote that his project was to trace "imaginative elements to their roots, and discover the kind of soil from which they have sprung." Even Brooks, as almost exclusively concerned as he is with psychobiographical narrative, ex-tends his "formula" of the decline of the New England mind from *belles lettres* to religion, politics, scholastics, and history (Parrington, 2: 1, 1: 13; Calverton, xi; Brooks, 528). In the metanarrative of their studies especially, these critics at-tempt to establish parallels between the narratives they have traced and those they have only implied. In this theory, the chaotic tendency of events is sub-dued by way of an analogy to history.

As suggested in the discussion of Parrington, though, wishing does not make it so. In fact, the strain between the teleological and anarchic representations of history reappears more vigorously the more assiduously it is denied, as the descriptions of the present assumed by these studies reveal. The proletarian literature that is destined to fulfill the teleological narrative of the development of realism by surpassing all previous versions of realism arrives on the scene with the subtlety of a locomotive. For example, listen to the uncharacteristically politicized vocabulary Calverton adopts in the following passage: "proletarian writers believe that their literature can serve a great purpose only when it contributes, first, toward the destruction of present-day society, and, second, toward the creation of a new society which will embody, like Soviet Russia to-day, a social, instead of an individualistic, ideal" (461–62). Calverton resorts to phrases such as "a great purpose," "a new society," and "a social, instead of an individualistic, ideal" to describe the proletarian writers' goals. The contrast to the considerably more clever and literate rhetoric that he uses to describe the southern agrarians could not be greater: "Full of intellectual TNT as their words are, they voice nothing more than the expiring spirit of a dead cause. At best, the plantation ideology having lost its economic *raison-d'être,* this group can do nothing more than stand apart, without the support of its environment, fighting a futile battle, modern Don Quixotes stabbing at steel windmills, hoping to destroy them by the gesture" (113). Engaged in both cases in the same critical task—describing and assessing the potential of a group of contemporary writers—Calverton musters much greater rhetorical strength for the group with which he is unaffiliated. The second description does not resort to slogans or negative definitions, and it communicates the scornful sympathy Calverton retains for the agrarians much more effectively than the first passage renders the exuberant, celebratory appreciation he assures us he has for the proletarian writers. After all, there is a significant difference between mocking writers for exemplifying the "expiring spirit of a dead cause" and praising them for having a "social" attitude.

This difference in tone marks a shift in analysis; it registers the critics' uncomfortable attempts to graft a teleological literary history onto a chaotic history of events. Since the proletarian writers inhabit the juncture between these two narratives, they are described in terms that are more adequate to their role in the conceptual narrative than evocative of literary qualities. Substituting for the historical necessity of revolution, they accrue all the ambiguous, apocalyptic significance due that concept. They represent the total identification of the intellectual with history, a maneuver that allows the literary historians to resolve—at least superficially—the problem of the intellectual's relation to history.

As the forced tone of this resolution hints, though, the problem persisted, and the literary historians had to employ other formal devices to investigate literature's role as a mediator among the "levels" of society. In particular, they balanced the diachronic narrative that stressed proletarian realism with a synchronic pattern, and, in so doing, they not only examined the past—they turned it into a utilitarian aspect of the present. This is the reason Van Wyck Brooks's famous slogan about the "usable past" made sense in the 1930s.[19] This critical quest allowed literary historians to consider moments of the literary past not only as partial fulfillments of the present, but also as proleptic analogies. Thus, the muckraking novels of the Progressive era or the short fiction of the western realists became sites at which critics could discuss the triumphs and disasters of the proletarian novel metaphorically. As high points in a history of failed attempts to capture the real, national, oppositional character of America, these eras represented the possibility and the necessity of successful cultural mediation, while also illustrating the rarity of such an achievement.

Although the pattern of waves established by drawing analogies between literary-historical situations does satisfy a certain desire for conceptual tidiness, it also rapidly reifies the systems of "literature" and "history" that it relates. This practice is habitual even with Parrington, who of the critics under discussion was least influenced by Marxist theories of history; he, too, discusses the interrelation of class dynamics and the development of American letters as systems. In the case of Ben Franklin, for example, he ties Franklin's rise to power to his agrarian roots and claims that Franklin's success "was the triumph of a rising class and a new social ideal" (Parrington, 1: 165). The intellectual's agency is objectified as the agency of a group, and any special effectiveness that the intellectual might have accrued as an intellectual disappears. In particular, the class analysis that one might expect to be central to writers on the left is simply not precise enough to account for intellectuals.

The moment when a nuanced sense of "class" exits the critical form is usually that at which the critics become most dogmatic about its utility—as an exemplary excerpt from the conclusion to Hicks's *The Great Tradition* demonstrates:

It has become increasingly clear, even to those who do not want to see, that the central fact in American life is the class struggle. The writer has a series of choices. . . . [Several undesirable options are presented.] If, however, the writer allies himself with the proletariat, there is no need of evasion or self-deception. He may be tempted to exaggerate the faults of capitalists or the virtues of the workers, but if he is wise he will find in facts his all-sufficient bulwark. Moreover, as this way of looking at life becomes an integral part of his imaginative equipment, he can not only perceive the operation of underlying forces; he can also rejoice in their play because of his confidence in what they will eventually accomplish. (305)

In spite of the fact that this paragraph argues for the primacy of an intelligentsia self-consciously aligned with the working class, the understanding of the class position of intellectuals necessary to theorizing such an alliance disappears from the form of the argument. Not only is the society that Hicks envisions the writer inhabiting a static, polarized, rational schema whose "forces" are immediately and obviously transparent, and not only is there a willful slippage between "the proletariat" as an ideology to which the writer is supposed to align himself and "the proletariat" as a social class from which the writer must not be separated, but also Hicks refuses to admit that his own observation of this scene has had any effect. He is so earnestly engaged in calling forth a revolution from below, or in inspiring a series of independent but unavoidable choices on the part of intelligent writers, that he actively suppresses recognition of the extent to which he is performatively summoning these changes rather than describing them.

One explanation for this remarkably unselfconscious dogmatism may be the widespread anxiety that leftist intellectuals felt in the face of mass culture. In an environment beginning to be saturated with the instant experts of mass culture but not yet supplemented by the sprawling multiversity of the postwar era, literary intellectuals had a legitimate fear of being replaced by technicians or managers of cultural production. This fear was often expressed in the extraneous aggressivity that characterizes some of their offhand comments about mass cultural phenomena such as the cinema ("an infantile product, uninspiring from beginning to end" [Calverton, 164]). Similarly, we might interpret the excessive dogmatism of some leftist intellectuals' pronouncements on class as a sign of anxiety—an anxiety that may have led them to insist hyperbolically on their own expertise. Their dogmatism about national culture may be a form of compensation for their fear that their culture is mutating under their eyes, and they may be anxious to claim for themselves some of the space previously inhabited by the traditional intellectuals. But other responses were also possible—as Dos Passos's experiments with the writer-as-technician theme will show. Perhaps it was in response to such challenges to their cultural legitimacy that literary historians on the left developed tools—such as the teleological literary narrative, the various models of an individual author's relation to history, the analogical model of society, the apocalyptic tone, the pattern of waves, the critique of mass culture, and the authoritative voice— that would locate their criticism centrally in the American tradition. Or perhaps these were simply the tools that came to hand as they struggled to lay the foundation for a socialist culture. Either way, a basic formal contradiction developed in their modes of situating particular intellectuals in the flow of history, and they repeatedly stumbled over the question of how to represent this relationship dialectically. This problem also appears in the overall picture of American culture that these historians developed: they charted the growth of an American literature whose maturation takes place in a different schema altogether from the pattern of historical events, and they attempted to apply an analogical model of the relationship of history to literature, without bringing the various levels of the society they describe into productive interaction. However, because this explanation quickly lost its dialectical character, the 30s critics end up with the obviously true, but ultimately uninteresting, conclusion that history influenced the writers they discuss.

This relatively unobjectionable form of historicism hardly seems an adequate inspiration for the kind of hostility that greeted the 30s critics in later years, since it is barely recognizable as a form of Marxism. Nor does the 30s critics' supposed exaggeration of "content" in an atmosphere of New Critical formalism adequately explain their expulsion from critical canons.[20] Instead, I would suggest that the shift in critical interest toward "form" signals a shift in the discourses of nationalism in the late 1930s. This latter development significantly altered the context in which the concept of a radical national culture made sense.

A Very Brief Look at Cultural Nationalism in the 1930s

In the early and mid-1930s, leftists defined national culture primarily in relation to time. We've seen that, like Calverton, Parrington, and others, Granville
Hicks described a "great tradition" of American literature that relates the recent
past to an imminently revolutionary future. This aspect of his study was not
lost on F. O. Matthiessen, who remarks in his review of *The Great Tradition* that,
for Hicks, "literature is inevitably a form of action."[21] Similarly, in Matthiessen's revisions of the action thesis, there is a sense of progress, change, or development as a nation through time; in his review, too, national culture is a state
of becoming. Matthiessen adds to Hicks's future tense his own appreciation for
literature that reflects "life itself as it has been lived"; he modulates the future
with the past perfect. Although their tenses differ, in the mid-1930s, Matthiessen and Hicks both measured American culture by its progress through time.

This sense of timing betrays one of the most important functions that the
concept of a radical national culture had in the period. During the 1930s,
left-wing intellectuals were concerned with understanding what differentiated their projects from the internationalism and alienation of the so-called
Lost Generation. While the bohemians of the Roaring Twenties saw American national culture generally as repressively petit bourgeois and Babbittish,
the literary generation of the 1930s began to identify a nascent anti-bourgeois
strain in American national culture. As Malcolm Cowley puts it in the preface
to his memoir of the 1930s, *The Dream of the Golden Mountains,* when he and
other exiles returned to the United States in the early 1930s, they suddenly
felt "that [they] were living in history."[22] That is, they experienced the shift
from the 1920s to the 1930s as a narrativization, as an entry into organized,
significant time. Modernity ceased to be represented as a series of abstract and
permanent losses (such as Hemingway's famous assertion in *A Farewell to Arms*
that the words Glory and Honor had lost their significance) and came to seem
a moment in narration. Furthermore, the exiles' reentry into history sparked
a reinterpretation of abstractions such as "the nation." While many 20s intellectuals had associated Americanism with capitalism and paid little attention
to the development of that association, 30s intellectuals worked to dissociate
capitalism and nationalism.[23] That dissociation took place when they isolated
what we might call progressive and regressive lines of history—for example,

when Hicks separated a "great tradition" of literary protest from the "mad advance" of capital.

Although literary intellectuals played a public role in this narrativization of American culture, they were not acting alone. For instance, the concept of the nation also became a major place for thinking about progress in the rhetoric surrounding the New Deal. In the social-democratic ideal of the later 1930s, the "nation" took on special significance as the site of economic planning, and therefore as the site of progress over chaos.[24] Thus, the leftists' insistence on a coherent narrative of national culture harmonized with a political agenda that emphasized the role of federal agencies. In the mid- and late 1930s, at several cultural locations, the concept of national culture seemed to offer a way to negotiate between history and the intellectual. Imagined as an alternative to the culture-less bourgeoisie, in its early phases of institutionalization, the concept of national culture remained available for insurgent cultural politics.

By 1941, however, when Granville Hicks finally had the opportunity to respond to Matthiessen's review with his own comments on *American Renaissance,* the terms had shifted. The Hitler-Stalin pact in 1939 had made it impossible for many left intellectuals—among them Hicks—to continue to associate themselves with the Communist Party,[25] and there was a widespread sense that the world that they had known was once again on the brink of crisis. One element of this crisis was that national culture began to be defined in terms of space (if not actual territory) rather than time, and form rather than content. For example, in *American Renaissance,* Matthiessen reduces his story of American culture to the five years of the so-called Renaissance, so that he can produce a basically synchronic account. Unlike Hicks, he does not feel compelled to summarize the interests of different periods and reproduce a sweep of culture. Despite the metaphors of "organic" growth that pervade his work, Matthiessen is ultimately more concerned with the Renaissance's exemplification of enduring features of the national culture than with the maturation or progressive alteration of that culture.

Hicks points out this aspect of Matthiessen's work when he comments on its "density" and "lack of clarity." *American Renaissance* seems to Hicks to resist the sensible order of narrative, and this resistance is most significant at the meta-critical level. According to Hicks, not only does Matthiessen not organize his critical account along narrative lines, but also he refuses to highlight his own points of disagreement with the thinkers whose works he describes. That is, he does not set up his own narrative of intellectual development; he perpetuates the illusion that he inhabits the same conceptual space as Emerson and Whitman. He fails, in Hicks's words, "to 'repossess' their discoveries, in terms of our knowledge and our convictions and our dilemma" in the present.[26]

At the same time, despite this serious criticism of Matthiessen's project, Hicks also betrays some of the same tendency to conceive of national culture in spatial terms. In his review of *American Renaissance,* he describes a turn away from history and toward religion in Matthiessen and other critics of his generation; this turn involves referring to the present as a "disaster." Although not sympathetic to religious thinking, Hicks, too, registers a fear that the future (in his old sense of an imminent historical necessity) does not exist anymore. He displays a fear that history has left him stranded—like an abandoned child—in the present. That present, as he understands it, is circumscribed by a culture "of which the Vichy regime may be a rough model," a culture in which the static realm of "order is achieved at the expense of liberty."[27]

This claustrophobic description of national culture reflects certain crucial features of the left's response to fascism in the late 1930s and early 1940s. In the United States, until the very late 1930s, fronts against fascism had primarily been of interest to intellectuals struggling to define a radical American nationalism that would counter fascist versions of nationalism. These efforts initially took shape in various coalitions across party lines, but these broke down extremely rapidly when internecine squabbling made solidarity too difficult to achieve.[28] Since homegrown North American fascism never became formal enough to inspire a significant opposition, the specter of counterrevolutionary nationalism seemed to many Americans a European problem; this "it can't happen here" attitude encouraged two related developments. First, in the late 1930s, members of the U.S. left began to apply the term "fascist" or "social-fascist" to members of rival leftist factions at least as often as they used it to describe genuine fascists; hence the word often degenerated into a casual insult and lost the more careful social analysis that it could have contained.[29] This sloppiness allowed a second development: the discourse of nationalism rapidly became the territory of liberal anti-fascists who promoted a proleptically bowdlerized version of the Frankfurt School's analysis of totalitarianism.[30] The totalitarian thesis rearranged the positions surrounding radical nationalism; while in the early 1930s, American national culture was understood to be a tradition of radical revolt against aristocratic elitism and petty materialism, in the late 1930s, it became more narrowly associated with the political ideology of individualism, as against the supposedly structurally identical determinisms of fascism and Communism. Since this view relies on a map of culture on which the United States is a lone isle of democratic freedom, it is not surprising that it encouraged a claustrophobic response among leftists. Understanding other systems as systems of "total" control, that is, as functionalist machines, proponents of the totalitarian thesis could only predict a future of stalemates. It was not change or progress that they imagined as a national goal, but simply the preservation of a tiny space of individualistic resistance.

This shift in the basic ways of conceiving of national culture from the early to the late 1930s does much to explain the hostility directed at the leftist literary historians. On this line of argument, we can read allegations that their analyses were necessarily reductive, or entirely dictated by party dogma, or incapable of aesthetic judgment, as evidence for a paradigm shift at the end of the 1930s, a shift completed after the end of World War II. At some point in the 1930s, American national culture lost its necessarily radical character in the eyes of leftist observers. Reconstructing their initial thesis reveals that in the 1930s the narrative of American national culture developed in literary histories helped leftists negotiate a position between modernist ahistoricism and fascism. In the ideological environment of the Depression, American nationalism was not always only equivalent to hegemonic repression. It was, instead, what Maria Mies has called a "struggle-concept."[31] That is, it was a concept adapted for its tactical utility, despite the problems entangled with it, and dropped when that utility eventually waned.

When we turn, in later chapters, to examine Canadian writings from the 1930s, it will be even more evident that "the nation" was a viable category for leftists during the 1930s. In Canada, cultural nationalism was a three-edged sword at least. It enabled critiques of British cultural imperialism, U.S. economic imperialism, and homegrown Tory diffidence.[32] Similarly, in the United States during the 1930s, "the nation" was a weapon on which many leftists relied, even as they watched it transform before their eyes into a justification for some of the worst atrocities of the hot and cold wars.

Chapter 2

"ALL RIGHT WE ARE TWO NATIONS"

Speed and the Stratification of Culture in *U.S.A.*

Between 1930 and 1936, during the most severe phases of the Depression, John Dos Passos published his *U.S.A.* trilogy. This trilogy ranges widely over the North American continent, exploring many social crannies and staking claims with a host of literary progenitors, not least of whom were the leftist literary historians examined in the last chapter. Their literary histories put forward the radically teleological view of national culture that forms part of the substructure of *U.S.A.*, although Dos Passos's trilogy implicitly refutes this teleology and projects its own darker, more open-ended and chaotic narrative. That is, *U.S.A.* positions Dos Passos on the margins of leftist culture, as an internal critic formed by the nationalism that he would oppose.

Of course, this view of Dos Passos's politics is not entirely new, and it could hardly be otherwise, seeing as it builds in part on the explicit commentaries Dos Passos makes on the political situation of his era. For example, *The Big Money*'s portrait of politico Mary French, drawn from real-life labor journalist Mary Heaton Vorse, is a famously cautionary one.[1] As many commentators have noted, Mary's betrayal and dejection certainly figure Dos Passos's disaffiliation from Communist Party politics. At the same time, the form of *U.S.A.* also modifies this explicit political commentary. The form, I will argue, articulates a much more fully engaged critique of the underlying cultural assumptions of the leftist literary community. The shape of Dos Passos's trilogy, its writerly technologies, its engagement with extant models of culture, and its struggle to define itself within and against these models display Dos Passos's entanglement with his ideological horizon, a horizon that includes the literary left.

More specifically, the form of *U.S.A.* reproduces types of speed—in its narra-

45

tives, in its montage of modes of writing, in its projected reading strategies—that take the acceleration of culture as a given. So, while the surface content of the literary historians' teleology is discarded in *U.S.A.*, the speed of that teleology, the foreshortening of distance or the acceleration associated with it, is not. The modes of perception of 30s literary histories became a necessary part of the ideological environment in which Dos Passos worked. By exploring the written technologies of speed, in particular, Dos Passos implicated himself in the cultural nationalism of the literary historians while also casting a critical eye on their various determinisms.

A Brief Cultural History of Speed

At the start of the twentieth century, speed was acquiring a new significance in the United States. In 1899, a New York cab driver became the first American arrested for speeding; the ticket charged him with careening along at the "breakneck speed" of twelve miles per hour. Only two years later, in 1901, the New York state legislature set the first automobile speed limit—at fifteen mph in the country and twelve mph in the city.[2] Balanced on either side of the century mark, these two incidents record an acceleration of socially acceptable speeds. What had been life-threatening in 1899 was status quo in 1901; very rapidly, people became accustomed to new speeds.

This shift was made possible, in part, by a host of new technologies that took advantage of the high power-to-fuel ratio of the internal combustion engine; of these, the automobile and the airplane ultimately had the greatest impact on social life. These inventions altered individuals' relations to time and space by making travel across great distances possible at great speeds—as well as inspiring new methods of production, new forms of international relations, and new areas of state regulation.[3] Furthermore, as a number of recent studies have demonstrated, these social changes also had a marked impact on cultural and intellectual life.[4] As early as 1900, the historian Henry Adams could see in technology a "sudden irruption of forces totally new."[5] Other early-twentieth-century cultural critics, such as Lewis Mumford and Stuart Chase, agreed that the United States had entered a frightening new phase of culture, and they, too, differentiated modern from pre-modern societies on the basis of their technological development.[6] The economist Thorstein Veblen argued that a new class of engineers and technicians now controlled U.S. society and that no social transformation could take place without their assistance. Pessimistically, Veblen concluded that the engineers were at present "fairly contented subalterns."[7] Nonetheless, the new class did find a political voice, briefly, in the Technocracy movement of the mid-1930s. Inspired by Progressive reformers and the ideas of Veblen and Edward Bellamy, among others, proponents of Technocracy argued for a more efficient society managed by technical experts. Although the Technocracy party always remained peripheral to the national political scene, many technocratic ideas crept into the social-democratic policies of the New Deal, and, overall, the fact that technicians organized politically demonstrates that debate concerning technology was by no means confined to the laboratory or the workshop in the early part of the twentieth century.[8]

It was this lineage of thought on technology and especially technologies of speed that provided Dos Passos with both the literal reference points and the metaphoric substructure of the *U.S.A.* trilogy.[9] The time frame of *U.S.A.* reflects Dos Passos's sense that the twentieth century marked the start of a new era, beginning as it does with the nearly simultaneous inauguration of a president and the century. Similarly, the trilogy is thickly peopled with representatives of the new class: engineers, scientists, public relations men, movie stars, and petty bureaucrats. Veblen himself even makes an appearance in one of the biographical sections, as do technologically minded celebrities such as the Wright brothers and Thomas Edison. The settings, too, indicate Dos Passos's interest in the new speeds; he often situates his characters in places where they will betray their dependence on modern transportation—in railroad stations, airports, and roadhouses. His plot lines continually subject these characters to the brutal and occasionally lethal pace of modern technology; characters die in plane crashes, are wounded by autos, and hopelessly chase trains receding down the track.

At the same time, the new technologies influenced Dos Passos's understanding of the writer's position in modern society. In a short essay written about the same time as *U.S.A.,* Dos Passos argues that "the importance of a writer, as of a scientist, depends on his ability to influence thought. In his relation to society a professional writer is a technician just as much as an engineer is."[10] According to this theory, the best interests of writers, like those of technicians, are necessarily opposed to those of bureaucrats, managers, and other servants of the profit motive. This latter group officiously strives to organize social energy—to separate, specify, and stratify creative labor until it finally produces efficient, profitable social machines, such as the newspaper. As technicians, then, writers require a certain "liberty" from such organizations so that they may fulfill their function of "trying to discover the deep currents [of historical change]";[11] as technicians, writers may be required to offer up the products of their labor to the social machine, but their best invention takes place on its periphery. In short, the three major elements of Dos Passos's argument are an analogy between the writer and the technician, an analogy between social organization and the machine, and the assumption that the "deep currents" of history flow in a liberated and non-mechanized manner. In his most prescriptive mood, Dos Passos aligns the writer/technician with the free flow of history and against the rigid machine.

These three categories—the writer/technician, the social machine, and a freely flowing history—also organize *U.S.A.* In the trilogy, as we shall see, the purportedly autobiographical "camera eye" sections outline a writer's development in stages analogous to the historical periods described in the narrative sections; this pairing of the writer/technician with history is set against both the stories of great failures in the biographies and the world of mass-produced writing in the newsreels; that is, the career of the historically minded writer is contrasted to the sacrifices of quality exacted by a machinic writing. Dos Passos is interested in exposing this opposition; he creates his own literary machine in order to force the reader to confront the possible incompatibility of writing and the machine.

Before turning to an analysis of Dos Passos's literary form, however, we should note more explicitly how his concern with technology strains against the narratives of the leftist literary historians. As I have suggested, Dos Passos all but adopted Veblen's description of the technicians as an emergent class that struggles with business in the interest of a more efficient social organization; his analogy between the writer and the technician simply extends Veblen's analysis to the publishing industry. This view directly contradicted the Third Period thesis of the early 1930s that insisted the revolution of *workers* against the owners of the means of production would establish an entirely new social organization and *soon*.[12] Although both the leftists and Veblen understood writers to be analogous to, or allied with, emergent classes and in contest with a dominant class, they diverged in their identification of the emergent class and, therefore, in their assessment of the overall tendency of the "deep currents" of history. While Veblen's view lends itself to the gloomy conclusion that the purportedly free flow of history is being constrained by the spread of bureaucratic machines, the leftist literary historians usually concluded that party organizations would help them direct the flow of a history that necessarily tends toward liberation.[13] That is, the contest between Veblen and the leftists centered on the possibility of historical change and the role social organizations might play in directing history.

In "The Workman and His Tools," Dos Passos does not resolve this dispute; instead, he declines comment on the question of history while referring to the writer's relationship with organizations as a "dilemma." "[H]onest technicians," he writes, try to "combat the imperial and bureaucratic tendencies of the groups whose aims they believe in, without giving aid and comfort to the enemy," and he can only conclude that, torn between these two, often incompatible goals, "in such a position a man is exposed to crossfire."[14] In 1935, this irresolution allowed Dos Passos to live with the contradiction of being an individualist who worked within the bureaucracy of the Communist Party's writers' organizations; he justifies his association with what seemed to him at the time the only satisfactory leftist organization by refusing to address his doubts directly.[15] Meanwhile, he reserved a fuller depiction of the problem and its possible resolution for *U.S.A.* In *U.S.A.,* I will argue, Dos Passos confirms neither voluntarism nor determinism. Instead, he takes advantage of the strain between the two positions to present his own more chaotic narrative of twentieth-century U.S. history and his own view of the increasingly unpredictable role of the writer or intellectual in that history. Finally, the complex form of the *U.S.A.* trilogy represents Dos Passos's effort to perform for the reader the social transformations—and especially those relating to speed—that he could not or would not resolve theoretically.

Speed in *U.S.A.*

Commenting on the organization of *U.S.A.,* Dos Passos once remarked that it worked because the subjective elements were "drained off" into the camera eye sections; then, the remainder of the text was free to represent objective forces or the supra-individual sweep of history. Whether or not this theory is verifiably correct and whether or not Dos Passos employs it successfully, it demonstrates that he hoped the different elements of the trilogy would represent portions of a dialectic between subject and object, or the writer and history.[16] In other words, whatever conclusions Dos Passos might be suggesting about the pace or flow of American culture will probably not be found in an isolated segment of the work but instead in the interaction among all its parts.

The four modes of writing in the trilogy—the newsreels, fictional narratives, biographies, and camera eyes—operate at different speeds and combine in a manner that complicates the question of an average or overall speed of history. We might say that they relate isolated episodes to "history" the way light particles are related to a light wave; the regular pace of the whole and the divergent, almost chaotic, tendencies of the parts are simultaneously suggested. Furthermore, each mode of writing plays out a similar contradiction in its formulation, so that each helps to describe a history that would not be apparent from the sum or average of the parts.

Dos Passos's model for this holistic writing was almost certainly Whitman, but the two were so differently situated in history that they necessarily employed different means of representing history.[17] "O, my body!" Whitman writes in "I Sing the Body Electric,"

> I dare not desert the likes of you in other men and women, nor the likes of
> the parts of you,
> I believe the likes of you are to stand or fall with the likes of the soul, (and
> that they are the soul,)
> I believe the likes of you shall stand or fall with my poems, and that they
> are my poems,
> Man's, woman's, child's, youth's, wife's, husband's, mother's, father's,
> young man's, young woman's poems,
> Head, neck, hair, ears, drop and tympan of the ears,
> Eyes, eye-fringes, iris of the eye, eyebrows, and the waking or sleeping of
> the lids,
> Mouth, tongue, lips, teeth, roof of the mouth, jaws, and the jaw-hinges.[18]

Echoes of Whitman's catalogues can be heard throughout *U.S.A.,* and yet there is an audible difference between Whitman's poem and this passage from the preface that introduces each of Dos Passos's three volumes:

> The young man walks fast by himself through the crowd that thins into
> the night streets; feet are tired from hours of walking; eyes greedy for

warm curve of faces, answering flicker of eyes, the set of a head, the lift of
a shoulder, the way hands spread and clench; blood tingles with wants;
mind is a beehive of hopes buzzing and stinging; muscles ache for the
knowledge of jobs, for the roadmender's pick and shovel work, the fisher-
man's knack with a hook when he hauls on the slithery net from the rail
of the lurching trawler, the swing of the bridgeman's arm as he slings
down the white hot rivet, the engineer's slow grip wise on the throttle,
the dirtfarmer's use of his whole body when, whoaing the mules, he yanks
the plow from the furrow. The young man walks by himself searching
through the crowd with greedy eyes, greedy ears taut to hear, by himself, alone.[19]

In a Whitmanesque fashion, the preface catalogues the intimate machinery
of the human body; it follows a young man walking quickly through the night
streets of a city. The young man's body yearns to spread itself out across the
social mechanism and merge with the laboring bodies of fishermen, bridge-
men, engineers, and dirtfarmers as they work the tools of their trade. This
young man's body is vibrant and articulated, and it represents a set of social
relations, but there the resemblance to Whitman ends. Dos Passos's bodies are
made up not of items but of motions, of the *"flick* of eyes, the *set* of a head,
the *lift* of a shoulder, the way hands *spread and clench"* (xix; emphasis added).
While Whitman's bodies lie sleeping or disassembled or stand on the auction
block motionlessly accessible to the scrutiny of his wandering "I," Dos Passos's
moving bodies delimit the realm of the narrative; his restive consciousness follows the motile young man who walks "fast but not fast enough, far but not
far enough" (xix). The narrative tries to keep step with him as he cannot quite
manage to catch up with the various subways, streetcars, and buses driving
every which way. He wants to go everywhere and be everything, but, like the
narrative, he cannot generalize himself. He remains "alone," his only link to
grander social processes: his ears. They catch the speech that binds together
the many places and times through which he could travel and organize them
into the nation. As the last sentence of the preface states quite bluntly, "mostly
U.S.A. is the speech of the people."

This use of "speech" accents the difference between what Whitman can say
in 1891 and what Dos Passos cannot in 1930. Whitman can claim that the body
itself is the poem, that it is the soul, that it must not be deserted or divided—

even if it could be. Such insistent faith in the immediate unity of body and poem nourishes his famous aesthetic self-confidence. Dos Passos's novels, on the other hand, read more somberly and employ a more intricate, less glorious voice. For Dos Passos, the body and the social order are in repetitious but non-synchronous motion, and his work is to register the mercurial "speech" that occasionally unites these uneasy partners.[20] Such a speech cannot be too easily located in one place or time—or else it will cease its translative function. Rather, like the anonymous young man, it wants to be everywhere and in everything; it is "of the people," not in the people. While Whitman's singing "I" electrifies an inert body, Dos Passos's "speech" rides the current already running the "body electric." For him, speech and speed evoke the free-flowing mobility that he associates, at least theoretically, with history itself.

Massifying Culture in the Newsreels

This preface is in constant friction with the other modes of writing in *U.S.A.* —each of which has its own velocity and its own implicit narrative of American culture. The sixty-eight newsreel sections, for example, describe the pace of a rapidly differentiating mass culture. Gathering snippets of popular songs, newspaper clippings, and dramatic headlines, these sections trace the invention of mass culture as a historical phenomenon. The first newsreel presents the image of a nation more or less unified; labor, churches, and the nation greet the new century while President McKinley is hard at work in his office, and the only battles take place far away in the Philippines. By the time the final newsreel of the trilogy rolls around, however, the early light-hearted humor has been replaced by irony. This tone emerges in the stark contrasts between folksy songs of suffering ("*while we slave for the bosses / Our children scream an' cry*"), glaring political violence ("POLICE TURN MACHINE GUNS ON COLORADO / MINE STRIKERS KILL 5 WOUND 40"), and the impoverished political rhetoric of a president who devotes his time to dedicating bird sanctuaries. By the end of the trilogy, the voices of mass culture speak for distinct groups that, rather than shouting or giggling in the single voice of the nation, articulate sharply differentiated concerns in distinctive manners. For Dos Passos, then, the spread of a stratified mass culture is part and parcel of an exacerbation of contradictions in the culture at large.

Nonetheless, the complete record of history is not encapsulated in the de-

velopment of the culture industry; instead, the media register the acceleration of one part of American society. In *U.S.A.,* the particular perspective of
the media always involves a distortion of some type, so that social conflict
seems simply sensational violence. For this reason, the tabloid headlines in the
newsreels grow increasingly more brutal as the trilogy progresses; progressively
greater numbers of scandalous murders, drownings, kidnappings, massacres,
and suicides are reported. Some of these, like the gunning down of Colorado
miners, have political consequences that resonate in several registers of the
trilogy, but most are the sensational, anonymous dramas of ordinary people.
The "GIRL DYING IN MYSTERY PLUNGE" and the "LUNATIC [who] BLOWS UP
PITTSBURGH BANK" are not personal tragedies; they are presented as inescapable facts of social experience. Parts of the social body continually break off and
self-destruct; dysfunctional misfits are produced and expelled at a tremendous
rate. For Dos Passos, these images are symptoms; the media's obsession with
sensational violence highlights the relish with which the public consumes the
evidence of its own decay.

The rapid historical development of a culture of consumption is also apparent in the advertisements that surround the "news" of the newsreels. In the
third volume, want ads, promotions of dancing lessons, celebrations of new
auto parts, tourist information for Detroit, and tempting statistics about the
number of people who have recently chosen to smoke Chesterfields all make an
appearance. Although sometimes humorous, the advertisements also acquire
an unpleasant edge once we realize that they are replacing the first volume's
more anecdotal clippings. In the early newsreels, humor is derived primarily
from descriptions of village eccentricities, as in the following example:

PLUMBER HAS HUNDRED LOVES

BRINGS MONKEYS HOME

> missing rector located losses in U.S. crop report let baby go naked if you
> want it to be healthy if this mystery is ever solved you will find a woman
> at the bottom of the mystery said Patrolman E. B. Garfinkle events leading
> up to the present war run continuously back to the French Revolution.
> (*42nd Parallel,* 287–88)

The superficial humor of the advertisements, by contrast, is aggressively modern and transparently motivated, and their audiences are clearly positioned as
normal, urban types, rather than local eccentrics. They ask, for example, "ARE

YOU NEW YORK'S MOST BEAUTIFUL GIRL STENOGRAPHER?" They condense and channel the population into manageable masses of girl stenographers or "likely lads," as the want ad lingo puts it.

In the newsreels, politics also follows this pattern of stratification. Whereas in the first volume, the relation of media to events is supposed to be one of complacent disengagement, in the last, almost all reportage stridently proclaims its ideological markings. In *42nd Parallel,* the "CZAR YIELDS TO PEOPLE" (76), but in *The Big Money,* the "imagination boggles at the reports from Moscow. These murderers have put themselves beyond the pale. They have shown themselves to be the mad dogs of the world" (441). Even the musical lyrics evolve from the fun love songs of the Jazz Age ("you great big beautiful doll") to soldier's campsongs and the Internationale, until what remains of the folk tradition is ideologically marked as populist by its persistence in a context of advertisement and filibuster.

On the one hand, then, mass culture in *U.S.A.* moves the national culture toward a controlled fragmentation or stratification. Yet, on the other hand, this narrative is also disrupted. For example, newsreels—like the one above that splices together a missing rector, a crop report, and naked babies—frequently but at irregular intervals include mini-collages within the collage. These startle the eye and require a sudden change in the pace of reading. Simulating the garbled effect of skimming a newspaper hastily, the mini-collages paradoxically teach readers to slow down and thus to experience anew the media's contradictions. The effort required to make sense of passages such as "missing rector located losses in U.S. crop report let baby go naked" involves identifying the links among the various phrases, since it is the ambiguity over whether the rector has been located or whether he located losses that makes the passage run together. From this series, the attentive reader isolates particular elements, while simultaneously appreciating the joke that this is a stream of mass consciousness that "run[s] continuously back to the French Revolution."

In a like manner but on a larger scale, the reader vacillates between micro- and macrocosm in the expanding and contracting time scheme of the newsreels. The first volume covers the fourteen years between the turn of the century and the U.S. entry into World War I, and one tends to read its newsreels for depictions of broad social trends. Similarly, since the third volume treats the ten or so years from the end of the war to the stock market crash of 1929, the implication is that news progresses steadily from event to event. In contrast, though, the second volume is concerned only with the four or five years of the war, and the sense of a regular chronology, of a reliable and hence invisible macrocosm, evaporates. Mimicking the pace of public events, Dos Passos's evocative re-creation of mass culture makes time bulge in certain places and grow slim and streamlined in periods when "nothing" (i.e., nothing violent or ideologically marketable) happens.[21] This narrative strategy leads readers to adjust repeatedly the magnification on the telescope through which they read history in *U.S.A.*

Finally, though, the question of whether history has a speed and what it might be remains unanswered by a consideration of mass culture or the newsreels alone. Although mass culture certainly has speeds—both very fast and very slow—no good reason surfaces to insist that these can be identified with the speeds of history. In fact, the ironies so evident in Dos Passos's arrangement of the newsreels suggest that they are not sufficient to chronicle history. Only in comparison to at least one other perspective could they offer a more total view; in the absence of any embodiment of a single speed of history, velocity must be calculated relatively.

Hollow Narratives

Complementing the frantic and generalizable pace of mass culture, the fictional narratives that make up the bulk of the trilogy focus on individuals. In *U.S.A.*, however, individuality is not the truth behind the veil, or an optimistic alternative to social determinism. As many readers have objected, the characters and the narratives are often empty of emotion or "hollow."[22] I would argue that this hollowness is not a flaw but, on the contrary, the sign of a goal achieved; the hollowness of his characters signals Dos Passos's deflation of an anthropomorphic theory of history.

For the fifteen characters to whom narrative sections are devoted in *U.S.A.*, being an individual means having one's whole life told in approximately 150 pages of un-purple prose. The actions and the dialogue are resolutely plain and plebeian, and when they reach emotional climaxes, these are most likely to be recorded as blanknesses. Take, for example, the homecoming of Charley Anderson, aviator and decorated war hero. Arriving in New York, he hops in a taxi and chats with the driver on his way to the hotel:

> "But, Jesus, I don't ever remember things bein' as quiet as this."
> "Well, why shouldn't they be quiet? . . . It's Sunday, ain't it?"

"Oh, sure, I'd forgotten it was Sunday."

"Sure it's Sunday."

"I remember now it's Sunday."

[end of chapter] (*Big Money,* 34; Dos Passos's ellipsis)

The repetitive character of this dialogue makes Charley's disappointment and exhaustion singularly evident. Even his disappointment over the non-eventfulness of the event is not an important psychological moment for the narrative; such ennui is typical for this character, as the diction indicates. All his events are reported with the flatness of journalistic prose; they are all equally unimportant.[23] A tension then results between the ordinariness of the scene to the character and the presumed significance of the scene to the novel. Since the novel does not by any means narrate all the episodes concerning a character, those that appear imply their own newsworthiness. In a scene like Charley's homecoming, the reader ends up questioning the principles of narration. If Charley's personal apathy is not the subject, what is eventful, significant, or exceptional to the novel, one asks.

The answer to this question is almost never "psychology," since emotional events are remarkably unstable quantities in *U.S.A.* For example, when Charley later meets actress Margo Dowling, the meeting is a high point in his narrative. Yet, Margo's narrative passes over the meeting with barely a ripple. Such disjunctions reveal that Dos Passos is not primarily concerned with the problem of perspective or with the event; his point is not to contrast perspectives on one event or even to express the emotional poverty of modern life. Instead, both narratives emphasize their recording of audible speech. When the normally transient spoken word is recorded, it becomes an object, and this object concerns Dos Passos.

This interest is especially apparent in the descriptive passages; these are packed with eye-catching hyphenless compound words. Peculiar-looking on the page, these words emphasize items so ordinary that a novelist commonly ignores them and an American speaker rushes through their pronunciation. On the other hand, in his references to the *linoleumsmelling companionway, diningsaloon, brasspolish, cigarettesmoke,* and *waterpitcher,* Dos Passos takes advantage of a peculiar virtue of English grammar—the ability to modify nouns with nouns. He captures the tendency of American speakers to glide over prepositions and makes that linguistic habit represent the flatness of the entire culture. As a result, his narratives do not progress at the deep, slow, autonomous pace of the individual; rather they proceed fitfully. They skate fluidly along clauses linked by conversational "and" upon "and" until they stumble periodically on an opaque print object like *linoleumsmelling.*

In the narrative sections, recorded speech and non-individual pacing are markers of the modern period, and as such they are important themes in their own right. Yet, at the same time, the narrative sections as a whole also contribute to Dos Passos's overall interest in the speed of history, since, in these sections, he charts a historical trend toward acceleration. From the first character to appear, Mac (the young Irish American who sells pornography from a horse and buggy), to Joe (the unlucky merchant mariner floating far on the periphery of World War I), to Charley (aviator, inventor, and dissipated owner of an airplane factory), to Margo (the super-ambitious vaudeville girl aiming for stardom in the motion pictures), *U.S.A.* traces a recognizable trajectory. Working conditions, ambitions, possibilities for women, sexual relations, and other features of modern life are changing quickly; the areas in which one succeeds are those that involve moving fast or talking fast or, in Margo's case, being "fast," in what is, for Dos Passos, the always important colloquial sense of the word. Though some of the characters gather enough momentum to accomplish their goals, the cultural speed-up punishes all of them in some fashion: they die in plane crashes or car crashes or lose their artistic impulses to the world of advertising or are dispirited by others' sell-outs. If there is a cultural or historical or collective speed, it is too fast for any one of them. Like the young man in the preface, they are always chasing a bus that has just pulled away from the corner.

At the same time, the narratives make it difficult to calculate any supra-individual speed, since, like the newsreels, they do not employ a regular or consistent clocktime as a reference. Not only do the narratives, like the newsreels, expand around incidents of particular interest—certain parties, Armistice Day, or moments of discovering vocation—but also the characters do not all occupy the same temporal scheme, as Barbara Foley has demonstrated.[24] We find the characters of the narratives proceeding at their own paces (none of which is the pace of the fully embodied and emotional Individual) while also engaging with a public cultural or historical speed. With this multiplicity, the narratives make it difficult to claim that this text is strictly determinist or strictly voluntarist in its orientation; rather they point to a gap and a doubleness repeated on many planes of culture in different vocabularies; they set both self and world, or public and private, or individual and society, or subject and object into simultaneous and destabilizing motion.

Reified Biographies

The "objective" mode of writing that most explicitly concerns the lack of synchronicity between the newsreels and the narratives is the biography. Scattered across *U.S.A.*, the twenty-five biographical prose poems examine public individuals, people who have managed, in different and heroic ways, to mediate the different speeds of history by embracing reification. For example, Dos Passos reduces the celebrity biographies to an approximation of the public's image of them; Rudolph Valentino actually becomes a series of "personal appearances." His biography insists that he takes the heady pace of the public world as his own and rides the wave of the newsreels. His identity is not genetic—it's photogenic; "he wanted to make good in the brightlights" is the phrase that repeatedly describes him (*Big Money*, 206-9). Sadly, the cost of this intense identification with his own moving-picture image is extremely high. Thoroughly absorbed in defending himself from an attack on his image, Valentino falls prey to a graphically described and deadly gastric ulcer. As Dos Passos would have it, the body expelled from his reified identification with publicity returns for its revenge.

For Dos Passos, the costs and benefits of mediating between two speeds, between mass culture and the fiction of individuality, always tally up to a loss; however, different types of loss may occur. In the biography of dancer Isadora Duncan, for example, it is not the body that suffers erasure; on the contrary, since the body was Duncan's medium, she became simply visceral. The biography charts how, in her admirable but melancholic drift into sensuality, Duncan abandoned communication with any community intangible enough to carry her beyond the personal, physical tragedy of death (*Big Money*, 170-76). Conversely, the biography of the Wright brothers describes the way that the public's identification of their discovery with newsy novelty meant the loss of any appreciation for the high ideals and sublime aspects of their "soar into the air" (*Big Money*, 293-98).

Despite these differences, though, in each case the biographical subject's negotiation between personal narrative and public culture is ultimately reified. For Dos Passos, socially circulating an idea—such as Frederick Taylor's theories of time and efficiency—necessarily involves one in the process of reification, a process that requires the loss of what he hopes will remain the free, if complex, flow of history. The regulation of time and speed required to negotiate between disjunctive elements of culture is, for Dos Passos, the major ingredient of the Depression-era social tragedy.

Language of the Camera Eyes

While the biographies evoke a loss involved in reification, the camera eye sections take the protracted development of reification as a topic. The territory that they explore is the capricious autobiographical subject's encounter with language. The artist-figure whose life story these Joycean passages suggest rarely appears in the first person, but each episode in his development, each linguistic event, positions him ever more precisely. His free-ranging, fuzzy consciousness takes shape as it discovers the cruelty of linguistic abstractions, so that, finally, the camera eye sections engage in a series of reflections on whether it is ever possible to negotiate between the differently paced streams of culture or history without loss.

The first records of childhood in the camera eye sections feature impressionistic experiments with words in several European languages: "O que c'est beau schön prittie prittie and the moonlight ripple ripple under a bridge and the little reverbères are alight in the dark . . . O que c'est beau la lune / and the big moon," the narrator prattles (*42nd Parallel,* 30). At this childish stage, language is a pleasurable, interlinked series of insignificant sounds. In the third camera eye, however, the disembodied narrative consciousness discovers meaning, and he discovers it as abstract and demeaning. Overhearing his mother use the word "greasers" to describe laborers shot in a nearby mill, the eye marks for the first time the social effects that the "speech of the people" can have; in this case, it allows his mother to minimize the killing—they're just "greasers" after all (*42nd Parallel,* 50). Speech, and especially colloquial American speech, contains within itself the legitimation of violence, the seeds of tragedy.

In the wartime camera eyes, speech becomes even more lethal; that is, it becomes less concrete and aural. Though the camera eye still takes delight in the incomprehensible soldierly slang that disrupts the inane routines of army life, he has by this time discovered writing as a profession. His relation to this discovery is ambivalent at best, precisely because he fears the reduction of avocation to profession and the concomitant reduction of speech to the written word. Finally, he cannot identify himself with this alienated language; the "pastyfaced young man," as he ironically refers to himself, "wearing somebody else's readymade business opportunity / is most assuredly not / the holder of any of the positions for which he made application at the unemployment agency" (*Big Money,* 54). Writing as a profession here means using readymade speech, a phenomenon as distasteful to the narrator as standardized ready-made clothes; both of these are suspect, reeking as they do of uniforms and wartime utilitarianism.

This reduction of mobile speech to readymade writing first horrifies the cam-era eye on aesthetic grounds and later on political ones, when not only the language spoken by the people but also the language that should be spoken to represent the people becomes abstract, frozen, reified. In the last volume, after a two-hundred-page silence from the camera eye, a newly politicized persona speaks, one who is committed to preventing the execution of Sacco and Van-zetti. When they are finally executed, the eye's persistent irony produces its bitterest fruit and its last hope:

> America our nation has been beaten by strangers who have turned our language inside out who have taken the clean words our fathers spoke and made them slimy and foul
>
> their hired men sit on the judge's bench they sit back with their feet on the tables under the dome of the State House they are ignorant of our beliefs they have the dollars the guns the armed forces the powerplants
>
> they have built the electricchair and hired the executioner to throw the switch
>
> all right we are two nations
>
> . . . .
>
> but do they know that the old words of the immigrants are being re-newed in blood and agony tonight . . .
>
> the men in the deathhouse made the old words new before they died.
> (*Big Money,* 469)

This final spurt of confidence in the renewal of the "slimy and foul" words fades a mere fifty pages later. In the last camera eye section, when visiting the striking Harlan County coal miners, the eye asks "what can we say to the jailed . . . we have only words against Power Superpower" (*Big Money,* 523). Words, especially foreign words, have lost the emotive, connective, human features of speech, and the artistic endeavor then subsides into pessimistic irony. After all, what are words in the face of the far vaster abstract circuitries of power? These,

Dos Passos indicates, operate at the languageless speed of electricity, communicating only instant death to the vicarious occupants of the electric chair. The lingering poetic consciousness of the camera eye, then, by its very redundancy, exhibits its own modernist obsolescence—or, better yet, exhibits what Dos Passos has come at the end of the trilogy to see as the alienation of immediate, transformative, revolutionary speech from the everyday practice of words.

Losing "speech" to words means, for Dos Passos, losing the possibility that history is a free flow, or a "deep current." Instead, American history comes to resemble precisely the type of organized machine that he had hoped to write against; lacking a single speed, embodying the process of negotiation between different speeds, history becomes a reified concept. This reduction of history is tragic in that it involves the loss that any reification might carry for Dos Passos, but, more specifically, it also includes the loss of his vocation as a writer as defined in the "Workman and His Tools" essay. If history does not have a free and mobile speed of its own any longer, then with what or whom can the writer/technician ally himself?

Ending with Vag

The parallel crises of a history without speed and a writing subject without vocation meet at the end of *U.S.A.* in a brief final section titled "Vag." This biography, or narrative, or epilogue picks up the nameless "young man" of the preface. It finds him thrown off a boxcar and onto the road, hungry and burning with desires encouraged by the endless talk of the radio, school, and billboards. While he tries unsuccessfully to catch the eyes of the drivers whose cars race by him, above his head a transcontinental airplane passenger vomits his lunch. Moving at entirely different velocities, these two men have no hope of communicating with one another. Each is locked into his own pattern of speech and speed.

Neither of these streams is especially desirable; the language in which each man speaks to himself is divested of speechy delight. The transcontinental man thinks in terms of "the concrete skyway; trains, planes: history the billion-dollar speedup"; meanwhile, Vag experiences a split between his visceral needs and the public language that addresses his desires. The words swimming in his exhausted corpus torture him with visions. "Opportunity . . . speed . . . shine . . . platinum girls . . . work": they are broad and intangible enough to lure him while also broad and intangible enough to deny sustenance to his body. Speed, in particular, the one word the two men share, is only a word. It is a concept characteristic of the years they have both endured, but it can only promise to abstract history further. Having abandoned the glittering promise of the Wright brothers' sublime invention, speed can only induce vomiting among the wealthy or strand the poor alongside the highway. It is finally only one among a cluster of slogans that differ in content but resemble one another in their effect on both the airplane passenger and the vagrant.

The last phrase of the trilogy completes this sense of deflation. Self-consciously employing a tired metaphor for history, Dos Passos ends *U.S.A.* by simply pointing "A hundred miles down the road" (*Big Money,* 556). There is no verb, no change, no motion imagined in this last phrase, only the road in its static form, and, consequently, there is no subject, no agent, no writer to direct our travel. We do not know if Vag is traveling down the road, if the narrator is encouraging us to spot a car coming over the horizon, or whether Dos Passos can imagine anyone covering this distance. Thus, of the three basic elements of Dos Passos's theory of writing, two have been reconfigured. By the end of *U.S.A.,* he is no longer assuming that history is a free flow, nor does he identify the writer with history any longer. The road, as history, is a cliché going—possibly—nowhere, and the writer does not seem to wish to travel it. In the end, only the analogy between social organization and the machine remains, and this, as we might expect, is a troubling topic for *U.S.A.*

Collision

As in "Vag," the sense of mourning evident behind Dos Passos's concern with speed erupts most visibly at climactic moments in the trilogy's structure—at the end of volumes, in the heat of war, in the narratives of characters whose era is seen to be passing. From this tendency, we can deduce that one of the practices of concern in *U.S.A.* is collision. If, as I have suggested, Dos Passos is distrustful of the social machine, then the places where various aspects of his own writing machine suddenly converge and explode with resonance are crucial; in the debris surrounding these collisions, we might locate a few vestiges of utopian historical consciousness.

Perhaps the most excessive of these conjunctures is the piece titled "The Body of an American"; this elegy to the Unknown Soldier buried in Arlington Cemetery closes the volume on World War I. Probing inside the coffin of a John Doe "raised in Brooklyn, in Memphis, near the lakefront in Cleveland, Ohio, in the stench of the stockyards in Chi, on Beacon Hill, in an old brick house in Alexandria, Virginia, on Telegraph Hill, in a halftimbered Tudor cottage in Portland, the city of roses," this speculative autopsy mourns the anonymous soldier not because he is unidentified, or because his anonymity allows him to represent any *one,* but because his coffin is the repository for too many lives, because his identity is transient (*1919,* 463). Throughout the passage, Dos Passos claims the body for an insurgent national collectivity—drowning out the protestations of the Voice of America (President Harding) who insists that the GI be made into the prototype of a more conservative patriotism.

Although Harding's reading of the corpse is made to sound presumptuous, Dos Passos's primary purpose in this passage is not to replace an abstract patriotism with an equally abstract radical republicanism. Rather he sets Harding's reduction of the man to the ideal type against his own sense of the many lives jostling for attention in order to demonstrate that their common denominator is a singularly uncommunicative body. The only concrete knowledge the narrator can retrieve about this soldier is the fact that "John Doe had a head" and "John Doe / heart pumped blood" (*1919,* 465). This knowledge provides absolutely no comfort in the face of death, but neither does it cancel out the importance of the political meanings attributed to the soldier's death; all it does is take Dos Passos to the rim of death, to the place where the collision among these meanings occurred. In this collision, a transformation from life to death took place. Unfortunately, however, this collision or transformation is to some extent unrepresentable; the description of the climax of this episode skips from "The shell had his number on it" to "The blood ran into the ground" (*1919,* 466). The collision that was the precondition for this scene remains outside the description.

Unless we pause to reflect on death per se, these collisions just behind the surface of the printed page ask us to inquire about the limits of perception. Confronting us with a possibly unrepresentable event, they alter and control the speed of perception by cutting cinematically and arrhythmically between different modes of speech. For example, the section begins with the rapid monotone of an official proclamation and then moves quickly into a second mode of writing that echoes the voice of a sentimental wartime correspondent. This equally official and suspect voice breaks off in mid-sentence, shifting

directly into an "enie menie minie moe" that emphasizes the arbitrary anonymity of the whole process of representing America with a single soldier's
body. Followed by a series of racist slurs and questions about the significance of
"a gunnysack full of bones," the montage demonstrates the inadequacy of any
one of these modes of perception. Only their common activity, their shared
desire to make the body of the American signify, is itself significant; with this
metatextual point, Dos Passos shifts our attention away from the content of the
messages about America and its debt to death and toward the mode in which
we perceive the message. He constructs montages whose organizing principle
is the collision between these equally inadequate modes of writing.

In such series of collisions, Dos Passos marks a major cultural shift. In addition to narrating the progressive stratification of a culture of speed, he hints
that that culture might be disintegrating; he amplifies voices that suggest a
shift from what Paul Virilio has called the "empire of speed" to "total war."[25]
According to Virilio, in the "empire of speed," social and especially military
domination is secured by control over highways, runways, and other avenues
of travel. The best example of this strategy is World War I, a "gasoline war"
which the Allies won by regulating the flow of fuel into the war zones. (Recall
the many conversations about oil during the armistice celebrations in 1919.)
After World War I, however, theorists of "total war" note a shift in military
strategy toward firmly planted command centers; rather than making military
strategy a matter of movement or speed, total warriors ensure domination by
controlling the flow of media into embattled territories. In this situation, the
entire culture becomes a war zone, in which the military struggles to direct
perception.[26]

Virilio's theses seem consonant with Dos Passos's work. After all, in the newsreels Dos Passos portrays the media's so-called barrage of images as an active
assault, and his use of collision as an organizing principle directs our attention toward the strategic aspects of such assaults. In the long run, he is most
interested in the circuits of transmission of speech. Especially in moments of
collision, the mechanical manner in which speech circulates is considerably
more important to Dos Passos than the messages about America being con-
veyed. Furthermore, he even reads the concept of "total war" back into his description of World War I. These passages rarely portray zones of conventional
fighting; instead, they dramatize the way the entire culture changes during
wartime. The characters roam to, from, and through war zones, establishing

a complex network in which they frequently run across one another. Scenes such as Daughter's death in a drunken airplane accident alter the meaning of warfare, suggesting that the technologies of speed on which the military once relied have now become a fatal form of entertainment, while the real business of war takes place on the ground, in the public relations offices, hospitals, and other bureaucratic centers that his characters occupy.

In Dos Passos's work, then, the "total war" thesis contains the vestiges of utopian thinking. Most important, it promises that, despite the abstraction of history, a total social transformation may still be possible. While the prospect of a society organized around bureaucratic and military transmissions of propaganda does not appeal to Dos Passos, aspects of the techniques employed by that society do—in particular the emphasis on collision. The paradox that disorganization can become an organizing principle is at the center of *U.S.A.* In the trilogy, the continuous cutting among the four modes of writing, the intersection of themes attached to one mode with those of another, the circulation of major and minor characters throughout one another's narratives, the punctuality with which autobiographical references are made, the recycling of a word (like *speed*) made heavy with significance—in sum, the sheer proliferation of collisions ultimately confuses what we might call the intended or organized collisions with the unintended ones. The quarantine of the "subjective" element to the camera eyes leads us to ask questions: In which direction are these collisions designed to propel us? Under whose or what's direction or lack of direction are they orchestrated? How can we imagine social transformation without an organizing consciousness? Beneath its complex formal structure, *U.S.A.* tends toward a new Brownian totality, toward a multiplicity of vectors, toward speed in excess of direction and difference in excess of contradiction, and this chaotic impulse supplements the reified currents of history.

Finally, behind Dos Passos's official despair at the stratification of society and the reification of history and the spread of repressive social organizations, he remains interested in these new chaotic patterns. Although as sociopolitical ideas, these tend toward the "libertarian" and are certainly not immune to stagnation,[27] these extra sparks of energy—the patterns emerging voluntaristically from his own text and from the social text—kept Dos Passos writing. In these chaotic collisions, he came closest to approximating his writerly ideal: accessing speed without the machine.

In the end, then, Dos Passos's *U.S.A.* displaces the strain between Veblen and the literary historians. The question whether one should be optimistic or pessimistic about history begins to seem irrelevant in the face of Dos Passos's rigorous anti-psychologism, and the question of the tendency of history seems moot if, as Dos Passos suggests, the movement of history is too multidirectional to chart. Although *U.S.A.* is thickly populated with technophilic characters, these become neither subjects of history nor positions with which the writer may fully identify himself. Instead, we can locate in Dos Passos's work a desire to multiply the subjects of history, to extend the privileges of this position to more than one category of persons—to the speeding writer as well as to the technician who serves the social machine, to the voluntarist *and* the economist, to the individualist *and* the determinist. In this fashion, Dos Passos excuses himself from contemporaneous debates about the revolutionary subject and intellectuals' collective responsibility to this subject. For Dos Passos, there is no single, coherent organizing consciousness or subject—and, hence, very little concept of responsibility.

Clearly, then, the figures of history presented in *U.S.A.* are at odds with the literary historians' vision of a coherent national culture that is moving progressively into a brighter future thanks to a revolutionary alliance between intellectuals and the working class. However, while pointing out this proto-poststructuralist position, I do not mean to suggest that Dos Passos willfully and independently surpassed the literary historians or the left movement because he was somehow able to remain a liberal individual, where the more orthodox leftists, tragically, could not. Rather, I hope to have demonstrated that, despite his critical posture, Dos Passos was interpellated within the problematic of the literary culture of the 1930s. Although he arrives at other conclusions, he addresses the central questions raised by the literary historians. He is concerned with the relationship between culture and history; he examines candidates for emergent subjects of history; and he accepts national culture as an organizing category of his work. Although he fragments and stratifies his trilogy into different generic voices, he is not dismissing the possibility that a national culture exists; he is examining the conditions of that possibility. He identifies characteristic strains that the incoherent entity known as "U.S.A." places on the subjects who are supposed to exemplify that culture—the emerging technophilic subjects, the ordinary "people." The fact that the literary historians' notion of national culture does not adequately describe these subjects' experience of the nation is important to his critique of the left, yet, nonetheless, his is very much a 30s-era critique. In particular, the ambitious question of what characterizes the totality of a national culture was central to the 30s left—even under the quite different circumstances we shall explore in the next chapter.

Chapter 3

A CONFLUENCE OF NATIONALISMS

Hugh MacLennan's Early Writings

While in the United States national narratives were firmly enough in place that they could be adapted or fragmented by the left-wing literati, in Canada during the 1930s the nation had only recently become a discursively solid entity— and not an incredibly solid one at that. After the majority of the provinces joined together in the Confederation of 1867, Canada had the status of a dominion within the British Empire. As a dominion, it had a slogan (*A mari usque ad mare*—from sea to sea) and a famous mounted police force, but it lacked the political independence of a sovereign nation. Not until the conclusion of the Great War did Canada acquire the political powers of a nation. After a strong showing by Canadian troops, in 1921 George V officially proclaimed Canadian colors (red and white) and a Canadian coat of arms that recognized the English, French, Scottish, and Irish as founders of Canada. In the 1920s, negotiations began that ultimately led to the 1931 Statute of Westminster; this statute declared Canada and other imperial holdings, such as South Africa and Australia, equal members in the British Commonwealth. According to the statute, the Canadian Parliament could make laws that would not be overturned by England and it did not have to obey laws made in London. With this statute, the British Empire transformed itself from a centralized power structure into one administered through national centers.

Despite its new national status, however, Canada had few of the practices of nationhood in place in the interwar period. Or, more precisely, it had a confusion of practices. As a dominion with national powers, Canada recognized a head of state separate from the head of government; the English king remained the symbolic head of state, while the Canadian prime minister led the government. This doubleness is recorded on Canadian currency; monarchs appear on the one-, two-, and twenty-dollar bills and coins, while prime ministers appear on five-, ten-, fifty-, and one-hundred-dollar bills. Similarly, during the 1930s, Canada continued to recognize imperial ties by using the Union Jack as its flag. From 1945 to 1965, it flew the Canadian Red Ensign—a Union Jack in the upper left, with the rest of the field red and the Canadian coat of arms on the reverse; not until 1965 was the red and white maple leaf flag adopted. The maple leaf and the beaver had been used as national symbols for some time—the beaver appearing on the first Canadian postage stamp in 1851, and the unofficial anthem, "The Maple Leaf Forever," having been written in 1867. However, these symbols were not uncontested. The Quebecois slogan *je me souviens* (I remember) originated in the late nineteenth century, as did Francophone anthems, flags, and colors.[1] In short, during the 1930s, three symbolic languages for the nation were available to Canadians: Anglophilic depictions of royalty, Franco-friendly gestures toward multiple origins, and the natural world. The monarch, the mosaic, and the beaver/maple leaf were all contenders for the status of national symbol.

Among intellectuals, this multiplicity of vocabularies was also apparent. During the 1930s, historians in particular began paying more attention to Canada as a separate entity. They began researching local phenomena such as the fur trade and the impact of the Saint Lawrence Seaway on North American commerce, and they developed a teleological narrative of nationalization. The national narrative began with a supposedly empty continent waiting to be enlivened by European explorers. Descriptions of the early hardships of the French settlements along the Saint Lawrence were followed by the British struggles with the French, the migration of Scots to the Maritimes, and the post-Confederation population of the Prairies. After the railroad linked the Atlantic and Pacific Oceans and Canadian troops brought glory to themselves and their home in World War I, the narratives of 30s historians conclude with projections of an equally glorious future.

Within this common framework, however, two theses emerged. Tory historians tended to stress the image of Canada as a "vast expanse . . . waiting for man, bearing in his hand the conjurer's rod of civilization"; especially in popular histories, they represented Canadians succeeding in direct proportion to their fealty to the Crown.[2] Drawing on the same material, Liberal historians tended to emphasize the multiple origins of the Canadian population, though they still agreed that "there is a Canadian history which is greater than the sum of these particular histories."[3] Typically, Liberals located this common history in the state, rather than in a definite cultural heritage. In fact, it was Liberal historians such as George M. Wrong who bemoaned the lack of imaginative literature in Canada; "Canada has not yet evolved her own types," Wrong wrote in 1938, "and her literature lacks this tradition."[4] In lieu of a national cast of characters or "types," both Tories and Liberals stressed Canada's vast mineral and agricultural resources, predicting prosperity and status as a major player on the international political scene for Canada as the twentieth century continued. Geography represented national destiny in these histories.

What Canada illustrates, then, is a clear divergence from the revolutionary model of nationalism. On the basis of U.S. and especially French experiences in the eighteenth century, students of nationhood such as Eric Hobsbawm have argued that nationalism develops first as a cultural revival among intellectuals, then as a political movement, and finally as a mass movement resulting in revolution and the establishment of a new nation-state.[5] However, in twentieth-century Canada, the political empowerment of the nation actually preceded a confused semi-national movement among intellectuals, and there seems to have been no mass national movement at all—and certainly no revolution. Instead of inspiring a mass movement, cultural nationalism among Canadian intellectuals was imported after the fact from other political arenas.

After all, the most popular artists and writers of the period were not primarily concerned with cultural nationalism. Ralph Connor, Mazo de la Roche, Martha Ostenso, Nellie McClung, and other romancers used Canadian settings, but, like similar U.S. novels of the time, such as the bestselling *Anthony Adverse,* their works were concerned with the staples of popular writing in many English-speaking nations: love, family, and virtue. Although these topics often took on a political valence, their politics were as likely to be feminist or broadly humanist as national in character.

Even among art writers, the historians' quest for a unifying national culture was unevenly received. As in the United States, cosmopolitan modernism was the order of the day in the 1920s—especially for poets, who often based their aesthetics on T. S. Eliot and European modernists rather than North American precedents.[6] The pattern of voluntary expatriation evident in the United States was even more common in Canada, where ties to English and French cultural centers were stronger. Many budding Canadian writers found cultural nationalism simply irrelevant in the 1920s; they considered it a political (or ethical) imperative that was best ignored.

However, by the mid-1930s, things started to change. Temporary exile in Paris or London often meant exposure to radical political movements as well as radical aesthetics, and when the money ran out and young writers who had learned to admire W. H. Auden and André Breton came home, "the traditional sense of the mimetic relation of literature to history" did not look the same any more, as Dermot McCarthy argues; modernist aesthetics and politics increased the sympathy of a new generation of writers to cultural nationalism.[7] In the new view, literature did not have to reproduce the doings of great heroes or picturesque locales in order to be national; on the contrary, by depicting the lives of ordinary working people in unspectacular locations, literature could help to direct national culture. In this spirit, a new kind of radical Canadian literature arose. While the few works written in an urban radical vein during the 1920s — such as Douglas Durkin's *The Magpie* (1923) or Raymond Knister's *White Narcissus* (1929) — are primarily concerned with portraying artist-figures and the struggle for an individual critical consciousness, later works in the same vein — such as Charles Yale Harrison's *Generals Die in Bed* (1930), Morley Callaghan's *Such Is My Beloved* (1933) and *They Shall Inherit the Earth* (1934), Irene Baird's *Waste Heritage* (1939), or Ted Allan's *This Time a Better Earth* (1939) — take up problems of social life, or at least the artist-figure's difficulties with social life. The later writers were more involved with countercultural political movements and represented these activities in the content and character of their writing. As is often the case, though, many of the more polemical of these writings have been excised from the literary-historical record, our only indication of their tone surviving in Cold War reminiscences such as Earle Birney's *Down the Long Table* (1955).

A thinly fictionalized autobiography, *Down the Long Table* describes the life of Gordon Saunders, an English professor facing a McCarthyist investigation of his morals; in the course of the investigation, Saunders recalls his adventures with Trotskyism during the 1930s.[8] An intellectual of working-class background, he fell in with Stalinists and Trotskyists out of feelings of loneliness and dissatisfaction. Converted through a combination of affection and rationality, he eventually agrees to go to Vancouver to organize a chapter of a Trotskyist splinter group among the unemployed. The majority of the novel concerns his political misadventures—including a confrontation with and the eventual murder of an informant—but major scenes are set apart for discussion of proletarian literature and the role of the intellectual in working-class politics. After considerable examination of the contradictions of these projects, the novel concludes with Saunders's long good-bye to literary and political commitment. In the end, he opts for an attitude of reluctant resignation; he desires action for social change but is utterly disheartened by the infighting, pettiness, isolation, impracticability, and violence of actual left-wing parties in Canada. Overall, the novel gives a condensed description of Birney's own adventures—and those of a number of his political companions—during the 1930s.[9] In its trajectory of discovery, enthusiasm, and involvement, and in its attention to Canadian scenes, *Down the Long Table* revisits a characteristically Depression-era confrontation with the politics of culture. It is only the sense of regretful discouragement and resignation that reminds us the text was written with the political hindsight of the 1950s. In the 1950s, this kind of panoramic assessment of the left movement as a whole could take place because the immediacy of that movement had faded; before that kind of hindsight was possible, though, leftist politics influenced the form as well as the content of a group of literary projects.

Among the leftist writers who took up the new content—the problem of the nation—and, despite their politics, have survived the vicissitudes of literary history, the foremost is Hugh MacLennan. Throughout his career, but especially in his landmark texts *Barometer Rising* (1941) and *Two Solitudes* (1945), MacLennan was understood to be fulfilling an important role: "that of interpreting a rapidly maturing society to its own people." He has been repeatedly called "a national spokesman," although this label can be either insult or praise depending on the speaker.[10] His basic project, it is agreed, was to figure the social forces at work in Canadian culture through conflicts among characters representing group identities. At least in his early works, these conflicts are generally understood to be resolvable, and a utopian conclusion of some type is projected. But in his best-known work, *Two Solitudes,* the conflicts among Scottish, English, and French Canadians are figured in the courtship between two characters of differently mixed heritages. Thus, MacLennan employs the conventions of the "national romance" in his efforts to present a narrative of Canadian national culture.[11] This genre presents numerous difficulties for contemporary readers—not least of which are narratorial didacticism and a tendency toward ethnic stereotyping—but in the context of the 1930s these issues were not the primary focus; instead, the effort to present a nation at all, especially a nation that had only recently emerged from the shadow of colonialism, was a daring and difficult act, and one that could indicate the author's leftist sympathies.

For example, in the opening paragraphs of *Two Solitudes,* MacLennan positions himself as a radical cultural nationalist vis-à-vis contemporaneous politicians and historians. Continuing the theme indicated in the epigraph from Rainer Maria Rilke ("Love consists in this, / that two solitudes protect, / and touch, and greet each other"), the novel opens with a description of confluence: "Northwest of Montreal, through a valley always in sight of the low mountains of the Laurentian Shield, the Ottawa River flows out of Protestant Ontario into Catholic Quebec. It comes down broad and ale-coloured and joins the Saint Lawrence, the two streams embrace the pan of Montreal Island, the Ottawa merges and loses itself, and the mainstream moves northeastward a thousand miles to the sea." [12] Like a Liberal historian, MacLennan draws our attention to a history of division between "Protestant Ontario" and "Catholic Quebec" so that he can narrate their merging and embrace. Then, he uses geography to figure this resolution. The strips of farmland bordering the river are bleak and frozen—reminding us of the decay of the seigneurial system which the novel describes. In the middle of this stream, downriver, is the island of Montreal—a place where "two old races and religions meet . . . and live their separate legends, side by side"; it is a place where MacLennan can listen for the "double beat" of "this sprawling half-continent" 's heart (10). That is, like a Tory, he looks for power centralized in urban capitals with a European flavor; he opposes heartland to uncivilized hinterland.

What distinguishes MacLennan's view, however, is the tone. Unlike the politicians and historians, MacLennan does not predict a necessary leap forward for Canada on the basis of her tremendous resources. Rather, in this introduction, as in his work generally, he stresses the conflicts and struggles that underlie the nation. Contrasting country to city, farmer to priest, French to English, he sketches the scene in a few large strokes. This breadth of vision indicates his commitment to the typicality of social realism. In *Two Solitudes,* as in most of MacLennan's work, the characters typify social groups, especially classes. MacLennan regularly sacrifices individuality to his historical thesis; depicting the peculiarities of particular psyches took a back seat to the portrayal of a new nation rising from the dust of a decaying empire in MacLennan's writing. Although less committed to modernist form than Dos Passos, like the author of *U.S.A.* and the literary historians, MacLennan attempts an ambitious exploration of the conditions of possibility for a radical interpretation of his national culture.

The Emergence of Cultural Nationalism

Before identifying himself as a social realist, however, Hugh MacLennan traversed several literary and political stages. He confronted Tory, Liberal, and orthodox leftist positions on nationalism before arriving at his final destination. Along the way, he experimented with Marxist historiography and the proletarian picaresque and participated in Popular Front groups and working-men's clubs. MacLennan did more than flirt with leftism; he wrote in the climate of leftist politics and developed the cultural nationalism for which he is best known while in conversation with the transnational subculture of the left. The blend of classicizing historical breadth and geographical mysticism that eventually became his signature obscures some of its leftist markers, but these conversations helped MacLennan differentiate his writing from most contemporary work on the Canadian nation.

It was as a youth in Nova Scotia that MacLennan began the first stage of his development: a confrontation with Tory Anglophilia. Strongly influenced by his teetotalling Calvinist father, he countered an imperialist education with rigorous study of the classics.[13] Equally important, as MacLennan reflects in the title essay of his 1959 collection *Scotchman's Return,* were his father's lessons in being a Scot. "All the perplexity and doggedness of the race was in him," MacLennan writes, "its loneliness, tenderness, and affection, its deceptive vitality, its quick flashes of violence, its dog-whistle sensitivity to sounds to which Anglo-Saxons are stone-deaf, its incapacity to tell its heart to foreigners save in terms foreigners do not comprehend, its resigned indifference to whether they comprehend or not" (146). It is resistance or antagonism to the Anglo-Saxon in particular that MacLennan prizes in Scottish culture. He spends much of the piece describing incidents in which a famous taciturnity is revealed to be not silence but indirect communication among insiders, a kind of code. From his father's cryptic prediction that when he goes to the Highlands he'll "understand" an unspecified something, to an Edinburgh local's abrupt "Ay!"—an exclamation that "assumed incorrectly that [the listener] understood that both himself and his country had been rebuked"—the details of the essay position MacLennan as an insider who has inherited the ability to decode statements indecipherable to non-Celts. His task as a writer, then, is to recode these observations into a publicly available language and comment upon them.

MacLennan considers himself uniquely available for this task of cultural translation because he belongs "to the last Canadian generation raised with a Highland nostalgia" and "to the last which regards a trans-Atlantic flight as a miracle" (153). Hinged to both the old identification with Scotland and a new North American technophilia, he can locate points of contact and rupture. He feels himself well situated to comment upon the ways in which Canada is and is not the Scotland of North America. He can imagine why persons of Scots origin make up 10 to 15 percent of the Canadian population—reasons that have much to do with the comparable harshness of Scottish and Canadian terrain.[14] Most important, as a returning Scotsman, MacLennan locates a basis for his critique of England. Identifying himself with an anti-imperialism of the margins, MacLennan discards early a Tory insistence that Canada "is" English.

This analogy between Canadian and Scottish situations on the margins of an empire that cannot decipher them remained powerful for MacLennan throughout his career. In several later essays collected in *Scotchman's Return,* MacLennan values intimacy and community over materialism and mass society, the "small town" over the "metropolis," and local borderlands over "Madison Avenue" (see "Oranges from Portugal," "If You Drop a Stone . . ." and "It's the U.S. or Us"). These concerns continue the comparison between Scotland's relationship to the United Kingdom and Canada's relationship to the United States. Even as late as 1973, MacLennan was warning that "unless we soon make up our minds about our future relations with the United States, we will drift or be pushed into such a position that our nation will become a mere territorial expression of American aspirations—as Scotland is a territorial expression of England" ("Scotland's Fate: Canada's Lesson," 260). Like the radical Scottish nationalist and Communist poet Hugh MacDiarmid, MacLennan found Highland localism a source of anti-imperial rhetoric.

In retrospect, MacLennan also found in Scotland a sense of himself as a writer of national epics. In a telling essay titled "On Living in a Cold Country," MacLennan dramatizes a scene from the end of his youth. He reports an encounter with a writer that took place during his first voyage to England. In contradiction to that writer's objection that "no important art has ever come out of a cold country," he describes how as a young man, from the ages of twelve to twenty-one he slept year-round in a tent. This experience is associated, for MacLennan, with his earliest intellectual developments—the translation of Latin, the discovery of communism in Plato's *Republic*, and so on. At the same time, as the writerly alter ego points out, "this avoidance of the house where your parents were sleeping" is yet another instance of a pervasive Oedipal complex (212); it is a protest against the father's domination made in the father's terms. By exaggerating the father's compulsion for self-discipline—a compulsion already and elsewhere established as "Scottish"—the young MacLennan made possible his own genesis as a Canadian writer. By out-"Scot"-ing his father, he came into his own in the confrontation with his "cold country."

The Scottish pride, however, did not in MacLennan's case turn into xenophobia or an isolationist racism. From his youthful identification with the tent outside the house and the defeated nation on the border of empire, MacLennan moved as a Rhodes scholar to the heart of the cosmopolitan world. These years reading classics at Oxford confirmed elements of his previous position, but also set these in a European context. While at Oxford, MacLennan traveled on the Continent and came to identify provisionally with the British against fascist forms of nationalism. While by no means an Anglophile, MacLennan learned to appreciate elements of English culture.

In another essay published in mid-career, "Orgy at Oriel," he recollects the purification he felt in Oxford rituals centered on drinking and emotional release. But, while recommending these metropolitan pleasures to fellow Canadians, he concludes that their institution at home is unlikely: "we need the healing grace of the orgy in this country but I confess myself at a loss to suggest what we can do about it," he writes (53). The pleasure of ancient rituals performed in a space uncontaminated by women appealed to MacLennan, but he finds it unlikely that such spaces can be reconstituted in the New World. He admires what he sees as the civilized masculinity of England and Oxford while recognizing its inappropriateness in other settings.

This sense of qualified identification with the imperial center continues in other reflections, such as "My Last Colonel," which consider the decline of modern-day English culture from its nineteenth-century heights. In this essay,

MacLennan recalls a more everyday after-tennis drinking orgy with a nostalgic army officer. The colonel bounces conversationally from topic to topic while getting himself and MacLennan extremely drunk. In his excesses, this figure signifies for MacLennan the dissolution of an organized, powerful imperial culture. The crowning cut arrives when, in the last paragraph of the essay, another elderly military gentleman informs MacLennan that this personage is "not received" by the very high society that preoccupies him (160). England, in this view, is a nation that is no longer vigorous and delays recognition of its own decay.

Though rejecting Tory aristophilia by historicizing it, MacLennan nonetheless found himself bound to some English ideals; especially when confronted with fascism in Italy and the jet-setting lifestyles of Saint Moritz, he expressed a marked preference for familiar "plebeian" cultures.[15] In later years, his comments on fascism would reveal the contrast he drew between that form of nationalism and his own conflicted identification with imperial culture. For instance, in letters written during the mid-1930s to Dorothy Duncan, his future wife, he mentions fascist nationalism repeatedly: fascists admire people who "think with the thighs"; like D. H. Lawrence and most college professors, Archibald MacLeish is "an unconscious Fascist"; Hitler represents "the third and final stage of Caesarism"; and the Japanese "are, relative to the West, what the barbarians were relative to the Romans." When urging Duncan that they will be happier living in Canada than in the United States, he writes at length of Nova Scotia, concluding that "at least there is no nationalism here and nationalism is growing in America by leaps and bounds. Americanization = Brave New World. It is spreading in Europe just as fast as in America these days."[16] Fascism, in these passages, is continuous with Roman conquest; it is making familiar inroads in Europe and the United States. Only Canada, in MacLennan's view, with its non-nostalgic investment in an older mode of colonial consciousness, offers an alternative to this dangerous form of nationalism.

In these essays and letters, then, we can see that studying at Oxford did for MacLennan exactly what education in the imperial metropolis so often does for colonials. It bound him, as a representative of a colonial elite, more closely to the imperial culture, while also establishing the boundaries and character of the colonial proto-nation. In his influential study of nationalism, Benedict Anderson argues that one of the main functions of education in the metropolis is to teach the colonial intelligentsia how European nation-states work—

an education that often, ironically, allows them to use that model in anti-imperialist struggles.[17] Certainly this is what happened in MacLennan's case. Building on his youthful identification with Scottish critiques of the British Empire, he learned at Oxford to identify with English tradition as against "thigh"-thinking anti-Westernism; then, he repositioned that form of nationalist consciousness in a critique of empire. Only in one important area does his education in nationalism deviate from Anderson's model. In MacLennan's case, the empire against which Canadian nationalism is deployed is not the British metropole but the more dangerous twentieth-century American one. It is American nationalism that reminds him of a fascist "Brave New World," and it is American cultural imperialism that he sees threatening Canada most directly. As we shall see, this change in empires makes a big difference. While many of the colonial elites Anderson studied returned home to use their classical training against the local masses, MacLennan struggled against other members of the incipient American elite. His classicism led him to ally himself more closely with the local masses—at least during the early 1930s.

Not surprisingly, MacLennan's anti-Americanism increased during his years of postgraduate study at Princeton. In particular, he confronted the liberal pluralism at the heart of U.S. and Canadian nationalist mythology. If liberal historians stressed the diverse origins of North American citizens while asserting that these persons can or should join together in a political unity, MacLennan increasingly stressed the conflicts within nations and asserted the priority of class struggles. In this, his most internationalist stage, MacLennan affiliated himself intellectually with the class consciousness of the Communist Third Period.

This anti-liberalism of the mid-1930s is difficult to separate from MacLennan's antagonism to the United States. As a graduate student, he routinely denounced the Princeton faculty for their "scientific" rather than humanistic methods of study. His letters to Duncan from these years are full of unfavorable comparisons between the United States and Canada, or the United States and England, many of which generalize from his Princeton experiences. For example, on June 6, 1934, MacLennan wrote, "in England and Canada we are all brought up in an atmosphere of trust. Instinctively I trust a man unless he shows himself untrustworthy. In the States this is not so." A month later, on summer vacation: "Nova Scotia seems so unbelievably quiet and happy after the States"; then, "Values seem so different here from what they were in the

States, where one felt so constantly on the defensive"; and "Princeton is the distilled essence of several great American qualities. Private enterprise, interference in other people's privacy, terrific energy and hard work, lack of balance, excitement, cowardice, courage and dishonesty of the most blatant kind, all exaggerated out of proportion. All I know is that there will be a crack-up soon among people who live that way."[18] In these mid-30s letters, MacLennan repeatedly asserts that America is to be admired for its vitality but criticized for the vulgarity of its materialism and the shortsightedness of its imperial fantasies. If English civilization is comparable to that of ancient Greece, for the young MacLennan, then America recalls ancient Rome; it conquers and subsumes England/Greece, only to extend itself to the edge of republican decadence.

This dissatisfaction with the United States was one among several elements that led MacLennan to an academic interest in Marxism. His biographer concludes that "his political 'conversion' constituted a significant part of his current rebellion against many things in his past"—including his father's conservatism, the industrial wasteland surrounding New York, and the intellectual aridity of Princeton.[19] While living in New Jersey, he began to frequent working-class clubs in New York where he could discuss politics with like-minded men, many of whom were anti-fascist exiles from Germany. He began regularly reading Communist commentary by John Strachey, as well as an assortment of radical magazines, such as *Action,* the *New Republic,* and *New Masses.* He also became involved in a Popular Front group and committed himself to giving several anti-fascist speeches.[20] Around the same time, he read and was strongly influenced by Marxist scholarship, especially the work of Russian classicist Mikhail Ivanovitch Rostovtzeff. In his influential study *The Social and Economic History of the Roman Empire* Rostovtzeff argued that the decline of Rome could be attributed to the class struggle; with the collapse of the aristocracy, he demonstrated, the empire came to rely on a corrupt urban merchant class that was weakened by its long-standing conflicts with the countryside. Like many middle-class intellectuals of the 1930s, MacLennan preferred a communist analysis that outlined social transformation in bold macro-historical strokes to a hands-on approach to immediate politics. This position allowed him to distinguish himself from liberals stressing the potential unity of U.S., Canadian, or even Roman culture.

Among the results of this combined interest in Marxist and anti-imperialist discourse were MacLennan's first published writings. His Princeton dissertation and an article drawn from it illustrate the uneasy fusion he forged; in these works, we find the highly polarized terms of social analysis that would remain with MacLennan throughout his writing career. "Roman History and To-day," a short article that appeared in *Dalhousie Review* (1935–36), argues that "we have reached the end of an era, though not of our civilization; and that the history of the Romans, whose vast civilization reached an end *for itself,* can throw much light on our own predicament to-day" (67). That is, like much of MacLennan's literary work, this article is based on a historical analogy between the classical and modern world. MacLennan asserts that the Roman empire decayed as a result of conflicts between the empire and the republic; he sees it as a society dominated by imperialist acquisitiveness and private enterprise. These forces and values are then put at odds with the concerns of the contemplative man and the slaves to such an extent that the society cannot persist. MacLennan sees some potential that this pattern will change in the modern era, because we now have two new elements in our society: machinery and the masses. Like Veblen, Mumford, and the technocrats, in machinery he finds the potential for an end to slavery, but unless the values of the masses and the state "are profoundly altered, the new era will not escape the old vicious circle" of empire, decay, and dark ages (78). In MacLennan's view, history is a cyclical process under the influence of massive forces, and the modern crisis in imperial power has opened a tiny window through which we might glimpse the possibility of the formation of a new kind of society.

This characteristically 1930s-era class analysis is developed at greater length in MacLennan's 1935 Ph.D. dissertation, "Oxyrhynchus: An Economic and Social Study." With a subtitle acknowledging his debt to Rostovtzeff, MacLennan's study uses papyrus fragments to reconstruct the social structure of an Egyptian town, Oxyrhynchus, that was "at least as typical [of Egypt proper] as Peoria is typical of the American Middle-West" (9). From a discussion of geographical constants—the river and the desert—MacLennan moves to a description of class structure and an analysis of large-scale change over the period being studied; he describes a city full of impoverished, stateless wanderers and led by middle and upper classes that have resorted to "economic and social cannibalism" (36). Oxyrhynchus for MacLennan represents a decaying empire dominated by aggressively private enterprise. Its history follows a logic of contradiction; MacLennan points to a "simultaneous growth and decay" in Egyptian society (23). Overall, the thesis is a reading of the past filtered by Depression-era social theory, a set of concerns that emphasized Marxist interpretation of culture.

This highly politicized class analysis did not sit well with Princeton academics. MacLennan's advisor insisted he rewrite the whole project, as neither his style nor methods were deemed acceptable.[21] It is likely that his anachronistic use of terms such as "bourgeoisie" and "proletariat" ruffled some feathers among the scientistic Princeton faculty, as perhaps did the strongly presentist overtones of the argument. After all, MacLennan suggests that provincial cultures of the 1930s, forced into a corner by economic depression and the decay of European empires, face a choice between revolution and barbarism. The lesson he would have readers draw from the Oxyrhynchus scenario is clear: if the working classes choose "to identify the self with the object of suffering," then we are all headed once again for the "masochism . . . of the Dark Ages" (87).

This confrontational presentism is also at work in MacLennan's first two novels, both of which remain unpublished. The first of these, "So All Their Praises," was finished in 1933, while MacLennan was still writing his dissertation, and he began the second, "A Man Should Rejoice," while completing the Ph.D. in 1934. Like the dissertation, both of these texts employ classical analogies for twentieth-century problems; both tie cultural change quite closely to the economic situation; both work on a large scale with typical rather than individualized characters; and both put forward a strong critique of fascism. Clearly these novels were attempts to mold his academic Marxism into a more presentable and public shape. In these works, as always, MacLennan is illustrating theses, especially the thesis that national cultures are irreparably divided by capitalism. That said, though, certain elements achieve a much grander and more thorough treatment in MacLennan's fiction than they did in his nonfiction prose—notably the emotional significance of the land. In the course of MacLennan's early fiction, he grows progressively more focused on geography while classicist historiography recedes further into the background. This focus on the land became increasingly central to MacLennan's depiction of Canadian national culture in the late 1930s and early 1940s.

"So All Their Praises" was completed in 1933, in the worst year of the Depression. A sprawling, semi-proletarian novel, "Praises" follows its wandering heroes, Michael, a British drunkard and writer, and Adolf, a young German; the two students begin in Freiburg, Germany, and end up on the east coast of the United States. This transition from old world to new establishes the political themes that are foremost in the novel. As the title borrowed from Shakespeare's Sonnet CVI indicates, MacLennan's main interest is to represent a modern consciousness—a consciousness aware of history but uncomfortable in it and to some degree inarticulate about its discomfort. "So all their praises are but prophecies," the sonnet goes, "of this our time." The argument of the sonnet and of the novel is that our ability to represent lags behind our experiences; thus, a chronicle of the present is particularly difficult to write. "For we, which now behold these present days," the sonnet continues, "Have eyes to wonder, but lack tongues to praise." With this allusion, MacLennan begins his argument for large-scale economic determinism. In this novel, economic relations continually motivate and frustrate the development of political speech.

Like "Oxyrhynchus," "So All Their Praises" begins in a moment when "the world was in a bad way," though, unlike the Egyptians, the denizens of Freiburg felt confident that "they were the ones who would make the world right" (1). They felt themselves part of an ancient continuum. Freiburg is "Freiburg, Freiburg-im-Breisgau, of the Holy Roman Empire" (6); the "old environment" has shaped European society, even though it is "gone" (23). Nonetheless, conditions have worsened with the Depression. Rootless and wracked by nostalgia, Adolf and Michael attempt to come to terms with the modern world. They abandon the hedonism of their university town and take jobs on a road crew where they confront communists who speak in faux Yiddish and discuss Nazism. Out in the world, they learn how the class struggle has deepened. Repeatedly, the narrator insists we view even the most casual social relations in class terms: "Although he knew that his own class of society had collapsed and had let himself fall out of it, he still felt himself a part of what had made him," Adolf reflects (27). Especially where love affairs are concerned, MacLennan confronts the stateless wanderers of Oxyrhynchus with modern middle-class cannibals.

While sketching the decay of these modern European empires, MacLennan also projects a timeless American utopia. After being laid off from the road crew, Adolf and Michael take a holiday on the Danube and, bumming around the wharves, they find a job on a Canadian rumrunner that transports them to Halifax. In the New World, the story focuses on Michael, who meets "one of the most intensely female women he had ever seen," a clear sign that the class-bound sexual norms of Europe will be shattered (80). Together, the triad of Michael, Adolf, and Sarah muses on the coming revolution, explores the Nova Scotia coast, and establishes a blissful retreat from the crises of Europe. The most paradisical moments arrive when they experience the land as simultaneously virgin and antique. Driving in the Nova Scotian countryside, they are overwhelmed by the grandeur of the scene: "The sun, the sky, the sea, the earth, ourselves, mile on mile of aromatic wilderness exhaling something of its essence into the sunlit atmosphere" (106). This landscape leads to brief reflections on "Canada, and in particular this little province, [which] seems to be just half way between the Old Country and the States" (106). Finally, on a mossy bank Sarah and Adolf consummate their attraction, in a scene that reveals something of MacLennan's idealism about the restorative virtues of the Canadian landscape.

After these scenes of sexual and geographical mysticism, the forces of history and private enterprise intrude once again; when the two men return to the rumrunner, they have dramatic confrontations with U.S. revenue officers.[22] With our heroes stranded on the sea, the novel eventually ends on a note of fatalism as Michael observes "on the horizon a very bright star . . . sloping inexoribly [*sic*] into the ocean" (262). The gap between events and consciousness remains unbridged. Political commitment is rejected and the Dark Ages threaten to return.

This first novel did not entirely satisfy MacLennan, as his letters from the mid-1930s reveal. While it conformed to the class-based analytical framework he had also used in his dissertation, its three central characters and frequent changes of scene gave it a dispersed feel. In his second project, MacLennan decided to focus more closely on a single individual and national scene, while still putting forward a class-based politics. In letters to Duncan he frequently mentioned a class type that had previously been unfamiliar to him: the American "man of action." "American men," he observed, "never seem to me to have much guts or sense of fair play—I mean, the real American bourgeois—and it is hardly their fault considering the way they have been brought up. . . . And in spite of all this America has a vitality which is thrilling if for no other reason than for the grand scale of its action, cruelty and cynicism. The ruthless man of action is at least a man, and in America there are plenty of them."[23] This ruthless figure provided the germ for his second novel.

Centering on David Culver, the son of a wealthy industrialist and an emotional Russian artist, "A Man Should Rejoice" replaces the stateless wanderers of "Praises" with an alienated artist/intellectual. Filled with "a longing to paint men as they worked on the American plan, not because they were beautiful or because they possessed the blood-vitality of Europeans, but because somehow or other they were the future," the main character David introduces utopian politics explicitly into the early portions of the novel (no page). He falls in love in a model socialist village and later becomes involved in a complex strike plot. Although both the village and the strike crumple in the face of fascism and authoritarian technocrats respectively, these political failures are not simply a backdrop for the development of an artistic sensibility; they are homologies for the hero's failure to find the strength to combat his capitalist father successfully. With this critical evaluation of politics, the only moment of genuine optimism occurs again in the wilderness: "I dissolved then, sap forcing open the veins of a maple tree in the Canadian spring," the hero gushes. The novel closes with the death of David's beloved, but even the significance of this moment is unclear. David wonders if his wife shares his vision of the forces of history, a vision that he does not know how to actualize. In one of the two variant endings, David remembers his past with courage and in the other he feels unutterably alone. Having abandoned Liberal and Tory certainties about the unifying power of tradition and tolerance, and having questioned the viability of utopian socialism in "Rejoice," MacLennan again saw the Dark Ages looming.

Publishing Nationalism

After leaving graduate school and returning to Canada to teach in the late 1930s, MacLennan began to complement the political cynicism of his early manuscripts with a newfound and more complete appreciation for his home. Especially in comparison to Americans, Nova Scotians seemed to him remarkably virtuous and concerned with their fellows. The cultural lag by which developments in the United States and/or Europe took some thirty to fifty years to reach Canada began to seem a viability rather than a liability to MacLennan; he began to see Canada as a possible site of resistance to American ultracapitalism. In particular, he began to write seriously of his childhood home, situating Nova Scotia globally. Rejecting Europhilia and liberal paralysis and critical of political idealism, MacLennan turned to radical nationalism.

The result of this exile's return was MacLennan's first published novel, *Barometer Rising* (1941). While referring to a global narrative of imperial contest, the novel's setting is limited to the city of Halifax and its time-frame to eight days. In both the historical record and MacLennan's novel, December 2 through December 10, 1917, were the days preceding and immediately following a catastrophic collision between the French munition ship *Mont Blanc* and the *Imo,* a vessel carrying relief supplies to Belgium. On Thursday, December 6, 1917, these ships collided in the Halifax harbor, causing a devastating explosion that leveled at least a third of the thriving city.[24] MacLennan witnessed this event as a boy, and his decision to narrate the explosion indicates his recognition of the historical significance of the Canadian scene. *Barometer Rising* makes the Halifax explosion a flash point in the development of Canada as a nation. A new kind of nationalism emerges from the rubble, dispersing the threat of the Dark Ages' return.

Barometer Rising begins with a cinematic zoom into the city of Halifax. A wanderer not unlike the young man of Dos Passos's preface climbs Citadel Hill and surveys the town; he observes the geographical situation—the harbor scooped by a great glacier, the hill and islands left as a legacy, and the peninsula on which the city lies. From these passages, we move to historical considerations: "even a landsman could see why the harbour had for a century and a half been a link in the chain of British sea power" (4). Because the harbor can protect fleets of ships, it has often served a purpose during wars between empires, as it is doing once again in the time-frame of the novel. To this observer, "Halifax seemed to have acquired a meaning since he had left it in 1914"; it is playing a role in the war, so it has entered modern history (5). The lights, motion, and crowds signal modernity, but the waterfront also has a more foreboding significance as the meeting place of as-yet uncharted forces. The sea here, as in the unpublished works, recalls for MacLennan the supra-individual forces of history.

In a similar moment of elevated, macro-historical observation later in the novel, the wanderer figure expands his vision from the significance of Halifax to a fuller realization of "what being a Canadian meant":

> Under the excitement of this idea his throat became constricted and he had a furious desire for expression: this anomalous land, this sprawling waste of timber and rock and water where the only living sounds were the footfalls of animals or the fantastic laughter of a loon, this empty tract of primordial silences and winds and erosions and shifting colours,

this bead-like string of crude towns and cities tied by nothing but railway tracks, this nation undiscovered by the rest of the world and unknown to itself, these people neither American nor English, nor even sure what they wanted to be, this unborn mightiness, this question-mark, this future for himself, and for God knew how many millions of mankind! (79)

At the heart of the novel is this macrocosmic vision of Canada as a social organization emerging from an "anomalous land"—as a nation caught between the United States and the United Kingdom but coming to know itself as "neither American nor English." Insofar as the novel has a thesis, it is the propagation of this vision of Canada as a nation in the process of forging itself, as an "unborn mightiness."

The character who experiences these visions is Neil MacCrae, a wandering radical of Scots origin. He is more clearly heroic than any of MacLennan's other central characters, since he is figured as an Odysseus whose return authorizes the foundation of the nation. "[I]f there were enough Canadians like himself, half-American and half-English," MacCrae muses, "then the day was inevitable when the halves would join and his country would become the central arch which united the new order" (218). Empowered by this sense of mission, he reaches out to his "Wise Penelope"; on the final page of the novel they stand together in the "rising wind" (219).[25] This new couple defines itself against both an autocratic, tradition-bound father and a weak doctor suffering from self-inflicted psychic wounds. The father-figure's authoritarian demeanor is coupled with an obviously misguided conviction that Canada is doomed to be a "second-rate" country; by foiling him, the couple also foils his Anglophilia. Meanwhile, the tender-hearted doctor is treated more sympathetically; the exigencies of the explosion offer an opportunity to thrust himself into action and test his mettle: In the aftermath, he performs hours of surgery and a crucial plot-function as well—revealing to MacCrae's Penelope the availability of her illegitimate child. Of course, this news requires that Penny and MacCrae marry and adopt the child, who is already biologically their own, so that the doctor has acted in some sense as a midwife to the "new order" as well as the surgeon who extracts the shrapnel of the old. Nonetheless, the doctor is not included in this resolution to the national romance. The new political family, as imagined by MacLennan, is unified in its future-orientation. The national couple proves its dedication to the community by rescuing rich and poor alike and reclaiming the baby that was already theirs. In this historical novel, MacLennan implicitly claims that the nation like the baby has already been born and has already thrown off the political obligations and conservative sexual morality of the colony. In a complicated subplot, MacLennan links his hero to a working-class radicalism that Liberals and Tories alike tried to exclude from their national narratives.

Although *Barometer Rising* was well reviewed in the United States and Canada, some critics noticed a strain in the form, where the documentary impulse to record local events conflicted with the typifying and didactic elements of social realism.[26] This formal dilemma also reveals a strain in the novel's politics. After all, despite MacLennan's Odyssean vision, Canada was not entirely unified in 1941, and certainly not around radical politics. The Communist Party, for one, was illegal during the war, and even social democrats like Frank Underhill found themselves in hot water for expressing their pacifist views. The war also increased tensions between Anglo- and Francophones when French speakers were conscripted to defend England.[27] It was as late as December 1939 that the Quebec Assembly adopted *je me souviens* as its official motto. Having moved to Montreal, MacLennan became increasingly aware of this latter tension and, in his most influential novel, more fully addressed the cultural dilemmas of Canadian nationalism.

First published in 1945, *Two Solitudes* is another national romance; love, in this novel, is a sociological phenomenon. However, instead of aiming for amalgamation, *Two Solitudes* represents the nation as a confluence of conflicting nationalisms. Class and ethnic tensions are explored, not forcibly resolved. The emphasis throughout falls on the hybridity of each group. Paul Tallard, the "French" hero, has an Irish mother, and his eventual bride, Heather Methuen, counts as "English" only so long as we include working-class Nova Scotians in this category—something that we have seen that MacLennan the Scot did not always do. In the end, the marriage of ethnicities is not the only goal of the novel; it is also an exploration of the conflicts and contradictions within each of the two "founding" white "races" in Canada.[28] The nation, in *Two Solitudes,* is a dialectic of nationalisms.

Of the four versions of national ideology represented in *Two Solitudes,* the racialized nationalism of the Francophone anti-conscription campaign is the first to surface. Paul's stepbrother, Marius Tallard, is vehement in his passion, breaking with his father and family, throwing himself into public speaking and political agitation. The reader suspects his motivations early on, however, when Marius reveals a guilty attraction to his Irish stepmother, a feeling quickly repressed and transformed into angry denunciation of his father and interethnic marriage. By the end of the novel, MacLennan has labeled Marius a proto-fascist demagogue; " 'The pure race is everything to him,' " his half-brother asserts (326). Not entirely without justification, this was an analysis adopted by many English-speaking observers of Francophone nationalism in Quebec during the late 1930s.[29]

By contrast, MacLennan gives a relatively sympathetic portrait of Athanase Tallard, Marius's pro-conscription father. Borrowing heavily from Ringuet's *Trente Arpents,* a contemporaneous novel of rural life in Quebec, MacLennan describes Athanase's origins in and conflicts with the rural community for which he bears a traditional responsibility as *seigneur*.[30] Athanase is a Francophone politician who has lost faith in Catholicism and the agrarian ideal; he turns instead to a vision of modified industrialization, hoping his village can modernize without falling entirely under the sway of alien cultures. These projects lead him to ask "how could Quebec surrender to the future and still remain herself? How could she merge into the American world of machinery without also becoming American? How could she become scientific and yet save her legend?" (70). As an intellectual whose grasp of issues is supposed to be rational rather than emotional, Athanase and the protective nationalism with which he is associated receive MacLennan's authorial endorsements.

This does not mean, however, that Athanase prevails—just the opposite. However sympathetic a character, Athanase and his idealistic nationalism still fall prey to the machinations of Huntley McQueen, an Anglophone financier with visions of a trans-Canadian economic empire. For McQueen, Canadianness is important only so far as it is profitable; in his analysis, Canadians "had definite advantages over the British and Americans, for they could always play the other two off against the other" (93). This opportunistic nationalism recalls Colonel Wain's assertions in *Barometer Rising* that Canada is a "second-rate" nation, pinned between the United States and the United Kingdom. But, even more powerfully, the portrait of McQueen recalls contemporaneous depictions of Prime Minister William Lyon Mackenzie King. MacLennan's McQueen is a wealthy, forty-something, church-going bachelor, tending toward fat and unconsummated romantic friendships with ladies of high society. Libelously close to the historical King's biography, this description reminds readers that, as a bachelor and ladies' man, King was friendly with American tycoons such as John D. Rockefeller, and, in details that MacLennan surely relished when they emerged after King's death in the 1950s, he seems also to have been a tormented Victorian who held frequent seances in order to consult the ghost of his mother on important sexual and political matters.[31] The longest-standing Canadian prime minister to date, King/McQueen's attachment to middle-of-the-road Liberal policies represents for MacLennan a pseudo-nationalism that ensured Canada's status as an economically dependent colony.

These three flawed forms of nationalism are contrasted in the later portions of the novel to the youngest generation's cultural nationalism. For instance, when the sentimental heroine Heather Methuen rebels against her fussy mother and the domineering McQueen by becoming a painter, she takes the requisite awe-inspiring drive through the countryside and discovers a sense of artistic purpose: "She wanted the lines and colours hard and brilliant, as they so often were in this part of the country" (261). She worries, though, that her efforts will look like "an imitation of A. Y. Jackson," one of the central figures of the Group of Seven (276). Well-known in Canada by the time MacLennan was writing *Two Solitudes,* the Group of Seven painters was widely credited with being the first distinctly Canadian movement in the visual arts, and through the 1960s and 1970s their paintings were considered icons of cultural nationalism in Canada (see fig. 2). Drawing on German expressionism, Scandinavian regionalism, and modernist abstraction, the Group made mythic the sparsely populated backwoods of the Laurentian Shield.[32] The Group's work reveals a geological drama of immense, inhuman proportions. "Theirs was a time of youthful hope and vim," painter and illustrator Thoreau MacDonald wrote in 1944, "of an art as Canadian as a cedar swamp or maple bush, healthy and still free from the vapours of older nations."[33]

This emphasis on the vigorous, athletic, even macho elements of the Canadian landscape clearly appealed to MacLennan, since it corresponded to his own somewhat mystical sense of Canada as a new order in a rough new land. In *Two Solitudes,* MacLennan translates the Group of Seven's painterly language into a verbal one by describing that landscape and by marrying Heather the painter to Paul, the budding writer. Paul is having difficulties with his writing; near the end of *Two Solitudes,* he bemoans his thwarted project, a proletarian novel entitled *The Young Man of 1933:* "Could any man write a novel about masses? The young man of 1933, together with all the individual characters

Figure 2 Bertram
Brooker's cover for *The
Canadian Forum* illus-
trates the famous
Group of Seven style.
July 1935.

Paul had tried to create, grew pallid and unreal in his imagination beside the
sense of the swarming masses heard three stories below in the shuffling feet of
the crowd. For long minutes he stood at the window. To make a novel out of
this? How could he? How could anyone? A novel should concern people, not
ideas, and yet people had become trivial" (307). Reflecting some of the problems Canadian writers had with the vacant scenes of the proletarian novel, as
well as MacLennan's own transitions as a writer, Paul soon adopts a new, painterly vision:

> Canada was a country that no one knew. It was a large red splash on the
> map. It produced Mounted Policemen, Quintuplets and raw materials.
> But because it used the English and French languages, a Canadian book
> would have to take its place in the English and French traditions. Both tra-
> ditions were so mature they had become almost decadent, while Canada
> herself was still raw. Besides, there was the question of background. As
> Paul considered the matter, he realized that his readers' ignorance of the
> essential Canadian clashes and values presented him with a unique prob-
> lem. The background would have to be created from scratch if his story
> was to become intelligible. He could afford to take nothing for granted. He
> would have to build the stage and props for his play, and then write the
> play itself. (329)

In this epiphanic moment, Paul recognizes that his literary mission is to specify his representation of "masses" with a representation of "the essential Canadian clashes and values"—a mission which, of course, is that of *Two Solitudes*. The nation must be presented not according to the already available cultural stereotypes, but "from scratch"; the vocabulary of cultural nationalism must be "raw" and fresh like the land itself. It must build up a scene and pay particular attention to the conflicts of English and French traditions.

Overall, in MacLennan's most famous novel, political conflict is displaced so that artistic visions of synthesis can take over, and immediate conflicts—such as conscription—are explained as the result of long historical processes, such as industrialization and the decline of feudalism. The class-based politics of the early 1930s are not repudiated so much as they are improved upon by inclusion in a synthetic national vision. Through cultural nationalism, MacLennan does his best to find a home and sphere of action for his wandering Odysseus. In the continuing dialectic of French versus English and fathers versus sons, he imagines a literary and cultural project that will outlast the radicalism of the 1930s. Although by 1960, critics were arguing that "MacLennan has flirted long enough with national-cultural chimeras to the detriment of his novels," in the 1940s and 1950s, many of MacLennan's readers agreed with the *Canadian Forum* that he had captured "the substance of Canada, her countryside, her cities, her conflicting cultures, and, above all, her people." [34]

The Cultural Politics of the Nation

In the 1930s, at least once in a while, MacLennan saw himself as a Canadian Dos Passos. In 1934, after reading *Three Soldiers* and *1919,* he wrote to Duncan that "Dos Passos' point of view seems singularly that of myself." [35] Certainly, both MacLennan and Dos Passos were well-educated upper-middle-class scholars attracted to the left on intellectual, rather than activist, grounds. In their writings, both adopted the stance that Malcolm Cowley called "the learned Poggius"—watching the decline of a modern Rome from atop distant hills.[36] Both used their distance from events to confront a more engaged and teleological view of the nation as necessarily radical, as thrusting forward into a shining future. That is, despite their sympathy for leftist goals, both came to stress the conflicts within nations and the lack of fit between national and socialist ideologies.

At the same time, both MacLennan and Dos Passos were committed enough to their respective national scenes that their works and ultimately their politics differ. For Dos Passos, the complexity of the emergent technocratic bureaucracy boded ill. He felt that whatever traces of a common language had once bound the nation together were dissolving, and he ended his trilogy with images of social fragmentation. In contrast, MacLennan retained a measure of hope for the future. For him, the issue was less what future was emerging than how competing cultural traditions could adapt together to the capitalist present. In *Barometer Rising, Two Solitudes,* and the post-1930s conclusion to his national trilogy, *The Precipice,* he depicts a nation cohering rather than dissolving.

These differing representations reveal the contrasting national situations in the United States and Canada during the 1930s. In the United States, radical intellectuals were disturbed as they watched a version of what they had been arguing for become institutional and bureaucratic; the skepticism of a Dos Passos must be measured against the bureaucratic rhetoric of Americanism in the 1930s. Mechanically reproduced and widely available, this rhetoric began to lose its appeal for some U.S. radicals during the Depression; it began to seem too closely integrated into the system of alienated modern technocracy than was bearable. By contrast, in Canada the state had only recently gained the possibility of independent action, and in a context heavily informed by European political traditions, Canadian intellectuals began to have a sense of new national horizons during the 1930s. While U.S. radicals began to arm themselves for an internal critique of an American world order, some Canadians felt liberated by the decay of the European empires. Consequently, the common project of chronicling the nation took different forms in the United States and Canada, as did the leftist subcultures generally. Even in a period when the Soviet Comintern increasingly attempted to dominate national branches of the Communist Party, and the struggle against fascism made international cooperation increasingly necessary, national conditions remained a major factor for both U.S. and Canadian writers on the left. Because the nation was the site of residual political vocabularies, it served as a *sine qua non* for leftists—even writers, like those considered in part II, who concerned themselves primarily with narratives of class struggle.

PART II   PROLETARIAN CULTURE

Chapter 4

SITUATING "THE WORKER"

An Overview of Proletarian Fiction

As the work of historians, literary and otherwise, reminds us, in the early part of the twentieth century, radical political movements targeted national audiences. To many observers, the Russian Revolution demonstrated that socialism could be established in one country, and on the strength of this precedent socialists organized national parties and sought places in national parliaments. Their goal was to reveal the existing power structure as a class power—thereby altering the shape of the nation. At the heart of the debate over national culture, in other words, was a theory of class relations.

Since Marxist theories of class, and especially those of the 1930s, have been widely and seriously misrepresented in the United States, it is important to clarify the significance of class categories for the 30s left before moving into a discussion of their literary deployments. In particular, in the United States, the ideological campaigns of the Cold War have encouraged many Americans to believe that all Marxist governments, theories, intellectuals, and sympathizers are totalitarian in organization and viciously reductive in their logic.[1] A dehistoricized version of poststructuralist critiques of subjectivity foregrounds the foundationalist epistemology and universal determinants that supposedly make it impossible for Marxist philosophers, politicians, and labor historians to understand class for what it is: an unevenly structured, relational field.[2] In this view, Marxism is not a critique of modernity but the epitome of destructively modernist logic. The effort to remake the world as a classless society—to make it politically new—is exactly what is thought to mar the Marxist project; the ideal of classlessness is seen as identical to the structure that perpetuates hierarchical and oppressive conditions in class societies.

By contrast, I will argue that it is not the case that Communist Party or

Marxist intellectuals necessarily understood class as an essence of individual or group identity. To the extent that it is dialectical in method, Marxism is not a theory of identity but of relations in a social space. Furthering Hegel's dialectical formulations of various possible human relationships, Marx famously described human history as the history of class struggle. The classes that struggle are defined in relation to each other, in the struggle; the working class recognizes itself as such because it sees reality as a process continuous with economic relations. Although there certainly are, as Fredric Jameson argues, many Marxisms, this latter view has been common to Western Marxisms in the twentieth century.[3] Certainly the dialectical understanding of class consciousness was foregrounded by Georg Lukács in *History and Class Consciousness;* Lukács develops a relational theory of how working-class consciousness contrasts to the reified consciousness of a middle class which takes a static, contemplative view of identity, society, and so on.

While not uncontroversial, Lukács's relational, processual view of class consciousness was close enough to other Marxists' thinking that we can find traces of it in official documents of the Third International. Adopted in 1928, the program of the Third International describes the world system of capitalism and predicts an impending crisis before outlining the party's major aim: to "abolish the class *division* of society . . . [to] abolish all forms of exploitation and oppression of man *by man.*"[4] In this document the existence of class divisions presupposes the oppression of one class by another. One class identity is necessarily defined in relation to another, and this relation is underwritten by hierarchies in work, property, education, culture, and society. Through a combination of these sources of power, classes emerge; the Third International officially recognized the conflicting interests of the bourgeoisie, intelligentsia, peasantry, petit bourgeoisie, and proletariat. Particular members of each class might adopt any of a range of political affiliations; the petit bourgeoisie, for instance, is described as continuously wavering "between extreme reaction and sympathy for the proletariat" (1005). Variations by historical situation and national condition are also recognized. The Third International identified different kinds of countries and different kinds of revolutions; in a semicolonial country such as India, for instance, the program recommends that party activists support the fight for national independence, rather than insisting on purely proletarian goals (1012).

In addition to stressing the relational and variable character of class identity,

Third International theoreticians also stressed its non-essential nature. Revolutions were described as bringing about "a mass change of human nature"—especially in the nature of the proletariat (1008). In the process of struggle, the authors of the program assert, the working class overcomes the limitations imposed on it by economic, political, and cultural exploitation. Similarly, other classes were considered likely to change in the transitional period between revolution and the establishment of full-fledged socialism—hence vigorous debates over the class affiliations of artists and intellectuals.[5] Because party theorists understood class as relational, variable, and culturally specific, they allowed for the possibility that it could and would alter dramatically in two stages: when the structure of class society was consciously understood and when the foundations for a new socialist culture were laid.

Of course, serious disagreements about how to effect these changes in the class division of society occurred regularly among Marxist intellectuals in and outside the Communist Party. The dictatorship of the proletariat (a strengthening of class division in order to further the eventual decay of class privilege); the role of party vanguards versus the spontaneous uprising of more or less politically aware workers; the role of bourgeois and intellectual allies in a proletarian party; as well as the relative importance of national versus class movements inspired major controversies. But a constant element of these internal debates is their commitment to an anti-essentialist concept of class. In the writings of Lukács, Trotsky, Rosa Luxemburg, Karl Kautsky, and even Stalin, class position and the possibility of politically effective class consciousness derive not from a particular type of work but from the position of that class in economic, social, and cultural systems that are subject to change.[6] Both the identity of social actors and the space which they inhabit are in flux. All that is taken to be solid in a naturalizing bourgeois discourse has the potential to melt into air. More recently these anti-essentialist spatial concerns have been developed by Marxist geographers working in the tradition of Henri Lefebvre, and the metaphorics of position, structure, and base have given way to a more supple vocabulary stressing a "socio-spatial dialectic" and uneven development.[7] It is this engagement of space and class that informs the following analysis of proletarian fiction.

The actual contemporaneous target of poststructuralist critiques of class essentialism, then, is not a "theory" of class identity, but rather the "effects" of what is presumed to be such a theory. The series of terrors referred to as

Stalinism is the target. As is well known, under Stalin, attempts to classify and punish individuals for their historically evolved positions in a system of economic privilege and/or an intellectual duplicity which they may or may not have understood resulted in famines, purges, show trials, and the kind of political shortsightedness that sacrificed Spanish and German anti-fascists to the survival of the Soviet Union.[8] Even after 1935, when the insistence on Third Period proletarianism gave way to the anti-fascist coalitions of the Popular Front in the Western national parties, rumors of class-based repression in the Soviet Union alienated the party's worldwide membership. North Americans who did not leave the Communist Party in the late thirties, when Stalin cynically betrayed the Spanish Loyalists and even more cynically signed a non-aggression pact with Hitler, dropped out in droves after the invasion of Hungary and the de-Stalinization campaign of 1956. Although recent scholarship based on archival materials made available after *glasnost* suggests that many Stalinist efforts were not as centrally administered or totalitarian as previous scholarship assumed, it is clear that the Third International's philosophical commitment to multiplicity, variety, and contradiction was not always fulfilled.[9] It is not clear, though, that Stalinism was a necessary "effect" of Marxist theory. At the very least, the question is debatable, and hasty elisions of class politics and the gulag should be avoided.

That position—that Communism and its ideological opponents, such as fascism, are essentially the same—builds on Hannah Arendt's influential theories of totalitarianism, although expanding her thesis well beyond its original formulation. Arendt described Stalinism as structurally similar to fascism and began research on a book criticizing Marx; however, she was also a careful and historically informed scholar strongly resistant to Cold War ideological exigencies. Arendt's admiration for republican government and the American revolutionary tradition did not involve asserting the permanence or necessity of class society, nor did it preclude intelligent discussion of "labor" as a part of the "human condition"; what we see in her work is evidence of a post-1945 shift toward politics and away from economics.[10] Like many of her contemporaries among the New York intellectuals, in the aftermath of the second world war, Arendt was more preoccupied with the crisis in public life inspired by genocide than with the economic crisis that had preceded and contributed to the war. Even in her postwar political philosophy, however, Arendt did not conflate intellectual traditions with the horrific events invoking them. Instead, she proposed to historicize Marxist concepts in the tradition of Western philosophy. Not by collapsing Marxism into historicity, but by retracing the genealogy of its central concepts, she hoped to identify anti-totalitarian roads not taken, such as those suggested in the work of Rosa Luxemburg. In combination with attention to socio-spatial dialectics of class, this kind of historicizing practice will help us recover the character and appeal that Marxist narratives about class had for American intellectuals during the 1930s.

The further one's historicizing moves from the Soviet Union, then, the more obvious it is that Communists outside the Soviet Union, far from being entirely under the monolithic thumb of the Comintern, were often unduly influenced by the conditions of local capitalist cultures. Like most of American society in the 1930s, for instance, the U.S. left did not always adequately appreciate the history of ethnic, racial, or gendered antagonisms among the working class, nor did it sufficiently question the widespread prioritization of industrial labor over rural and domestic concerns. The 30s left was also obviously off base when it apocalyptically proclaimed the imminence of revolution in the industrialized nations. Throughout the Depression, the U.S. left overrated the political coherence of the dispossessed workers, underrated the ideological resilience of consumer society, and often misunderstood how variously the local cultural traditions it was trying to employ were interpreted. The left's focus, however, on the figure of the worker had less to do with a supposedly totalitarian drive to reduce human diversity to a single master narrative than with a quite contrary impulse to make a mark on North American culture by foregrounding "new" or poorly represented social categories and spaces.

When placed in conversation with contemporaneous essentializing discourses, the situated character of Marxist conceptions of class becomes evident. In the United States during the Depression, sudden changes in the economic status of white working-class men made class more transparently inessential than in more stable conditions, but, while Marxist rhetoric stressed the uneven distribution of breadlines and evictions, many non-Marxist discourses became more essentializing, ahistorical, and aggressively punitive than usual. Major rhetorical trends contemporary with the 30s left included, first, a heightened paranoia focused on the mob. While President Hoover urged Americans to respond to the Depression with local charity, many middle-class citizens found this a difficult ideal and responded to the crisis with Victorian fears about the immorality of the poor. Parents warned their daughters not to speak to dangerous hoboes; newspaper editorials and chambers of commerce represented the unemployed and underemployed working class as unstable, irresponsible, and violent. The national government even deployed troops against hunger marchers in Washington, D.C.[11] A second trend was noblesse oblige toward the deserving weak. Expressed in the paternalism of relief workers toward their clients or the election strategies of Roosevelt and other members of the New Deal elite, this rhetoric replayed the fears of mobocracy in a quieter key; many New Deal administrators saw themselves as temporarily stepping in to serve the nation with their special talents. Well-meaning and well-educated, their commitment was to planning and regulating the economy for necessarily disempowered Others.[12] Finally, some social and political leaders employed a third type of rhetoric: divisive scapegoating that allowed members of the working class to locate enemies among their ranks. Famous pseudo-populists such as Father Coughlin represented the working class as the target of foreign conspirators. These efforts to represent class as a traditional and necessary identity were often as effective as representations of the working class as victim or mob.[13] None of these approaches could legitimately be called non-essentialist, since all relied on psychologization of groups in isolation from the institutions which define them.

In this context, Marxists stressed systemic not individual responsibility for economic crisis and offered remedies for the short and long term including cross-class alliances and a sense of empowering solidarity across nations. The U.S. left like its peers around the world focused on the non-essential nature of current class identities and accentuated the strength of class-conscious individuals within the working class. Recollecting why they joined the Communist Party, many Americans mention the empowering effect of this message; they recall the uplifting sense that one could change what had seemed essential and escape from the ghettos.[14] This utopian remapping was crucial to the Communist movement during the Depression; it provided the basis for hope for a new world and energized a range of efforts to create a socialist culture within the shell of capitalism.

In arts and literature, left intellectuals sought to preserve and enhance this spatial imagination. Their central symbol in this effort was the so-called "positive hero"—the burly, disciplined worker who was a member of a group of fellow laborers (fig. 3). Usually depicted with pneumatically bulging muscles and on a superhuman scale, the figure of "the worker" promised a bursting

Figure 3 Figures of "the worker" from the *New Masses,* January 1930.

of restraints. The potential of that body was the potential to reconfigure the space which it inhabited. This spatially symbolic figure appeared in labor propaganda, post office friezes, drama, reportage, diaries, film, and perhaps most famously, in the controversial proletarian novel. Even in this genre, however, the worker symbol was not monolithic or even entirely consistent. Like any other recurring literary figure, it was deployed, contextualized, and interpreted in a variety of ways. The symbol played several roles in contemporaneous debates about the politics of culture, and, in practice, radical novelists revised this element of the genre as often as they manipulated its other elements. In order to make sense finally of the relational nature of class categories in general and the spatially symbolic quality of "the worker" in particular, then, we will need to trace our way through the dialectic between formula and revision that typified leftist cultural politics during the 1930s.

Theorizing Proletarian Culture

Although a major element of 30s cultural politics, the Communist Party's efforts to create a new socialist culture by fiat were controversial on the left; the worker figure in particular was often contested. Since the 1920s, when something like the proletarian novel was first proposed, theoreticians have asked what it means to represent working-class subjects, authors, or ideologies. Do any of these categories have coherence? What are their effects, if any? How fully is the scope of class-based cultural activism delimited by other struggles? Where is the boundary between present configurations and future utopias to be drawn? These questions shaped the debate over proletarian culture.

Communist Party intellectual Mike Gold was one of the first Americans to call for a proletarian culture. In "Wilder: Prophet of the Genteel Christ," he denounced the "daydream of homosexual figures in graceful gowns" that he took to be central to the decadent writing of established modernists such as Thornton Wilder.[15] Gold sought instead "the speech of a pioneer continent," in a literature written by and for radical workers. He calls for novels of "the modern streets of New York, Chicago, and New Orleans," novels that will describe "the cotton mills, . . . and the child slaves of the beet fields" (352). Written in the style of "the clean, rugged Thoreau, or vast Whitman," these novels will authentically depict modern America and the life of the working class, and by doing so, they will necessarily lead to greater sympathy for Communism, as the ideology of the working class. Proletarian writers in the tradition of Walt Whitman will, Gold insists, infuse American culture with powerful images of the need for revolutionary change.[16] By representing the power, strength, and certainty of the American working class, proletarian culture will help create the conditions for that class to gain power.

Gold's appeal to budding proletarian writers became an official party line in the early 1930s. Although the Soviet literati were in transition between a proletarian aesthetic and what later was codified as socialist realism, in 1931 the CPUSA committed itself to proletarian culture. At this time, the Workers Cultural Federation published its manifesto "ART IS A WEAPON" in the *New Masses.*[17] This manifesto linked the project of creating an empowering proletarian culture to a larger cultural analysis. According to the party line at the time, culture was a legitimate terrain for struggle since the capitalist class was already making use of culture to promote its view of the world. The 30s left, in other words, understood culture as a zone of contest, and they saw opposition as the extant condition of culture. The capitalist class, in their view, was already using culture offensively; culture was already a war zone. The manifesto writers argued that "[t]he most cursory glance at American cultural institutions *will reveal them at once* as instruments of capitalist domination" (emphasis added). For the Workers Cultural Federation, schools, churches, press, sporting events, radio, and movies are all obviously instances of "the industrialization of art." Propaganda, in this context, is not a special disruption of aesthetic function but rather the usual mechanism for the diffusion of culture. In this scenario, the left's role was simply to energize its own side of the contest. Announcing its slogan in the title, the "ART IS A WEAPON!" manifesto proposed that culture was a battle in progress.

On this battlefield, two tactics are possible. First, there is the mechanism of diffusion through which the dominant "imperialist culture" of the Americans is exported to "foreign countries" such as "Cuba, Haiti, China, the Philippines." This external imperialism, aimed at preventing "the development of an independent national culture," directly parallels what later came to be called "internal" colonialism, or the cultural domination of minorities within the United States.[18] The prototypical instance of this process is African American culture, which the Workers Federation considered as much under siege as external colonies. These twin imperialisms, then, indicate how the diffusion of culture can be a repressive maneuver; if unopposed, the dominant capitalist culture would blanket the world and silence minoritarian opposition.

The second tactic, however, offered the means for opposition. Outside the homogenizing, imperialist culture lies Soviet Russia; the manifesto describes the Soviet experiment as "a striking contrast" to capitalist instrumentalism. The Soviets are supposed to have "given complete cultural, as well as political autonomy to the numerous nationalities that were formerly oppressed." In other words, Soviet culture is imagined here as the pinnacle of an emergent multiculturalism—the operative metaphor being the island.[19] Soviet society is pictured as an island in the homogenous ocean of capitalism, while, similarly, radical American working-class organizations make up an archipelago of "[l]ittle cultural islands." From such islands, radicals can perform their own projects of cultural diffusion; they can speak to African and Latin American allies; they can "hold out the hand of comradeship." In other words, the Workers Cultural Federation imagined a flat sea of capitalist culture, dotted by proletarian islands. By joining these islands with human bridges, the Communists sought to create the foundations for a worldwide opposition.

Once Gold and other proponents of proletarian culture were authorized by this macrocosmic analysis, a network of support for sympathetic artists emerged. Clubs for painters, poets, novelists, and dramatists formed and congresses to discuss their problems and accomplishments were called. More than a hundred novels that could plausibly be called proletarian appeared during the 1930s—a remarkable number, especially when one recalls how drastically the publishing industry was affected by the Depression. Information on the

readership of these works is notoriously difficult to collect, but many of
the proletarian novels were reviewed in major mainstream publications of the
period as well as in the partisan leftist press. One contemporaneous study demonstrates that these novels were not only available in public libraries during
the 1930s but also reasonably well read.[20]

Despite these successes, Gold's particular vision of proletarianism did not go
uncontested. Gold himself stepped down from the *New Masses* as editor in the
early 1930s, and responsibility for discussion of the issue was ceded to less out-
spoken columnists such as Granville Hicks and Joseph Freeman. In a six-part
series published in 1934, Hicks evaluated revolutionary novels published in
the United States so far and concluded that they were only partially successful;
in his view, the effort to celebrate simultaneously the strength and oppression
of the working class was producing a flawed literature—something of use, but
only for the moment.[21] Even while encouraging the writing of more revolutionary fiction, Hicks viewed it as a temporary scaffolding around the more
inspiring vision of socialism to be revealed after the revolution.

By 1935, it was possible to adopt any of three very different positions on proletarian fiction, each of which had been endorsed by official spokespersons of
the Communist Party. Although all the literary critics agreed that art played
a political role and could serve as a weapon in the class struggle, some, like
Gold, saw proletarian literature as a vehicle for depicting working-class life and
inspiring working-class writers. Others, like Hicks, were concerned with the
appeal the novels would have as literature for potential allies outside the party,
and even outside the working class. Still others, here represented by the manifesto writers, wanted a proletarian literature that would counteract the influence of the dominant capitalist culture—that would, in short, promote communist ideology. These various goals were each modified in time as the debate
over proletarian fiction and political literature in general continued.

It was in 1935 at the American Writers' Congress that one of the most famous and cogent attacks on the subject matter of proletarian literature was
launched. Here, Kenneth Burke argued that left-wing writers would be more
successful if they substituted "the people" for "the worker" as the linchpin of
revolutionary symbolism.[22] Burke asserted that left-wing writers had placed
too much faith in a kind of "over-simplified, literal, explicit writing of lawyer's
briefs" and thus blinded themselves to the repulsion the worker symbol generated in an American context. His recommendation was that left-wing writers

seize the means of representation and use the inclusive "people" symbol "as a psychological bridge for linking the two conflicting aspects of a transitional, revolutionary era, which is Janus-faced, looking both forwards and back." That is, Burke accepted that the goal of leftist literature is to construct a "bridge" between cultural islands, but he suggested that this would be more effectively accomplished if writers were less, rather than more, concerned with the working class.

At the Writers' Congress, responses to Burke's suggestions were not entirely friendly, but they were not bald-faced, hostile rejections either. A German comrade correctly remarked on the geographical limits to the "people" symbol by pointing out that in his country it had already been appropriated by the fascists, while the leading American Communist literary theorist at the moment, Joseph Freeman, defended the "worker" symbol, arguing that "the proletariat takes over all that is best in the old culture" while supplementing it with their own culture, which includes the "worker" symbol.[23] While accepting the need to speak to an audience in its own terms, Freeman defended the party's class-specific rhetoric.

Meanwhile, the worker symbol was also being questioned in the Congress's other major confrontation. Edwin Seaver's paper extended the ideological definition of proletarian literature, arguing that, regardless of subject matter and authorship, the "worker" symbol was in operation when the novel proposed a pro-worker ideology.[24] In the discussion period, this led Mike Gold to insist again on subject matter, proclaiming that "a great body of proletarian literature will show the concrete facts. It will show our face." Seaver responded that a middle-class writer need not know all the concrete facts of working-class life but can solve this problem by being "equipped with the Marxian analysis." Malcolm Cowley suggested that middle-class authors can enter into an "alliance" with their working-class subjects, and Meridel Le Sueur hoped the debate would inspire "a new experience, a communal relationship."[25] Clearly, the problem of what constituted a proletarian novel was not resolved at this congress; even among the party faithful there was not a monolithic consensus about what counted as working-class subject matter, authorship, or ideology or who would adjudicate the matter and how. The proletarian literature debate operated by way of both formula and revisions in the mid-1930s.

Around the same time, however, another more challenging form of opposition began to emerge among the young intellectuals publishing *Partisan Re-*

view. Initially a Communist-sponsored periodical, in its first issues *Partisan Review* supported proletarian literature and published a number of stories and critical articles on the topic. By 1937, though, after a short-lived merger with Jack Conroy's independent *Anvil,* its editors became disenchanted with party cultural policies and turned toward Trotskyism and later away from Marxism altogether.[26] Their position, which became the dominant post-1945 view, was that leftist fiction had sacrificed aesthetics to politics. Joining Hicks's argument with a version of Trotsky's remarks in *Revolution and Literature,* they argued that art interests the middle class more than the working class and that faulty proletarian novels are boring to the first group and insulting to the second. A more effective political art would focus on changing the sensibility of its readers without necessarily having any political "content" at all. A particularly influential version of this attack on the ideology of the proletarian novel was developed by Philip Rahv, who argued that proletarian literature was "the literature of a Party masquerading as the literature of a class."[27] Rahv's position was that the Communist Party's claim to represent the consciousness of a class was not only false but cruelly deceptive. Politically committed writing, in this view, always involves a certain degree of bad faith, so long as it relies on realist aesthetics and the psychology of belief. Turning toward individualist and avant-gardist ideals, the *Partisan Review* circle specifically discounted the compatibility of ideology and literature.

With the advent of the Cold War and McCarthyism, most American literary intellectuals dissociated themselves from working-class subject matter and ideologies. Even when the tide turned back again with the New Left, a renewed interest in authenticity as a source of cultural critique resulted in a second wave of reaction against proletarian fiction. It became increasingly important for intellectuals to contrast the actual composition of the working class to the party structures, genres, and ideologies that claimed to speak for them. Displacing Old Left alliances between urban intellectuals and the industrial working class, many 1960s radicals preferred rural folk culture and alienated explorations of mass society to the rhetoric of class.[28] An author's authentic rendering of psychological conditions rather than the documenting of social conditions earned praise in the 1960s and 1970s; Nathanael West, Henry Roth, and Henry Miller replaced Dos Passos and Richard Wright as the heroes of the New Left. Fragmented postmodern consciousnesses found even the provisional coherence of the "worker" symbol inhospitable, and the famous divide between labor and the new social movements widened.

Culminating this series of revisions to the proletarian thesis is a poststructuralist position. For some, the very project of describing a sociopolitical reality linked to a possible and alternative future is epistemologically unsound and repressively monologic. For instance, in *Authoritarian Fictions,* Susan Suleiman defines the *roman à thèse* as the limit of realism; operating according to an unambiguous, dualistic system of values, early-twentieth-century political fiction in Suleiman's view addresses rules of action to the reader and authorizes its own position through reference to an external doctrine.[29] According to Suleiman, it is not the specifically class-conscious ideology of proletarian fiction which renders it authoritarian, but simply the project of promoting any ideology at all.

The assumption that all political fictions and ideologies are complicit in the same totalitarian master narrative, however, obscures the fact that within this supposedly monolithic movement there was an active debate over the subject, sources, and character of class-based fiction. Furthermore, as James Murphy and others have demonstrated, these were internal differences; all of the subsequent positions on this genre were foreshadowed by the debate that took place within leftist culture during the Depression.[30] Neither the intellectual nor the political culture of the North American left was simply a reflection of centrally controlled and philosophically dishonest policy. It was rather "a vast, sprawling, fragmented, intensely various experience," as Vivian Gornick has written; the ideology of class consciousness made sense to people from a variety of origins, and they experienced their commitment to this ideology in a variety of ways and abandoned it for yet another diverse set of reasons.[31] Not surprisingly, then, theoretical challenges to the central symbol of the revolution—the "worker"—were part of this culture. While using this symbol, Communists and other leftists questioned the viability of the worker symbol, pondered how to make it more effective, and worried about who it might exclude. While considering the way these debates played out in literary practice, we will want to attend to these variegated tensions and avoid reproducing the premature foreclosures which have so often so hastily been attributed to our subject matter. In particular, it will be important to mark the various spatial imaginaries made visible by the situation of the "worker."

Reading Proletarian Fiction

Most commentary on proletarian fiction describes the genre as formulaic, unimaginative, and dogmatic. Malcolm Cowley's remarks in *The Dream of the Golden Mountains* are typical in this regard:

> [M]ost of the [proletarian novels] have essentially the same plot. A young man comes down from the hills to work in a cotton mill (or a veneer factory or a Harlan County mine). Like all his fellow workers except one, he is innocent of ideas about labor unionism or the class struggle. The exception is always an older man, tough but humorous, who keeps quoting passages from *The Communist Manifesto.* Always the workers are heartlessly oppressed, always they go out on strike, always they form a union with the older man as leader, and always the strike is broken by force of arms.[32]

Like later structuralist readings, this account reduces the proletarian genre to four elements: the presence of a positive worker hero, a plot involving confrontation and/or political conversion, a narrator who redundantly repeats the ideology of a central character, and an ending that coercively calls the reader to action.[33] These elements of characterization, plot structure, narration, and ideation consistently recur in critical accounts of the genre.

Very few proletarian novels, however, conform to this formula. Considering each of the four supposedly constitutive elements in turn demonstrates that the presence of only one—and that presence partial—has been sufficient to include a novel in the genre; furthermore, novels exhibiting all four qualities are extremely rare. Nor is there a marked chronological development; although the Communist Party officially withdrew support for proletarian fiction in 1935, numerous novels with some proletarian elements appeared after that time and no significant decrease or increase in the distribution of proletarian characteristics occurs at this marker. The more closely these novels are examined, then, the more variable the genre appears.

Nonetheless, some clustering is apparent. As others have noted, the body of work grouped under the title proletarian fiction can be subdivided into categories such as stories of bottom dogs, strike novels, depictions of the great mother, narratives of intellectual anxiety, historical fiction, collective novels or documentaries.[34] It is also true, as Cowley charged, that some topics and themes rarely appear, especially the working-class love story, betrayal or spy narratives, and anti-heroes. Still, a closer examination reveals that even these themes did find their way into the genre on occasion. In short, a comprehensive analysis of proletarian fiction published in the 1930s reveals the genre to be unified less by a set of essential and permanent qualities than by certain characteristic tensions.

For instance, only a few of the novels commonly considered proletarian actually take a burly worker hero as the central character. Mary Heaton Vorse's *Strike!* (1930) gives a roving labor reporter's views of a violent strike in the textile mills of Gastonia, North Carolina. Chunks of each chapter report local history that this northerner is unlikely to have known and speculate on the feelings of the workers he observes. As a result, simply constructed worker characters appear on the margins of the narrative; these characters have only a few driving passions and a few thoughts (such as love for a daughter, or self-pity). They are types of strong, stoic workers but they are not the center of the plot or the narration. Similarly, Myra Page's *Moscow Yankee* (1935) and Clara Weatherwax's strike novel *Marching! Marching!* (1935) also include macho proletarians engaged in heroic fistfights and soul-searching, but these positive heroes are contrasted to other figures who struggle in other ways—old women in rocking chairs who hide political pamphlets from the police, for instance. An even clearer example is Pietro di Donato's *Christ in Concrete* (1939); this novel depicts the coming-of-age of a young Italian boy who lost his father to a construction accident and who adapts himself to the adult worker role in order to support his family. He is delicate and sore, suffering in the transition from conflicting longings; he yearns not only for muscular work, but also for "the gray eyes and contemplative lips of a thinker" like his scholarly neighbor.[35] In short, the presence of a masculine worker hero in a text does not always signify an obsession with virility or even an affirmation of the priority of class struggle.

Furthermore, the majority of proletarian novels do not employ this figure. Far more common than the hymns to the innocent young worker that Cowley describes are novels with various types of "weak" heroes. Fielding Burke, Agnes Smedley, Myra Page, Josephine Herbst, Meridel Le Sueur, and Catharine Brody describe heroines struggling with love and family as well as work and torn by their contradictory commitments; like other women writers during the Depression, they confront the constriction of gender roles inspired by the economic crisis and do their best to fuse the struggle for survival with the struggle for some kind of gender equality. Arguably, proletarian novels written by women and focusing on combinations of gender and class issues constitute a distinct genre.[36] Other writers—such as Donato, Mike Gold, Erskine Caldwell, and James T. Farrell in *Studs Lonigan* (1935)—focus on young people who are only peripherally integrated into the system of wage labor and are not yet steeled by the struggle. Still others invent heroes whose struggles with ethnic or racial inequality complicate their class identity—a topic explored more fully in chapters 5 and 6. Sometimes, the heroes of proletarian novels, in addition to their other deviations from the worker type, are proletarian in neither origin nor ideology. A number of radical novels concern homeless drifters whose travels expose the social conditions of the nation during the Depression; Tom Kromer's *Waiting for Nothing* (1935), Edward Anderson's *Hungry Men* (1935), Edward Dahlberg's *Bottom Dogs* (1929), Nelson Algren's early novels, and, to a lesser extent, Jack Conroy's *The Disinherited* (1933) are instances of this tactic. Their weak, underemployed heroes display few of the characteristics of the muscle-bound worker whose anger grows to the boiling point during a strike. They are at the mercy of a hostile world and buffeted about almost comically, except that, like Woody Guthrie's autobiography *Bound for Glory* (1943), these novels integrate the adventures of life on the bum with a radical moral. Joining the men singing his song, Guthrie watches a "great big cloud of black engine smoke" hovering over his train "like a blanket for the men through the storm."[37] In the closing pages of *Bound for Glory,* the train and the song both become images for the strength in solidarity available to "weak" men. Not surprisingly, this image of the hipster drifter exploring voluntary poverty has retained a certain appeal for latter-day beatniks. While we may consider it slumming in the "proletarian sublime," it is also important to note the transformation that accompanies that slumming.[38] In order to make the proletarian novel available to refugees from the middle class, the authors of this "bottom dogs" subgenre displace the burly "worker" symbol with various forms of weak and mobile subjects. Ultimately, it is not the specific qualities of a hero that define the proletarian genre but the distinctive pattern of tensions between weakness and strength, activity and passivity, youth and maturity.

As this first conclusion suggests, the generic view of 30s proletarian writing is somewhat more accurate with respect to plot structure. Most proletarian novels are narratives of conversion or confrontation. As Suleiman argues, the intersection between the *roman à thèse* and the *Bildungsroman* often results in the story of a political apprenticeship, while the intersection between the *roman à thèse* and the adventure story results in a pitched battle between representatives of different classes or political factions. Where there is a strong narrative line, it usually follows one of these two patterns. Nonetheless, within these categories there is variation and, as the more episodic narratives in the "bottom dogs" cluster suggest, some alternate patterns were possible. Most of these variations are less focused on the transformative alterations of conversion or confrontation than on tensions with dominant plots in genre fiction. In particular, fusions of proletarian and sentimental fiction proved fruitful for many women writers.[39]

In fact, most of the novels that do employ the conversion or confrontation plots use these in a modified form. Most conversions are incomplete or ineffectual; that is, heroes of whatever political stripe rarely experience a clean reorganization of their ideological world around the principles of Marxism-Leninism. Instead, like Mike Gold's young hero or Agnes Smedley's autobiographical heroine, they experience various phases of enlightenment and backsliding, often vacillating between political and quasi-religious ideas—Gold's hero approaching Jewish messianism and Smedley's a mix of psychoanalytic and subaltern nationalisms. Or, as in Jack Conroy's *The Disinherited,* the conversion can disempower the hero—leading to unemployment and further wandering rather than invigorating struggle and historical self-consciousness. As Daniel Aaron argues, Conroy's novel is as much a picaresque as a proletarian fiction.[40]

Confrontation narratives are a little more reliable. They do typically involve an older or wiser leader who enters the local scene from outside the world of the novel and delivers a rousing speech at some crucial juncture, as Cowley suggests. However, the dynamics of this process are not as simple as they sound; some of the more interesting proletarian novels pay close attention to the tensions involved in moving from conversion to confrontation, from idea to action; a more detailed examination of the speech scene in Fielding Burke's *Call Home the Heart* (1932) is instructive on this point. In this scene, Fred Beale, a character based on a real-life Communist organizer from the North, is speaking to a crowd of North Carolina millworkers early in the organizing effort. The heroine and her middle-class lover are in the audience, and most of the scene is filtered through her consciousness. We do not hear the early naturalist portions of the speech that recounted "familiar things; their struggles, their hardships, their fight for the union." Instead, Burke turns up the volume only when the speaker begins to translate these local problems into a leftist vocabulary, when he begins "to speak to you of communism." Then, she pays close attention to the effects of these attempts to bridge cultural islands. After the introduction of the word "communism," she writes, "a gasp went over the audience; a gasp of dazzled relief." As the speaker continues, shock becomes comfort ("He didn't sound like he was going to knock the Bible anyhow") and an invigorating pride tinged with eroticism ("Some of the women had risen, their weariness forgotten, and pressed softly nearer the speaker's stand"). At this point, the main character's role in the scene becomes important, and we begin to hear reflections like these:

> Ishma looked at the faces where here and there she could see them, pallid and straining, in the dim light of the lanterns. She knew the yearning and thirst that was on them, stirring through the lines and scars of an ever losing battle. Faces like these had hid in the catacombs, bearing a light that no darkness could put out. That hunted light had encircled thrones. Faces like these had whitened in the dungeons of serfdom, while bleeding fingers had dug away the foundations of feudalism. That bleeding strength had overturned kingdoms. Was this starved feeble handful part of an unconquerable host? Would they win again, and the mountain in their path be levelled? Or would they fall and rot, more fertilizer for its rank, material blooming?[41]

In such passages, the soon to be converted heroine is both in and outside the crowd. She translates the politicized language of the speaker into a folk vocabulary—or, more precisely, into a middlebrow vocabulary representing the folk. Her comparisons of the millworkers to renegades hiding in the catacombs and serfs fighting against feudalism recall middlebrow reformers' thesis that Appalachian mountain culture was a fossil of Elizabethan culture.[42] These reformers understood folk life as necessarily anti-modern and did their best to encourage mountain people to resist the incursions of what they saw as the corrupting influence of mass culture and industrialization. Elements of this cultural position recur in Ishma's reflections throughout the novel.

Similarly, the evangelical language of "the inconquerable host" is a frequent feature of the interior monologue in *Call Home the Heart.* Echoing the crowd's earlier relief that the speaker was not going to "knock the Bible," such phrases situate Ishma firmly in a regional folk identity. Many outside observers during the 1930s associated textual fundamentalism with the cultural islands of the South.[43] In some cases, this image of an ethnically and religiously homogenous folk community served as an example of resistance to the corruption of a secular modern world. Phrases such as "more fertilizer for its rank, material blooming" served similar purposes, marking the sacrifice of the folk community's mountain home to the destructive inroads of capitalism.

This proliferation of vocabularies reveals the point of the speech scene in *Call Home the Heart.* Burke did not insert this scene in order to preach to the reader, nor was she creating a vehicle through which to express a series of dogmatic positions the truth of which would be immediately adopted by the characters and the readers, as Cowley would have it. Instead, the effect of such a scene is precisely the opposite: it highlights the many acts of translation involved in the construction of a confrontation and a conversion. The links between idea and action are many and delicate. The presence of a strike plot— even one as well documented as the Gastonia strike—by no means renders a proletarian novel transparent in structure.[44] It is instead the tensions among various extant ideological languages and implicit plots that the conversion plot explores. These languages are associated with regional identities and their confrontations are played out by way of picaresque wandering or invasion narratives, but it is translation between languages and spaces that is the point.

For instance, we find other generic hybridizations of the conversion/confrontation formula in Catharine Brody's novels. Concerned primarily with psychological adjustments that working-class and lower-middle-class women make, Brody's novels remap the proletarian novel onto the working-girl romances popular during the 1930s.[45] In *Nobody Starves* (1932), a strike does occur, but it takes a role peripheral to ultimately lethal marital squabbles. Similarly, Brody's *Cash Item* (1933) takes working girls who want to marry as its subject, and the plot documents their changing responses to potential suitors. This kind of novel—one in which shifts in the lead character's emotional landscape reflect shifts in social organization—is also represented by James T. Farrell's *Studs Lonigan* trilogy. Farrell pays considerable attention to Studs's half-articulated desires and fears and is particularly skillful at interweaving these with fantasies originating in the mass media. Strikes and discussion of politics are rare in Farrell's trilogy, as he is primarily concerned with depicting a modern psychology of evasion and urban disorientation.

Another prominent generic translation occurred when the presentist intellectual and sociological concerns of conversion and confrontation plots met historical fiction. Only a few historical novels appear in the proletarian genre, but Guy Endore's *Babouk* (1934), Arna Bontemps's *Black Thunder* (1936), Dalton Trumbo's *Johnny Got His Gun* (1939), William Cunningham's *Green Corn Rebellion* (1935), and the earlier volumes of Josephine Herbst's trilogy are important contributions. These works often involve some kind of confrontation, such as a slave uprising or the American Revolution, but detailed description of these events takes a back seat to critical reflection on their representation. In *Babouk,* for instance, Endore draws analogies between slavery in eighteenth-century Haiti and race relations in the twentieth-century United States, but the point of these comparisons is less to assert the identity of past and present racisms than to insist on a fresh interpretation of the problem. Frequent authorial intrusions insist we read the uprising against the narrow interpretation of rights motivating French revolutionaries and subsequent historians. "History" in this novel is clearly ideological, and historical memory for Endore is clearly a weapon in the class struggle.[46] "Our historians," he ironizes at the climax of the story, "who always shout reign of terror when a few rich people are being killed and see nothing much worthy of comment when poor are slaughtered by the thousands in the miseries of peace, cry out unanimously: The pen cannot describe the cruelty of these savages!"[47] In *Babouk,* as in Herbst's trilogy, struggles in the present are authorized by rewriting the history of the confrontations that shaped one's culture. Especially in the later years of the Depression, under the influence of Popular Frontists interested in recovering American radical traditions, proletarian novelists explored tensions between the transformative impulse of conversion/confrontation and a sense of recurrence fostered by historical consciousness. These translations ultimately involved spatializing history—depicting the past as a territory recaptured by rewritings.

Making good use of historical interpretation, however, involved experimenting with the relationship between the narrative voice and the events narrated. According to narratologists, ideological fiction is characterized by a redundancy at this juncture; the narrator validates certain politically correct sentiments voiced by particular characters or insists on a corrective interpretation of events depicted. Thus, a closed, monologic world is created which allows no space for a dialogue of voices or a discrepancy between points of view or a multiplicity of political vocabularies.[48] In this view, the proletarian novel denies the potential of art by collapsing the open-endedness of social reality. Concentrating on historical inevitability and an ideology of progress, it produces an "impossible" aesthetic.[49] Of the charges laid against political fictions and the proletarian novel in particular, this is probably the most serious for contemporary readers.

However, it is more difficult to agree with Cowley and others that the proletarian novel is "always" the same, always tedious and redundant, once we begin to examine the actually existing array of relations between narrative voice and characterization in these fictions. While there certainly are numerous examples of narrators who affirm the political decisions made by leading characters—a not unsurprising feature of a genre that included a number of thinly fictionalized autobiographies—it is not difficult to find exceptions to this rule. Some argue that women's radical fiction necessarily fractures the ideological consensus between different levels of narration, while others have found numerous examples of works by men that also violate the redundancy model.[50] Furthermore, even the affirmative or redundant narrators fall into several categories. Redundancy is not "always" the same, nor does it produce a single effect.

Among the fictionalized autobiographies, for instance, *Daughter of Earth* (1929), *Jews without Money* (1930), and *Call It Sleep* (1934) are markedly different. In Smedley's episodic *Daughter,* the narrative voice waits for the main character to grow up and into socialist feminist ideology. Childhood and young adult experiences, including relationships with parents and men, are described in terms that Marie Rodgers, the central character, will eventually adopt as her own. Smedley traces the harshness of family life back to the miserable conditions in Western mining towns and her mother's efforts to supplement a tiny income by taking in washing. We might call this an empathetic redundancy: the narrator emphathizes with the character's struggles and affirms the ideological explanation of these struggles that she ultimately accepts, after much difficulty.

By contrast, Gold's *Jews without Money* is a circular narrative that concludes with a conversion which seemed always in the works. This story of Lower East Side tenement life in New York takes pains to show that there were radicals in the community all along; the main character's intellectual development is less a discovery of new truths than a clarification of the stories and arguments he has heard all his life. Yes, it is redundant when the narrative concludes with a celebration of revolution-as-messiah, but it is the redundancy of a literary world fulfilling its own premises; it is a formal tautological redundancy rather than an emotional one.

Henry Roth's quasi-proletarian novel *Call It Sleep* is set in the same territory as *Jews without Money,* and like *Daughter of Earth* it is much concerned with family violence and psychology. But Roth's novel is structured around a symbolic redundancy; the narrative voice in *Call It Sleep* is much less dominant than in the other two novels. It is an alienated consciousness reflecting critically on childhood and working-class culture, much as modernists like Faulkner reflected doubtfully on aristocratic culture. Roth's narrator finds the social relations of the Lower East Side vulgar and vicious. It is only charmed by the faint traces of aesthetic pleasure it can locate in surreal sexual experimentation. But the narrative does not completely validate this distantiation. In the climax, after a family argument, David, the main character, runs along the trolley tracks and accidentally electrocutes himself. The narration of the scene alternates between his poetic reflections while in a state of liminal consciousness and snippets from conversations throughout the neighborhood. Someone tells dirty jokes, a whore describes an abortion, a young stud gets ready to go out on the town, and a Communist propagandist makes apocalyptic predictions. Filtered through hallucination, the propaganda transforms into a series of rude jokes about the "red cock" that rises at dawn, and the artistic consciousness of the semi-detached narrator begins to change. Instead of reflecting the prejudices of the presumably adult subject of memory, it begins to transcode elements of the social environment, celebrating a more mystical sense of communal entanglement. This vision both results from and resolves the child's crisis. When he is jolted with electricity, he can witness the neighborhood in action around him and that vision energizes him to return to it. In this shared suffering, recovered through trauma, there is a rare and heroic unity. The narrative voice learns from the child-subject. Instead of redundantly organizing a story that conforms to discursive categories, Roth reworks the narrative voice around the central symbols of the story. We might call this a potential or symbolic redundancy; the ideological referents are present in both the narration and characterization but their relation occurs at a more abstract level.

These variants in redundancy reveal that monologism is itself not monologic; there are several ways to produce self-affirming narratives within the proletarian genre. Furthermore, there are of course alternatives to redundant narration possible within the confines of the proletarian novel. For instance, Tess Slesinger's *The Unpossessed* (1934) offers an ironic reproduction of the structure of the proletarian novel while satirizing the sterility of the intellectuals who, mule-like, keep trying to reproduce a hybrid, declassed culture.[51] Drawing on her own relationship with a CP organizer, Josephine Herbst's narrator expresses doubt about her more ideologically rigid characters in *Rope of Gold* (1939), drawing parallels between the dissolution of a marriage and a loss of political certitude.[52] Farrell's narrator is even more explicitly critical of the limited consciousness of its main character, Studs Lonigan; the interchapters contrast his world to that of his mother, African American and Jewish neighbors, and a local Communist, suggesting that Studs's world should be opened up. In such novels, ideological authority is neither expressed directly nor confirmed. Occasionally, as we shall see in chapter 8, in the case of Nathanael West and friends such as A. J. Perelman, even comic writing on proletarian topics was possible. In texts such as *The Day of the Locust* (1939) ideological consensus between narrator and character was not only unachieved, it was satirized. While retaining political commitment, some comic writers were able to disrupt the internalization, seriousness, and assumed depth of character typical of realist political fiction. The relation between narration and characterization could hardly be considered redundant in these works, since they rely on the gap between the two for their comic effect. Overall, the inescapable redundancy that categorical descriptions of the proletarian genre invoke is much more rarely in evidence than explorations of the limits of so-called didacticism. The narratological tension between story and discourse is maintained in 30s political fiction.

Finally, we need to consider the concluding gestures of proletarian fiction. Cowley's parody describes the genre as always ending in debacle; registering a distaste for narratives of failure, he sighs, "always the strike is broken by force of arms." Of course, this description contrasts to false optimism with the force of "real" events, real repression. Joining realism with utopianism requires, in post-proletarian critiques of the genre, a coercive ending. The disjuncture between ideal and real, between the brutality of strike-breaking and the utopian vision of a new society supposedly results in a narratorial call for action on the part of the reader—action that will address that disparity—and the unfolding of a definite path into the future.[53] In generic terms, this "happy" ending is thought to coerce the reader, leaving him or her no options for interpretation of the present other than those provided in the ideologically rigid text.

Of course, most novels reviewed and treated in criticism as proletarian fiction do not have this kind of ending. Many of the "bottom dogs" variety conclude with the hero continuing his aimless wandering, only mildly enlightened by earlier experiences. Several join Donato's *Christ in Concrete* and render politically ambiguous conclusions; it is not clear in *Daughter of Earth,* for instance, whether the heroine's psychological breakdown will allow her to continue working in independence movements or whether some form of psychotherapy is being offered as a complement to politics. Furthermore, when political outcomes are predicted in proletarian novels, they are not always triumphant; a sense of deflation, even hopelessness, can be detected in *Call Home the Heart,* as Burke describes the way that racism compromised the strikers' solidarity. William Cunningham's *Green Corn Rebellion* goes a step further—making it clear that the uprising of populist farmers ran counter to the forces of history; his novel ends with the hero going off to fight in the very war he opposed. In short, the endings of proletarian fiction are by no means always optimistic or militant calls to action; the tension in American socialist realism between utopian projections and "realistic" descriptions of social conditions is not so hastily resolved.

Nonetheless, some works, such as Clara Weatherwax's *Marching! Marching!* or Herbst's *Rope of Gold* do fit the bill. Both of these novels end in the middle of a political conflict, with the outcome still undecided and the tension rising. Police oppose the strikers and violence seems imminent. The reader's sympathies are enlisted in the striker's cause, since the other side is rarely characterized, and the pattern of escalating confrontation in the plot suggests that there is at least a potential for future conflicts of this nature to result in victory for the strikers. The last sentence of *Rope of Gold,* for instance, describes a minor victory; a "brother" flings back a word of encouragement to the friends of the union, creating a moment of tension with the National Guard poised to attack, until he finally "eased down on the other side and walked up the steps to the fellows inside." [54]

The question to ask about this kind of conclusion, though, is not whether it coerces the reader, prohibiting her or him from escaping a logic of binary alternatives and foreclosed futures. Certainly that is what these novels, like most explicitly realist texts, do; they depict a certain version of social reality and project an outcome of the pattern of conflicts within that social scene. Perhaps they are not as often interested in foregrounding their discontent with their own solutions to the dilemma as more formally ambitious fictions, but their basic dilemma is not substantially different.[55] Instead of condemning these texts for daring to imagine a future qualitatively different from their Depression-era present, it may be more useful to ask what these so-called coercive endings did for the left movement. What was their effect? Why was this gesture integral to the project and reputation of proletarian fiction, even if it was implemented less frequently than Cowley and others assumed?

The Effects of Proletarian Fiction

As we have seen, the proletarian novel was hardly a singular entity. These fictions were not written strictly along the lines dictated by a monolithic formula prescribing essentialist class identities. Rather, ongoing dialectical relations between formula and revision informed this genre. Engaging both social and spatial situations, proletarian fictions were a major part of the U.S. left's efforts to map their cultural geography.

Insofar as there was a proletarian novel, it most likely described a hero in crisis. Struggling with a mismatch between his or her psychological and economic roles, this hero encounters an array of interpretations of this conflict. Often the interpretations that make up this array are mapped onto a local geography—with out-of-towners confronting immediate neighbors confronting a local elite. After exploring this array, the hero usually undergoes a translation from one position to another. This transition is not a simple exchange or erasure; one place on the map is not simply obliterated because the hero moves elsewhere. Instead, the shift of issues experienced by the hero is the occasion for explicit commentary—generally on the part of the narrator. This commentary may take a number of forms, but in all cases it draws our attention to the fact that the novel is part of the reader's continuing confrontation with the world. The novel's didacticism, in other words, throws the reader back into his or her social world. Any actions or effects this maneuver might produce for the reader are unclear within the bounds of the text. Futurity, as we have seen, is often depicted as continued confrontation and probable failure. It involves meeting the social equivalent of death face to face. It is in the space between this confrontation and the utopian vision of the classless society that proletarian fictions ultimately leave their readers, having moved from isolated psychological crises to a generalized social or conceptual one.

The continuing concern of this genre, then, is the position of particular consciousnesses—their situation. These novels map terrains of action, drawing attention to conditions in which different kinds of subjects were emerging. Gastonia, Akron, the Lower East Side, Colorado mining camps, Cuban sugar plantations, and Chicago tenements became in these novels sites of literary attention; the social relations invoked by these names were added to a cultural geography that had previously found little of interest there.

Further, the proletarian novelists suggested that these sites were not entirely isolated. Presenting these sites for the reader's consumption involved bridge-building. As Kenneth Burke's commentary suggested, the human bridge between cultural islands that the literary left sought to construct linked local conflicts. These were then recoded at the conceptual level into a political vocabulary of class relations addressed to a national audience. As didactic texts, the proletarian novels invited readers to test their own social maps against those described fictionally.

Thus, the major effect of the proletarian novels was to articulate a literary version of working-class identity as a situated consciousness—as a socio-spatial dialectic. In dramatic contrast to the essentializing character of contemporaneous non-literary discourses on class, these texts made an effort consistent with Marxist theory of the period to display the potential for transformation latent in marginal social and geographical locations. While few of the political commitments made by the proletarian novelists continue to attract many U.S. writers today, this literary project has not been entirely abandoned. Judging the "Best of Young American Novelists" in 1996, Robert Stone described a "resurgence of realism"—particularly a regional, humanist, empathetic realism that places working-class heroes and heroines at the center of its narration.[56] While texts by Dorothy Allison, David Guterson, Cormac McCarthy, and other late-twentieth-century American novelists may sometimes exhibit problems similar to those we can identify in proletarian novels—a tendency toward class orientalism for instance—they also share with the proletarian novels a tendency to challenge urban or suburban middle-class claims to speak adequately for the nation as a whole.

Chapter 5

SPATIAL PHOBIAS IN *NATIVE SON*

Richard Wright's Revisions of the Proletarian Novel

In *American Hunger,* the volume of Richard Wright's autobiography that describes the 1930s, Wright includes an episode that occurred after his first visit to the Chicago John Reed Club, a major branch of the Communist cultural organization which helped promote proletarian culture. Inspired by his newfound sense of community and audience, the young Wright pounds out "a wild, crude poem in free verse," until his mother enters his room:

> She hobbled to the bed on her crippled legs and picked up a copy of the *Masses* that carried a lurid May Day cartoon. She adjusted her glasses and peered at it for a long time.
> "My God in heaven," she breathed in horror.
> "What's the matter, mama?"
> "What is this?" she asked, extending the magazine to me, pointing to the cover. "What's wrong with that man?"
> With my mother standing by my side, lending me her eyes, I stared at a cartoon drawn by a Communist artist; it was the figure of a worker clad in ragged overalls and holding aloft a red banner. The man's eyes bulged; his mouth gaped as wide as his face; his teeth showed; the muscles of his neck were like ropes. Following the man was a horde of nondescript men, women, and children, waving clubs, stones, and pitchforks.
> "What are those people going to do?" my mother asked.[1]

His mother's horrified questions ("What's wrong with that man?" and "What are those people going to do?") allow Wright to borrow "her eyes" for a moment. From this vantage point, Wright gains a defamiliarized view of the socialist-realist "worker" symbol to which he had become accustomed. To his mother's eyes, the workers' vigor and strength are menacing; the violence they promise is at odds with her fundamentally religious view of the world. "She was a gentle woman," he writes. "Her ideal was Christ upon the cross," and this Christian gentleness does not mix well with the muscular aggression of the proletarian imagery (65).

Throughout his work, Wright frequently analogizes religion and African American folk culture, and this scene in his Chicago bedroom is no exception. Here, his mother's "disgust and moral loathing" at the sight of the *Masses* cartoon represents the incompatibility of the central image of the proletarian novel with African American cultural traditions. Wright broods on this problem and discusses it with his comrades at the John Reed Club, until, finally, his affection for African American culture and the woman who nurtured him lead him to revise his sense of literary purpose. From the solitary exuberance of his initial "wild, crude poem," he turns to a more socially conscious and dialogical project: "I would address my words to two groups," he decides; "I would tell Communists how common people felt, and I would tell common people of the self-sacrifice of Communists who strove for unity among them" (66). The rest of his autobiographical narrative describes the difficult negotiations that this project required. Positioned between the Communist Party and the African American community, Wright was continually revising the representations that each group made of the other and continually experiencing the difficulties of translation. The strains that these efforts produced are evident in his nonfiction and in his most famous novel, *Native Son*. This novel substantially revises the discourses on local culture that were popular with proletarian novelists, and—after a brief consideration of Wright's critical reception—I shall argue that it makes difficult translations the precondition for any possible alliance between the masses and intellectuals, or between African Americans and Communists. Thus, the incomprehension and horror with which his mother interpreted the *Masses* cartoon ("What are those people going to do?") ultimately became the generative question of Wright's literary and political project.

Their Eyes Were Watching Baldwin: Wright's Reputation

Although Wright's dialogic posture—interpreting African Americans to the left and vice versa—has received some attention, most Cold War interpretations of his work have downplayed this aspect.[2] The standard studies of the 30s left granted Wright only a peripheral role, greatly underestimating his actual significance to left-wing culture, while studies of African American intellectual life peripheralize him because he was a Communist.[3] In the body of criticism devoted specifically to *Native Son,* this pattern is repeated. Wright is seen almost exclusively in terms of his position in the African American literary canon, and the Communist elements of his work are almost always described as limits to his understanding of African American community life, not as moments of dialogue or translation.

This thesis has been a constant in Wright criticism since James Baldwin articulated it in the early days of the Cold War. In two important essays, "Everybody's Protest Novel" and "Many Thousands Gone," Baldwin placed *Native Son* in the tradition of the protest novel. Most significantly, Baldwin compares Wright's novel to both *Uncle Tom's Cabin* and the works of "the militant men and women of the thirties"; these writings shared, in Baldwin's words, "a certain thinness of imagination, a suspect reliance on suspect and badly digested formulae, and a positively fretful romantic haste."[4] The "formulae," according to Baldwin, included the assertion "that the aims of the Worker and the aims of the Negro were one," while the "romantic" quality meant preferring "the good of society" to "niceties of style of characterization."[5] In other words, Baldwin objected to Wright's novel because he saw it as the result of a debilitating intrusion of reductive politics into literature. For Baldwin, a good writer is more properly concerned with issues of psychology and the positive attributes of the community that nurtured him. He does not situate that psychology among sociological concerns.

Despite the anxiety of influence that clearly motivates Baldwin's attacks on the older writer, his theses have remained the starting point for most criticisms of Wright's work.[6] Baldwin's oppositions between ideology and psychology, between romantic, formulaic protest and celebration of one's community, between the "Negro" as "Worker" and the "Negro" as "human being" continue to structure Wright's reputation. Furthermore, Baldwin's assertion that Wright is "the most eloquent spokesman" for "the militant men and women of the thirties" has remained a major thesis for many feminist critics. The major feminist readings of Wright condemn him for his presumably easy acceptance of a presumably acceptable Communist misogyny; in response, advocates of Wright defend him simply by inverting Baldwin's opposition and insisting that Wright was completely opposed to the Communists.

After the close of the Cold War, however, many of Baldwin's oppositions seem considerably less self-evident than they may have in the 1940s and 1950s. Not only does the contrast between sentimental or "romantic" literature such as *Uncle Tom's Cabin* and authentic explorations of the (male) psyche have a particularly sexist ring, but also the single-handed rejection of any political or ideological fiction seems untenable.[7] It is a commonplace today to state that all writers are entangled in ideology and that exploring the human psyche is no less an ideological project than exploring social problems. In other words, our current understanding of what it means to be a "spokesman" for the "militant men and women of the thirties" (or anyone else, for that matter) differs from Baldwin's. While Baldwin uses the term to indicate an unusual and objectionable degree of ideological commitment, today we might be more prone to use it to indicate an interesting performative doubleness in the writer's relationship to ideology. We might understand spokespersonship as speaking for and speaking to the 30s left—encouraging dialogues, translations, revisions.

Following from this sense of spokespersonship is a different understanding of the role that writings by "militant men and women" play. In particular, this development can lead us to reevaluate the proletarian novel—or, to use Baldwin's terminology, the "protest novel"—of the 1930s. I argued in the previous chapter that the proletarian novel did not, as Baldwin asserts, rely on the vilification of local cultures or insist on replacing them with the abstract universals of Communist orthodoxy. On the contrary, the proletarian novel was often structured around the effort of local communities to speak for and to the nation at large; these novels attempted to diffuse what they considered the innate radicalism of "cultural islands" into the broader culture. This attempt focused most often on Appalachian and other white communities, but it did not necessarily exclude African Americans. For example, the burgeoning left-wing folk music movement of the late 1930s and early 1940s relied extensively on African American musical traditions. Most famously, spirituals such as "We Shall Overcome" and "We Shall Not Be Moved" became standards of the labor movement in the 1930s and later contributed to the early phases of the civil rights movement.[8] This positive and reciprocal relationship between cultures certainly did not, as Baldwin asserts, always involve pretending "that the aims of the Worker and the aims of the Negro [or other folk communities] were one." The basic dynamics were not reductive identification but rather diffusion and translation from "the Negro" into "the Worker." Further-

more, critiques of racism and inequitable race relations were a key element
of leftist culture.[9] In part because the membership of left parties included a
wide range of people who for reasons of race, class, religion, or ethnicity did
not fit into melting-pot Americanism, left parties were often far ahead of their
time in criticizing the racial hierarchies of American culture. Nor was Wright
the only writer concerned with these matters; Arna Bontemps's *Black Thunder* (1936), Guy Endore's *Babouk* (1934), Claude McKay's *Banana Bottom* (1933),
Myra Page's *A Sign for Cain* (1935), and, somewhat later, Chester Himes's hard-
boiled detective fiction all addressed the intersection of discourses of race and
class from a vantage point sympathetic to the left.

In sum, Baldwin's understanding of Wright as the "spokesman" for the radicals of the thirties needs to be complicated. I will argue that, far from blindly
accepting the dictates of a lily-white Communist Party leadership, Wright
made adapting the language of class struggle to African American urban conditions the basis of his literary and political life. In particular, in *Native Son,*
Wright explores the relationship of the "Negro" and the "Worker" symbols in
order to reformulate the model of cultural geography employed by the proletarian novelists. As part of the ongoing conversation between the Communists
and the African American community that Wright hoped to facilitate, he took
on three tasks: he reconceptualized the space of African American culture, revised narratives of cultural contact, and refigured the nature of the alliance
supposed to emerge in interracial social spaces. Wright's execution of these
tasks is evident in *Native Son* and in the historical and theoretical documents
that surround that text.

The Politics of Place in Folk Culture

In "Blueprint for Negro Writing," a short manifesto published four years
before *Native Son,* Wright outlined a few of the principles that informed his
fiction; although these theses were neither definitive position statements nor
stances that Wright held for the duration of his life, they illuminate his modifi-
cations of theses proposed by theoreticians and practitioners of the proletarian
novel.[10] While the latter often assumed that folk culture resembled an island
on which some form of native radicalism had been preserved, Wright assigned
different political and spatial meanings to local traditions.

First, in "Blueprint" Wright argues that African American writers have a rich culture to draw from—a culture based on parallel developments in religion and folklore. Although, overall, Wright is hardly enthusiastic about the influence he thinks religion has had in African American life, he does take a more nuanced view of it here than he is generally credited with: he argues that "the Negroes' struggle for religion on the plantations between 1820–60 assumed the form of a struggle for human rights. It remained a relatively revolutionary struggle until religion began to serve as an antidote for suffering and denial" (55). In other words, Wright sees the political potential of religion as something that varies according to the social relations of which it is a part; when religion is a mode of expression for an oppressed group, it is a "revolutionary" and cohesive force, although when it becomes hegemonic, it seems "an archaic morphology" (55).

This two-part structure also characterizes Wright's analysis of folklore—although in this case the political sequence is reversed. Broadly speaking, Wright understands folklore as an artistic form ("[b]lues, spirituals and folk tales recounted from mouth to mouth"); as a social practice ("the whispered words of a black mother to her black daughter on the ways of men," "the confidential wisdom of a black father to his black son," and "the swapping of sex experiences on street corners from boy to boy in the deepest vernacular"); and as a companion to labor ("work songs sung under blazing suns"). Wright sees all these forms as embodying "the memories and hopes of [African Americans'] struggle for freedom" (55–56), and, thus far, he is in agreement with the usual leftist analysis of local culture. His assessment of the immediate political significance of this lore, however, is where he differs most substantially from his contemporaries. Wright argues that African American folklore has been warped by "the Jim Crow political system of the South" and that it therefore expresses a potentially destructive form of nationalism. Far from being a subdued "internal colony," in Wright's view, African Americans have developed viable social institutions in order to defend a way of life and nurture an active culture in an inhospitable soil. Wright's assessment of this kind of nationalism is that it is not in itself a sufficient political strategy; he sees nationalism as the extant state of African American culture, but a state which writers "must *possess* and *understand*" in order to move forward to "revolutionary significance" (58–59). That is, he sees nationalism as latent within African American culture and the conditions for what he calls "social consciousness" as latent within nationalism. While religion moves from a revolutionary moment to a reactionary one, the nationalism expressed in African American folklore can, in Wright's view, shift from reaction to revolution. African American culture, then, is not an isolated island for Wright so much as it is an active conflicted arena the writer must negotiate and understand.

In proposing this more voluntarist analysis of the political potential of African American culture, Wright was not entirely alone. His theses reflect some of the concerns of the late thirties—especially the left's efforts to differentiate radical and fascist nationalisms—and two other articles appearing in the same issue of *New Challenge* as his "Blueprint" echo his line of reasoning.[11] Like Wright, these authors challenge theses based on analyses of white folk culture and argue that African American intellectuals are responsible for allying themselves with the masses; together they can separate a radical version of cultural nationalism from its proto-fascist counterpart.

Wright's unique contributions to the revisions of the proletarian theses are more apparent when he provides figures for the contradictory political significance of African American culture. In *Twelve Million Black Voices: A Folk History of the Negro in the United States,* for example, Wright countered the proletarian novelists' image of folk culture as an "island."[12] While the proletarian's image might suggest a Robinson Crusoe-esque individuality and the insular safety of a natural paradise, Wright's lyrical and evocative "folk history" employs the discourse of the built environment to figure folk culture. Throughout *Twelve Million Black Voices,* he describes the "place" of black folk culture through images of the sharecroppers' "one-room shacks," one-room schools, and one-room churches; then, he follows this list with a description of the shock black farmworkers felt when they migrated to the cities and learned "that there are not enough houses" (100). His implicit thesis is that the segregated boarding-houses, rooming-houses, apartment-houses, and kitchenettes of northern cities shaped early-twentieth-century urban African American culture as fully as rural life in the South did. These small spaces are not naturally isolated like islands, nor are they awaiting the construction of bridges from the outside. Rather, these one-room buildings are social islands, their confining shapes reinforced by social practices of discrimination. The continuity between rural and urban forms of confinement—between the shack and the kitchenette—is important because it underlines the social element of these limits. One cannot easily escape a confining space if one remains within the borders of the society that constructs and replicates it, Wright stresses.

Thus, by depicting the social side of the socio-spatial dialectic, Wright revises a tendency toward romanticism latent in the proletarian novelists' spatial
imaginary.

Does this revision go too far, though? Some readings of Wright's interest
in confinement interpret these domestic images as analogies for the holds of
slaveships—a reading that suggests Wright misogynistically also links maternal spaces with enslavement.[13] In this view, in order to escape confinement
and appropriate the power of birth for the Communist symbolic order, Wright
has to punish a figure of black women: referring derogatorily to the last phrase
of *Twelve Million Black Voices,* where Wright proclaims the emergence of African Americans into "conscious history," Houston Baker asserts that "a Marxian
problematic forces the writer to devalue women, therefore, in both folk culture and 'conscious history.' "[14] This, however, is not the only possible interpretation of the spatial imagery in *Twelve Million Black Voices.* We might also
understand Wright's images of confinement as dialectical counterparts to the
expansive, reborn freedom of the narrative voice. This voice is self-consciously
collective, lyrical, poetic, and imagistic, suggesting that Wright associated African American folk life with both confinement and spacious, free-floating spiri-
tualism.[15] In passages such as the following, Wright makes an appreciation for
the pleasures available within the spaces of domestic life essential to his narrative style:

> Our black children are born to us in our one-room shacks, before crack-
> ling log fires, with rusty scissors boiling in tin pans, with black plantation
> midwives hovering near, with pine-knot flames casting shadows upon the
> wooden walls, with the sound of kettles of water singing over the fires in
> the hearths. . . .
>
> As our children grow up they help us day by day, fetching pails of water
> from the springs, gathering wood for cooking, sweeping the floors, mind-
> ing the younger children, stirring the clothes boiling in black pots over
> the fires in the backyards, and making butter in the churns. (62)

Here, Wright is not attempting to confine women to the home or to relegate
them to a back room of history; on the contrary, this scene roots his lyricism in
an appreciation of birth, childhood, and motherhood. The sociological studies
cited at the start of *Twelve Million Black Voices* underscore this positive relation to the mother.[16] Unlike Daniel Moynihan and white liberals of the 1950s

and early 1960s, Wright was not pathologizing African American matriarchy. Unlike the proletarian novelists, he was not interested mainly in using the island as a platform from which to speak to a national culture; he began with a knowledge of local culture, supplemented it with sociological research, and returned to the folk by way of aesthetics. He positioned himself as speaking both to leftist romantics and to an African American folk culture associated with the mother. His relationship to the "Marxian problematic" did not force him "to devalue women" or folk culture so much as it encouraged him to figure an African American urban life shaped in part by women and promising further development. Finally, Wright saw the space of African American culture as something he as a writer could struggle to reclaim in a radical mode. Characteristically, he did not state this concern overtly in theoretical statements but dramatized it in *Native Son.*

One of the central questions of *Native Son* is this: To what is Bigger Thomas, the central character, native? Does "native" indicate that Bigger belongs to the spaces he inhabits? That these shape him definitively? That they confine him? Or does the title ironically emphasize his displacement, his isolation, his alienation from the land of his birth? In "How 'Bigger' Was Born," an essay chronicling the process leading up to the publication of his novel, Wright describes the way these questions came to cohere for him in the mid-1930s. After moving to Chicago, he began to see urban versions of the "bad nigger" who resisted Jim Crow in the South; when reading crime stories in the paper, he began to see white versions of the "bad nigger"; and within the labor movement, he began to see Russian and German versions of the same figure.[17] "Here, I felt, was *drama,*" he concluded. The figure of the resistant rebel exemplifying a social condition without necessarily realizing his position offered a powerful dramatic conflict—he could describe not only the hero's battles, but also his developing consciousness; furthermore, the whole project offered analogies of an international scope. Ultimately, translating between the black, white, and European versions of Bigger Thomas's drama of entrapment became the basis of Wright's most important literary projects. The dilemma of his nativity became the basis for a transnational effort.

The basis of Wright's analogies in *Native Son,* in other words, is his depiction of space. The novel, of course, begins in the Thomas's kitchenette and describes the elaborate ritual behavior the family has developed in order to cope with their close quarters—the boys turning their heads to preserve their

mother's and sister's modesty while dressing, for example. From the kitchenette to the pool-room to the movie theater to the white employer's kitchen, the
first scenes of the novel remain in the confining places Wright designated in
Twelve Million as the circuit of the black urban folk. Even Bigger's room at the
Dalton's house is symbolically crowded: the walls are covered with "pictures
of Jack Johnson, Joe Louis, Jack Dempsey, and Henry Armstrong [and] there
were others of Ginger Rogers, Jean Harlow, and Janet Gaynor" (60). Although
Bigger's initial response is delight at the spaciousness of the room, it, too, feels
confining after he violates yet another "taboo"—entering the white girl's bedroom.

In addition to, or perhaps parallel to, Bigger's sexual anxieties in the scene in
which he murders Mary Dalton are his anxieties about place. Even before the
confrontation with the blind Mrs. Dalton (which leads him to kill her daughter), he fears transgressing the spatial boundaries of his folk culture: "Was this
really [Mary's] room? Was she too drunk to know? Suppose he opened the door
to Mr. and Mrs. Dalton's room?" Bigger asks himself while hauling the intoxicated Mary upstairs. When Mrs. Dalton appears as he is caressing Mary, "he
wanted to . . . bolt from the room. . . . He wanted to move from the bed, but
was afraid he would stumble over something and Mrs. Dalton would hear him,
would know that someone besides Mary was in the room" (83–84). While in
the grips of this intense claustrophobic anxiety, Bigger displaces his asphyxia-
tion and stifles Mary, and thereafter he experiences almost all spaces as con-
finements. He hates the closeness of his family's room; he feels trapped in the
basement where the furnace is burning Mary's body: "He had to get out into
the air, away from this basement whose very walls seemed to loom closer about
him each second, making it difficult for him to breathe" (100, 114). He feels
he has to kill his girlfriend Bessie because "[h]e could not leave her here and
he could not take her with him" (221); that is, he does not know where to put
her; there is no place for her. After murdering Bessie, Bigger creeps through the
buildings of the South Side, listening to conversations through walls, studying
maps printed in the paper that show the "tiny square" of the Black Belt that
the police have not yet searched; he feels the rooms and the city itself closing
in on him (239). Then, when Bigger is captured and imprisoned, his confinement is complete.

Wright notes in "How 'Bigger' Was Born" that he stretched the probabilities
of space in the prison scenes; although he "knew that it was unlikely that so

many people would ever be allowed to enter a murderer's cell," he chose to introduce them anyhow because he wanted "to elicit a certain important emotional response from Bigger." That the desired response was almost certainly a claustrophobic panic is implied when Wright next states that his goal was "to 'enclose' the reader's mind in a new world" (xxxi–xxxii). In other words, by associating African American culture with confining spaces, Wright chose to portray the psychic scarring those spaces can induce by duplicating their effects in the reader's experience of the novel. Specifically, he depicted the space of African American urban life as the site of psychological crisis.

The source of this crisis becomes evident when we note that these recurrent images of enclosure are contrasted early in the novel with images of freedom of motion. Bigger and a friend dream of flying while they watch a tiny airplane spell out "USE . . . SPEED . . . GASOLINE," (19–20), and later they daydream about living out a scene in a high-society movie they're watching—dancing, driving, and keeping clandestine appointments with giddy young women. Clearly, Wright is interested in the way that mass culture and technology are confronting social restrictions in the fantasies of black youth.[18] In the many references to hard-boiled fiction and film, the novel highlights the conflict between the dream of speed and Bigger's immobile confinement in order to revise the discourses on nativism associated with the proletarian novel. In part, these scenes function as references to famous passages from leftist novels of the thirties. The airplane flying overhead recalls the conclusion to John Dos Passos's *U.S.A.*, while the episode in the movie house is reminiscent of James Farrell's *The Young Manhood of Studs Lonigan.* Wright rewrites these passages in order to emphasize the particular problems encountered when mass culture meets black folk culture.

Unlike Dos Passos and Farrell, Wright does not pretend to examine mass culture in general; as an African American who is always aware of his limited access to the dream-life offered by mass culture, he finds that mass culture is always in dialogue with previously extant cultural forms. The scene that makes this point most clearly is Bigger's writing of a ransom note for the recently murdered Mary Dalton. As others have pointed out, when penning the note, Bigger writes in the hard-boiled tradition; he draws on a reservoir of phrases, such as "Get ten thousand in 5 and 10 bills and put it in a shoe box," that he had read "somewhere" (167). At the same time, he marks the note as a product of local conditions with African American vernacular speech: "Do what this letter say," he writes.[19] This scene illustrates Bigger's rewriting of tough-guy practices and Wright's rewriting the proletarian novel. By leaving the "s" off the end of "say," Bigger and Wright point to the formation of a new culture—an urban culture in the midst of establishing its own practices. This urban culture is the one that Bigger is "native" to, and it is a social formation recognizable more by its linguistic practice than its location. Responding claustrophobically to the confined space imported from the rural South, and excluded from the absolute mobility of white mass culture, the Bigger Thomases Wright describes invent their own procedures for writing themselves into culture. For Wright, it is this new African American practice that needs to be put into dialogue with Communism—that needs to be translated and diffused.

Translating between Cultures

For many leftist novelists, as the next chapter will discuss, writing a political text could involve adopting a narrative of assimilation. Bridging the local and the national, translating the local community's vocabulary into what they conceived of as a more widely comprehensible political vocabulary involved proletarian writers in such unlikely experiments as rewriting the gospel song "Give Me That Old Time Religion" as "Give Me That Old Communist Spirit."[20] Despite the dissonance such a translation may produce for contemporary listeners, and despite their own thematization of the difficulties of translation (in novels such as Tess Slesinger's *The Unpossessed* that reflected on the genre), few 30s leftists imagined that such a project would be terribly difficult. It was simply a matter of finding a good translator.

For Wright, however, translating between African American and leftist culture was not such a one-directional or effortless procedure. In *American Hunger,* for example, the transition from folk to mass culture is figured in terms of Wright's own travels from the South to Chicago. This transition, however, does not simply replace his old bad life with a good new collective one: "My first glimpse of the flat black stretches of Chicago," the memoir begins, "depressed and dismayed me, mocked all my fantasies" (1). The city was gray and ugly, and living there forced him to confront the difficulties he would encounter when attempting to translate between cultures. At his first job, working at a Jewish delicatessen, he has an embarrassing miscommunication with one of his bosses almost immediately. When she asks him to go to a neighboring store to fetch a can of chicken à la king, he misunderstands her thick accent. Memorizing the sound she uttered, he asks the clerk for "a can of Cheek Keeng Awr Lar Keeng," hoping his pronunciation would not offend. This difficult transaction humiliates and angers Wright, and at first he can only attribute his boss's impatience to racist attitudes. Then, later, in a parenthetical insert, he informs us that he "had misread [her] motives and attitudes" because of his own ignorance of the cultural and linguistic practices of the city (4–5). In other words, for Wright, the translation of "chicken à la king" into "Cheek Keeng Awr Lar Keeng" and back is an occasion for reflection, for repeated and retrospective wonderment.

Eventually, this wonderment at the difficulty of cross-cultural communication becomes one of the major themes of his autobiography—as the epigraph to that volume indicates:

> Sometimes I wonder, huh,
> Wonder if other people wonder, huh,
> Sometimes I wonder, huh,
> Wonder if other people wonder, huh,
> Just like I do, oh, my Lord, just like I do!

Identified by Wright as a "Negro Folk Song," this epigraph locates wondering about cultural translation as a practice of African American culture. At the same time, the "huh" punctuating each line of the song recalls the "work songs sung under blazing suns" Wright described in "Blueprint," and we see the problematic of labor inscribed as well. In short, Wright's autobiography stresses the work involved in cultural translation. The song that serves as its epigraph is no more univocal than the novel he wrote during the period of time the autobiography describes.

In *Native Son,* Wright returns to and reflects further on the process of translation. As noted earlier, the novel's basic technical challenge is to "enclose" the reader in the thoughts of an intellectually rather limited character while also suggesting political conclusions other than those articulated by that character. That is, the novel struggles with the problem of translating between Bigger's and Wright's agendas. Many critics have objected to this element of Wright's project—from an early and entirely hostile review that expresses disgust with Wright's Communism, to later controversies over the novel's supposed didacticism.[21] Conflating Wright's work with what they assume to be the practice of the proletarian novelists, these critics object to Wright's narrator's moralizing and especially to what they view as his pre-packaged translation of Bigger's experience. If, however, we attend to Wright's revisions of the proletarian novel, we find that Wright makes the difficulty of just this kind of translation the subject of his novel.

For example, the attention to dialect that the "chicken à la king" episode demonstrates is continued in *Native Son.* As one critic has noted, Wright separates his characters into social groupings by the way he records their use of dialect. When Bigger and his family speak black English, Wright employs white English spelling to record their speech, but when black characters who accept whites' definitions of their social roles are speaking, Wright marks their speech with "eye-dialect," a visual emphasis of their speech patterns. For example, when Bigger is hiding in an empty kitchenette, through the wall he hears several frightened men discussing his situation:

> "Jack, yuh mean t' stan' there 'n' say yuh'd give tha' nigger up t' the white folks?"
> "Damn right Ah would!"
> "But, Jack, s'pose he ain' guilty?"
> "Whut in hell he run off fer then?"
> "Mabbe he thought they wuz gonna blame the murder on *him!*" (235)

Not only do these characters make the same vital mistake that the Daltons do—finding it impossible to imagine Bigger as capable of committing an act as rash and individualistic as the murder of Mary Dalton—but also the transcription of their speech indicates their adherence to Uncle Tom roles. Their speech is represented with the same "Ah"s and "fer"s that Uncle Tom uses in Stowe's novel. In such passages, Wright defamiliarizes this dialect by positing Bigger as the auditor of the scene. Crouched in the kitchen next door, Bigger hears this speech in much the way some white people might hear black English—as a variation on "standard English"; Wright uses eye-dialect to show how Bigger learns the necessity of translation.

Conversely, the numerous scenes in which Bigger reads newspaper accounts of his own exploits foreground another act of translation. When Bigger reads the first account of Mary's disappearance, he compares the journalists' dry recitation of clichés with his own vivid memory, until the photograph of Mary recalls his own "sweaty fear at her head lying upon the sticky newspapers with blood oozing outward toward the edges" (195). That is, when Bigger seeks verification of his safety in the objectivist language of the newspapers, this flight returns him to the particularity of his own experience, although this experience is still, to some extent, delimited by the newspapers. He imagines her bloody head framed by "the edges" of the paper. That final image combines Bigger's memory and mass cultural production and sends him into crisis—panicking further. This fundamentally dialectical structure emphasizes Wright's sense that translation between discourses is not only multidirectional, but also complex, difficult, and crisis-inducing.

These two examples have concerned Bigger's translations of the materials around him, but we should also note that the novel performs two other translations; Mr. Max, the Communist lawyer, retells Bigger's story in court in a public, politicized language, and the narrator continually interprets Bigger's interpretations of Max's retellings. The first of these translations has been most controversial, with readers objecting strenuously to the "transparently propagandistic" elements of Max's speech and Wright's "hammering home sociological points in didactic expository prose."[22] If, however, we see Wright's novel as engaged in a dialogue with the proletarian novel, the effects of this speech will appear otherwise.

In proletarian novels, such as *Call Home the Heart,* characters often attend a speech made by a Communist organizer and experience a radical transformation during the oration; that is, they identify with the speaker's articulation in general terms of their own local problem. In *Native Son,* however, Max's courtroom speech serves a different function. Granted, Max speaks "in general terms" and considers Bigger as "a test symbol," and, granted, his speech is positioned at the end of the novel so that its general terms will summarize the action the reader has already witnessed (359, 354). However, the speech does not act as the inner truth of Bigger's experience, or the propagandistic moral;[23] Max does not use Marxist jargon or present a "stereotyped Communist vision of black and white workers marching together in the sunlight of fraternal friendship."[24] Instead, Max's speech provides a "background," a context, and a narrative for Bigger's crime. Max attempts to portray the "mode of *life,*" or the culture, in which Bigger lives by describing some of the historical circumstances surrounding African Americans in the 1930s, and neither the range of his vocabulary nor the length of his speech are implausible for a lawyer. This passage is very clearly marked as the translation, not the propagandistic core, of Bigger's life.

In addition to presenting the Communist lawyer's speech as a translation of the events we've already seen narrated, Wright makes it quite clear that Max's "general terms" are not a sufficient translation. Not only does the speech not effect the conversion or radical transformation that it might in some proletarian novels—the judge does not pardon Bigger—but also Wright insists on the fact that Bigger "had not understood the speech," although "he had felt the meaning of some of it from the tone of Max's voice" (370). This is a dramatic departure from the proletarian novel, where the hero almost always recognizes him or herself in the Communists' abstract vocabulary and achieves some form of class consciousness. This departure indicates Wright's insistence on translating the abstract vocabulary back into Bigger's language; it reinforces his interest in the several directions of translation and in the difficulty of speaking to several audiences at once. Ultimately Max could not speak both to the court and to Bigger, so, finally, he convinced neither.

Bigger's semiconscious appreciation of the "tone of Max's voice," however, suggests a site where this other translation might take place. Characteristically, the narrator interprets Bigger's feelings for us; like a Flaubert of the 1930s, Wright's narrator rewrites his character's feelings into those of a symbolic individual. In a sentence structure repeated innumerable times throughout the novel, the narrator relates a feeling or response specific to the situation to the abstract, general "he": "He could hear his breath coming and going heavily. He had not understood the speech, but he had felt the meaning of some of it." With this structure, the narrator combines Bigger's emotion-laden mode of translation with Max's generalizing. The narrator attempts the dialectical feat of simultaneously translating Bigger the particular and Bigger the general into Bigger the individual.

Even this translation is not without its difficulties though. At several moments, Bigger's unassimilated experience breaks through the master narrative with an ironic laughter.[25] And, more fundamentally, the novel is organized around an ultimately untranslatable event: the murder of Bessie. A close examination of the passage in which Bigger kills Bessie reveals the limits of the narrator's power to translate the causes of this horrific event: "He straightened and lifted the brick, but just at that moment the reality of it all slipped from him. His heart beat wildly, trying to force its way out of his chest. No! Not this! His breath swelled deep in his lungs and he flexed his muscles, trying to impose his will over his body. He had to do better than this" (222). The entire scene is told in simple sentences by a narrator who speaks for Bigger, generalizing. Also, the passage is clearly marked as a translation, as an insertion of fantasy where "the reality of it all" used to be. Then, when the physical presence of Bigger threatens to erupt into a resounding "No!" the narrator finds it is necessary to impose a "will" on the "body." Thus, the scene begins with the conflation of translation and discipline. It continues: "Then, as suddenly as the panic had come, it left. But he had to stand here until that picture came back, that motive, that driving desire to escape the law. Yes. It *must* be this way. A sense of the white blur hovering near, of Mary burning, of Britten, of the law tracking him down, came back. Again, he was ready. The brick was in his hand" (222). The whole weight of the narrative must bear down on Bigger before he can plausibly accept the necessity of killing Bessie. The narrator retraces Bigger's progress from the murder of Mary Dalton through his flight into the kitchenettes until the necessary claustrophobia replaces his bodily "No!" Then, fantasy sets in again: "In his mind his hand traced a quick invisible arc through the cold air of the room; high above his head his hand paused in fancy and imaginatively swooped down to where he thought her head must be. He was rigid; not moving. This was the way it *had* to be" (222). Here, the narrator insists on interpreting Bigger's hesitance as planning, but reading against the grain and recalling the novel's dedication ("To my mother, who, when I was a child at her knee, taught me to revere the fanciful and the imaginative"), we might read Bigger's "fancy" and imaginative swooping as hinting at another more maternal mode of behavior. The intrusion of this mode into the plot causes Bigger to become "rigid" and unmoving. Far from debilitating, this paralysis is in accord with Bigger's intuitive, bodily "No!"; his willful return to the posture of confinement is the mark of his resistance in this passage. But this moment does not last; he succumbs to the narrator's sense of necessity: "Then he took a deep breath and his hand gripped the brick and shot upward and paused a second and then plunged downward through the darkness to the accompaniment of a deep short grunt from his chest and landed with a thud. *Yes!* There was a dull gasp of surprise, then a moan. No, that must not be! He lifted the brick again and again, until in falling it struck a sodden mass that gave softly but stoutly to each landing blow" (222). Abandoning himself to action, to the forward movement and reckless mobility of the speeding airplane pilot, Bigger kills Bessie with a brick. However, in this gesture, a semiotic grunt escapes from his chest—a syllable that the narrator interprets as the final "*Yes!*" but that is so quickly followed by Bessie's own inarticulate sounds that it transforms into a new kind of "No." At the height of the narrator's disciplinary triumph, Bigger's wordlessness escapes translation.

This resistance to translation continues and Bessie's murder remains a recurring gap in the text. Neither Max nor the narrator can invent a plausible justification for Bigger's actions; neither can subsume the event into a master-narrative. Once the murder begins, the narrator can no longer attribute Bigger with any further emotions concerning it; only action, not reflection or collective wonderment, is comprehensible at that point. Similarly, Max comments on his inability to discuss Bessie: "I have not forgotten her. I omitted to mention her until now because she was largely omitted from the consciousness of Bigger Thomas" (367). Like the narrator, Max has only the flimsiest arguments available to explain Bigger's murder of Bessie, and he shies away from using them.

Finally, then, the conspicuous horror of Bessie's mangled body represents the untranslatable residue, the irreducible difficulty in translating between the particular and the general, between the private kitchenette and the public courtroom, between an urban African American culture and Communism. And, if a sometimes suspiciously easy translation characterizes the proletarian novel, then Bessie's corpse also represents Wright's resistance to that form.[26] By carefully marking the inadequacy of his means of disposing of Bessie's body, Wright focuses on the difficulties the proletarian novels characteristically gloss, drawing our attention to the fact that the brutal acts that black and white men inflict on black women inhibit the progress of any future alliance among these groups.

Alliances and Anger

Wright's complication of the translations that take place between Bigger and Max and between Bigger and the narrator does not mean, however, that he sees the kind of alliance proposed by the proletarian novel as necessarily impossible. On the contrary, his call in "Blueprint" for black intellectuals to "*possess and understand*" the culture of the black masses closely parallels proletarian novelists' call for a militant, class-conscious intelligentsia allied with the working class, and his excitement about the "*drama*" of German, Russian, and white Biggers requires the possibility of that alliance. Throughout *Native Son,* these themes appear. Wright establishes the commensurability of Bigger's anxiety as an African American and Max's as a Jew;[27] he even briefly mentions a further parallel in Peggy, the Dalton's maid, whose Irishness leads her to sympathize with Bigger (332, 58). Later in an angry response to a reviewer who suggested that such cross-cultural alliances were impossible, he added Mexican Indians to his series of interlinked oppressions.[28] As his career progressed and the Communist Party's line on issues of race and ethnicity changed, Wright devoted a great deal of his personal energy to promoting alliances between first and third world. In short, for Wright, the prospect of alliances between oppressed groups remained a crucial one; even while writing his study *Black Power* (1954), he remained suspicious of the kind of separatist nationalism described in "Blueprint."

The most central element of Wright's interest in alliance, though, was not intercultural. Instead, as *Native Son* demonstrates, Wright was primarily concerned with portraying the difficult translations that take place across class lines in African American culture. The narrator's efforts to recuperate Bigger and Bigger's resistance to recuperation dramatize this struggle, representing the continuously strained alliance between intellectuals and the masses. Wright's later novels were considerably less popular (although they have their partisans) in part because they lack this sense of immediacy, contact, struggle, and dialogue. In these novels, Wright is too clearly writing to white America and sidelining the struggle between black intellectuals and the black masses in the effort to speak for a united front of African Americans. *Native Son,* on the other hand, is positioned nicely on the cusp between what Native American writer Thomas King has called "polemical" literature and "associational" literature.[29] While, like a polemical novel, *Native Son* challenges whites to discard stereotypes about African Americans (most notably the myth of the black rapist), the novel also depicts African American culture appreciatively; it invites alienated African Americans and white Americans alike to associate themselves with this rediscovered culture. In particular, it invites white Communists to reevaluate their misrepresentations of African American culture, thereby furthering a possible dialogue between these two groups.

One final image will suggest the particular character of this alliance as Wright conceived of it in the late 1930s and early 1940s. In *Twelve Million Black Voices,* most of the one hundred and eighty-six photographs that accompany the text are drawn from the Farm Security Administration's extensive files.[30] In general,

Figure 4   Russell Lee's "Mother and Children" from *Twelve Million Black Voices,* edited by Richard Wright. (Reproduced from the Library of Congress, Farm Security Administration collection, LC-USF34-38618)

they are skillful photographs that portray a wide range of contrasting textures and shapes. Soft frontal lighting brings out the warmth of skin, and interesting compositions place their subjects solidly in particularized landscapes. Russell Lee's "Mother and Children," for instance, depicts a gently smiling woman in her late thirties holding a droopy-eyed boy in her lap while close by a serious, alert young girl in a freshly starched cotton dress looks on (fig. 4). The expressions in the three figures' eyes and their interlocked arms form a complex triangulation of light and shadows that contrasts with the right angle of the grimy windowsill trailing off the page behind them. Overall, the picture suggests the intimacy and comfort of a family life persisting in this inhospitable environment, and the relationship of the photographer to this family grouping appears to be one of sympathy, if not actual pity. Finally, there is both a gentleness and a sense of cultural distance and suspicion in the eyes of the subjects as they pose for him—particularly in the eyes of the little girl.

By contrast, the one photograph in the volume that was taken by Wright is much starker. "Sign" (104) depicts the window of a Brooklyn brownstone whose decorative trim frames an advertisement for an apartment. "JUST OPENED TO COLORED," it reads. The brutal ironies of the sign and the social relations it encodes are the subject of the photograph. The harsh lighting produces a dark, triangular shadow pointing to the first "O" in "COLORED" and accentuates the contrast between the white sign and the blackness of the room behind it. No leering landlord's face appears; the sign alone is sufficient to recall the dynamics of ghettoization and urban crowding that Wright discusses in the text.

Although the fact that Wright was not primarily a photographer probably has something to do with the simplicity and starkness of this photograph, there are traces too of a more sociopolitical rage in this scene. The high level of contrast in the photograph suggests that it was taken near midday, and one can easily imagine Wright being suddenly arrested by the sign during a mid-morning stroll. How enraging for the novelist, this spokesperson for "Negro writing" and the militant men and women of the thirties, to be interpellated as "COLORED" and summoned back to the kitchenette. In an instant, he photographs the sign's linguistic violence and appropriates it for his own use.

While this re-creation of the scene behind this photograph is only hypothetical, it suggests the nature of the alliance Wright sought. The photograph demonstrates that Wright did not position himself at a distance like Russell Lee, who could comfortably pity the black madonna, because Wright, too, was the object of racism. He concerned himself instead with capturing the linguistic practices that marginalized both the black intellectual and the black masses. In so doing, he expressed a certain anger at being treated like one of the masses, but that is one of the difficulties that fuels his alliance. Identifying fully with neither the African American mother nor with the white leftist on the other side of the lens, Wright provides the documents that would inspire each to speak to the other. In his photographic "folk history," in *Native Son,* and in his theoretical and autobiographical works, he willfully made himself the site of controversy, dialogue, and exchange. He wrote an African American countertext to the proletarian novel that reconceptualized the space of folk culture, the processes of cultural translation, and the alliances that might follow this translation, and he did all this with a righteous anger that still chills readers today.

Chapter 6

EVADING THE GARRISON

Class and Ethnicity in Canadian Regional Fiction

In 1939, in the pages of one of Canada's most respectable academic journals, the *Dalhousie Review,* it was possible to claim that "there is no proletarian literature . . . in Canada."[1] Surveying recent writings in English, Ruth McKinzie concluded that Canadian writers were singularly resistant to the political goals of proletarian fiction and that class was not a major theme in her national culture. Since the late 1930s, essayists such as Robert McDougall and Robin Matthews have examined McKinzie's claim and, overall, they have been inclined to agree with her.[2] Thematics of geography and survival have often seemed more dominant in Canadian literature than those of class struggle. Views like McKinzie's, then, have helped to solidify a version of Canadian exceptionalism by describing Canada as a homogenous petit-bourgeois society faithful to the traditional values of the British aristocracy but mercifully spared the conflictual extremes of the mother country's class hierarchy, thanks to the self-selection of colonizers. Influenced by this exceptionalism, generations of critics have imagined Canadians as pseudo-European conservatives, struggling to maintain their values in a hostile New World wilderness. McKinzie's thesis, in other words, bolsters the myth of the "garrison mentality" eloquently described by Northrop Frye:

> Small and isolated communities surrounded with a physical or psychological "frontier," separated from one another and from their American and British cultural sources: communities that provide all that their members have in the way of distinctively human values, and that are compelled to feel a great respect for the law and order that holds them together, yet confronted with a huge, unthinking, menacing, and formi-

dable physical setting—such communities are bound to develop what we may provisionally call a garrison mentality.[3]

Seeking a national mythology for Canada, many cultural critics have stressed the "great respect for law and order" inspired by the "formidable physical setting" of the Canadian wilderness. They have defined Canadian culture as *a priori* non-revolutionary.

While appreciating the resistance that such a view provides to a hasty subsumption of smaller national literatures into a supposedly universal or international ideal, I also want to recall Frye's proviso that "[t]he garrison mentality is that of its officers: it can tolerate only the conservative idealism of its ruling class, which for Canada means the moral and propertied middle class."[4] Loosely paraphrasing Marx's remarks in *The German Ideology,* Frye reminds us that the ruling ideas of a nation are generally those of its ruling class; he does not, however, suggest that competing ideas were not available. On the contrary, Frye reminds us of the existence of another sort of "mentality" active outside the garrison.

Certainly, it is the case that during the 1930s, persons outside the "moral and propertied middle class" took a considerable interest in class issues. From strikes among Montreal dressmakers, to protests against the wages paid to men in government relief camps, to parliamentary debates over punitive tariffs, the Canadian Depression-era political scene was repeatedly punctuated by the politics of class. Successful new populist parties on the left and the right gave voice to these concerns and ensured their institutionalization in provincial governments. Socialist and Communist organizing was most active in urban and industrial areas, but members of the Communist Party of Canada (CPC) and other leftist groups were spread from coast to coast. Recent immigrants—especially those designated "nonpreferred" by Canadian immigration policy—were particularly active in radical parties. Areas with large concentrations of Ukrainians, Finns, and Jews tended to show strong support for communism through polling habits, social organizations, and activism. Though only a portion of the immigrant communities usually involved themselves in radical politics, throughout the 1930s mainstream groups tended to identify radicalism with these "dangerous foreigners" from southern and eastern Europe.[5] As a result, traditional parties attempted to control leftist parties through a variety of semi-legal means. Harassment, streetfights, infiltrations, arrests, and deportations occurred; during World War II, despite the alliance with the Soviet Union, some Canadian Communists were even placed in concentration camps on the grounds that they might betray their country.[6] In sum, there was no shortage of class-based political activity in Canada during the Depression, though—as in the United States—this fact has sometimes been obscured by the exclusion of non–English-speaking radicals from the canon of Canadian culture on the basis of their attachment to an "other" ethnicity.

Among Canadian intellectuals, this pattern of political engagement is also evident. As in the United States, the economic crisis startled many intellectuals and led them to consider their position in society more actively. Of those who associated themselves with radical politics, some of course had artistic inclinations. Especially in urban centers, Canadian radicals organized clubs, invited speakers, produced plays, wrote reviews and manifestos, published periodicals, and engaged in protests designed to illustrate the uneven effects of the Depression on different classes. Many of these projects explicitly or implicitly supported the proletarian aesthetic being developed in the United States, the Soviet Union, France, England, and elsewhere. For example, Oscar Ryan, a Communist Party member and one of the founders of the Progressive Arts Clubs, energetically supported proletarian theater; his wife, Toby Ryan, recalls their productions of U.S. and Canadian materials with proletarian themes in her memoir *Stage Left*. The radical Canadian periodicals discussed in the next chapter regularly reviewed proletarian writings by André Malraux, Josephine Herbst, Edward Dahlberg, Christopher Caudwell, John Dos Passos, and others. The League for Social Reconstruction (the intellectual wing of the social-democratic party Canadian Commonwealth Federation or CCF) organized radical book clubs and reading circles across the country.[7] And of course, Communist periodicals published urgent manifestos encouraging young writers to develop a specifically Canadian body of proletarian writing.

Even the non-Communist *Canadian Forum* sponsored a short story contest for young radicals in 1937; its literary editor, Earle Birney, reported on the entries as follows: "it is surely the business of proletarian literature to make art out of the half-realized emotions and incoherent thoughts of workers, some clear, coherent and moving representations of their lives."[8] Apparently, few of the entries met this criterion. Although as a Trotskyist suspicious of a proletarian art produced for profit under capitalism, Birney repeatedly criticized U.S. and English proletarian writers for their stereotyped depictions of workers and self-serving politics, he clearly took an interest in the project and, like others, hoped to see an effective radical aesthetic develop.

Unfortunately, as Birney concluded, despite all this activity designed to call forth a Canadian proletarian literature, McKinzie was right; only a few literary works that recognizably met the proletarian criteria appeared in Canada during the 1930s. Despite the dozens of strikes in Canada during the 1930s, there were few strike novels. Despite the tens of thousands of homeless drifters, there were very few novels of the "bottom dogs" variety—exploring life on the bum as Nelson Algren and Edward Dahlberg had in the United States. Despite the presence of active leftist political parties, there were almost no conversion narratives documenting their attraction for workers or intellectuals. Although some retrospective writings in these genres appeared later (as Dick Harrison has demonstrated, the Depression remained "a principal landmark," especially for prairie writers who continued to document its effects into the 1970s and 1980s), relatively little Canadian fiction written during the 1930s resembled the narratives of class struggle being written in the United States in the same period.[9]

Neither did Canadian authors of the 1930s revise the proletarian genre in the ways that some American writers did. Explorations of the limits of class discourse like those produced by Richard Wright and other African American writers were rarely found in Canada. The combination of race and class was not represented as claustrophobic in Canada in the same way, though narratives of entrapment were quite common in Canadian literature. Race was simply not a primary site of political critique in 30s Canada; the strongly polarized and ghettoized society described in *Native Son* was not duplicated in the Canadian imagination. Although of course African Canadians and other visible minorities experienced considerable racial discrimination in this period—including, for example, racist immigration policies and the non-enfranchisement of Japanese, Chinese, East Indian, Native Canadian, and many other nonwhite residents—the concerns of these populations did not gain nearly as much prominence in Canada for white radicals as issues like the Scottsboro case did for leftists in the United States.[10] Racial discrimination was widely conceived as being a specifically American problem, and it would be another thirty years before a body of literature by visible Canadian minorities began to disrupt this view.

Instead, in Depression-era Canada, radical writers produced narratives of class struggle cross-cut by ethnicity. Ethnicity was of central concern not only to immigrant writers but also to anyone seriously trying to describe the Canadian situation. A geographically vast country with a small population, Canada had actively promoted immigration since the mid–nineteenth century. While the majority of immigrants—then as now—came from the United Kingdom and the United States, since the 1880s, increasing numbers have arrived from southern and eastern Europe. In the wake of World War I and the Russian Revolution, poor peasants were joined more often by better educated and wealthier urbanites. These people settled into already established communities (rather than the isolated homesteads of earlier years), so when suddenly thrust into an ethnic hierarchy in which they were not on top, they had some resources to fight back. The post–World War I immigrants continued to organize politically even after immigration all but ceased in 1930. For many recent immigrants, the double barrier of ethnicity and class was a double incentive to political action.

Of course, in telling this story, we must remember that "ethnicity" is never a single experience. Who counts as "ethnic" changes over time and varies with the immigrants' national origin—the Irish, for instance, barely registered as ethnically marked in the 1930s, while Poles almost always did. Sometimes ethnicity has little to do with immigration, since some groups retain their identities in addition to or instead of assimilating. Finally, as we shall see, the workings of "ethnicity" have also varied by region.[11] In different regions of Canada, ethnicity filtered class narratives in different ways.

In this chapter, I will be looking at the three Canadian regions that produced clusters of radical writers during the Depression. A region for my purposes is not an empty geographical unit awaiting inhabitants but rather an invented identity (like ethnicity) defined by the way that particular populations live, work, and manipulate power in that geography. A region is the effect of a dialectic between space and its social uses. Some of these combinations being more appealing to writers, the Canadian regions were not evenly represented in Depression-era literature, but from the three we will examine—Quebec, Toronto, and the West—certain trends are evident.

The vast majority of Canadian fiction written during the Depression considers scenes delimited by ethnic communities and introduces questions of interethnic solidarity more or less centrally. In many cases, the boundaries of the ethnic community are also those of a class identification, and pursuing interethnic relations also involves crossing class borders. However, this is not always the case and certainly does not happen in the same constricted, regulated fashion that it does in Wright's fiction. Canadian narratives concerned with the politics of ethnicity almost always include some confrontation with the possibility of assimilation. Ethnicity, in this context, differs from race in that it is potentially temporary, or something that can be switched off and on in different social contexts. Thus, if the question for Wright was how to combat the double constraint of race and class oppression, the question for many Canadian writers is what the consequences might be of avoiding a working-class life by assimilating, by switching off certain versions of ethnicity. Paradoxically, their answer is that class identities are analogized to ethnic ones; they can, potentially, be left behind. In fact, some argue that the assimilation tactics immigrants learned in left groups helped participants to move into the middle class, thus defusing the political potential of both ethnicity and class in Canada.[12]

In other words, the spatial imaginary of Canadian radical fiction differs from that of the United States. If U.S. proletarian fiction is premised on the projection of long-standing local conflicts onto a national screen, Canadian concerns about the instability of the national scene and the comfort of the local scene make this dynamic difficult to achieve. Instead of being confined by the microcosm, Canadian radicals worked in conversation with the "garrison mentality." While often protesting the confines of insular homogenous communities, Canadian radical writers find more elements to enjoy in the garrison's spatial arrangement than Wright did in the confines of urban ghettos. The contrast between an unknown vastness and a protective fortress recurs in the Canadian writings. However, what differentiates the foot-soldiers' narratives from those of the officers is the fact that the ethnic garrison is not always a panic-inducing problem for the soldier; home has its attractions. Instead of imagining an explosive alteration of the local scene or its continuation *ad infinitum,* Canadian radicals tend to imagine quiet evasions—escapes into the equilibrium of the night.

Quebec: Ethnicity as Entrapment

The province of Quebec is the place in Canada where the boundaries of region and ethnicity have most often been represented as corresponding most closely. Even after the English conquered the French in 1760, Lower Canada remained culturally semi-autonomous. Well over three-quarters of the population in this region has consistently been French-speaking, and until the 1930s the majority of the population lived in rural areas, continuing a pre-industrial way of life dominated by the Catholic Church. Religious leaders encouraged local residents—*les habitants*—to resist urban temptations and perpetuate a conservative, hierarchical society. Despite these efforts, however, consumer products did infiltrate rural areas and interest in farming was declining by the time the Depression hit. Encouraged by the provincial government and the railroads, some small farmers migrated further north to colonize the Abitibi area, but this difficult enterprise only succeeded in a minority of cases. Similarly, the church leadership organized massive relief efforts but was unable to break the cycle of unemployment. By the end of the 1930s, two-thirds of the impoverished Quebec population lived in urban areas and the church's influence was on the wane as parishioners turned to secular, especially political, organizations for answers to the economic and social dilemmas they faced.[13]

This transition from a predominantly rural to a predominantly urban society changed the nature of Quebec as a region. Although Francophones remained the majority, when they moved to either of the province's two urban centers— Montreal or Quebec City—they left behind relatively homogenous, family-centered communities and joined the significant immigrant populations that had also clustered in these areas. The Jewish population of Montreal, for example, had expanded tenfold between 1891 and 1911 and there was a sizable neighborhood of eastern European Jews speaking English, Yiddish, and Slavic languages in central Montreal during the Depression.[14] Italians and other predominantly Catholic groups had also immigrated to Quebec before the doors to Canada were closed on most immigrants in 1930. Newly urbanizing Francophones generally did not live in the same neighborhoods as new immigrants or the English Canadian elite. Residential segregation by ethnic group seems to have been quite common in this period. In Montreal, the poet Irving Layton recalls, three-way streetfights erupted when boundaries between Anglo, Francophone, and Jewish neighborhoods were crossed.[15] Internal migration and urbanization, in other words, increased rather than reduced consciousness of ethnicity.

As Layton's anecdote reveals, the heightened consciousness of ethnicity among Quebec Francophones during the Depression did not necessarily encourage greater tolerance of in-mixing. Instead, proximity often led to a process of political othering. Conservative Catholic intellectuals, such as Abbé Lionel Groulx, struggled to maintain their influence and promoted a form of nationalist politics emphasizing racial homogeneity, moral purity, and, not infrequently, anti-Semitism.[16] Catholic unions were formed that discouraged class-based activism and coalitions with non-Francophones. Perhaps not surprisingly, social-democratic and socialist political organizing was most successful among the most recent immigrants—especially Jews in the garment industries—and Anglophone intellectuals. The influential CCF "Brains Trust" utilized the talents of prominent Montrealers such as the lawyer F. R. Scott, but efforts of the CCF, the Communist Party, and various socialist splinter groups to engage a significant Francophone following were much hindered by that population's nationalist sentiments. The CPC was particularly unwilling to address Francophone concerns by acknowledging nationalist claims. After 1925, the Comintern's Bolshevization policy meant even tactical support for nationalist movements was significantly reduced.[17]

Of course, there were nonetheless a few Quebecois involved in the leftist movements—as the passage of the controversial Padlock Act in 1937 demonstrates. Designed to prohibit left-wing public assemblies, the Padlock Act authorized police to padlock any building in which a politically undesirable meeting was scheduled and to arrest persons on the scene; before its repeal in the 1950s, this measure was widely applied to close down dramatic performances and literary readings as well as more explicitly political rallies.[18] Such measures reveal that, although leftist parties did not make large strides in provincial politics or have much success in Quebec unions, they were a strong enough public presence to be considered a threat. Some of this threat was realized during the 1960s when the left-wing Front de libération de Québec, analogizing Francophone and third-world nationalisms, kidnapped a government official.[19]

During the 1930s, though, much of Quebec society was polarized by both class and ethnicity while politically recognizing only ethnicity. The majority of the resources were owned by a small Anglophone elite concentrated in a few neighborhoods in Montreal, while mutually antagonistic immigrant and Francophone communities performed the majority of service and working-class labor. The waning influence of the church left many Francophones without a stabilizing sense of community, and that loss, combined with the unevenly distributed economic effects of the Depression, led to an increase in in-group identification. Economically motivated shifts in the distribution of rural and urban populations greatly exacerbated the development of an ethnic consciousness that portrayed itself as regional—that claimed Quebec as a Francophone homeland.

In this climate of intraregional conflict, leftist literary intellectuals tended to represent ethnicity as a problematic limit to class solidarity. Of the realist novels published on Quebecois themes during the Depression, most commit to some form of socialism—be it of an empathetic or a more self-consciously ideological variety. There were, of course, relatively few novels in this vein—since the population of Quebec was small and since the literary tradition was dominated by what Antonio Gramsci called in the not entirely dissimilar Italian context "traditional intellectuals"—that is, intellectuals trained by or otherwise supporting the church, intellectuals who conscientiously resisted modernity, industrialism, and the politics associated with these developments.[20] Still, during the 1930s, a small strain of Quebecois social realist fiction developed, a strain that would flourish in postwar years with the writings of Gabrielle Roy, Albert Laberge, and others.[21]

Foremost among the Quebecois social realists of the 1930s was Philippe Panneton, a doctor who wrote under the pseudonym Ringuet; Panneton did a great deal to displace the *mythe agricole* that dominated the work of traditional intellectuals. An admirer of Anatole France and Voltaire, he constructed an anti-romantic but humanist portrait of rural Quebec.[22] His well-received novel *Trente Arpents* (1938; translated in 1940 as *Thirty Acres*) describes the economic struggles of a farm family living on one of the small strips of land along the Saint Lawrence that the French crown had parceled out to settlers in the eighteenth century. Doubly burdened by responsibility for a failing farm and commitments to educate his son in the priesthood, the central character trusts his funds to the local notary, a peripherally religious figure who eventually absconds with all his money. Thus betrayed by a society whose workings he does not understand, the farmer decides to follow the example of a more sophisticated neighbor and relocates his family in a New England industrial village. There, the young adapt to a newly modern and commercial life, while the aging *habitant* yearns for the soil and the religious community of his youth.

Although this story traces the life of a single family, the emphasis in Ringuet's novel falls less on individual psychology and family conflict than on collective portraiture. He depicts a way of life in the process of disappearing without becoming overly sentimental about its passing. He certainly does not urge its preservation as Catholics like Abbé Groulx did; at the same time, he is clear about the exploitation and isolation associated with industrialism. The pleasures of New England factory life are few for the *habitants;* modernity is not progress. Ultimately, while depicting the rule of the church as hypocritical, Ringuet also shares the priests' fears of an anonymous mass society. He describes a transition from an economically insecure but ethnically unchallenged situation to a wealthier but less historically and culturally enriched one. After the migration, Quebecois identity takes shape through nostalgia; focusing on his loss, the ex-farmer retreats from the local scene.

Of course, Ringuet's is a literary resolution; actual Quebec migrants did not always subscribe so passively to nostalgia for impossibly preindustrial relations. In 1937 French Canadians were important participants in one of the important labor conflicts of the period—a shoemakers' strike in Maine; although priests agitated against the strike, ethnic solidarity seems to have aided class-based organizing in this case.[23] However, in Canadian fiction, the rise of a nostalgia-based Quebecois consciousness that complemented rather than confronted the *mythe agricole* was a prize-winning narrative because it offered tools with which nontraditional intellectuals could combat the power of the church.

More controversial and more pointed, however, were depictions of urban Francophone life, such as Jean-Charles Harvey's *Les demi-civilisées* (1934; translated in 1938 as *Sackcloth for Banner*) and Roger Lemelin's *Au pied de la pente douce* (1944; translated in 1948 as *The Town Below*). Both of these novels depict life in Quebec City during the Depression—in the Upper City and Lower City respectively. The site of a major French fortification, Quebec City is set on a hill; within the walls of the old fort are the centers of prestige and power—elite residential sections, provincial government, military training grounds, the famous hotel Chateau Frontenac, as well as an Ursuline convent and school. Below the walls, on the steep hill sloping toward the Saint Lawrence river and on the opposite bank live the working and lower middle classes. Thus, both the terrain and the history of its usage—as garrison and provincial capital which excludes those who service it—literalize the city's two-tiered social structure.

This local topography figures in both novels. In *Les demi-civilisées,* Harvey tells the story of Max Hubert, a would-be radical intellectual who migrates to the city from the country for education and employment. Although his initial commitment to the church allows him access to the Upper City, once he strays from the fold he has difficulty finding a job that will allow him to express his personality. Eventually he starts up a review with tainted money loaned to him by the father of the woman he loves. When he publishes an article on the activities of a modern-day Christ—an article that attacks the hypocrisy and insularity of the Francophone religious elite—Quebec high society conspires to separate him from his career and his lover. After being forced to join a convent rather than be given in marriage to a crude man she despises, Max's sweetheart dies in his arms.

This novel scandalized the city, and Harvey lost his job as a reporter at *Le Soleil* immediately following its publication. As was apparent to many of his readers, this narrative, through the conventions of sentimental romance, criticizes the Quebec elite for its "intellectual colonialism" and for being "morally castrated" by the church; Harvey describes the Upper City as a "truncated pyramid" lacking a top, though having a large, squashed base.[24] Max's goal is to form an intellectual vanguard that will escape this cultural confinement and revitalize some kind of Christian socialism. It must be a Quebecois vanguard—he imagines political and cultural assimilation to the United States, for example, as destruction (177–78)—and it must act in the name of tradition and custom.

Like Ringuet, then, Harvey vacillated between liberal nationalism and class-based socialism. His opposition to what he saw as a stagnant bourgeoisie led him to oppose their version of separatism while expressly supporting the Popular Front, but only a few years later, after the Hitler-Stalin pact, he was arguing that political systems based on equality are "non seulement injustes mais contraires à toutes les tendances biologiques de la nature."[25] His primary concern was to counter the influence of the church with political ideologies of one stripe or another, and socialism was one possibility.

By contrast, Roger Lemelin's *Au pied de la pente douce* is more clearly committed to depicting social life in class terms; in fact, one could read the novel as the prehistory to a political conversion. In his introduction to the Canadian Library edition, Glen Shortliffe compares the novel's world of proletarianized *habitants* to Erskine Caldwell's *Tobacco Road* and James T. Farrell's *Studs Lonigan* trilogy.[26] Like his U.S. counterparts, Lemelin gives priority to scene and social pattern over character. Also, like the inhabitants of Harvey's Upper City, the people of the lower town are entrapped; the church and the class system restrict their options and condemn them to repeat a limited number of narratives. The social world of the novel is internally divided among Les Mulots (workers), Les Soyeux (literally, the silky ones, the middle class), and Les Gonzagues (the pious). The plot follows Denis Boucher, a talented Mulot whose gifts offer the possibility to a clerkship or other lower-middle-class employment. After conflicts with his family, Denis falls into a love triangle formed by himself, his best friend, and a middle-class, convent-educated girl. By the end of the novel, after the death of two innocent Mulots, Denis's ambitions are still murky but the narrator insists we view him sociologically:

> He had a vision of his past, and the meaning of it was becoming clear. The parish had betrayed him in a different way from what he had thought. Not through love but through a kind of segregation [*séquestration*]. He was the victim of the unfortunate somnolence of a class of people for whom education means a shoe or a hat. So long as the horizons the parish imposed had not been rent by the lightning flash, a youth like himself, possessed of a real superiority but rendered restless by ambition, had seen fit to discover his enemy in love, and had preferred to look upon that sentiment as coming from his flesh rather than from his heart. . . .
>
> The young ones of St. Sauveur, deprived of a field of action which might have provided their country with a body of strong and capable young men, were obliged to content themselves with the semblance of moral torture, from want of anything better to do. (259)

The aristocratic element recurs here in the mention of Denis's "real superiority," but it is tempered by the emphasis on the constriction that deprived him and his peers "of a field of action." The church—or, more locally, the parish—is to blame in this novel, because it authorizes the political wrangling that allows the corrupt Soyeux to remain in control. In *Au pied,* Lemelin urges the reader to sympathize with a constricted life and with the desire to escape it. Here and there, literature is offered as a way out—as when Denis and his beloved discuss their mutual affection for Lamartine; through literature, one can retain ties to tradition and language while also, as this novel demonstrates, depicting the uneven effects of the class system within the Francophone community.

While all three Quebec authors discussed so far examined the conflict between ethnicity and class consciousness within the Francophone community, there were also some writers thinking about interethnic contact and coalition. Typically, these authors wrote in English for an English Canadian audience and in the name of a cultural nationalism similar to MacLennan's. Distinguishing between an exclusive loyalty to one's own ethnicity and a political nationalism based on pluralism, they tended to be carefully internationalist when writing in English, as the work of two-time winner of the Governor General's Award Gwethalyn Graham shows.

Both *Swiss Sonata* (1938) and *Earth and High Heaven* (1944) are anti-fascist novels set against the backdrop of the war to come, and both stress an internationalist form of tolerance that we are cued to read as socialist. *Swiss Sonata* is a coming-of-age novel set in an expensive Swiss boarding school; the girls at the school are designated and controlled by their family and national origins. German girls torture Jews and Catholics psychologically, and Vicky—the Torontonian heroine—derives much of her moral heroism from sympathy for a Quebecois peer dying as an indirect result of her severely restrictive convent education. Early in the novel Vicky's position is identified as "subtle Bolshevism" by a hostile teacher, and since the progress and argument of the plot involves the teachers, not the students, being schooled in social realities, it is Vicky's position that wins the day. Herself the illegitimate daughter of an American slattern and an Englishman who fled in shame to Canada, Vicky represents and speaks for tolerance of an international hybridism already in progress. The novel furthers this position through a series of analogies. Vicky's mixed origins are a microcosm of the conflicts in the school, which reflect those of multilingual Switzerland, which also stands in for bicultural Canada, which in turn represents a world on the brink of interethnic war.

Ethnic tolerance and especially anti-anti-Semitism are also the themes of Graham's second novel. Set in Montreal in 1942, *Earth and High Heaven* describes the problems encountered when a wealthy Westmount Protestant falls in love with a Jewish lawyer from small-town Ontario. Here, again, the main character is marked as a leftist (this time because she is a newspaper-woman who supports Labour and has joined a union). The moral heroine argues with her conservative father about his prejudices, and her love for the Jewish lawyer is partly motivated by their mutual attraction to socialism. French Canadians do not figure in the novel, except as the voiceless masses; like *Swiss Sonata*, *Earth* is concerned with delineating moral choices made by members of the Anglophone elite about membership in their own social world. Graham is interested in leftist politics as a bond across ethnicities, a bond that ideally also allows ethnically marked persons to cross class boundaries.

Thus far, we have seen that Quebec fictions of the 1930s represent ethnicity and class as a double bind. Class identities are clearly reinforced by ethnic ones, and in situations where those identities are also revealed to be bounded, where one desires to cross boundaries, the potentially mobile person experiences a dilemma. As Francophone authors describe it, the dilemma is as follows: working-class ethnics cannot assimilate to the middle class because doing so would require leaving behind traditions and customs that are an important part of their identity. Yet, at the same time, that working-class ethnic life is sti-fling, impoverished, and under attack by the forces of modern industrialism, so one cannot remain comfortably within the ethnic traditions. Out of this double bind, entrapment narratives result, and this psychological condition is fictionally refigured as an element of social geography.

These narratives, I would argue, illustrate the political stalemate left-leaning Francophone intellectuals experienced during the 1930s. Feeling that they could not participate in internationalist or social-democratic politics domi-nated by Anglophones without betraying their ethnic communities, they also rejected excessively homogenizing versions of ethnicity that resembled fas-cism. Projecting their own dead end onto the community at large, they told stories of entrapment by ethnicity and class.

For authors like Graham who wrote about ethnic positions that they did not inhabit, though, the problem was a slightly different one. For Graham— and, as we shall see, for several Torontonian authors—a segregated social geog-raphy was not a metaphor for entrapment but rather an invitation to cross borders. From the position of the dominant elite, the problem was their own intolerance of difference, and, at least intellectually, the solution was a cos-mopolitan socialism. The question of traditions abandoned or altered by such in-mixing was rarely considered, as the implicit ideal was assimilative. In *Earth and High Heaven,* for instance, there is no mention of the possibility that the Westmount heiress could convert to Judaism and abandon *her* origins; instead, the marriage hinges on her Jewish lover adopting her cosmopolitan ideal. Not recognizing the stalemate her position produced for others, then, Graham im-plicitly contributed to it.

Of course, there were other options for Quebec intellectuals concerned with issues of ethnicity; the binary opposition between ethnic identity and leftist politics did not produce stalemates in all situations. After 1945, a new gen-eration of writers began delving more fully into class and ethnically based tradition as a source of political nourishment. In part because the recent war had made such sources of strength apparent in various resistance movements, A. M. Klein and Gabrielle Roy could begin writing narratives such as *The Second Scroll* (1951) and *Bonheur d'occasion* (1945; translated as *The Tin Flute* in 1947). These narratives are much more concerned with detailing their local terrain. Their social geographies are less constricted and more open-ended; there is a sense of mobility in Klein's hero's quest in the Holy Land and Roy's exploration of Montreal street life. Ethnic communities in these later novels are communal in a socialist sense; they emblematize care, not division and entrapment, as in the Depression years.

Toronto: Fantasies of Placelessness

If the U.S. proletarian novel involves a projection from a local to a national stage, then clearly the Quebecois writers' concern with the limitations imposed within the province preclude that spatial imaginary. In Toronto, however, the preclusion took the opposite form. Several radical Torontonian writers chose the church, the military, and other hierarchical institutions as representations of the social totality. Focusing on class alone, they became less ethnically and geographically specific the more they were committed to radical politics. By ignoring local specificity, they tried to claim national grounds. However, as our reading of Graham's fiction forewarns us, this evasion of ethnicity in favor of class alone was clearly an indication of English Canadian hegemony.[27] Claiming the grounds of national culture meant adapting to the English Canadian fantasy of that group's invisibility and universal appeal. Lacking consideration of its own origins, this purportedly unmarked language of the "center" often became a vacant placelessness, rather than the expansive universality that was intended.

This pretense that English Canadian culture spoke for the entire nation was not simply a literary habit; economic and political conditions conspired to make English Toronto a cultural capital. During the Depression, Toronto replaced Montreal as the financial hub of Canada, and throughout the period the majority of Canadian industrial production took place in the surrounding areas of Ontario. Not surprisingly, numerous labor struggles arose in this area during the 1930s. When the CIO attempted to internationalize, the double threat of American and Communist infiltration meant that even supposedly pro-labor Liberals like Ontario premier Mitchell Hepburn did their best to keep them out.[28] Relief efforts for the laborers and unskilled workers who were most vulnerable were made, but the welfare state that Americans might now associate with the area was not established until after the Depression. Instead of a Canadian New Deal, Torontonians experienced a retrenchment of elite power. The strongly Anglophilic and urban character of the region increased, as did ethnic segregation by neighborhood, occupation, and social class.[29] Since most Franco-Ontarians lived in rural areas at this time, the primary divisions in the urban center were between English Canadians and southern or eastern Europeans. These latter groups made distinct contributions to the Canadian political scene; in Toronto as elsewhere, in comparison to English Canadians they were strongly represented in leftist political parties and labor strife of the period. For instance, on July 15, 1939, a festival of Ukrainian music and dance sponsored by the Communist Party–affiliated Ukrainian Labor Farmer Temple Association drew 10,000 spectators to Toronto and raised significant amounts of money for education, organizing, and publications.[30] In this respect, Toronto resembled a number of cities in the American Midwest, such as Chicago and Detroit, which had politically active populations of so-called white ethnics.[31] In both countries, southern and eastern Europeans working in ethnically specific organizations were major supporters of radical politics.

In fictions written by left-wing Torontonian intellectuals, however, class hierarchies are more central than ethnic ones. The central concern, as in Quebec fiction, is with wasted talents and wasted lives, but the waste proliferates everywhere—it is not represented as located in particular communities. Morley Callaghan's Depression-era fictions, for example, describe moral crises inherent in cross-class relationships. *Such Is My Beloved* (1933) is the story of an earnest young priest who flouts petit-bourgeois convention by befriending two prostitutes in his parish. The majority of the novel is devoted to his soul-searching and struggles with his peers and superiors about how to save these women, and when they are arrested despite his efforts, he finally goes mad. Clearly, the import of the novel is that during the Depression, even more than at other times, cross-class solidarity is necessary; sadly, the hierarchical structure of the church does not allow for enough flexibility to practice the requirements of faith. As its title indicates, Callaghan's next novel, *They Shall Inherit the Earth* (1934), tackles similar themes. The responsibility a young man of bourgeois origin feels for his working-class wife and neighbors conflicts with his fear that he has inherited his family's ruthlessness and insanity. A politically committed faith and love are again at issue and again their application is constricted by hierarchy—here of the family.

In both of these novels, Callaghan contrasts religious responsibility to politically motivated positions such as Communism. In both novels, a peripheral Communist straw-man appears. In *They Shall Inherit,* the narrator "longed to free himself from his distress by losing himself in his [Communist] friend's disinterested hope for the poor of the world," but finds, not surprisingly, that he cannot (103). Personal morality and individual history make it impossible for him to access what he views as the impersonal, dislocated, abstract ideals of Communism; the best he can do is align himself with the "meek" heirs of the earth by adopting a similar attitude himself.

The idea that Communism involved absenting oneself from local and personal concerns rather than screening these for a larger, national audience is also apparent in Hugh Garner's somewhat later slum novel *Cabbagetown* (1950). Though written in the 1940s, the novel is set in the Depression and offers an interesting glimpse into social life among the Anglophone poor in Toronto. Cabbagetown is a (currently gentrified) neighborhood in Toronto that during the Depression was one of the most impoverished areas of the city. Garner's novel splices together the conversion narrative of a smart young man who falls in love, gets radicalized, and eventually fights in the Spanish civil war with narratives of class assimilation and naturalist decline. After designating the neighborhood as "the largest Anglo-Saxon slum in North America," Garner pays little attention to the ethnic register of the area, but considerable attention to the nest of political positions represented locally (vii). Wobblies, Communists, socialists, cynics, fascists, Tories, racists, and hopeless fatalists are characterized—with class being the main obstacle to their integration. In particular, Garner's novel spotlights working-class radicals' suspicions of their would-be middle-class allies: "Too many ex-preachers in the ranks," an ex-Wobblie says of the CCF, "too many fruity professors. They want to change the working stiff's morals more than they want to fill his belly" (373). With ethnic differences sidelined, the left is here imagined as involving an unworkable clash of class cultures. In the frame of the novel, CCF moral standards are imagined as a renunciation of masculinity and thus of the potential for love. To Garner's speaker, as much as for Callaghan's, socialist commitment involves entry into an abstract "moral" hierarchy, and thereby a loss of more tangible concerns. Only when the local hierarchy is abandoned and the hero arrives in Spain are such resistances overcome. In Spain the men are all "drawn together by a strange social osmosis" (414). Members of all classes, factions, and nationalities fight together in the common cause.

This tendency to commit to socialist politics only outside the local scene also appears in other Toronto novels. Of these, Charles Yale Harrison's *Generals Die in Bed* (1928) and Ted Allan's *This Time a Better Earth* (1940) are the Canadian fictions that most closely resemble the U.S. proletarian novel in tenor. Both are war novels that use military structures to reveal social ideals; the action in both novels takes place off Canadian soil, where the Canadianness of the narrator can be occasionally asserted, without being scrutinized. Both are strangely placeless, sceneless novels that rely mainly on dialogue and employ very little description, and both are openly pro-Communist.

Harrison's *Generals Die in Bed* describes conditions among the Canadian troops in World War I. It follows a soldier from his first days in the barracks, into battle, and through his being wounded and sent home. As the title suggests, the point of this depiction of the traumas and indignities of a soldier's life is the implicit comparison to the relatively comfortable situation of officers who die in bed rather than in battle. It is a grim, angry novel that details conditions in the military as if detailing unfair labor practices in a southern textile mill; since excerpts of the novel were published in the *New Masses* in 1930, its aesthetic was clearly deemed compatible with the calls for proletarian literature that periodical's editors were making in the same issues.

Harrison's next novel, *Meet Me on the Barricades* (1938), is much more cautious in its leftism—concerning as it does the delusional fantasies of a musician who finds that Trotsky, the Moscow trials, and Spain have turned him into "an ideological Marco Polo" (69); set in New York, this novel also abandons even a superficial commitment to representing English Canada. Despite Harrison's interest in housing issues and the politics of who lives in what kind of space, in his fiction he makes location merely a vacant place in which ideas echo. New York has no more influence on this novel than Toronto did on the previous one.

Harrison's strategy in *Generals* also worked for other authors. Set during the Spanish civil war, Ted Allan's *This Time a Better Earth* makes many of the same moves as Harrison's World War I novel. The novel uses relations among men of the International Brigades to figure social relations—though in this case they are utopian rather than oppressively hierarchical. "[T]here was no place in the world for us as long as the world was what it was," the narrator reflects in the opening sequence (5); escaping the ugliness of things as they are, men representing various national and subnational groups join together in the Brigades to fight for a better world. They imagine a dramatic transformation of culture will result from the bridging of national, regional, racial, and ethnic islands. Bob Curtis, the Torontonian narrator, forms relationships with a Francophone Canadian, a Boston Brahmin, a Chicago union leader, a Brooklyn wiseacre, and an African American who is symbolically blinded and thus unable to see color; although the narrator occasionally insists defensively that he is Canadian and not American (as the African American insists he is not a Moor), race, color, ethnicity, political faction, and so on are explicitly effaced in the fight against fascism. The anti-fascist slogan *"No Pasaran"* is written in a dozen languages on the walls of the barracks, and the military hierarchy is reformulated as functionally necessary. All racial and ethnic concerns are subsumed in the common cause.

So, in Allan's novel, we see the clearest version of what the Communist ideal represented in English Canada during the late years of the Depression. The goal was to surpass the isolation of ethnic difference, and replace regional and national identifications with those of the "earth." Perhaps not surprisingly in a country ravaged by drought, a vision of responsibility to soil and life on the soil was repeatedly offered as an alternative to the small-scale isolation on a politically defined bit of territory. In *They Shall Inherit the Earth, This Time a Better Earth,* and, as we shall see, Frederick Philip Grove's *Fruits of the Earth* and Bertram Brooker's *Think of the Earth,* a grounded pan-ethnic internationalism is imagined. Difficulties with this vision were more or less apparent to different authors, but insofar as it had an appeal, it relied on the hegemonic position of English Canadians whose dominance has historically allowed them to disregard the question of the possible desirability of the persistence of ethnic difference. Or, more precisely we might say, the pan-ethnic position operated *as if* it were the position of the dominant group, since many of its proponents (such as Allan) were not themselves WASPs. (In the film he later wrote and acted in, *Lies My Father Told Me* [1975], Allan describes conflicts between his secular and orthodox Jewish relatives in Montreal.) Here is the crux of the matter: the Communist pan-ethnic ideal appealed most to persons marked and constrained by ethnicity in Canadian society; yet, in their efforts to articulate a non-ethnic national support for internationalism, persons like Allan also implicitly supported the hegemony of English Canadian invisibility. In certain respects, at least in its Torontonian version, Communist pan-ethnicism came to resemble an assimilation narrative.

The West: An Emergent Regional Identity

If in Quebec ethnicity was usually represented as a limit to class politics and in Toronto the invisibility of English Canadian ethnicity provided a weak base for class analysis, the different history of the Canadian West made possible the most coherent Canadian literary alternative to the U.S. proletarian novel: a new regional realism. While Ontario and Quebec had some sense of dominant and residual regional identities before the Depression, a distinctive Western identity arguably emerged in fiction during the 1930s.

For our purposes, "the West" includes five distinct geographical zones: the flat prairies stretching through Manitoba to the Rockies, the parklands just north of the prairies, the boreal forest further north, the Rockies themselves, and the coastal zone of British Columbia. Throughout this varied terrain, a number of small urban centers arose in the early part of the twentieth century; although sparsely settled by Europeans in the nineteenth century, Winnipeg, Regina, Calgary, and Edmonton boomed thanks to the influx of immigrants after 1900. The majority of the region's population until the Depression consisted of farmers living in isolated communities on the prairies, and immigration policy filtered out persons of "non-preferred" national origins.[32] Immigration policy favored persons from eastern Europe, Scandinavia, Germany, and the British Isles who claimed to be skilled agricultural or domestic-service workers, but there were of course persons of other ethnicities—especially Asians and Native Canadians—living in the West, but the so-called white ethnics dominated. In cities, preferred and non-preferred immigrants often lived in enclaves, and in rural areas the tremendous isolation also reduced assimilation. The result was that both urban and rural communities experienced a high degree of ethnic concentration.

When the Depression hit, immigration all but came to a standstill. In the West, the high level of debt farmers had been carrying meant that capital was concentrated in Eastern financial centers. To pay interest on debts, farmers poured more of their resources into high-cash crops such as wheat, and the drastic fall in wheat prices as well as the drought hit them doubly hard. The protective tariffs imposed by Washington and Ottawa did not help the farmers sell their excess; in fact, they were economically devastated with record numbers on relief.[33] For many, the only option was to leave the farm. Some resettled in the northern parkland and boreal forest regions, and many joined the urban poor. As in Quebec, urbanization tended to increase ethnic antagonisms rather than the reverse.

The political situation in the West reflected this polarization. On the left and the right, politics became strongly regional and strongly ethnic. Farmers' parties such as the United Farmers of Alberta or the farmer-labor alliance that developed into the CCF were strong critics of Eastern domination; in Alberta, this tendency developed a step further. In 1935, an evangelical minister and high school principal with a popular radio show swept the new Social Credit Party into provincial office, where it remained for some thirty-five years. The Socreds argued that Eastern bankers were to blame for the Depression and that the only way to prevent unfair interregional domination was for the one-party provincial government to manage its own currency. Wildly popular with the Protestant small-town petit bourgeoisie, the Socreds were also committed to ethnic homogeneity, including some forms of anti-Semitism and anti-Catholicism.[34]

Support for left-wing parties was also drawn on ethnic lines. At a time when membership in the Ku Klux Klan rose to the tens of thousands in a predominantly left-liberal province such as Saskatchewan, many immigrants supported parties to the left of the Liberals.[35] The CCF had strong support among eastern Europeans and Scandinavians, and 80 percent of the membership of the CPC was reportedly Ukrainian or Finnish.[36] The most recent immigrants from eastern Europe were often fleeing political conditions as well as economic deprivation, and they tended to be better educated and more politically involved than the generation that had preceded them. Across the region today one still finds evidence of the Labor Temples, co-ops, bands, reading libraries, and other organizations that these groups founded. Of course, not all the Ukrainians, Poles, and Scandinavians in the Canadian West leaned toward the left. There were also passionate nationalists in these communities, devoted to restoring monarchies and ethnic purity.[37] However, because of their focus on the old country, these latter segments of the immigrant community were not always well known in Canada, and the mainstream Canadian media regularly attributed a dangerous interest in socialism and Communism to the new immigrants.

Although—or perhaps because—this political and ethnic consolidation of regional identity was taking place in the Canadian West during the Depression, literary representations of that region tend to avoid much explicit mention of politics. Instead, they focus on representing social and geographical conditions. They represent persons of marked (i.e., non-English) ethnicity as victims more often than actors, and they describe ethnic hierarchies as being at least as powerful as class politics.

Nonetheless, it is clear that these fictions register the influence of the social forces that led to an uprise of regionalist politics during the Depression. The intellectual historian R. Douglas Francis has argued that the Western realists were reacting to the utopian depictions of the region used to recruit settlers in the pre–World War I period. By portraying the harshness of the land, the restrictive social life, and the possibility of economic disaster, painters, novelists, and historians began to clear away the European standards of picturesqueness used to market the region and identified the elements of what would become a Western mythology focused on transcending suffering.[38] What I would add to this thesis is some recognition of the particularly ethnic dimension to this spatial imaginary: while depicting social confinement in a large land, Western realists also proposed a commitment to ethnicity as a way out of communities divided by class. While inhabitants of Quebec and Toronto tended to see ethnicity as a (surpassable or insurpassable) limit to solidarity, some Westerners saw alternatives. Hence, in their narratives, one finds the most thoroughgoing alternative to the proletarian novel.

The Western Depression novel that deals with these themes most openly is John Marlyn's *Under the Ribs of Death*. Published in 1957 but set and written during the 1930s, Marlyn's is a radical novel about Hungarians in Winnipeg; the main character is an ambitious young man in perpetual conflict with his anarchist father. Influenced by Horatio Alger–like stories, the young Sandor hopes to escape the ghetto and become a wealthy assimilated businessman, but instead he finds himself apprenticed to a devious loan shark who preys on his own community. Ironically, his business involves building housing; he makes money by enclosing others in the vicious cycle of ghettoization that he despises. Nonetheless, despite his best efforts, Sandor is not accepted by the Anglo-Canadian establishment, especially after the stock market crash. Only by the end of the novel, after fathering a son, does he finally gain an appreciation for the cyclical and supportive nature of Hungarian family life. Included in his appreciation is his father's (and later his brother's) study of Kropotkin,

Bertrand Russell, and other radical intellectual heroes. The assimilationist narrative of upward mobility—transcending class-based claustrophobia by leaving ethnicity behind—is rejected in this kind of narrative. The happy ending for Marlyn is a renewal of class politics *and* ethnic pride. Sandor rejoins his neighborhood without feeling confined.

In another Western urban narrative written from outside the ethnic community, the moral is similar. Claudius Gregory's unique allegory *Forgotten Men* (1933) follows a young man working among the poor in an unnamed North American city. Along the way, the young man acquires twelve friends—the first of whom is faithful Peter and one of the later of whom is the betrayer Jude. Sent to prison for sedition, the hero dies in the shadow of a cross, though his Society of Forgotten Men persists. Although in the postscript to *Forgotten Men,* Gregory disclaims the "socialistic" content of his program for the redistribution of wealth and stresses the "localized" nature of his plot, he also acknowledges that the novel was strongly influenced by pamphlets produced by the printer, Thomas Dyson Lisson. The publisher of radical tracts such as *World Reorganization or Downfall, and the Remedy* and *Is Fascism the Answer: Italy's Law of the Union Compared with the N[ational] R[ecovery] A[ct],* Lisson was apparently an independent radical favoring the regeneration of Canadian society around social-democratic principles similar to those of the New Deal. Also, like *Under the Ribs of Death,* Gregory's novel offers a vision of a community of like-minded persons working for the elimination of poverty as an alternative to the rabidly competitive nature of a class society. This picture is structurally similar to the vision of ethnic community as well as to the Social Gospel flavor motivating prominent Canadians such as J. S. Woodsworth, the founder of the CCF. In both cases, there is a particularly Western sense that one can start social life anew and escape the pressures of a divided society precisely by becoming more local and embedded in the particular.

The more famous rural narratives from the Depression West, however, were somewhat less hopeful. Frederick Philip Grove's *Fruits of the Earth* (1933), *Two Generations* (1939), and *Master of the Mill* (1944), Sinclair Ross's *As for Me and My House* (1941), and even Bertram Brooker's peculiar *Think of the Earth* promote a paralytic mythology of the prairies. They depict small towns in a big land, and their heroes are alternately confined within a rigid morality and liberated by mystical appreciation for the grandeur of the open spaces.

Certainly, Grove's Scandinavian homesteaders experience this double consciousness. As in *Settlers in the Marsh* (1925), his first and most successful novel, the heroes of his Depression trilogy struggle with an alienating landscape. Sexually repressed and isolated, they battle the elements in hopes of eking out a living that will allow them to improve on the family home-life they left behind in the old world. Thus, their struggles result both from the harshness of the land and the cultural/religious standards of taciturnity and extreme self-reliance. Of course, these standards read rather ironically here, given that Grove himself had adopted a false Swedish identity to replace his original German one after political troubles as a young man.[39] Resembling somewhat the mysterious B. Traven who also emigrated from Germany and melted into a new world peasant society, Grove described the prairie way of life and the challenges it offered to the new immigrants who continued to flock there despite the difficulties. Implicit in his narratives is an appreciation for the potential community into which his isolated heroes stubbornly resist incorporation.

The couple at the heart of Sinclair Ross's *As for Me and My House* also have a conflicted relationship with their local community. Told through the diary of an unhappy minister's wife, this celebrated novel documents the windstorms and tempests in a teapot eroding social life in a small prairie town ironically named Horizon. Feeling constrained by the conventional expectations of their neighbors, the couple chafe at the borders of their lives and seek escape through art, music, flirtations, and rambles along the train tracks. Ultimately, however, it is only an episode in which they briefly adopt a Catholic Hungarian orphan that allows them a sensation of freedom befitting the expansive geography. The boy's wild passion for riding, his dark good looks, and his sensual appreciation for new clothing inspire the couple—though also making them jealous competitors for his love and targets of the town busybody. Until the boy is cruelly taken away by priests, his stereotyped ethnic vibrancy represents an escape hatch from the confines of class society. In the wake of the energy produced by exoticizing the Hungarian boy, the couple eventually gathers enough courage to plan their retreat to the city. A shabby bohemianism is as close as they get to imagining a community of like-minded people, but still the structure of the narrative fits our pattern. For Ross, as for the other Western realists, one accesses the glories of the region (as, say, in Ross's narrator's husband's paintings) only when supported by friendly local people sympathetic to one's background. Outsiders represent either a threat to that community or the possibility of its establishment elsewhere. The split between the vastness of the land and the closeness of the towns and ghettos built upon that land is not resolved by trumpeting forth the problems of the local to a national audience; only by consolidating local communities around a productive sense of ethnicity do the urban and rural Western narratives conclude.

The one exception, if we can apply this term to a variant on such a small body of works, is Irene Baird's *Waste Heritage* (1939). Baird's novel is set in Vancouver and various prairie towns during the sit-down strikes that led to the 1935 On-to-Ottawa trek. (Organized partly by Communists, the trek led men from across the West to the national capital to demand relief; it ended in a bloody confrontation in Regina in which dozens of trekkers were arrested and one RCMP officer was killed.) The novel documents conditions among the trekkers, drawing attention to their conflict and sympathetically portraying their desires for a home life. It is unique among Canadian novels of the period in taking topical reference as its subject and in limiting itself almost entirely to the world of the trekkers. There is almost no effort here to specify the men's origins and family life; instead, their relations to one another within the community of homeless men drive the plot forward. It is as representatives of larger social conditions, not as emblems of ethnic types, that allegorically named characters such as the hero Matt Striker function. The allegorical names for places, however, are transparent; the novel deals with events that took place in knowable (and well-known) locations. For this reason, more than any other Canadian fiction of the decade, *Waste Heritage,* with its vaguely humanist sympathies and depiction of an exemplary topical conflict, comes closest to the American model of the political novel. It depicts local class conflicts with documentary specificity and publicizes them as prototypical. Indeed, a number of contemporary commentators noted the resemblance between Baird's work and a more celebrated West Coast writer whose activist novels were concerned with life among migrant laborers—John Steinbeck.[40]

Overall, however, the Western novels written during the Depression place more faith in ethnic communities than unemployed strikers as models of semi-socialist care. These communities are seen as the basis and perhaps salvation of a regional lifestyle that contrasts sharply to what is often imagined to be a vindictive, corrupt urbanism. Ethnicity supplements—sometimes even supplants —class as the foundation of politics in these narratives. Although this concern only rarely resulted in depictions of ethnic and class-based political activity, these regional writings reflect much the same concern with reformulating a more moral social order that one finds in the political movements of the period.

Class Participation

While it is certainly the case that there was no proletarian novel in Canada, there was definitely a literature concerned with class and crisscrossed with ethnic and regional issues. This literature developed in a context of intense class politics and conflict and indirectly reflects many of the concerns of the period. In particular, Canadian social realist fiction illustrates a concern with evading the confines of conservative tradition—by supplementing it with personal ambition or ethnic exoticism.

Furthermore, in these works, we find a concern with the multiple and non-essential nature of class identity; class is represented as a site which one inhabits not only because of one's occupation or family origin, but also because of one's ethnic background and political ideology. It is something that can change as one educates oneself; it can flicker on and off in the course of a narrative, even while it still operates as a limit to one's social interactions. Contrary to some representations of the 30s left, then, this subculture was not universally concerned with an exclusive concept of class identity early in the decade, only to subside into a soft populism later on. Instead, actual representations of working-class life and politics from the period reveal that a considerably more flexible and relational notion of class is being employed. The concept of "class" makes sense in these narratives in relation to other social norms that can also be understood as iterated rather than originary.

Clearly, the more confining notion of the "proletariat" or "proletarian fiction" was revised from within the leftist community, and this was not the only shibboleth the 30s writers took on. Among 30s leftist writers of varying skill, we find a number of difficult questions being asked: What is tradition? How important are ties to family and community versus ties to workers? Can romantic love overcome divisions within one's class? Are the sacrifices involved in political commitment worth the trouble? Can fascism and racism ever be defeated? How can we make a better earth?

In the 1990s, in a consumer culture, after the victories of civil rights, after the Cold War, not all of these dilemmas resonate as powerfully as they did in the 1930s; some even seem hopelessly naive or tainted by a modernist arrogance.

But in the dark years of the Depression, sacrifice was the order of the day for many, and concepts such as family, community, and ethnicity did not involve all the political baggage that they do today. These concepts were available to persons on the left struggling, albeit in a conflicted manner, to gain power in their culture.

Of course, as we shall see in part III of this study, the burgeoning mass culture challenged efforts to base a new life on modified ethnic or racial or class communities. It may be that the entire project of proletarian culture was too closely tied to nostalgia—for a folk life left behind in Europe, for preindustrial Appalachian traditions, or the phantasmatic safety of home—and this may be why assimilation through language skills or the spatial or class mobility of the 1940s and 1950s replaced that project. It is also inescapably true that self-deception and acceptance of Soviet imperialism under the cover of internationalism was part of 30s radical culture. The case of Ukrainian Communists who refused to believe, even when presented with compelling evidence, that their comrades in the Soviet Union were starving in a man-made famine is an instructive one.[41] Too often, an ideological foreclosure became the basis of the proletarian aesthetic and middle-class authors did "slum" among the working class in order to shock their own peers into more radical behavior.

But—and this is a big but—it is not the case that all of these effects or intentions were necessarily prefigured in the original acts. If we take quite seriously Foucault's assertion that "we generally know what we do, sometimes we know why we do what we do, but we rarely know what what we do does," then it is necessary to accept the difference between the earnest assertions of 30s radical writers and the cynical politics of the Hitler-Stalin pact.[42] In the context of the Depression, in the United States and Canada, writers of many classes, races, and ethnicities made an impressive effort to evade local garrisons and describe the world as if a genuinely classless society—in which no heritage is wasted and plenty does not encompass poverty—were possible.

PART III   MASS CULTURE

Chapter 7

PROVINCIAL AVANT-GARDES

Confronting Mass Culture in U.S. and Canadian
Literary Periodicals of the 1930s

Like the proletarian novelists, most leftist magazine writers of the 1930s doubted that artistic production would continue to flourish under capitalism. Not infrequently these doubts surfaced in their film criticism; for example, when describing the plot twists of a new Douglass Montgomery picture, a *New Masses* critic descends into sarcasm: "Don't anticipate me, but you're right. The baby has been born during his absence. And now everything is different. Are we downhearted? No! This is a new bit of life, we have created it and we must look after it, for Life Goes On."[1] According to the critic, this "pathetic attempt at grappling with life" lacks the "vitality and warmth and deep emotional content" of serious art. More generally, he concludes that Hollywood's habitual substitution of formulaic cliché for realism will trivialize narrative, possibly leading to the eradication of all genuine art.

This representative and unfavorable comparison between Hollywood and real art found more complete theoretical expression at the end of the 1930s in an often-quoted article by the art historian Clement Greenberg. In "Avant-garde and Kitsch," Greenberg argues that artistic culture may not survive the modern period. Because the ruling class no longer supports the tiny, self-conscious avant-garde necessary to cultural innovation, the "ersatz culture" of Hollywood, Tin Pan Alley, and advertising has taken over. This abominable "kitsch" imitates the effects of art by inartistic means and for inartistic goals; that is, through mass production, it creates imitations of pleasure and beauty for profit. Since, finally, neither the impoverished avant-garde nor this industrialized kitsch can produce a full-fledged artistic culture, Greenberg concludes, "we look to socialism *simply* for the preservation of whatever living culture we have right now."[2]

Although many leftists of the thirties agreed with the spirit of Greenberg's analysis, they often disagreed on the exact means through which socialism would preserve culture.[3] Some, like Greenberg and the literary historians discussed in chapter 1, wanted to educate socialists about their cultural heritage, while other more activist-minded persons hoped to create a new, socialist alternative to mass culture—or at least to make room for socialism in the space between the avant-garde and mass culture. This latter view was expressed by the Canadian modernist poet and scholar A. J. M. Smith in the preface he wrote for an influential 1936 anthology of new Canadian poetry titled *New Provinces.*

In this preface, Smith uses terms that are at once characteristic of the Canadian literary scene of the 1930s and evidence of his debt to left-wing culture. Seeking a "useful" poetry that "will facilitate the creation of a more practical social system," he criticizes "pure poetry" that is "unconcerned with anything save its own existence," and he continues by heaping scorn on the "sentimental . . . idealized, sanctified, . . . inflated . . . definite, mechanically correct, . . . obvious . . . [and] commonplace" verses of popular poets.[4] His concern with "sentimental" poetry is typical of Canadian literati of the period, as are certain aspects of his more contentious views on cultural nationalism: "Poetry today is written for the most part by people whose emotional and intellectual heritage is not a national one; it is either cosmopolitan or provincial, and, for good or evil, the forces of civilization are rapidly making the latter scarce" (xxix). As in his later, controversial *Book of Canadian Poetry* (1943), Smith here divides Canada's poets into a native or "provincial" tradition and a modernist or "cosmopolitan" school.[5] This division marks Smith's participation in Canadian literary culture, since it does not dismiss "provincial" writing so much as it describes that writing's continuing struggle with "the forces of civilization." Also, in the 1920s and 1930s, it was quite usual to set the concept of "civilization" in opposition to "culture," and use of this opposition usually indicated the author's preference for authentic, local culture over mass-produced, mechanized civilization.[6] In other words, by associating the "culture" in the "culture and civilization" thesis with provincialism, Smith offers a particularly Canadian critique of mass civilization. In his analysis, mass civilization is an invading "force" that must be resisted, while provincial culture is one of the sources of opposition on which he will draw for the "useful poetry" in the aptly titled *New Provinces.*

The Canadian elements of this analysis become even clearer when we compare Smith's essay to Greenberg's. While Greenberg views socialism as a museum for the preservation of culture, Smith emphasizes its creative aspects. Though the geopolitical differences between 1936 and 1939 (the date of Greenberg's essay and a year of important disappointments for leftists, such as the Hitler-Stalin pact and the defeat of the Spanish Loyalists) may account for some of Greenberg's pessimism, the overall structure of his analysis suggests less topical sources as well. Where Smith saw the conflict between modernist and sentimental provincial culture as the major division, Greenberg identifies a conflict between kitsch and the avant-garde. This terminological shift suggests that the major difference between the U.S. and the Canadian critic is his position *vis-à-vis* mass culture. Although both Smith and Greenberg sought a socialist culture that was neither avant-garde nor kitsch, neither "pure" modernism nor sentimental commonplace, they do not share terms for describing mass culture or a socialist resistance to mass culture. While Greenberg views mass culture as pervasive, Smith sees it as invasive; while Greenberg's hope for socialism stresses the development of critical consciousness, Smith seeks an enhanced provincial realism; while Greenberg wants to preserve, Smith wants to create.

This series of contrasts also appears in the literature of the 1930s. During the Depression, both the United States and Canada experienced a boom in magazine publication and especially in the publication of left-wing magazines.[7] (This parity contrasts to the book publishing industry, which nearly crumpled in Canada during the 1930s, while remaining fairly strong in the United States.) When writing for magazines, many writers self-consciously experimented with their medium and paid special attention to the issues of culture that interest us here; in Canada, these issues were highly politicized since Canadian publishers developed an early analysis of cultural imperialism and demanded that tariffs be levied on U.S. imports.[8] In this vigorous, politically charged literary marketplace, then, left-wing writers in both countries established their own subculture—a subculture marked by its proximity to both national traditions and the incipient transnationalism of the mass media.

The U.S. Left: In Pursuit of Objectivism

Left-wing culture in the United States during the 1930s had a number of distinguishing features. Although many of the writers and artists who became politically active during the Depression had only a superficial knowledge of politics and only committed themselves politically for a few years, they none-theless helped to shape socialist culture in the United States. First, their Mani-chean sense of commitment contributed to the Communist Party's promi-nent position in the United States; many considered joining other smaller left parties akin to drinking "near-beer," as Dos Passos quipped.[9] According to this pattern, intellectuals not inclined to join the Communists usually became fel-low travelers. They either committed themselves entirely or circulated around those who did; few other centers of left-wing activity received their respect. This political centralism was also evident in the geographic arrangement of the left; the Communists' traditional association with immigrant groups who gravitated toward the large urban centers in the Northeast and the artistic pres-tige of Greenwich Village in the interwar years helped to concentrate leftist culture on the East Coast. Literary intellectuals often experienced difficulties inhabiting cities, such as Chicago, that did not boast a substantial bohemian population.[10]

The leftist periodicals published in the United States during the thirties re-flect these political and geographic tendencies. The major publications in the literary scene were the Communist-sponsored *New Masses,* some friendly lib-eral journals of opinion such as the *Nation* and *New Republic,* and, in the sec-ond half of the decade, the more theoretically inclined *Partisan Review.* While publications affiliated with other parties or regions, such as the Trotskyist *Mod-ern Quarterly* or Chicago's *Anvil,* were available, as the decade progressed and political lines were drawn more fixedly, most of these either folded or merged with the larger publications.[11] The periodicals that survived sometimes dem-onstrated the particular obsessions of their editors, but this tendency was not as pronounced as some historians of the period have suggested.[12] In practice, each of these magazines published work from a variety of viewpoints, and, since individual writers were usually not tied to journals through editorial re-sponsibilities, contributors often published in several supposedly hostile pub-lications. For instance, women writers such as Meridel Le Sueur, Josephine Herbst, Agnes Smedley, and Mary Heaton Vorse published simultaneously in *American Mercury, New Masses,* and *New Republic.* Individual writers were able to publish widely because the actual effect of leftist periodicals, and especially those with a literary focus, was not to propagate a particular political line; instead, these magazines had primarily cultural effects. They introduced new writers, reviewed new works by established writers, dramatized significant recent events, and produced theories of contemporary culture. In short, the leftist literary periodicals published in the United States during the 1930s tried to encourage a vigorous socialist culture through improved distribution of culture more often than they tried to direct the production of that culture. Creating culture remained the task of individual persons working simultaneously but separately.

Of course, none of the leftist or liberal periodicals in the United States ever circulated as widely as the mass market magazines. The *Nation*'s circulation, for instance, hovered around 36,000 for the entire decade, while magazines such as *McCalls* and *Good Housekeeping* regularly boasted circulations in excess of one million over the same period.[13] Nonetheless, historians of the publishing industry have often noted that the opinion magazines had an influence on the public discourse that was out of proportion to their subscription rate.[14] Their influence was great enough that even conservative trade magazines such as the *Saturday Evening Post* reported on left-wing writers' groups, reviewed leftist novels sympathetically, and occasionally invited radical critics to contribute columns.[15] Nonetheless, the major site of interaction between mass and socialist cultures was within the socialist magazines themselves. Here, leftist periodical writers hammered out four prose strategies for transforming their medium—each of which imagined mass culture as the objective precondition of its project.

The type of prose most often taken to be representative of the 30s left is, not surprisingly, the proletarian short story. Shorter versions of the proletarian novel, these social realist stories typically portray a working-class character's struggle to substitute radical activism for the passive fatalism inspired by mass culture. They worked to represent social conditions directly, and their defenders argued that they hastened the "death of the euphemism" by pointedly offering commentary on everyday life.[16] These stories were most likely to appear in the periodicals closely affiliated with the Communist Party. The *New Masses,* for instance, published numerous excerpts from forthcoming radical novels, such as Charles Yale Harrison's *A Child Is Born* or Dos Passos's *1919,* as well as more or less thinly fictionalized accounts of recent strikes and other political battles.[17] Leane Zugsmith's "Room in the World," for instance, describes a desperate unemployed man who makes sandwich boards for his family to wear while picketing his former workplace. The crux of the story occurs when his daughter cries because a classmate she admired, a girl who "looked like Shirley Temple," saw her on the picket line.[18] The conflict between popular images of bourgeois femininity and the display of class-based suffering required by radical culture humiliates the daughter, a fact that only the sensitive mother who narrates the story understands.

The division of characters with incorrect political and cultural allegiances from a wise narrator is often sharp in proletarian stories, and too often it leads to the uneasy synthesis seen in Zugsmith's piece. In the final paragraphs, the wise mother—afraid to anger her husband—"found the tone she had lately learned to use . . . a casual conversational voice." That is, the mother becomes the locus of rationality and draws the family together by explaining the hotheaded father to the wrong-headed daughter and vice versa. As is often the case in proletarian fiction, with this conclusion, Zugsmith employs the basic tropes of sentimental fiction for a nostalgic critique of mass culture. The moral authority of the mother, the family as image of solidarity, the home as site for renewing one's faith—these gestures combine proletarian radicalism with sentimentalism.[19] Although this strategy produced a number of promising experiments—especially by women writers—the analogy between narrator and parent often reduces the story to a message or a moral. The narrator's role, as in Zugsmith's story, is to replace mass culture's vulgarity with a more proper political etiquette; however, the reader rarely learns exactly how that writing/narrating subject managed to escape mass culture's pernicious influence.

Many writers in the 1930s commented on the exaggerated distance between mass culture and socialist culture assumed in the proletarian stories; in fact, this issue became a refrain in postwar commentary on the failings of the 1930s.[20] Even during the 1930s, though, a second type of prose developed around this theme. Particularly in the more theoretical *Partisan Review,* a number of pieces were published that commented on cultural politics; often adopting a satiric tone or constructed around an ironic plot twist, these pieces draw attention to the double binds produced by different forms of class consciousness. Most of these stories draw attention to difficult confrontations between working-class or otherwise marginalized persons and mainstream politics; typically, they suggest a moral conclusion.[21] In an especially interesting variant on the parable structure, writers such as Barney Conal used the form to make metacommentary on socialist culture a part of that culture; Conal's "Notes on a Character," for example, self-consciously refers to its protagonist as a "character" and charts the shifts in that character's allegiances.[22] The story begins with the narrator recounting that Tommy appreciates his new wife because "he thought she had 'class'"; that is, he liked the fact that she read books. As the story progresses, his wife's desire to establish a family life appropriate to her "class" comes into conflict with Tommy's "sport's-world culture": "She only believed in the desirable things she couldn't reach. He, it turned out, believed only in what was, no matter what" (47). In other words, the wife's desire for upward mobility contrasts with Tommy's fatalism, an attitude, the narrator points out, that is bolstered by his reading of the *Daily Sun* and the *Saturday Evening Post,* and his playing of baseball and basketball. With these details, Conal points out that Tommy is aware of cultural differences and that his knowledge is not created by mass culture so much as it is enhanced by mass culture.

In the second half of the story, the "character" confronts Communist culture: "I looked at some of their stuff," he tells the narrator, "but it don't get me . . . it's too deep" (49). Initially, he continues to read the *Daily Sun,* since he finds that the writers in the left magazines "talk too much" and use obscure language to mock people he respects, such as the police. Yet, by the last paragraph of the story, Tommy is jailed for punching a cop at a demonstration; "he had switched his allegiance" from his wife's "class" to "these baffling, battling groups who would not sell out." The key factors in this switch are Tommy's admiration for the Communists' "action" and his need for "a crowd, as he used to know when he was a kid" (51). In other words, it is in the sociological rather than the literary sense that radical culture attracts Tommy. He feels comfortable when its practices overlap with the pragmatism and camaraderie of his "sport's-world culture," and only then do his verbalized opinions begin to change. In the last sentence of the story he rescinds his earlier objection to socialist culture with the statement that "Some cops are damn fools" (51). This conclusion, then, rejects an implicit premise of proletarian writing—the assertion that socialist culture is an alternative to or replacement for mass culture. Instead, Conal describes a radicalism that originates in and transforms mass culture. Finally, he implies that socialist writers should take advantage of the radical potential in mass culture.

Of course, "Notes on a Character" is not itself an example of the kind of writing that Conal might desire, since it appeared in *Partisan Review,* a periodical that preached to the converted—and to the intellectuals among the converted, no less. Furthermore, the story shares a basic technique with proletarian writing: it, too, separates the narrator almost completely from the dynamics it describes. The narrator of "Notes on a Character" translates the experiences of the inarticulate character and generalizes freely from the particular: "it was as though all the capitalist-trained and ignorant, honest masses had spoken," the narrator concludes after Tommy makes an unusually blunt statement of his dilemma (49). One is never in any doubt that the narrator is a socialist who encourages Tommy's progressive radicalization. This split between the righteous narrator and the erring characters is not quite as pronounced here as in Zugsmith's story—perhaps because Conal exhorts the radical audience to listen to his character and learn from him; he is not quite as interested in disciplining the character into rationality. Nonetheless, phrases such as "the capitalist-trained and ignorant, honest masses" do imply that the narrator is somehow free from the training in ignorance provided by capitalist (read, mass) culture.

A third way in which radical writers in the United States attempted to soften the moral and lessen the opposition between the subject and object of narration is evident in documentary stories. *Partisan Review* published excerpts from James T. Farrell's *Studs Lonigan* trilogy that followed this format, as well as several pieces by Edward Newhouse and Nelson Algren about the life of transients.[23] Often episodic in structure and impressionistic in character, these thinly veiled autobiographical pieces paradoxically attempt to eliminate the narrator altogether—or at least to relegate the narrator to the extreme margins of the narrative. For instance, in "A Jazz-Age Clerk," Farrell uses an internal monologue to describe the highs and lows experienced by a jaunty young clerk on his lunch hour.[24] This monologue interweaves the young clerk's consciousness with the language of popular songs and films, suggesting that the clerk assesses the world (and the women) around him according to the standards provided by mass culture:

> He saw an athletically built blonde, and she was just bow wows, the kind to look at and weep. He jerked his shoulders to the jazz rhythm of another song:
>> *I'm running wild, I'm runnin' wild*
>> *I lost control . . .*
> Now if there would only be some mama like that in the restaurant, and if he could only get next to her. (9)

The clerk desires the woman who corresponds to an image provided by mass culture ("an athletically built blonde"), and this image in turn recalls a jazz song. Thus, both the desire and the language in which the clerk expresses his desire derive from mass culture. This derivation, however, doesn't mean Farrell positions the clerk's thoughts as by-products of mass culture; in fact, Farrell explicitly states that the clerk's use of mass culture is a means of "expressing his feelings." His expertise in the selection of fragments of mass culture helps him speak to the world, and he shapes that world by offering it new slang and linguistic experimentation. To highlight this side of mass culture, Farrell makes frequent use of "jazz-age" idioms such as "bow wows," "mama," and "get next to," with the result that mass culture appears in the story in two modes: as a constraining and as a creative feature of the clerk's consciousness.

The two-sided legacy of mass culture contrasts with other more limited cultural options presented in the story. At one point, a "slatternly peroxide-blonde waitress" lets out a dull "What'll you have?" that suggests the kind of working-class fatalism Conal described. The clerk refuses to sympathize with her, insisting instead, rather defensively, that he lives a high life in the dance halls. Later, he encounters the living version of the high life he desires. Walking into the lobby of a fancy hotel, "he felt as if he were in a moving picture world" and he begins to imagine "a movie with him the hero." As at the lunch counter, though, the clerk soon feels a moment of shabbiness intrude when he fears the bellboy will eject him from the lobby. Quickly inventing an excuse for his presence, he is shocked to find that the bellboy passes him without a glance; he discovers he is not visible to the inhabitants of this movie palace—not to the bellboy or to the beautiful women about whom he fantasizes. This final fantasy is disrupted, however, by an awareness of time. The story ends with the clerk anxiously rushing back to the office, and the reader concludes that here is a third and perhaps most "real" alternative to mass culture: the world of work and the clerk's perilous position in it.

Although an alternative culture based on knowledge of the working world is only implied here, and, although Farrell offers a complex view of mass culture, the clerk's consciousness is still isolated in a fantasy realm in this story; that is, Farrell implies a theory of false consciousness. Self-awareness remains an unpleasant disruption of the clerk's fantasy, and Farrell does not portray the clerk receiving and approving images that correspond more closely to his situation; he portrays the clerk as always desiring something far beyond his reach. In short, the documentary form has difficulty exploring the object of the story, the clerk, without reintroducing the subject, or the evaluative narrator. Since the form does attempt to eliminate the latter, it is open to the charges of insincerity, manipulation, and propagandistic intent that have been leveled against it.[25] The presence of a subject positioned outside the pervasive jazz-age culture that the story describes reads as a betrayal of the form, if not also of the object.

The fourth type of leftist prose from the United States—reportage—also encounters the problem of faithfully representing the object. In this form, writers explicitly articulated their partisan views and attempted to demonstrate that the events they reported corroborated these views. That is, in theory, reportage recaptures the object by making the writer one object among many. One of its more innovative practitioners, Meridel Le Sueur, put the problem this way: "If you come from the middle class, words are likely to mean more than an event. You are likely to think about a thing, and the happening will be the size of a pin point and the words around the happening very large, distorting it queerly. It's a case of 'Remembrance of Things Past.' When you are in the event, you are likely to have a distinctly individualistic attitude, to be only partly there, and to care more for the happening afterwards than when it is happening." [26] Though striving to proportion their writing like an event, and thereby to recapture the real object, reporters like Le Sueur found that most modes of writing at their command shrank the event down to "the size of a pinpoint." Furthermore, as a result of their "distinctly individualistic attitude," they themselves were "only partly there." To be fully there, to equate the writing subject with the object, required words and concepts that were small, unobtrusive, almost transparent—the very opposite of the self-indulgent formal extravagance of Proust's purportedly middle-class work, *Remembrance of Things Past.* By articulating this theory, however, Le Sueur was not encouraging a pseudo-objective journalistic style like that used in the mass media; rather, her discussion of the difficulty of pursuing objectivity aims at making the conditions of writing one of the objects of writing.

This emphasis on the self-conscious writing subject is characteristic of left-wing reportage, though not all reporters articulated it as theoretically as Le Sueur. Many of these first-person, subjectivist reports are more concerned with representing their outrage at recent events. With titles such as "They Killed My Son," "I Handed Out Relief," "My Uncle Was a Miner," "On the Picket Line," "We Are Mill People," and, again, "I Was Marching," these pieces stress the representative character of a situated subject's response.[27] Important series—such as Josephine Herbst's reports from Cuba, Agnes Smedley's views of the Chinese situation, and Mary Heaton Vorse's coverage of textiles organizing—clearly fed these writers' fictional projects, as well as providing news.[28] Reportage, then, offered an intermediate zone between the subjective and the objective. Tillie Lerner's "The Strike," for example, begins with Lerner's reflections on writing and emphasizes her solidarity with struggling workers by revealing her own labor process. "Do not ask me to write of the strike and the terror," she writes; "If I could go away for a while, if there were time and quiet, perhaps I could do it."[29] Defending herself from the immediacy of the event because she fears it will silence her, Lerner finds she must turn her attention to the linguistic codes that organize her own and others' writing. As a result, she begins to distinguish typographically among the newspaper headlines ("LONGSHOREMEN OUT") and slogans the strikers use to steel themselves ("H-E-L-L C-A-N'-T S-T-O-P U-S") and the quiet observations one person makes to another ("we're through sweating blood"). She demarcates these different types of language because the disparities among mass culture, socialist culture, and the private voice anger her, stimulate her, and lend her both subject matter and form.

Recognizing these disparities—recognizing that the alliance between subjects and objects of representation had not yet been achieved—was a necessary feature of socialist culture in the United States in the 1930s, and for this reason the tone that dominates the prose of the period is anxiety. In pieces by Zugsmith, Conal, Farrell, Lerner, and others, the narrators anxiously pursue the object and attempt to wrest it from mass culture; thus, they continually reflect the anxiety produced in a contest between cultures. At their worst, these efforts devolve into the personal sorrow of the frustrated, lonely intellectual,[30] but at their best these experiments enabled many writers—and especially women writers—to describe what they saw as a new alliance between themselves and the working class, and between the subject and object of their writing.[31] Although the writers of reportage, like the proletarian short story writers and the documentarists, did not always accomplish their goals, all of these experiments with prose clearly register the U.S. intellectuals' common desire to transform their medium. And, more specifically, they reveal the shared hypothesis that writing in and against the pervasive mass media would alter the political possibilities of writing.

The Canadian Left: In Pursuit of Realism

In comparison to the United States, the Canadian literary left of the 1930s made a more lasting mark on its national culture. Although—or perhaps, be-cause—there was no New Deal in Canada, the 1930s saw the introduction of a long-lived social-democratic party in which intellectuals played a signifi-cant role, the Cooperative Commonwealth Federation (CCF, later the New Democratic Party, NDP). This party did something that was never a real pos-sibility for leftists in the United States; it won elections and lastingly altered the political environment of the nation from inside the power structure.[32] In specifically cultural matters, left-wing Canadian intellectuals also set prece-dents by actively supporting new cultural institutions, such as public interest radio broadcasting, and some of this work helped pave the way for a perma-nent structure of governmental support for cultural workers in the 1940s and 1950s.[33] Some of this work may also have led Canadians to resist the kind of McCarthyism that erased many writers of the 1930s from cultural memory in the United States.[34] Left-wing poets and novelists, such as MacLennan, Earle Birney, Dorothy Livesay, and those associated with *New Provinces,* remain im-portant figures in Canadian literary history. In all, the 30s left has remained a significant reference point in Canadian literary culture.

The political structure of the Canadian left in the 1930s probably had some-thing to do with its relative success. Because the Canadian political scene had two major left-wing parties—the CCF and the Communists—a greater range of roles was available for intellectuals to play than in the United States, and left-wing ideas gained somewhat greater legitimacy in the public discourse.[35] Also, although support for both parties was most concentrated in Toronto and Mon-treal, intellectuals from all regions of Canada showed hostility to U.S. cultural imperialism.[36] Despite regional differences, Canadian intellectuals generally preferred what A. J. M. Smith called provincial culture to imported mass cul-ture. This situation resulted, in essence, in a fusion of national and socialist cultures in the left-wing aesthetic.

Of left-wing Canadian magazines, the *Canadian Forum,* which supported the CCF, was the only one to survive the Depression. Their survival hinged in part on the editors' emphasis on specifically Canadian writing and politics, since these issues appealed to a politically heterogeneous selection of readers. However, the other Canadian literary periodicals with a left-wing orientation,

Masses and *New Frontier,* also exhibited nationalist sentiments. Although these were officially internationalist in their content, both magazines justified their existence through cultural nationalism. *Masses* wanted to find and encourage a Canadian proletarian literature, and *New Frontier* wanted to widen the Canadian audience for left-wing literature.[37] The latter project not only involved informing the Canadian public of interesting new works by French, Russian, U.S., and British authors; it also involved a strong focus on publishing poetry, fiction, and commentary by rising stars in the Canadian literary world, such as A. M. Klein, Dorothy Livesay, Leo Kennedy, Morley Callaghan, and Ted Allan. These periodicals also arguably played a role in promoting literary modernism in Canada.[38] Certainly they cleared room for some of the important postwar literary magazines, such as *Preview* and *First Statement,* that took an interest in social realist verse.

Whatever the differences between the three major leftist magazines in Canada, though, all three shared a basic project.[39] All concerned themselves with creating a socialist culture in Canada, rather than simply distributing it, as the U.S. periodicals did. This emphasis on creation may have had something to do with the fact that these magazines were not supplementing a flourishing book publishing industry, nor could they rely on sympathetic reviews in liberal magazines; instead, these magazines were the major site of left-wing literary activity in Canada during the 1930s. Left-wing writers founded these magazines in order to have an outlet for their work, and hence they were often their own most frequent contributors. Editors published their own material, and the creation and distribution of socialist culture fused together in Canada. Perhaps for this reason, the writer/editors of Canadian periodicals usually published exclusively in their own periodicals or, if they did publish elsewhere, they chose a Canadian competitor. Encouraging Canadian literary culture was a priority for left-wing Canadians, since they were interested in formulating a national resistance to mass culture. As Smith's preface to *New Provinces* indicates, this resistance combined modernist techniques with provincial realism for a distinctly Canadian socialist culture.

Perhaps the unique qualities of leftist prose in Canada emerge most clearly in the reportage. As in the United States, reportage was most frequently featured in the farther left periodicals. The Communist-affiliated *New Frontier* published more work in this genre than did *Canadian Forum*—accounts of the Spanish civil war and key labor struggles being the most common topics.[40] For example, Dorothy Livesay's "Corbin—A Company Town Fights for Its Life," an account of striking coal-miners in British Columbia, begins with anxiety about borders.[41] Livesay describes the subterfuges she had to resort to when visiting the mining town. The border she crosses between provinces emphasizes the specifically Canadian location of the report. Livesay specifies the site (Corbin, British Columbia) and her own point of origin for the trip (Crow's Nest Pass, Alberta) and emphasizes the distance of both of the cultures she describes from any metropolitan or imperialist centers of power. She records local dialect, quoting extensively from the miners' conversation and paying particular attention to the differing accents of workers from Czechoslovakia, Nova Scotia, and Ontario. When she is not quoting dialogue, her descriptions of the events of the strike are summaries rather than syntheses or interpretations; she spends much of the report recounting details about how much food the miners allow themselves in rations—explaining how they survive from day to day. In other words, while Le Sueur and Lerner concentrated on the reporter's anxiety about writing, Livesay grounds her report in her desire to go native, to fit into the mining community. The primary task of her report is a precise rendering of the particularities of the local situation and the character of the local resistance to invaders.

As Livesay tells it, the force invading Corbin is not her but the company, "Corbin Collieries, Ltd., an American firm" (203). The firm is described here by way of systemization; it controls water, electricity, sanitation, schools, medicine—all from outside the town. But most significantly here, the "American firm" controls the newspapers: "They would not print our facts," a miner's wife tells Livesay, "but lies that came from the other side. . . . it makes you sore to think that people on the outside don't know what happened" (204). The miners in this case are not presented as the childish victims of the mass media, as in the United States; on the contrary, they are fully aware of the extent to which the newspapers misrepresent them. They even lament the fact that other people, "on the outside," might believe "the other side." In a notably Canadian formulation, the "outside" here is also the "other side," and it is the miners' inside knowledge that enables them to criticize the invasions of the media.

At the same time, the incursions of the American firm and its media representatives also contrast to the miners' sense of a national culture. Represented by the police and by government relief programs, the nation supports the company's interests. The police attack the miners, and the distribution of relief removes the workers from the town, allowing scabs to fill their jobs. The result of this dilemma is that the miners view the national government as an invading force as well: "I used to be patriotic," one woman tells Livesay, "I'd stand up on my little Maple Leaf in front of anyone. But I learned my lesson. We all did" (206). A sense of solidarity within the town—and with other nearby mining towns providing some support—helps Livesay distinguish nationalism from patriotism. The miners are secure in their national distaste for "an American firm," but this does not mean they patriotically support the Canadian government. Instead, a nationalism growing out of regional or provincial culture, Livesay suggests, fosters a genuinely socialist culture; she goes on to describe how the experience of solidarity led the one-time Maple Leafer to a newfound appreciation for articles in *The Worker,* a Communist labor newspaper.

Most of the themes present in Livesay's reportage also appear in the fiction published in left-wing Canadian periodicals, and, as in the United States, this fiction took three basic forms, the first of which concentrates on describing the conditions of working-class life. Like the proletarian stories, these sketches usually employ a radical narrator who interprets working-class life. Both the *Canadian Forum* and the Communist periodicals published this kind of piece, although they were somewhat more likely to appear in the latter; *Forum* pieces tended to focus more on the moral of the situation than on the character of the work.[42] For a good example of the more radical workday fiction, we can examine Winnipeg scientist Dyson Carter's "East Nine."[43] Carter's story, however, focuses less on narrowing the gap between the subject and object of the story than on creating an empathetic relation between the reader and the characters. Carter's essentially realist aesthetic aims at involving the reader in a specific community of sufferers. Language in these stories does not hinder the intellectual subject as often as it cements local cultures together, and "realism" here usually indicates an authentically local use of language.

Like several of Carter's other *New Frontier* stories, "East Nine" is set in a hospital ward for recipients of worker's compensation. Like Livesay's Corbin, this ward also represents a self-sufficient, multiethnic community defending itself against invasion. The most important invader here is Carl Thorsen, a Norwegian who was horribly maimed in a sawmill. Thorsen speaks only a few words in the story. After the accident, his wounded consciousness is represented exclusively by a chaotic gaze that was "unreal and without meaning as some trick movie shot with crazy perspectives" (71). The narrator reporting this phenomenon clearly prefers a familiar realist perspective to this "crazy," media-inspired rambling. The story itself is written in a style that produces a visceral sympathy for Carl's suffering in the reader; the tone recalls Livesay's sympathetic interest in the miners' diets.

In "East Nine," the ward community discovers common ground when its members resist further invasions into their territory. The first visitor, the boss directly responsible for Carl's accident, is represented as feeling guilty and defensive, and the men on the ward bond together by mocking him. The narrator intrudes into the boss's consciousness only to note that while exiting the ward he is mentally composing a want-ad for a worker to fill Carl's position. The message is clear: the mass media are the boss's tools, while irony and solidarity are the workers' weapons. Other intruders include a doctor, Carl's father, the memory of Carl's wife, a Jehovah's Witness, and death. The doctor and the Witness receive much the same treatment as the boss, while the father and the memory of the wife remind the men of their shared pain. After Carl raves deliriously about them, they become mythically proportioned counterimages to the mass media for the men: "Never again would they see a fair Norwegian woman," Carter writes, "without the memory of that ghastly night rising to blur their vision" (78). In the end, though, these symbols drive some of the men to religious quibbling, and the real strength of their community appears again only in their resistance to death. When Carl catches pneumonia, Wardle, a Communist organizer, investigates the causes. He gathers facts and writes a petition; these activities do not save Carl, but they unite the men and provide the basis for a final lyrical apostrophe to the dying man written in a collective voice.

This collective voice moralizes freely: "Fellow man, worker, comrade, farewell. The motor is repaired, the plane sings, the bee-hive profits mount. No longer wretched, no longer of this earth, rest. We of East Nine who struggle and have yet to die, salute you" (85). The moral here is not a lesson that the characters need to learn; it is an ironic statement directed toward the society at large. In a parody of religious bombast, Carter dramatically opposes the false names used by the world outside the ward — motor, plane, profits — to the single, ironic fact of death. The language of motors, planes, and profits means death for the men of East Nine, and this ironic translation is the only alternative Carter offers to the "crazy" perspectives that would direct our attention elsewhere. Using a collective and ironic voice, Carter invites the reader into the hospital community and insists that the reader participate in the construction of the moral by reading through the story's irony to a realist narrative of cause and effect.

Carter's editors at *New Frontier* noted that his stories were popular with their readership, and, perhaps as a result, other left-wing Canadian writers also chose to sound an ironic note especially when exploring working-class subjects' investment in mass culture—often from the perspective of a slightly bemused but empathetic middle-class narrator.[44] As their titles indicate, these stories frequently took longing as their theme: "When I'm a Man," "Lots More of Something Else," "The Dress," "The Party," and "The Enchanted." Rather than equating mass culture with death and insanity, prolific short story writers such as Mary Quayle Innis figured the more attractive side of mass-marketed images. Tackling a topic similar to Farrell's in "Jazz-Age Clerk," Innis's story "Holiday" describes a woman on relief who spends her free afternoon in a department store, looking for "something nice to take the bad taste out of her mouth."[45] Wandering among the cosmetics, bath soaps, powder puffs, and velvet dresses, she convinces herself that the "store was for everybody" despite considerable evidence to the contrary. Although clerks refuse to serve her and usher her away from the merchandise, although a pompous matriarch lectures her for bringing her baby out among so many germs, she continues to cherish the illusion of the democracy of the marketplace. In short, Innis assumes that the reader will understand the woman's thoughts to be false consciousness while continuing to empathize with her regardless of the structural irony. Unlike Farrell's story, however, the majority of "Holiday" is not given over to replicating the ebbs and flows of the woman's stream of consciousness, nor does it reproduce the relentlessly modern language of popular music and advertising. On the contrary, Innis's character demonstrates an almost childish lack of knowledge of the names and functions of the products that surround her: "A salesgirl at the corner of the counter sprayed a lady with perfume out of a tall crystal atomizer and a few of the tiny drops fell sparkling on Nettie's shoulder. She smiled and sniffed them appreciatively. That was nice. Rose, it smelled like, though you couldn't tell. They had such funny names" (140). The tone insists on Nettie's old-fashioned naiveté, and colloquialisms such as "rose, it smelled like" have a faintly Victorian ring. This suggests that Innis's interest is not in creating an accurate, up-to-date portrait of a working-class mother or in celebrating the mother's role, as Zugsmith does. Instead, Innis provokes the reader's sympathy for this woman on the basis of her desire for beauty,

her love for children, her need to rest. To evoke this kind of bond, Innis relies on what one critic has called a "moderate realism";[46] that is, she employs
a near-omniscient narrator who explains the state of mind of the character,
justifies the actions of that character, and positions the encounters with other
characters as illicit interruptions, and this narrator accustoms the reader to uncomfortable material in the contemporary setting. The task of this moderately
realist aesthetic is to create a community of feeling between the reader and
object of narration, rather than to rationalize the subject's distribution of the
object, as in U.S. stories.

By 1936, stories like Innis's—ironic stories about the state of mind of the
unemployed, impoverished man or woman—were so common that the well-
known short story writer Morley Callaghan could write of their continued proliferation, "[i]f this keeps on it will appear that either all the young writers of
the country are out of work, or that they all feel a little frustrated, a little cynical, or even defeated, and that living in this country doesn't leave one with
a strong feeling." In contrast to this projection of writerly insecurity, Callaghan urged "a lustier crowing."[47] Such a crowing would involve opposing the
"strong feeling" of their own country to the frustration provoked by encounters with an invasive mass culture.

When writers such as Marion Nelson answered Callaghan's challenge, they
often turned out stories presenting the dilemma of intellectuals. Focusing on
the writing subject, these stories are also concerned with desires, but here
the desires do not involve commodities so much as they do a sense of social
and political certainty; they highlight the middle-class subject's confusion.
Leon Edel's "The Eternal Footman Snickers," Robert Greer Allen's "The Rest
Is Silence," and Marion Nelson's "What's Wrong with Us, Webb?" follow this
pattern. Nelson's story, in particular, is a stream-of-consciousness representation of Webb, an indecisive young teacher who "didn't even know which
side was his own."[48] On the eve of his resignation from a post at an exclusive
boys' school, he feels torn between his service to wealthy chair-warmers and
a romantic notion of rescuing the working classes. The story follows his vacillating sympathies, as he applies his derisive wit first to "the school's soundest
advertisement"—its playing fields—then to his radical girlfriend's seriousness
about politics, then to a slightly more radical fellow teacher, and finally to his
pompous supervisor. The political outcome of the story is ambiguous, at best,
since Webb concludes by plunging himself back into his work, laughing and

comparing his fantasies of radical heroism to "a bunch of carrots before the nose" (12).

Interpreted in terms of cultural or aesthetic options, however, the conclusion is more certain. Webb's elitist scorn for bread and circuses is a constant theme—from the first mention of the school as an advertisement to the final metaphor of carrots; the young teacher views everything around him—the school, his girlfriend's tears, his friend's politics—as a pitched battle between image and reality, and it is clear he will always choose "reality." This aesthetic preference for realism leads him to scoff at the other teachers, "whose leisure was by preference given to the reading of comic strips and to the cracking of dull jokes concerning them" (10). For Webb, the culture of comic strips is too clearly associated with capitulation to the hierarchy of the school to be pleasurable, and he comes to prefer the other radical teacher's probing history lessons for their aesthetic and, eventually, we are led to hope, their political appeal.

In the terms of the story, this combination of realist aesthetics and political skepticism makes it difficult for Webb to appreciate what he views as a fantastic socialist culture, but the following passage demonstrates how the aesthetic might begin to alter the politics: "Webb's strong point was his sense of humor. He amused people, he said witty things, often without thought. Frances [the girlfriend] had suddenly wanted him to grow serious. Once, he remembered, she had wept at a joke of his—something or other about Ethiopia, the details escaped him now. She had wept bitterly and he had comforted her, only dimly understanding her pain then. After that she began to give him pamphlets and a string of novels about people on relief" (8). The passage describes Webb's incomplete understanding of politics and shows how he uses wit to compensate for his lack of comprehension, but, significantly, the passage is also a memory. Webb remembers that he had a partial understanding, and his aesthetic preference for realism makes him uncomfortable with the thought that he has been deluded and has only insufficiently reached the real. In that gesture, in that brief desire to improve himself by understanding his girlfriend's real "pain," Webb offers a glimmer of hope. Once he begins applying a realist aesthetic to his own self-image, once he begins to separate his own self-advertising as a witty fellow from his real purposes, Nelson implies, the road to political engagement begins. Since Nelson is faithful to the principle of internal monologue, the narrator does not conclude what those real purposes may be for Webb, but the story does suggest that asking the title question, "What's Wrong with Us," is a necessary step for intellectuals seeking an alternative to mass culture. As long as Webb refuses to identify his problem, he remains unallied—without a "side"—and therefore outside the community of people already writing "pamphlets" and "strings of novels about people on relief."

Although Nelson's, Innis's, Carter's, and Livesay's versions of realist prose are not entirely consonant with the more obviously modernist poetry of the *New Provinces* anthology, when taken together, these literary experiments do highlight a basic difference between the literature found in U.S. and Canadian periodicals of the 1930s: the difference between pursuing the object in itself and pursuing the local reality that unites subject and object. This difference, I have argued, results from the different positions of U.S. and Canadian writers vis-à-vis mass culture. While left-wing writers in the United States viewed mass culture as a pervasive feature of their environment and anxiously experimented with literary forms that would describe its effect on working-class consciousness, Canadian writers saw mass culture as an invader from the south and sought sources of resistance to that invasion in regional culture. As a result, socialists in each country developed different aesthetic and political styles.

The Persistence of National Culture

Once we identify the different aesthetics operating in the United States and Canada during the 1930s, one question remains: If the different positions in relation to mass culture can explain the different aesthetics adopted by left-wing writers in the United States and Canada, what explains the different relations to mass culture? Most cultural historians interested in such a question have concluded that the two countries have different national cultures that frame every cultural product of the country. Some consider the difference primarily political and call attention to the contrast between a nation founded by revolution and one founded by treaty; or between two- and three-party political structures; or between different forms of federalism; or—speaking more particularly of the thirties—between a Communist-dominated left and a social-democratic left. Others emphasize ethical differences—contrasting U.S. individualism and Puritanism to a Canadian sense of community and social gospel. Still others discuss economic, technological, geographical, climatic, or historical factors that differentiate the two nations.[49] Margaret Atwood has famously pointed to a particular relationship to the land as a unique feature of Canadian literary culture.[50] The implication of these studies is that any difference between U.S. and Canadian writers' positions in mass culture simply reflects a difference in the national cultures.

The problem with this absolutely nationalist position is that it tends to relegate to obscurity marginal cultures that developed in both countries. For example, Atwood suggests that certain left-leaning writers cannot properly be considered Canadian, because they "connect [their] social protest not with the Canadian predicament specifically but with some other group or movement: the workers in the thirties, persecuted minority groups such as the Japanese uprooted during the war."[51] Of course, this statement irritated a writer like Dorothy Livesay, who had devoted herself to both causes as well as to a lifetime of writing, publishing, and teaching Canadian literature.[52] In Atwood's view, Livesay and the other writers of the thirties leap too quickly from personal concerns to "The World"; that is, Atwood charges them with bypassing intermediate categories such as the region and the nation.

By contrast, I hope to have demonstrated that, whatever the problems inhering in the internationalist political theory of the thirties, the "nation" was an important category in socialist cultural practices of that period. Furthermore, examining writings that, by their very medium, often circulated across political borders, suggests that the national differences are relative rather than absolute. U.S. and Canadian left-wing cultures developed in relation to one another and are usefully studied together.[53] The practices of one cluster of writers and editors often inspired a response from their peers across the border—be it a mimetic or an oppositional response. In the end, one finds that mass culture, socialist culture, and national culture are categories that help to define one another. Only by clarifying the interrelations among them will we understand with any certainty the significance of any single element of the shifting terrain of the transnational culture of the thirties.

Chapter 8

PROLETARIANS WHO RESEMBLE HORATIO ALGER

Parody in Nathanael West's *A Cool Million*

If the periodical writers' attempts to appropriate the territory between mass and avant-garde culture concentrated on reformulating the significance of the former, Nathanael West's efforts leaned toward the latter. His first novel, *The Dream Life of Balso Snell* (1931), follows Snell on a surreal, nocturnal journey into the anus of the Trojan Horse, while his second novel, *Miss Lonelyhearts* (1933), describes the travails of a modernist artist-figure who is employed as an advice columnist and cannot entirely bear the evidence of mass suffering that his job requires him to confront. In these works, and even more so in his third novel, *A Cool Million* (1934), West exhibits a typically avant-gardist combination of suspicion and fascination with the institutions of culture—classical, mass, and, increasingly, leftist.[1] Although his work was poorly received during the 1930s, in later years, this tendency made West the darling of critics who were, if anything, more panicked by the imperialistic tendencies of mass culture than the left of the 1930s. Like Henry Roth, West was rediscovered in the 1960s in the following terms: "If Nathanael West appears to us from our present vantage point the chief neglected talent of the age, this is largely because he was immune to the self-deceit which afflicted his contemporaries; he knew what he was doing. Despite his own left-wing political sympathies and the pressures of friends more committed than he, he refused to subscribe to the program for proletarian fiction laid down by the official theoreticians and critics of the Communist movement."[2] Like many of his contemporaries, Leslie Fiedler praised West for refusing "to subscribe to the program"—that is, for rejecting the laughable proletarian fiction preferred by the "more committed" left-wing writers of the 1930s. Such comments reveal that West could be rediscovered only if he was understood to be an ironic avant-gardist critic of the "age" from which he emerged.

If our portrait of the "age," however, is not what Fiedler suggests—that is, if my descriptions of the genres and major writings of the 1930s have been convincing so far in arguing for the complexity, reflexivity, and relatively non-programmatic nature of many writings from this period—then, no doubt, we should rethink the relationship of a "chief talent" such as West to that "age." If the literary culture of the 1930s was not completely programmatic, then perhaps West did not refuse "to subscribe to the program," but rather shared aspects of the "program" that Fiedler would rather we did not remember as being part of the "program."

This more intimate relationship with the literary left is evident, I will argue, in the character of West's interest in mass culture. His parodic appropriations of film, comic strips, dime novels, and other popular forms have been well documented, but often these are understood in a framework that assumes West's isolation from his American contemporaries and his proximity to European leftists sympathetic to modernism.[3] By contrast, I will argue that West's parodies of mass culture demonstrate his engagement with the American left; in particular, his famous appropriations of Horatio Alger stories in *A Cool Million* doubled as references to contemporary American debates over proletarian fiction.[4] These are by no means adulatory references, but they do reveal West's understanding of the political—and occasionally, utopian—role proletarian fictions could play. Seen in this context, West is not a writer whose serious literary achievement rests on the suppression of his left-wing political sympathies, but, on the contrary, a writer whose singular encoding of his sympathy with "the program" of "his age" is at the heart of his literary production. Identifying these codes clarifies the politics of West's parody while also expanding our sense of the political and cultural options available to U.S. writers during the Depression era.

Representing Horatio Alger

"Only fools laugh at Horatio Alger and his poor boys who make good," West wrote in an unsuccessful screenplay drawn from *A Cool Million;* "[t]he wiser man who thinks twice about that sterling author will realize that Alger is to

America what Homer was to the Greeks . . . the Bulfinch of American fable and the Marx of the American Revolution."[5] That is, unlike earlier readers who saw Alger as a Progressive reformer, an immoral sensationalist, or a happy medium between the dime-novelist and the Sunday school pamphleteer, West saw Alger through the lens of the Depression; he saw Alger as the representative writer of capitalism, as a compiler of its myths, and an analyst of its major traits.[6] Unlike some of his contemporaries, however (who were prone to suggesting that those down-at-the-mouth about capitalism read Alger to boost their spirits), West appreciated Alger in an ironic mode; he juxtaposes "that sterling author" to major writers of other civilizations—Homer, Bulfinch, and Marx—so he can expose the puffery of this comparison. Thus, West articulates the avant-gardist truism that the cultural achievement of capitalist America is less satisfying than that of older civilizations; he expresses what one commentator has described as an aesthetic outrage at the shoddiness of American culture.[7]

At the basis of this aesthetic outrage, though, was a very 30s understanding of the concept of culture. As Warren Susman has argued, during the 1930s the concept of an actually existing American culture gained special currency.[8] In this decade, it became increasingly common to view American culture as the fullest development of a machinic civilization—the prototypical aesthetic form of which was the slapstick comedy. During the Depression, Susman argues, these comedies were especially popular because they allowed middle-class Americans to work through the shame of economic failure. These comedies usually began with the ritual humiliation of the hero and concluded with his eventual escape from adversity through commitment to a positive ideal—be it science, the New Deal, the Popular Front, or the nascent war effort. Despite the dehumanizing roles they offer, slapstick comedies functioned nostalgically in a context in which film was rapidly dissolving the vaudeville circuit.

That is, the slapstick comedies of the 1930s make reference to the codes of a previous generation; they follow the formula that cultural critics of the Depression attributed to Horatio Alger's stories. They describe the inevitable success awarded to a young man as a consequence of pluck and luck. Of course, these values differ from those expressed in the actual Alger stories; during the Depression, procapitalist propagandists preferred their own mythic misrepresentations of Alger to more literal transcriptions of his genteel anxiety about proletarianization.[9] But, since the references to Alger in *A Cool Million: The Dis-*

mantling of Lemuel Pitkin also make Alger a spokesperson for capitalism, it is clear that West, too, was using Alger for contemporary comic purposes.

West's most obvious parody of the Alger narratives involved inverting their plot. In *A Cool Million,* a series of chance encounters result in West's hero losing his money, his teeth, an eye, a thumb, his scalp, and a leg; this bad luck and the unabated humiliation of the hero invert the ideology of success. By the time the novel finally concludes with the hero's death, West has carried this theme to its limit and permanently prohibited any comedic expurgation of shame. Instead, West centers his narrative on the difficulty of translating shame into commitment. Rather than allowing the reader to identify with the humiliated hero until the moment of his commitment to a positive ideal, West turns humiliation into a spectacle. No comfortable resolution is offered, because West's major project in parodying Alger is to unravel the ideologies that claim comfort, commitment, and success will necessarily result from suffering.

Lingering in the background of this strongly critical strain, however, is West's abiding interest in maxims, adages, slogans, and clichés—in short, in codes. At this level, the Alger narratives parallel other codes that appear in the novel— advertising jingles, academic treatises, political stump-speeches, fair-barkers' patter, and interior decorators' jargon—each of which offers tangible evidence of the mechanization or commodification of language. Clearly, the critique of commodity fetishism is a major theme of the novel. However, West's sense that American culture is structured around the loss of linguistic depth and authenticity should not obscure the pleasure he takes in employing these commodified formulas. To take one fairly minor example, toward the end of the novel in one of the many passages lifted from Alger, West introduces a character who describes himself as a "rip-tail ringer and a ring-tail squealer." [10] Although—as I will demonstrate below—West is very much interested in satirizing discourses of nativism, the passage also exhibits a weird alliterative pleasure in manipulating the good-old-boy elements of this code. West repeats the folksy phrase several times, drawing attention to its formulaic qualities, and the fact that it is a formula enhances rather than reduces its appeal. Like Duchamp's urinal, or Picasso's wood-print contact paper, this mass-produced found object has a surreal quality that West foregrounds. It represents a kind of linguistic playfulness that contrasts strikingly to the acts of brutality also performed by this character.

By pausing to appreciate these found objects, West offers brief glimpses of a utopian pleasure inhering in mass culture. In particular, the citations from Alger allow him to explore the satisfaction provided by transparent genres—the pleasure of grasping structures and predicting their unfolding. For West, the utopian element of this pleasure is not the certainty that the plot will trigger a positive commitment but, instead, the possibility that completion and commitment lie just beyond the horizon. This uncertainty, I will argue, provides the first point of comparison between Alger and the proletarian novel: both forms contain for West a residue of utopian freedom.

The Proletarian Novel and the Ideologeme

In order to explore the Alger stories and the proletarian novels together, West reduces both forms to their basic units of ideology—that is, to ideologemes.[11] These ideologemes consist of both conceptual and narrative elements, and West examines both of these features. By revealing the commonality between the basic structures of the Alger narrative and the proletarian novel, however, West is not staking out a neutral aesthetic middle ground between fascism and communism, or between right- and left-wing politics, as a number of critics have suggested. Instead, he is proposing a fundamentally materialist understanding of the social role played by narrative; he is pointing to the similarities in the way that both Alger and the proletarian novelists attempted to resolve social contradictions. Thus, his famous examination of "the dream life of the masses" is, in the end, less a psychologizing of politics than a rendering of the political unconscious.[12]

Like Alger's narratives, the proletarian novel is recognizable as a site of ideological investment because of the disparity between its reputation and its actuality. As demonstrated in chapter 4, many commentators falsely characterized the genre as the story of working-class triumph that centers on the adoration of a brawny proletarian leader and too often becomes visibly conceptual. In other words, the proletarian novel often sounded objectionably close to propaganda. Propaganda, in this theory of literary value, is necessarily opposed to the more properly aesthetic exploration of some universal human experience; it introduces an unsuitable element of historical contingency into works that could and should—for example, in Fiedler's view—offer an immunity from history.

As demonstrated in earlier chapters, however, this reputation does not accurately describe the writings generally understood in the 1930s as proletarian novels. Many of these novels were written explicitly in criticism of Communist Party policy; many are devoted to the exploration of the difficulties, not the inevitability, of organizing effective working-class resistance; and many describe the decidedly harsh toll capitalist economics takes on a less than brawny proletariat. By no means do the majority—or even a sizable minority—of the proletarian novels match the portrait too often casually invoked by literary historians. Like Alger's success story, then, the proletarian novel has been reduced to a concept and rejected for its undemonstrated, but presumably scandalous, lack of literary value; whether this concept is a bald affirmation of capitalism, as in the case of Alger, or the contrary, as in the case of the proletarian novel, the basic reduction of form to formula has been the same.

West's play with the proletarian and Alger-ian ideologemes depends on these critical reductions; as with Alger, he adopts and inverts the stereotyped version of the proletarian novel. His hero, in *A Cool Million,* is scrawny rather than brawny; his Party is Fascist rather than Communist; and its victory is a horror rather than a triumph. Also, his party's organizing tactics include lynching and demagoguery rather than the self-actualization of the working class. By inverting these elements of the proletarian novel, West parodies the overt message of the form—that success will follow collective struggle and organization.

However, West's parodies of the proletarian novel differ from the critics' reductive definition in one important way: as with Alger, West is at least as interested in the operation of the genre as a code as in the specific content being expressed. His central Communist character, for instance, is a fat man, "enormously fat": "On his head was a magnificent bowler hat. It was beautiful jet in color, and must have cost more than twelve dollars. He was snugly encased in a tight-fitting Chesterfield overcoat with a black velvet collar. His stiff-bosomed shirt had light gray bars, and his tie was of some rich but sober material in black and white pin-checks. Spats, rattan stick and yellow gloves completed his outfit" (114). From the bowler to the Chesterfield jacket and spats, this figure precisely duplicates the cartoon caricature of the capitalist familiar from the pages of the *New Masses* and other leftist publications during the 1930s (see fig. 5). Thus, we are meant to conclude, it is all the more ironic that he is a double agent operating simultaneously on behalf of the Communists and the international Jewish bankers. This aspect of his character is revealed through two quick phone calls he places to contacts who are housed

Figure 5 Cartoon capitalists from the *New Masses* often doubled as figures of genteel culture. January 9, 1934. (Burck)

on Union Square and Wall Street, respectively. Although this character, this nexus of cliché, appears very briefly and only a few times in the novel, each of his appearances helps to establish the commensurability of popular representations of conspiracies. This single unstable figure simultaneously represents the clichés of anti-Communism, anti-Semitism, and a vulgar anti-capitalism, because his figure is pure code. Behind the facade of reporting an incident of Fascist organizing, in the passage quoted above, the real point of his conversation is the manipulation of his code names and coded locations. As Operative 6384XM/Comrade R, he encapsulates the novel's central process: the translation between presumably incommensurate concepts, a translation that takes place on the basis of their common character as codes.

Finally, then, the political charge of *A Cool Million* lies in the relationship of these coded ideologemes to the social contradictions of the Depression. The three major ideologemes that West explores in the novel include (*a*) a concept of character as a bearer of ideology; (*b*) the emblematic setpiece; and (*c*) the plot that hinges on magical necessity. These ideologemes reveal contradictions latent in the contemporary social discourses surrounding sexuality, ethnicity, and the commodification of culture, respectively. Further, each of these nodes is shared by the proletarian novel and the Alger stories, and West's choice to exploit them reveals ways in which the proletarian cultural project was continuous with mass culture. In this respect, then, *A Cool Million* illustrates the negotiations among cultural formations characteristic of the suburb of dissent.

The Gentle Boy, Whitman, and the Worker

In *A Cool Million,* then, West inverts Alger's prototypical plot; all of West's hero's efforts to succeed lead only to pain. This inversion addresses the social role that Alger's stories played during the Depression—the role of lessening middle-class "shame" about "failing." The hero who moves West's plot forward, however, is less the inversion of Alger's hero than an exaggerated type of the weak proletarian hero.

In a persuasive explication of Alger's fictions, Michael Moon has argued that their "boy ideal" is the locus of a "generative contradiction" between late-nineteenth-century social discourses on gentility and the "dangerous classes."[13] Alger's boy heroes typically combine the physical handsomeness of a gentleman with the hygiene and clothing of the ragged poor. That is, Alger's stories begin with the disparity between "the gentle boy" and the dangerous proletarian, and they proceed until the boy has risen to the petit-bourgeois social plane for which his handsomeness befits him. Especially in the early stages of this process, the narrator is positioned as a homoerotic spectator who decodes the meaning of boyish beauty.

When framed in this way, Alger's gentle heroes rightly appear to be attempts to resolve some of the contradictions inherent in a nostalgic, ethical interpretation of the economic system. By insisting that it is wrong to leave deserving (i.e., potentially petit-bourgeois) boys in the gutter, Alger's narrator implies that the boys' virtues were appreciated in some previous natural aristocracy.[14] This view, however, involves a continual displacement of social harmony backward into an imagined past, and it means transmuting systemic economic problems into an individual matter of virtue. Alger attempts to paper over these troubling displacements with an appeal to beauty. In his stories, the boy's beauty is the sign of his timeless spiritual depth, of his lasting moral worthiness. In other words, Alger solves the conflict between past and present, and between individual and social virtue, by positing the body as mediator. The problem, however, is that this resolution sponsors a new crisis: the possibility that the bodily beauty of the boy will enter into a narrative of seduction, rather than remaining outside narrative as the permanent symbol of virtue.

With this understanding of Alger's "gentle boy" ideologeme, it is clear that West's hero Lemuel Pitkin is a parodic exaggeration, rather than a simple reversal, of its social role. As already noted, West mercilessly attacks the body of his hero—reducing him to such a toothless, eyeless, thumbless, legless, and scalpless state that any question of his handsomeness is moot. By dismantling his hero while insisting all along that Lemuel was "refusing to be discouraged or grow bitter and become a carping critic of things as they are," West prohibits any analogy between physical and moral conditions (171). He makes Alger's appeal to beauty an impossibility.

At the same time, West accentuates the homoerotic subtext of the Alger novels and the crisis of repressed desire that this subtext introduces. To parody both a genteel horror of homosexuality (or, more specifically, pederasty) and the genteel discourse of "saving" boys that structures pederastic desire in Alger's novels, West inserts a scene in which Lemuel impersonates a gay prostitute. Midway through the novel, Lem is captured by pimps and prepared for an encounter with an Indian prince with a lisp: "My, wath a pithy thailer boy," his admirer remarks, in one of the only positive references to Lem's appearance. This potential seduction breaks down, however, as soon as Lemuel's body does. When Lemuel "realized what was expected of him, he turned pale with horror," and his false teeth fell out of his mouth. This event terminates the prince's desire (131). At this moment, the prince's and Lemuel's horrors appear isomorphic; each panics when asked to place the body in a new narrative—be it one of seduction or one of dismemberment. West reveals the limits of the "gentle boy" ideologeme implicit in Alger's stories; it literally falls apart when openly confronted with the implicit seduction narrative.

I do not read West's attack on Alger's gentility in this scene, however, as a resistance to homoerotic desire generally. Instead, West is demonstrating that this particular version of homoeroticism depends on the repression of the commodity form. The punchline of the scene relies on the fact that Lemuel's seemingly "real" teeth are manmade and, worse yet, exchangeable, replaceable. When knowledge of their status as an object of exchange becomes inescapable, Lemuel can no longer function as the perfectly unified beautiful body, that is, as the object of the prince's desire. Thus, the breakdown of this moment of homoerotic desire is identified with the critical exposure of the mechanism of capitalist exchange.

Furthermore, within the ideologeme of the "gentle boy," interchangeability also has another resonance; it highlights the fact that West has self-consciously chosen Alger's genteel hero over the favorite hero of contemporary leftists: the muscular worker. The year after West's novel was published, Kenneth Burke made his famous critique of the worker symbol, claiming that it repulsed the American masses and should be replaced with the symbol of "the people." [15] Burke, too, highlighted the interchangeability of ideologemes. Like Alger's "gentle boy," the "worker" symbol was sufficiently reified by the mid-1930s to be exchangeable.

Usually, the worker symbol was considered the negation of the gentle hero. In a pivotal review of Thornton Wilder's work, for instance, the prominent Communist critic Mike Gold objected to the "genteel spirit" of Wilder's plays and novels. In his words, Wilder offered "a daydream of homosexual figures in graceful gowns moving archaically among the lilies"; Gold ridiculed Wilder's cosmopolitanism, his infatuation with the past, his "irritating and pretentious style pattern," and, above all, his inability "to express America." These weaknesses are contrasted to Gold's admiration for "the intoxicated Emerson, . . . the clean, rugged Thoreau, or vast Whitman." In Gold's lineup, the latter group of writers represents the native virility and truth-telling style necessary for descriptions of contemporary America. [16]

Ironically, Whitman was the author most often proposed as an antidote to the bourgeois "daydream of homosexual figures"; for theorists of the proletarian novel as for literary historians, Whitman was "a great figure, the greatest assuredly in our literature," "the founder of the new American literature," and "the first genuine force in the creation of an American art." [17] Leftists of the 1930s saw Whitman as an important forerunner of their own projects; for them, Whitman represented the "worker" and not Alger's genteel hero.

The irony of this choice was not lost on West, who includes a parody of this macho representation of Whitman in *A Cool Million*. Of course, as a parodist, West does not correct Gold's misrepresentation of Whitman by comparing it to a more biographically accurate portrait of the poet. Instead, he juxtaposes the macho image to a slightly older representation: West's Whitman figure, Sylvanus Snodgrasse, is distinguished "by his long black hair which tumbled in waves over the back of his collar and by an unusually high and broad forehead. On his head he wore a soft, black hat with an enormously wide brim. Both his tie, which was Windsor, and his gestures, which were Latin, floated with the same graceful freedom as his hair" (106). As others have noted, this

description clearly recalls the 1855 frontispiece to *Leaves of Grass*.[18] This walking lithograph approaches Lemuel and proposes to write an ode about him "in
the real American tradition." "Fie on your sickly Prousts," he exclaims, "U.S.
poets must write about the U.S." Obviously, the point of such a passage is that
Snodgrasse's own expression of a virile, heterosexual American nativism is a
pickup line. This point is followed by a brief parody of Whitman's style—especially his famous "vastness," which he shows to be a matter of assembling clichés that describe Greece as "immortal" or Rome as "the eternal city." In short,
Snodgrasse is a drag Whitman who exposes the repressed model of gender and
sexuality underlying the proletarian novel.

So, West's Whitman figure shows how the proletarian novel overlaps with
Alger's stories. With this point in mind, we can locate this overlap in other 30s
writings. For example, *Jews without Money* (1930)—Mike Gold's own attempt
to write a proletarian novel—also explores the gentle boy ideologeme. *Jews* is
the largely autobiographical story of a smart little boy coming of age in New
York's East Side tenements. The novel is structured around a character with
the potential for rising "above" his circumstances, and this character is explicitly marked as heroic because of his weakness/childishness—not his manly
virility. In fact, on the final pages of the novel, the narrator remarks that he
has purposefully excluded the painful transition into virile manhood from his
account: "At times I seriously thought of cutting my throat. At other times I
dreamed of running away to the far west. Sex began to torture me. I developed
a crazy religious streak. I prayed on the tenement roof in moonlight to the Jewish Messiah who would redeem the world. . . . And I worked. And my father
and mother grew sadder and older. It went on for years. I don't want to remember it all; the years of my adolescence."[19] These are the fears and fantasies
that preceded the author-figure's conversion to the "workers' Revolution . . .
the true Messiah"; and they reveal the same strains that Alger's boy is designed
to resolve. The disparity between the Messiah and work, between ethics and
economics, is the central conflict of the novel, and here, too, the conflict is
resolved through reference to the body. For Gold, however, the truth of the
body is pain, not beauty. Gold's hero contemplates suicide; sex is a "torture"
for him; and he cannot be saved. At one point, the hero is beaten by a possible
benefactor, a Hebrew schoolteacher who "was cruel as a jailer . . . [and] had
a sadist's delight in pinching boys with his long pincer fingers; he was always
whipping special offenders with his cat-o-nine-tails" (43). In short, in Gold's

narrative, "saving" the "gentle worker" is an act of sadism, and, as in Alger's stories, the seduction of the boy results in a new crisis—the fleeting entertainment of homoerotic desire.

West, however, rejects the appeal to pathos on which Gold's accusation of sadism rests. In fact, he parodies Gold's kind of pathos in *A Cool Million*'s final scene. Reduced to utter destitution and severely dismantled, Lemuel takes a job as a stooge for a vaudeville act; his part in the show involves sitting quietly while comedians beat him with rolled-up newspapers until parts of his commodified body pop off. Then he chooses a replacement from a box in front of him, until the comedians demolish him with a huge hammer labeled "The Works" (172–73). Here, it is Lemuel's job to be gentle and, as in the earlier whorehouse scene, the joke lies in the interchangeability of his parts. In this scene, however, the point is not to induce and parody horror but to prohibit pathetic identification. West insists on the fact that the spectators were "convulsed with joy" at the sight of Lemuel's suffering (174). Instead of allowing the reader to empathize with the humiliated hero, West makes the reader a victim of his irony. He forces the reader to laugh at the spectacle of suffering until the reader becomes uncomfortable with the fact that suffering has been made the subject of a vaudeville show.[20]

Then, in one last twist, West displays the limits of ironic victimhood. The possibly infinite regression of the audience's increasing self-consciousness stops only when the show stops. After demonstrating great endurance, Lemuel stands up to deliver a speech: " 'I am a clown,' he began, 'but there are times when even clowns must grow serious. This is such a time. I . . .' Lem got no further. A shot rang out and he fell dead, drilled through the heart by an assassin's bullet" (177; West's ellipsis). This attempt at self-articulation marks the end of the ideologeme of the "gentle boy/worker" and the end of the audience dynamics perpetuated by that hero. When the hero ceases to be the mere bearer of ideology and begins to articulate ideology, the novel shifts toward the ideologeme of the didactic setpiece.

Thus, through the hybrid ideologeme of the "gentle boy" placed in the position of the "worker," West unravels—or, better, dismantles—the resolutions to social contradictions offered by Alger and the proletarian novelists, and, instead of offering even "the clown" as an alternative hero, he relentlessly disallows any resolution. Each hero, he implies, generates more contradictions than can safely be contained—and not least of these, for West, is the representation of a pederastic desire that requires the commodification of pathos. Therefore, to locate any more workable imaginary resolution to the contradictions of the Depression we must turn our attention away from the ideologeme of the hero.

Ethnicity in the "House of Nations"

As Gary Scharnhorst has noted, West had to invent the fascist diatribes in *A Cool Million,* since Alger did not write characters who mouthed "political manifestos" or who were articulators as well as bearers of ideology.[21] However, this invention does not mean that the Alger stories were free from didactic setpieces. On the contrary, Michael Moon has persuasively argued that the boardinghouses where Alger's heroes congregate represent Alger's fantasy about the source of social regeneration.[22] In these scenes, Alger reformulates the nineteenth-century rhetoric of domesticity that considered the family and the home as centers of power. Alger transplants the genteel "home" of domestic fiction to cheap New York boardinghouses, and the many setpieces distinguishing among different levels of boardinghouses function as markers of the ideologeme of the "family." Thus, the family unit in Alger's story remains the locus of reproduction, although it is a reproduction that specifically does not involve women. Alger's "family" is all male, and the cohesion of this homogenous group often depends on tricks played on peripheral female figures. With these alterations, Alger adjusts the domestic family to his own purposes.

The structure of Alger's version of the family ideologeme is duplicated in the proletarian novel. Descriptions of the camps set up by strikers in proletarian novels such as *The Disinherited* and *Strike!* parallel the boardinghouses; they are public spaces established outside of the traditionally female-controlled space of the home, and they unify another family predominately composed of men —the Party or the union. As with Alger, the continuation of the new "home" generally depends on magical reproductions of the social unit, and, finally, women appear in these novels most often either in the character of the Revolutionary Girl or the Great Mother. The former is usually made a martyr of some type, while the latter is generally grieving for the loss of a heroic son.[23] In other words, here, too, the "family" ideologeme represents women as the victims of a homoerotic conflict/contract among men. When women wrote proletarian novels—as quite a number of them did—they usually revised this pattern, but their revisions restored the motherly roles accorded to women in the domestic parables more often than they imagined alternatives to the family.[24]

For West, however, the troubling aspect of Alger's and the proletarian novelists' family ideologeme was not its gender homogeneity. Although the many rape scenes in *A Cool Million* draw attention to the traffic in women in these genres, West's more pressing concern is with ethnic homogeneity. Throughout his novel, West deploys vicious stereotypes of many ethnic groups—but especially Jews—in order to comment on the conditions of their production. That is, he demonstrates how the "family" ideologeme comes to represent ethnically homogenous social and national collectivities.

The family appears at several sites in *A Cool Million,* but most prominently in Wu Fong's house of prostitution. The descriptions of this house are self-consciously marked as episodic intrusions by the narrator: "Let me now say that Wu Fong's establishment was no ordinary house of ill fame," and "Before I take up where I left off in my last chapter, there are several changes in Wu Fong's establishment which I would like to report," he remarks (93, 126). These passages are set off from the picaresque flow of the narrative, and the attention to the decorations of rooms in the whorehouse indicates that the house is a site rich in codes. There are setpieces figuring the formation of intentional communities that stand in for the family.

Since West refuses to adopt the pathetic mode, these scenes do not focus on the degradation of female prostitutes and the suffering they endure. Instead, the whorehouse is named the "House of All Nations," and the scandal it provokes is the marketing of ethnicity.[25] The house initially features girls from different nations situated in rooms decorated, by a Jewish antique dealer, in the styles of their homelands. Wu Fong, the Chinese proprietor, is particularly pleased to acquire a "genuine American," as she is sure to be a favorite with his non-Aryan clients. He quickly installs her in "a perfect colonial interior," dresses her in a brown chintz gown, and has "an old Negro in livery" serve her buckwheat cakes for breakfast. In other words, the House of All Nations is also the house of all racist clichés.

Among the ironies explored in this setpiece is the regulation of racial purity within the "family" of Americans. West makes it obvious that producing this stereotype of the genuinely American interior requires deploying the concomitant stereotypes of the greedy Jew, the crafty Oriental, and "the darky" (94). Placing this version of national character in a whorehouse also suggests that this racist typecasting is not an incidental by-product of the economic system but is, in fact, the commodity being sold; non-WASP clients like the Indian prince purchase the sign of the very ideology that peripheralizes them when they visit the prostitutes. Their desires make them complicitous in their own exclusion. By emphasizing complicity, West is also suggesting that readers do more than sympathize with the victims of racial exclusion, as is evident in his treatment of Jews throughout the novel. West insistently positions Jewish businessmen behind the other racist stereotypes he is parodying: Asa Goldstein, the ubiquitous antique dealer, provides the furnishings for the "House of All Nations"; Ezra Silverblatt is the official tailor of a fascist party; and Seth Abromovitz helps run a legal system that favors New England Christians. These characters do not suggest that Jewish greed is responsible for the production of racism, as some have argued; instead, they demonstrate some of the contradictions involved in marketing assimilation to an ethnically diverse population.[26] West insists on the imaginary character of the "family" of nations.

Of course, this kind of association between prostitution and a corrupt moral and economic system was a well-established literary tradition by the 1930s. Major writers of the realist and naturalist schools, such as Zola, Maupassant, Crane, and Dreiser, to name only a few, had already made famous use of this association, and West's whorehouse might be understood as a reference to their work. The prostitution image has also been central to Marxist theory; one recalls the famous comparison of the wife and the prostitute in Engels's *The Origin of Family, Private Property and the State*.[27] In the 1930s, many left-leaning critics drew on this comparison in their analyses of mass culture; castigating the products of Hollywood and Tin Pan Alley as kitsch, they preferred the supposedly more authentic products of precapitalist American culture. For instance, many leftist novelists, cultural critics, and musicians considered Appalachian folk music an innate cry for justice that represented the *a priori* fusion of authentic Americanism and radicalism.[28] Prostitution and corrupt ethnic stereotyping were generally opposed to narratives favoring authenticity.

This context helps explain West's second description of Wu Fong's establishment. Inspired by the Hearst papers' "Buy American" campaign, Wu Fong redecorates the "House of All Nations" in strictly American motifs. These include "Pennsylvania Dutch, Old South, Log Cabin Pioneer, Victorian New York, Western Cattle Days, California Monterey, Indian, and Modern Girl," and each room is furnished authentically and occupied by a genuine representative of the version of Americanism being marketed (126). The primary irony of the scene lies in the extension of the logic of the ethnicity market: the "Buy American" campaign includes buying American girls. But it is also important that so many rooms are required to represent genuine Americanness; the authentic folk identity comes in eight flavors. Furthermore, West is explicit about the fact that among these folk identities some are less acceptable than others; the California Monterey girl, Wu Fong predicts, "was bound to be a losing proposition. The style, he said was not obviously enough American even in its most authentic form" (127). Clearly, in West's view, an appeal to native or folk culture as an antidote to degenerate mass culture might also be "a losing proposition," since not all folk cultures are created equal.

Finally, on the issue of folk authenticity, West's trump card is indigenous culture. West refuses to allow even Native American "nativism" to represent a comfortable authenticity. Not only does Wu Fong's marketplace of ethnicity include an "Indian" room, but also West associates the major Native American character with the theses of his own European intellectual heroes, Spengler and Valéry.[29] He also endows this character with a name, Israel Satinpenny, that suggests he is entangled in the same cycles of complicitous production of his own oppression as the Jewish businessmen. In sketching Satinpenny's background, he suggests that the chief realized the value of his native heritage only through a Europhilic education at Harvard. By the time all these details culminate in Satinpenny's long didactic speech denouncing the "surfeit of shoddy" in Euro-American civilization, it is clear that for West a folk or ethnic authenticity is always self-conscious and hybrid, if not actually complicit in its own prostitution. Even the Native American cannot stand as the figure of the untainted authentic folk.

In the end, after replacing the folk/family ideologeme with that of prostitution, West reinvents the family at just the site that a Satinpenny would least expect. In the elaborate setpiece describing the Chamber of American Horrors, Animate and Inanimate Hideosities, he takes an up-close look at the "shoddy" mass culture that Satinpenny descries and examines its utopian potential. This chamber is the site of an Algeresque "family" reunion; after a long separation, Lemuel and his official benefactor, Shagpoke Whipple, meet up with an old Native American friend and with the notorious Sylvanus Snodgrasse. The only person missing is, typically enough, Betty Prail, the "genuine American" prostitute. The site of this reformulated family is also explicitly marked as a reworking of the leftist thesis on folk culture when the narrator remarks that the contents of the chamber included "innumerable objects culled from the popular art of the country and of an equally large number of manufactured articles" (162). The animate portion of the chamber—a brief sentimental play-let and a pageant involving the sadomasochistic beating of Quakers—provides West with yet another occasion to parody the pathetic voice of the proletarian novels. Linking the animate and inanimate portions of the chamber, we are told, was the responsibility of Sylvanus Snodgrasse, the Whitmanesque poet. He made "a little speech in which he claimed that the former had resulted in the latter." These outright statements of the Marxist analysis of commodity fe-tishism "were not very convincing, however," the narrator adds (164), and so West rapidly dispenses with a major aesthetic problem that plagued the pro-letarian novel—how to articulate a didactic message. West baldly states that the didactic speech is as inadequate as Alger's family, the proletarian folk, and the pathetic playlet in articulating a critique of commodity culture. For West, the inanimate objects are capable of demonstrating their own hideosity on their own terms.

What then are these objects? West draws our attention to plaster sculptures, a gigantic artificial hemorrhoid, trompe l'oeils—such as paper that looked like wood, "wood like rubber, rubber like steel, steel like cheese, cheese like glass, and, finally, glass like paper"—and instruments with multiple or camouflaged purposes—such as "pencil sharpeners that could also be used as earpicks, can openers as hair brushes . . . flowerpots that were really victrolas, revolvers that held candy, candy that held collar buttons and so forth" (163). While the speeches and plays failed to demonstrate anything of significance to their audiences, through a mere description of these objects, West displays the magi-cal transformations they effect. Most importantly, the objects are arranged in regressions that become circles (from "paper" to "paper"); that is, the trans-formations of the inanimate objects parallel the transformation of living labor into commodities. By arranging the objects in this way, West suggests that they offer an immanent critique of the methods of their own production. They are "the popular art of the country," and they alone will voice the innate "cry for justice" associated with folk culture.

In *A Cool Million,* passages such as the Chamber of Hideosities—the setpieces that are inanimate portions of the novel's plot—indicate the closing of the "family" ideologeme. By this point in the novel, West has amply demonstrated that the sexually and racially homogenous "family" is, at best, an unstable resolution to the contradictions of a national folk culture, since that "family" is always marketed. The family—be it a homogenous or heterogeneous domestic arrangement, or a union—is not outside the market, and it projects an ethnic exterior to compensate for its own implication in the market. Jews, women, and African Americans are all, for West, victims of the contradictions of the family ideologeme, and the only authentic alternative he can offer rests on the inanimate objects of mass culture, because these display the transformative power at the root of American consumer culture. However, to understand how and why West is using these objects, we must turn to the narrative device that is most concerned with transformation and magic: the plot.

Magic Wishes and the Conclusion

It is well known—or, I should say, often assumed—that both Alger's stories and proletarian novels employ plot formulas.[30] The aesthetic faux pas of the formula is, supposedly, that it makes outcomes obvious and predictable—that it reduces narratives of possible freedom to narratives of necessity—and therefore reveals itself too obviously as the result of ideology. In Alger's novels, the formulaic qualities become obvious when the "family" of men begins to reproduce. As Michael Moon has demonstrated, this reproduction is essentially magical; Alger's boy heroes acquire little boy babies through mysterious agencies, and they watch their money increase through the fetishistic properties of "interest."[31] A similar event occurs in the proletarian novel. There, the reproduction of the union "family" generally requires an equally mystical conversion of a major character to the cause of labor—or an unlikely victory on the part of the strikers. The conclusion to Gold's *Jews without Money* can serve as our example here: "O workers' Revolution, you brought hope to me, a lonely suicidal boy. . . . O Revolution that forced me to think, to struggle and to live. O great Beginning!" (224). This apostrophe is posited as a miraculous salvation and a tautology. The novel's last word, "Beginning," leads us to believe that the circle is completed, that an initial premise has been fulfilled.

Although Gold's tautology and Alger's differ in their content (one returning us to childhood and the other to a spiritual origin), they are structurally similar. In each case, the novel concludes with a wish-fulfillment. For some, this structure calls up a contradiction between the realist and utopian strains, since the articulations of the wish and the fulfillment take place on different planes.[32] If, however, you consider narratives as always resolving and provoking contradictions, these wish-fulfillment plots might not appear to be aesthetic failures as much as they seem bearers of residual utopian desire. In addition to straining the realist aesthetic, the "magic" ideologeme that concludes these narratives joins a myth of freedom to a plot of necessity.

West was interested in both freedom and necessity and their magical joining. He demonstrates that the reproduction of "interest" is by no means the realm of freedom when he repeatedly calculates the debts Lemuel incurs in his bouts with the law: "Suppose you had obtained a job in New York City that paid fifteen dollars a week," a warden tells him. "You were here with us in all twenty weeks, so you lost the use of three hundred dollars. However, you paid no board while you were here, which was a saving for you of about seven dollars a week," and so on (99). These figures never add up in Lemuel's favor, and the accumulation of debt inverts the necessary accumulation of interest that structures Alger's novels.

Similarly, West parodies the basic necessities of the proletarian plot simply by changing the ideology of the victorious party. While in the proletarian novels, the Communists are supposed to win, in *A Cool Million,* the fascists are triumphant. The novel's last scene is a political rally called by the ex-president, Shagpoke Whipple, who proclaims that "through the National Revolution [America's] people were purged of alien diseases and America became again American" (179). The occasion for this vicious tautology is Lemuel Pitkin's birthday, since, after his assassination in the theater, Lemuel became a national hero; he became "the American Boy."

At the most literal level, this scene parodies the leftists' wish-fulfillment by insisting that their narrative necessities apply equally well to fascist circumstances, but, more generally, it also points to the role that magical transformations play in the production of wishes and their fulfillment. The real targets of West's ironic energies in this scene are the codes used to celebrate the now mythic Lemuel Pitkin. West mimics the pompous voice affected by parade commentators; he parodies the inverted grammar, the serious caesuras, the martial vocabulary, and even the apostrophical "oh"'s of Gold's novel in the "Lemuel Pitkin Song." Finally, a eulogizing oratory concludes the novel: "Simple was his pilgrimage and brief, yet a thousand years hence, no story, no tragedy, no epic poem will be filled with greater wonder, or be followed by mankind with deeper feeling, than that which tells of the life and death of Lemuel Pitkin" (179). This passage simultaneously deflates bloated and sentimental nationalistic rhetoric, groans at the superb obviousness of circular narratives such as Gold's, and indicates that West is interested not so much in Pitkin as in the story, tragedy, and epic poem that tell his life. The transformation of *A Cool Million*'s hero into myth ironically fulfills the novel's initial wish—that Lemuel succeed. Of course, he succeeds on a different plane than usual. He becomes the story of success, and his apotheosis becomes the last in a series of magical transformations. Like the inanimate paper that turns into glass, or the victrola that was really a revolver, Lemuel's story emblematizes the stories, tragedies, and epic poems that articulate and fulfill wishes. His transformation from penniless nobody to emblem for the nation demonstrates that transformation is a basic unit of narrative; it is transformation that leads to a feeling of closure. This, in turn, allows us to see how narratives themselves transform into something quite different; Lem's story shows that Alger can become proletarian as easily as a victrola can become a revolver. When this transformation continues, until the proletarian novel becomes a folk tale, and the folk tale becomes mass culture, and mass culture is exemplified by Horatio Alger, the structure of West's novel emerges. West constructs a regression that becomes a circle and so parodies the engagement of Alger and the proletarian novelists in the same cycle of commodification. By pushing his readers toward this metafictional plane, West reveals narrative to be a culturally determined object, and in that knowledge lingers the faintest trace of utopian possibility.

West and the Left: Revising Literary Periodization

In sum, then, with his interest in Whitman, the family, and commodification, Nathanael West was very much in sync with "his age" and not—as Fiedler and others have asserted—a rebel genius isolated from his peers. West was engaged in major debates of his period over the comparative merits of folk, mass, and proletarian cultures, and his definitions and symbols of these cultures all demonstrate his contemporaneity. Furthermore, his most prominent theme— an aesthetic outrage at the commodification of culture—is fueled by the Marxist critique of fetishism, while West used leftist modes of writing to dismantle the ideologemes employed by his left- and right-wing contemporaries.

Also, as the revisionist narratives of John Dos Passos and Richard Wright demonstrate, this posture of being more Marxist than the Communists is itself a signal of West's embeddedness in his age. The position has long been associated with the *Partisan Review* of the late 1930s and 1940s, but increasingly we now recognize that the editors of this journal were not alone in launching internal criticisms of leftist culture. Especially in the late thirties, an array of writers such as Josephine Herbst, Edmund Wilson, Nelson Algren, Kenneth Burke, S. J. Perelman, and many others took sides with neither *Partisan Review* nor the Communist *New Masses*—choosing instead to explore a variety of positions along the periphery of the officially committed left. Like these writers, West worked out a different sense of commitment than is generally associated with the 1930s today—a sense that twenty-twenty hindsight may suggest was a central feature of "his age." This commitment did not involve sacrificing literary quality to political utility, or individual originality to collective mediocrity. Instead, writers like West spent the 1930s thinking through the terms of these oppositions, struggling in their work to resolve these contradictions, and struggling in their lives to ameliorate them. West's career demonstrates that, like members of any minority culture, leftists of the thirties were a varied lot, and they experimented with many different kinds and degrees of "commitment." In retrospect, West's own avant-gardist stance is only one of the more interesting versions of this common project.

Chapter 9

THE EMERGENCE OF PUBLIC CULTURE

Dorothy Livesay's Documentary Poems

For the most part, both the periodical writings and *A Cool Million*—like most leftist writings from the 1930s—have been judged "failures" by critics trained under the influence of New Criticism. The efforts of leftist writers to transform the territory between mass culture and the avant-garde have seemed less successful to critics than the more formally sophisticated projects of European modernists. But one genre produced in the 1930s has not fared quite so poorly in the critical world: the documentary. In fact, in popular culture, the 1930s (or more properly, the "Depression") continues to be represented almost entirely through the filter of the documentary lens.

This is not to say that documentaries have not been criticized—for their sentimentality, for their sociological bent, or, later, for their epistemology. They have, and generally the history of the documentary, like that of the 1930s, is a tragic narrative. However, the failure attributed to the documentary is not the same type of failure attributed to other genres from the 1930s. The documentary's failure is generally understood to be formal, as much as political. Thus, most histories of documentary conclude that James Agee and Walker Evans's explosion of the form in *Let Us Now Praise Famous Men* (1941) is the highest achievement of the form. For example, Alfred Kazin sees *Praise* as "a revolt against the automatism of the documentary school . . . an attack on the facile mechanics and passivity of most documentary assignments," while William Stott writes that it "culminates the central rhetoric of the time, and explodes it, surpasses it, shows it up."[1] In this view, Agee and Evans sublated the possibilities of the documentary, and, when the thirties waned, that form mercifully gave way to more complex and less tendentious aesthetic projects. Also, at that point, the left-wing politics and culture associated with the documentary were supposedly happily subsumed under the broader banner of liberal anti-Communism.

However, if we tell the story of the documentary in a manner that is not circumscribed by the category of nation—that is, if we tell the story of 30s documentaries, in particular, so that this narrative includes Canada—Kazin's and Stott's conclusion is not so self-evident. In Canada, the documentary was not so easily equatable with self-righteous Northerners' attempts to exploit the poverty of rural, black Southerners for political purposes, nor did its form prove an aesthetic dead end. In fact, most of the major Canadian writers of the 1930s experimented with some form of documentary at one point or another; most struggled to establish a relationship to the "real" that would fall outside the generic patterns of realism and act in a transformative, dialectical manner on the reader. F. R. Scott's parodies of the genteel orthodoxy of the Canadian Authors Association, Morley Callaghan's Catholic social realism, and Dorothy Livesay's documentary poetry all bear witness to this effort. Of these, Livesay's is the most significant for our purposes, since her documentary work emerged most directly from her accumulated literary and political experiences in the 1930s. Furthermore, Livesay's work proved an important link between the cultural experiments of the 1930s and the more prolific Canadian literary community of the postwar years. Livesay was a prominent figure in Canadian literary life both before and after World War II, although she was not afforded quite as much recognition as perhaps would have been hers in a less masculinist and prose-centered critical environment.[2] Nonetheless, Livesay has worked consistently to make room for a responsible, committed, imaginative, and internationalist left-wing literature in Canada. Here, I will focus on her development in the prize-winning volume *Day and Night* (1944) of a documentary aesthetic that combined elements from mass culture and the avant-garde and laid the groundwork for a new cultural formation—something I am calling a "public" culture.

Discovering Documentary

In one of her several autobiographical writings, Livesay offers the following account of her Columbian discovery of the documentary aesthetic:

> All these three social work years I had abandoned writing any poetry which was personal. But in New Jersey, so near New York, in trips to

> Greenwich bookshops I delved about—perhaps seeking some relief from the orthodox Marxian literature I had been consuming for so long— *Masses, The Daily Worker,* and countless pamphlets and political tracts along with some heavier economics and Engels, Lenin and Stalin. What was my astonishment and unbelief to find some slim volumes of English poetry—revolutionary poetry but full of lyricism and personal passion! C. Day Lewis first, then Spender, then Auden and MacNeice. There was nothing like it in America or Canada, but it was a movement that followed exactly where I had left off with my Paris thesis—it threw Eliot aside and proclaimed a brave new world. I think I must have wept over this discovery, but there was no one of my friends and comrades who would have taken any interest in it. All I could do was write a poem myself, celebrating the new horizon.[3]

In a pattern followed by many North American intellectuals, Livesay represents herself as a New World adventurer who crosses imaginary oceans to reconquer Europe and, in particular, England. At the same time, as we might expect, such a narrative of discovery also involves a certain amount of evasion; Livesay finds it necessary to avoid recognition of Genevieve Taggard, Muriel Rukeyser, Langston Hughes, John Wheelwright, Sherry Mangan, A. M. Klein, F. R. Scott, Leo Kennedy, and the many other contemporaneous North American poets who would doubtless object to her statement that "there was nothing like [Auden et al.] in America or Canada." And, like the Puritans who invented storybook tales in which the "Indians" were delighted to receive them, she rather blithely assumes in this account that the English poets did not have their own cultural conflicts, that they easily "threw Eliot aside." Furthermore, we can detect an element of self-aggrandizement in the claim that "there was no one of my friends and comrades who would have taken any interest in" the new poetry.[4] With these qualifications in mind, however, Livesay's statements still reveal something interesting about her poetic evolution. For her, it was important to emphasize the solitary, innovative aspects of her discovery of "revolutionary poetry." We can see that Livesay needed to tilt the dialectic between "personal" and "public" voices often understood to be the generative contradiction of her work.[5] She explains the appeal of the English writers by setting their "personal passion and lyricism" against the "orthodox Marxian literature" she had been reading—and against her own youthful "personal" poetry. The conclusion she suggests is that the old personalism has been transformed;

the British writers' "personal passion" promises her a "brave new world" or a "new horizon." Of course, by 1977, the year this account of her discovery was published, the phrase "brave new world" necessarily brought Aldous Huxley's dystopian novel by that name to mind, and Livesay's use of this phrase also functions in part as a disclaimer for her youthful enthusiasm for Stalinism. However, this familiar post–New Left qualification should not obscure the equally utopian strain of her poetic discovery. For Livesay, discovering the Auden group meant adding another continent to her map of cultural geography. Their work added a "new horizon" to her world and offered her a new poetic destination.

Also, all discussion of Livesay's metaphoric travel aside, we should note that this shift in aesthetic was associated with a new physical and cultural location: this redrawing of mental maps took place in New Jersey and would probably not have had the same impact on her if she had stumbled across C. Day Lewis and Auden in Toronto. In New Jersey, Livesay seems to have had a strong sense of herself as a foreigner. In particular, by her account, this cultural relocation involved a heightened racial consciousness. In her memoirs and poems about the United States, and in a radio play entitled "The Times Were Different," she comments on the discrimination against African Americans that represented to her the worst aspects of U.S. culture. An important aspect of these scenes, however, is that Livesay consistently recounts these "public" problems in terms of her "personal" experiences. She describes a landlady making racist comments after Livesay had invited an African American friend to her apartment, and she intimates that a young coworker fell in love with her to spite their boss's fears of miscegenation.[6] In other words, the traveler's sense of anecdote became central to her interpretation of the new poetic; she uses the tension between her personal experiences and public issues to describe the culture of the United States. In particular, by concentrating on the lack of fit between her "personal" feelings and foreigners' presumptions about her personality (like the landlady, white Americans seem generally to have assumed that she would share their racism), Livesay transforms the role of the personal in her writing; she makes her personal sense of alienation a matter of public interest.

This shift points to ways in which Livesay reformulates the concerns of the documentary prose writers. In her poetry of the late 1930s and early 1940s, she posits the "real" at the base of Canadian realism less often in terms of spatial location and land; instead, developing her New Jersey "discovery," she turns to experiments with cultural consciousness as a site of resistance. Also, her concern with the issues of "personal" versus "public" culture helps her to evade the subject/object split so evident in many U.S. writings of the period. For Livesay, the problem of the writer's position in mass culture was displaced by the question of how to represent the many, simultaneous voices of the public. Her efforts in this direction took shape in what she called documentary poetry—a form that refers less to the experiments in documentary fiction than to film and, especially in Livesay's work, to music.[7]

In a critical essay published in 1971, when Livesay was working toward a Ph.D. in Canadian literature, she argues that the documentary poem is "deeply representative of the Canadian character."[8] A dialectic between facts and feelings, this genre requires research as well as social concern and generally involves a long narrative structure with a topical theme. Its basic elements, Livesay asserts, are "descriptive, lyrical and didactic" modes of writing. These ultimately combine, forming the documentary voice—which she also identifies strongly with the situation of the Depression: "it could be proved that since the 1930s our narratives have followed the experimentations originally made by [National Film Board director, John] Grierson in film: they are documentaries to be heard aloud, often specifically for radio." In other words, Livesay specifically identifies documentary poetry with a transformative use of the mass media; it represents to her a socially committed combination of residual oral traditions and the dominant technologies of culture. From these contradictions, the documentary draws its ability to address an emergent public culture.

Livesay's essay traces a genealogy of documentary poetry in Canada—beginning with nineteenth-century poet Isabella Valancy Crawford and stretching through the early modernist poets such as E. J. Pratt to mid-twentieth-century realists such as Earle Birney and Anne Marriott. Throughout she makes frequent mention of her own documentary radio play, *Call My People Home*. Like her account of discovering Auden, however, this essay is probably less revealing as a literary-historical analysis or as an answer to the riddle of Canadian identity than as an indication of the ways in which Livesay wishes to remember and value her early work. Indeed, the terms Livesay uses to describe documentary poetry offer a most revealing synopsis of her poetic preoccupations during the thirties; her poems from this period can be logically grouped into "descriptive, lyrical and didactic" categories that culminate in the more widely appreciated documentary efforts of the 1940s and 1950s. Most of these earlier poems have received little critical attention to date, and examining them here should help clarify the significance of the documentary aesthetic for Livesay in particular and for the emergence of a new type of "public" culture generally. In the jumble of cultural contradictions evident in Livesay's New Jersey discovery lie hints of the cultural preoccupations of the postwar literary scene in North America.

The Proto-Documentary Poems: Voice Training

The poems I will examine in this section were the building blocks for Livesay's more famous work—most of which was published between 1944 and 1950, although written earlier; they were not all chronologically prior to the documentary works, but they are logically prior. That is, like the properly documentary poems, they are concerned with developing a new voice out of the contradictions of "personal" and "orthodox" materials—or out of what Margaret Atwood called Livesay's opposition between self and world.[9] However, in these proto-documentary poems the "public" voice is not fully developed. It occasionally conflicts with the "mass" voice—whether conceived of in the political sense as "the masses," or in the cultural sense as the object of mass media—and it sometimes stumbles under the weight of its own poetic heritage.

The most easily categorizable poems that Livesay wrote in the 1930s are the "descriptive" poems, of which "Depression Suite" is a fine example.[10] The suite consists of seven sections—each of which allows a precisely positioned voice to describe a primary dilemma; the voices range from "the wall, the enemy / Who keeps our hands from striking free" (177) to a middle-class "coward" to a harried secretary, a jilted vagabond, a deluded lumberjack, a modern Christ figure, and a radical poet. The poem first appeared under the title "Depression Suite" in the "Thirties" section of the *Collected Poems* (1972), which suggests that Livesay compiled what she considered various representative fragments from that period for the retrospective volume. The point of the poem is more descriptive than propagandistic, as the title indicates. The title distances the author from the material by insisting that its contents are historically situated in the "Depression," and the emphasis on the harmony of themes in this "Suite" focuses our attention on the structure, not the message. The poem's immediate social impact is not Livesay's primary concern.

Instead, the writing in this descriptive vein is sociological; Livesay experiments with the professional concerns and the linguistic conventions of the career in which she was employed throughout the 1930s: social work. This poem and others like it—poems that explore such matters as an unwed mother's hostility to her less than helpful boyfriend—report case histories. Of course, popularizing case histories was not a unique invention of Livesay's; a number of other 30s writers were experimenting in this vein, although usually in prose. Often these efforts attempted to dramatize social problems such as unemployment by narrating the dilemmas of particular individuals or families, and almost as often they found themselves stumbling against the boundaries of class. It was not unusual for middle-class social workers and writers to conclude that the life of the workers was finally inaccessible to them.[11]

In Livesay's work, however, the problem of class presented in the popularized case-history is as much a matter of writing as it is a sociopolitical one. For instance, in "Depression Suite," she explores the question of what is relevant to the standard narrative of the case history. She pares down the lives she describes to basic problems, so that the secretary's life story, for example, is suggested by the posture she adopts at her desk where "the fear / Like rigid tentacles, like arms / Gripping her back" (178), and the vagabond's condition is summarized by his hunger for sex. She ruthlessly condenses complex narratives to the physical needs. The relevant features of the case end up being only those that express what the social worker sees as the problem. In other words, Livesay's poem shows that the writer of a case history has difficulty negotiating the leap from the particular case to the general problem—usually with the result that the particular is reduced to the general. The secretary becomes the type of the secretary, and no other information about her is relevant to the form.

Livesay does not reproduce this problem unwittingly in her work. On the contrary, she made it the theme of "Case Supervisor," a short story contrasting roles available to social workers. Two basic types appear in the story: the sympathetic younger women who give extensively of their love and money without understanding the overall social problems, and the hardened bureaucrats who ultimately dehumanize themselves and their clients by scrimping on benefits to individuals for the sake of the greater good. These equally unattractive options both appear in "Depression Suite," first in the second section, where a silent, sympathetic observer wants to "nurse a little cloud / And yet not mention it aloud" (177), and later in the last section, where the poet's voice sets itself against a "skimpy relief investigator" (182) who underestimates the needs of her clients. In both "Case Supervisor" and "Depression Suite," these two types represent the two most common ways of solving the dilemma of the case history: the sentimental preference for the individual and the statistical attachment to the abstract. For Livesay, neither social work nor social science offered an entirely satisfactory means for describing a human life.

Although this dilemma limits the success of Livesay's case-history poems, it does allow her to develop one of her recurring motifs—the images of muted or thwarted voices.[12] If she could not describe another life fully from her vantage point as a social worker, she could describe her own troubled situation as a writer. As a result, silence, or the strangled word, is not a negative theme in her work; on the contrary, it reinforces her role as a poet. Valorizations of silence appear consistently in her work—from her early imagist poems on nature to the more assertively public social poetry of the 1930s and 1940s; for example, a poem of the mid-1930s entitled "Invitation to Silence" invites the reader to "hear the thunder of non-broadcast sounds."[13] Silence, in such a context, represents contact with the primary semiotic rhythms, not the absence of words or language; it is the basis of an authentic—here, "non-broadcast"—communication. As such poems indicate, ignoring the clutter of words and listening to silence is crucial to Livesay's aesthetic.

In "Depression Suite," the image that condenses the contradictory role of a writerly celebration of silence is the lavatory wall:

> If there are prayers, it is the walls
> That hear them, lavatory walls
> And smart swift taps that spurt.
>
> If there are tears, and cigarettes
> It is the walls that hold such
> And then erase the hurt.
>
> If there are girls who still have left a song
> The midnight scrubber does not heed
> But mops it up like dirt.
>
> This is the wall, the enemy
> Who keeps our hands from striking free. (177)

As the site where prayers and tears and cigarettes become "dirt," the wall represents the contradictions of displaying personal sorrow in the public bathroom. The wall hears the songs of weeping women and records them temporarily in a form of resistant graffiti—yet, it is also "the enemy." The wall's conventional resolution of the public/private split through anonymity does not work; it "keeps our hands from striking free." That is, the wall isolates the women and keeps them from striking together, because it substitutes graffiti for "song." Writing their protest on the wall is one of the only ways the women can express themselves, but, Livesay suggests, even as it allows the comfort of release, this act thwarts and silences them. The act of gripping the pen constricts their hands, substituting for the "striking" fist.

Such a suspicion of writing was not an unusual sentiment for Livesay to express in the mid-1930s; she claimed several times that she had ceased to write personally at all during this period. Recall the first line of Livesay's discovery narrative: "All these three social work years I had abandoned writing any poetry which was personal." It was more than apparent to her that describing a problem is not the same as solving it—even if the problem is how to express her own dilemma. Faced with the dead-end project of uniting private/personal and public/general realms of experience through simple description, she returned to modes which were suspect but familiar.

The second type of proto-documentary poems from the 1930s—the lyric poems—shares many of the virtues of the imagist poems in Livesay's first two collections, *Green Pitcher* (1928) and *Signpost* (1932). They use sure, precise, concentrated images; they cut directly to the point, and they stop just in time. Significantly, though, where the earlier poems generally describe the poet's desire for communion with nature or a lover, the poems of 1930s typically express appreciation for another voice. Most often the poet has lost contact with this voice and adopts an elegiac tone to mourn her loss. The lyric is then structured around a comparison of the present deprivation to a past or future fullness; the poem imagines a transition from personal loss to public fulfillment.[14]

This structure of concerns corresponded well with Livesay's interest at this time in the Spanish civil war. In her essay "Canadian Poetry and the Spanish Civil War," Livesay identifies three themes of the Spanish conflict: disgust with the Western powers' nonintervention, the Fascists' betrayal of the Christianity they claimed to espouse, and a view of the war as a final showdown between civilization and barbarism.[15] These political judgments reveal that Livesay, like many others, saw the war in Spain as a contest between "the world" (that is, Europe) and a set of noble ideals (the Loyalists' efforts to preserve democracy). Especially in the later years of the war, when the Soviet Union's politically motivated betrayals of the volunteer battalions were more widely known, the sense that one was living in a present deprived of the past's virtue must have been overwhelming, and, for a poet such as Livesay, the correspondence between this political situation and the basic structure of the lyric poem was more than obvious.

For Livesay, the assassination of Spanish poet Federico García Lorca provided an appropriate and timely subject for a lyric poem on Spain. Her elegy "Lorca" mourns the death of this radical poet's unifying voice and sets itself the task of reasserting connections between the sorry present and an ideal world.[16] The initial images evoke confinement, constriction, and loss: congealed veins, dead eyes being closed, beds shrinking "To single size," and a descent "down from heaven / Into earth's mould." Then, this world that lacks the poet's singing voice is opposed to a world of articulate possibility:

> If you were living now
> This cliffside tree
> And its embracing bough
> Would speak to me.

Briefly, in the next section, the poet's desire for Lorca's words leads to the marvelous sense that "You are alive!" in the simple objects Lorca celebrated. But, in the poem's final stanzas, this sense of presence, of the song that "outsoars / The bomber's range," is again slipping from the poet's grasp; Lorca's voice returns to the heavens leaving her behind in a transformed relationship to what she earlier called "earth's mould." The spirit of Lorca, then, is understood to be existing in the mythic or lyric time hinted at in the italicized lines interjected like catechistic responses between the descriptions of the poet's communication with him.

> *While you—*
> *You hold the light*
> *Unbroken.*
>
> . . . .

> *You make the flight*
> *Unshaken.*
>
> . . . .
>
> *You hold the word*
> *Unspoken.*
>
> . . . .
>
> *Light flight word*
> *The unassailed, the token!*

These brief stanzas organize the poem—providing the magic threes and the singsong rhythms of fairy tales and suggesting that the poet and his words are a "token" that may compensate for a world of death and chaos and loss. "Lorca" places the poet's public voice in an illocatable utopia just beyond the reach of everyday life.

This gesture is characteristic of lyric poems; the mystical illocatability reduces the world to one poet's appeal to another—that is, to a solitary cry. The difficulty with this mode of writing is that Livesay is concerned with making this solitary cry a public voice. "Lorca" was intended in part as a commentary on the Spanish situation, but it is difficult to decode this aspect of the poem, since all public voices are represented by the poet's voice. Even when she praises Lorca's ability to speak publicly, she suppresses possible conflicts among voices:

> For you sang out aloud
> Arching the silent wood
> To stretch itself, tiptoe,
> Above the crowd . . .
>
> *You hold the word*
> *Unspoken.*

Other voices are "the crowd" or, at best, the "wood," and they are "silent." They do not even seem to exist in that state of marvelous thwartedness that Livesay celebrates in other poems, since that virtue is reserved for the "you" who holds the word unspoken.

After "Lorca," Livesay continued to push at the boundaries of the lyric, seeking ways to express public voices and situate them more precisely. An interesting example of this second type of lyric is "For Paul Robeson: Playing

Othello." [17] Similar in conception to "Lorca," this poem also apostrophizes a kindred spirit, celebrating the transformation from silence to appreciation of natural objects to an expansive condition. Also, like "Lorca," "Robeson" is centrally concerned with voice in both its subject matter and its form.

In "Robeson," however, the public voice emerges from the poem's scenery in a different manner than it does in "Lorca." "Robeson" begins with the image of "warming waves of sound" that "Fall through a sea of silences / Fall and resound." Here, silence is not crowded or blocked out by "the wood" or "the wall" so much as it is supporting the word on the "warming waves of sound." Contrasting "sound" and "a sea of silences" rather than the "word" and "silence," as in "Lorca," in "Robeson," Livesay creates a considerably less polarized landscape. In "Robeson," persons inhabit their place, harmonizing with the rhythms of both sound and silence; both human and inhuman noises "fall and [punningly] resound" in comforting cycles—united by non-semantic aspects of language, such as the rhythm of the sea.

In the poem's second stanza, Livesay attaches the resounding waves to a specific voice, a voice that extends "our world's first tongue" to "echoing circles" that "reach, embrace, rejoice!" This lateral reach across the earth's surface contrasts to the "tiptoe" arching above the wood in "Lorca," and the difference strongly influences the way we imagine the auditor of the voice. In "Lorca," the poet seems an invalid confined to her narrow bed, but in "Robeson," the poet is one of the "fallow forms" lying across "wind-combed, sandy beaches." She is an organic being who is traced and disturbed by this voice; she is related to the voice by a mellow sensuality. The wide inclusiveness of the voice in "Robeson" does not demand that the poet organize, translate, or mythologize it, just that she feel and record it.

This intimate relationship between the public voice and the auditor continues in the third stanza, where Livesay imagines four other listeners, each in a unique psychological and physical location. All of them

> Lose littleness, grow in the world they share.
> . . . given of beneficence
> Learn to breath its air.

The voice here does not become a "token" for the solidarity that might once have been possible; it is itself the creation of an expanded community of "beneficence." Through its extension on the radio waves, the voice unifies a community of isolated listeners. Their private but simultaneous experience sets them in relation to one another, much as the land on which they all reside does. In the poem, mountains and shoreline are juxtaposed closely as in the dramatic vistas of Vancouver, where Livesay was living when she wrote "Robeson." This geographical situatedness allows Livesay to locate her generalized perception of Robeson's voice in a particular place, just as the transformation of the ocean waves into radio waves locates her in a particular technological era. She condenses the general and particular, the personal and public into a single image.

In the last stanza, however, when Livesay turns from the situation of listening to the public voice and begins to reflect on the individual who gives the voice its "noble bearing," this promise of a dialectic breaks down. When she begins to contemplate the man, the wave image vanishes, and Robeson becomes more a symbol than a unifying voice. Like *Othello,* the play he reads, his presence evokes basic oppositions: dark skin and illuminated, sunlit words; love and murder; balm and pain; joyous humanity and wilderness. In other words, meditating on the immediate, socially situated parodoxes of race pulls Livesay away from her dominant wave imagery, and a much less compelling account of her moral indignation substitutes for her previous auditory and sensory imagination. The social concerns disrupt the lyric qualities of the earlier portions of the poem rather than flowing organically from them. In the end, in "Robeson," although she was successful in situating the lyric more precisely in a social location, the form was not entirely adequate to her desire to unite description with social commentary and personal with public concerns.

To satisfy her need for a poetry capable of public commentary, Livesay also experimented in the 1930s with a more didactic mode. Relying more heavily on thesis than image, these poems offer the reader a blunt statement of the poet's outrage in general terms; they aim at startling, angering, and motivating the reader to action. A poem such as "Montreal" is typical.[18] "The beauty of this city is haphazard," it begins, followed by the corollary that "the ugliness of this city is a planned and calculated thing!" The first two stanzas flesh out these propositions with examples: the way children huddle four to a bed or "Men stand knowing they live like this / So that the boss may live in bliss." The concluding stanzas urge the reader to encourage "All those born under ugliness" to build a city of conscious, purposeful beauty. The poet and the reader, as "thinkers," cannot build that city themselves, but they may celebrate the new world in which "The hammer beats, and the sickle has its song."

In such a poem, the thesis drives the poet forward. The emphasis is on vigorous teaching and not on creative learning or a memorable image. A number
of readers have commented briefly on this matter, most of whom object to the
very idea of didactic poetry. F. W. Watt, for example, claims that Livesay "accepted almost overnight the Marxian answer to the current social chaos, and
dedicated her art to the revolutionary cause" with the result that she began
to write "hortatory chants and indignant diatribes for the insurgent proletariat." [19] Such objections suggest that Livesay's imperative mood is by definition antipoetic, and Watt's use of the word "proletariat" implies a criticism
of what he considers her equally inappropriate political judgment. However,
Livesay's political poems have consistently had some credibility among critics
subscribing to a different theory of poetic value. Dennis Cooley, for example,
argues that Livesay's political conversion also involved a crisis of language and
literature. This crisis coalesced for Livesay in "the realization that the word
and the world do not coincide, that the world we seem to inhabit is misnamed
and that we cannot take the pure lyric (or, more accurately: the signifying system we know as lyric) for granted." [20] As a result, she began to experiment with
new names for the world—names, such as "proletariat," that disrupt the more
contemplative, individualistic, private world of her lyric poetry.

Cooley's view offers some interesting possibilities for rethinking the didactic poetry, since he suggests we need not see it as a betrayal of the autonomy
of poetry or as the intrusion of politics into culture. Instead, poems such as
"Montreal" comprise a distinct aesthetic. The imperative tone and the presence of abstractions such as "proletariat" or "hammer and sickle" are common
features of this aesthetic, but it also has a distinct voice. Cooley mentions that
the didactic poems add "sub-literary, or anti-literary" speech to poetry, creating "a rude babble of public voices." [21] Crossing the traditional boundaries
of literary culture, Livesay reaches beyond the subcultural ghetto in which she
began, translating concerns from her social work and political organizing into
the middlebrow literary culture—much as the proletarian novelists did. However, this long reach does not mean she has adopted a fully "public" aesthetic
in these poems; it is, in fact, possible to read the outraged, imperative tone in
poems such as "Montreal" as the residue of a personal revelation. These poems
convey a sense of discovery and a self-righteous delight in identifying a general principle: "the ugliness of this city is a planned and calculated thing," she
reports. The discovery of this horror is still fresh enough in the didactic poems

to be taken personally; perhaps this is why these poems were not especially powerful for readers outside Livesay's political subculture, for readers who had not experienced a similar revelation. The didactic poems do not communicate her crisis in language as well as they reflect it.

If, however, the didactic poems did not become a major poetic mode for Livesay, they did extend her range of concerns and clarify her poetic purpose. Through these poems, Livesay developed her sense of vocation; she began to understand her task not only as the refinement of images and the precise rendering of concrete location, but also as the detailed description of the social conditions and the engagement of poet and auditor in a mutually participatory process. These didactic poems helped Livesay make use of her lyric and descriptive talents. Through them, she established the poetic problem that would lead to some of her best work: the challenge of linking a general, public voice to an intensely private, specifically situated reservoir of images. This is the problem that almost all her work from the 1930s addresses and that found its most complete expression in the documentary poem "Day and Night."

Documenting the Thirties

The long title poem of a collection that won Canada's prestigious Governor General's award, "Day and Night" was one of the pieces Livesay wrote after her return from New Jersey. Lying in bed, suffering from a nervous breakdown, she poured out this poem in a dramatic new style. Drawing on her various experiments in proto-documentary writing, she began to balance those voices against one another until her long poem became a composite record of the cultural negotiations a writer had to make in the 1930s, until it reproduced the "babble of public voices." Amid this babble, she acclimated the concept of documentary to poetry.

"Day and Night" opens with a lyric voice moving from an urban skyline into the factory: "Dawn, red and angry," marked by shafts of steam and screaming whistles, reveals a "moving human belt" where "Men do a dance in time to the machines."[22] In this context, the two central adjectives ("moving" and "human") are doubled-edged; Livesay suggests at once that the men's ritualized movements resemble a dance, and that witnessing that dance moves her to sympathy for people restricted to dancing with machines. This ambiguity shows how Livesay negotiated social and aesthetic debates of the 1920s and

1930s—such as the famous conflict between the cinematic aesthetics represented by Russian filmmakers Sergei Eiseinstein and Ziga Vertov. Livesay's appreciation for the quirky poetry of mechanization corresponds roughly to Vertov's famous image of the dancing camera and tripod in "Man with a Movie
Camera," while her moral dilemma over dehumanization is not unlike Eisenstein's in "The Strike"—a film which makes extensive use of images from the
countryside (such as a dying bull) to suggest the factory's brutal effects on the
workers. In other words, in the opening stanza of "Day and Night," Livesay's
lyric voice internalizes contradictory positions on a common dilemma of the
1920s and 1930s: the problem of the machine.[23] By choosing the ambiguity of
the lyric voice, she retains ambivalence about the machine's role in human
life, and she makes this ambivalence the center of the poem, the source of its
central image: dancing in the furnace.

This image recurs throughout the poem in different tonalities. As in some
of the most compelling poems of her youthful imagist phase, the image holds
its clarity, remaining apt in each incarnation. From the first description of the
"red and angry" dawn to the subsequent references to the way "The furnace
glows within our hearts" (158) until work and sleep and love are fiery rituals,
the image never becomes an allegory for the workers' situation; it is always an
immediate, literal description of what the poet sees and, especially, of what
she hears. Dancing in the furnace is not a pattern of concepts that is repeatedly
defined but a pattern of associations with an auditory component. From the
first, it involves an attention to the whistles and screams, the humming and
whirring of machines. The patterns of sounds are in the same liminal condition as the men's dance—they are painfully close to being artful, and thus the
image becomes entwined with typically poetic concerns about the sound and
rhythm and pattern of language.

The second section of the poem develops this concern with sound.[24] In lines
of three or four syllables, a new voice calls out the steps of the workers' dance:

> One step forward
> Two steps back
> Shove the lever,
> Push it back
>
> While Arnot whirls
> A roundabout

And Geoghan shuffles
Bolts about. (155)

At first, the imagery and the simple, unvaried rhythms recall the folk dances that the ethnically marked workers might be assumed to perform—the "round-about," for example. At the same time, when these short lines are placed in the context of the longer, more image-laden lines describing the outside of the factory, they sound more like foreman's instructions shouted over the din of machinery. This latter possibility begins to seem more probable as the section continues and the strict rhythms grow more ominous, violent, and oppressive: "A writhing whack / Sets you spinning / Two steps back" (155).

In these stanzas, Livesay replaces lyric ambiguity with a didactic dialectic. Livesay borrowed the phrase "One step forward / Two steps back" from her reading of what she called Lenin's "admirable warning: we may have to take one step back in order to take two steps forward—something to that effect. In dealing with capitalism I reversed the image."[25] In the poem, Livesay reversed Lenin's formula to portray the workers' situation under capitalism as a perpetual and forced regression. She contrasts the social machine that produces robotic men to the whirling of folk dancing and to the regular progress of socialism.

Yet, Livesay's task in these lines is not limited to the articulation of a thesis. She gives her attention as a poet to the rhythm of Lenin's slogan until the repetitive declarative phrases also begin to recall the singsong she experimented with a few years later in poems such as "Abracadabra" or in the beginning of her radio play on the 1930s, "The Times Were Different." This collective voice differs from the didactic mass chants she wrote in the early 1930s—one of which climaxes with one group roaring across the stage, "There is hunger in Germany," only to be answered by another group shouting, "Hunger in Canada," followed by "Terror in Germany / Terror in Canada," and so forth.[26] In the mass chant, the short, declarative lines are the only voice, and they acquire a sense of melodramatic importance that they do not have in "Day and Night." In "Day and Night," the adaptation of Lenin's slogan is only one of several voices in the poem, and the lines themselves can be read in several different tones. In the documentary poem, Livesay makes use of the fervor of the didactic mode but alters it—using it to produce an image rather than to convey a message. In this manner, Livesay sidesteps the problem with abstract vocabulary that accompa-

nied some of her earlier endeavors, while maintaining the force and basic structure of her leftist convictions. Finally, for Livesay, the process of multiplying
public voices was more important than adhering to particular positive theses.

In Livesay's poems, the articulation of theses is almost always less important
than an arrangement of voices into oppositions. As she wrote in the same letter to Paul Denham quoted above, "everything I write contains pairs of opposites . . . Hegel's theses, antithesis leading to synthesis—Marx and Engels was
it, analogy of the water, boiling, turning into steam. Revolution! A new society
being born." The way Livesay phrases this idea is significant; she understands
dialectics and politics by way of an image—water becoming steam; this suggests that, for her, Marxism was less a theoretical explanation of the world
than an image for the world. That is, Marxism seems to have appealed to her
in part because it involved organizing thought in patterns that she already recognized, that corresponded to her own formal interest in oppositions. As she
notes, pairs of opposites, including day and night, appear in some of her earliest poems, and this pattern of thought was attractive to her before she became
politically active. For her, the appeal of dialectical materialism seems not to
have been based on theoretical insight or social life that was superadded to her
interest in literature, but instead it seems to have developed directly out of her
experience as a writer.

Not surprisingly the opposition between day and night in a poem by this
name is important. Reverberating with theoretical as well as cultural and racial
connotations, the phrase "day and night" is first introduced in the poem's third
section. This section combines the longer lyric lines and the short, pseudo-
didactic phrases of the previous two sections. Thus, initially, the phrase acts as
a synthesizing agent—pulling together the contradictory poetic problems of
the first two sections. Furthermore, when it appears in the third section, it is reversed; the first articulation of "Day and night" is followed on the next line by
"Night and day" (155). This treatment of the phrase suggests that the opposition between day and night is part of an ongoing pattern of double passes, and
that this process has an exterior. The terms of the opposition can be viewed
in contest and in harmony—as opposites and as elements bound together in a
single totality. In other words, the reversibility of the phrase indicates a shift in
poetic concern; it points to Livesay's move from lyrical and didactic passages
on factory life to another kind of issue.

Moving outside the perpetual interchange of day and night, of steps forward and back, Livesay considers love in the third section. In the voice of a lonely worker, she writes

> I called to love
> Deep in dream:
> Be with me in the daylight
> As in gloom. (157)

The hope that love might unify "daylight" and "gloom" is the theme of this section, though this is not a synthesis the poet can support herself—as the tone of the proposition makes clear. The plaintive, self-conscious poeticism of the word "gloom" instead of "night" hints that Livesay is parodying an excessive faith in "love." The parodic register is even more audible when we recall the tone of the Cole Porter song "Night and Day" that Livesay has also indicated was on her mind while writing "Day and Night." The popular Porter song featured the longing for love that haunts a young man "In the roaring traffic's boom, / In the silence of [his] lonely room."[27] In alluding to this song, Livesay reminds us of the potency of this private crooning desire while also highlighting its absurdity as an answer to social problems by contrasting it to "the knives against my back . . . [and] the steel's whip crack" (157). The voice in Porter's song seems utterly oblivious to such concerns, and Livesay implies that her poem is a richer document since it can hear both the dance tune and the dance of man and machine.

However, we should not conclude from this reversal of Porter's sentiments that Livesay scorned popular forms of writing and entertainment. On the contrary, like many writers of the 1930s, Livesay was preoccupied with the ambiguous territory between avant-garde and kitsch. The fourth section of "Day and Night" demonstrates her attempt to integrate popular forms with her own poetic practices, and her efforts are not simple appropriations. This section also contrasts two voices—the first similar to that of the case-history poems. Like those descriptive works, the first stanza of section four quickly sketches a life story from the point of view of a working-class person. "We were working together, night and day," a white worker says of himself and a black coworker. "We were like buddies, see?" he continues, "Until they said / That nigger is too smart the way he smiles. . . . Therefore they cut him down, who flowered at night / And raised me up, day hanging over night" (157). Recalling images of lynching, the phrase "day hanging over night" figures the iniquity

of the bosses' attempts to divide the workers. From the previous section, we
know that day and night are equal, two moments in a perpetual series of re-
versals, and that it is not possible to raise day over night, or white over black.
This political point is condensed into the less prominent but equally important issue of cultural equality. Livesay's use of New Jersey slang and colloquial
expressions such as "We were like buddies, see?" in this context suggests that
linguistic and cultural parity is, for her, a foreshadowing of a more egalitarian
social order.

The second part of section four extends the night and day opposition further by countering the white worker's version of the situation with an African
American spiritual:

> Lord, I'm burnin' in the fire
> Lord, I'm steppin' on the coals
> Lord, I'm blacker than my brother
> Blow your breath down here. (157)

She confronts the problem of speaking for a racial other—a problem which
her experiences of racism in New Jersey had underscored—by mimicking the
collective voice of the spiritual. Of course, it was common for leftists of the
1930s to interpret spirituals as songs expressing a desire for liberation, and they
usually preferred precisely the slow, serious type of spiritual presented here.
Paul Robeson's deep, professionally elocuted, and minimally accompanied arrangements of this material were landmarks of leftist culture. The originality,
however, of Livesay's use of the spiritual lies in the way that she opposes it to
the Porter song and to folk dancing. These several uses of song as a public voice
render differences of dialect while minimizing exoticism.

This effort at an egalitarianism of theme and technique is substantiated further by Livesay's framing references to the biblical characters Shadrach, Me-
shach, and Abednego. Immediately before and after the spiritual, she mentions
the prophet Daniel's three companions in Babylonian captivity. In the Bible
story, these three refuse to bow down to a colossal golden statue and so are
thrown into a furnace, where their faith protects them from a fiery death. Not
only does this reference relate the spiritual back to the poem's central theme
by establishing the parallels between capitalism, slavery, and hell, but also the
unity of the three names (never separated, all distinctly biblical) suggests that
solidarity is a crucial part of the saving faith. Thus, the black and white voices

agree on a fundamental principle, though they articulate it through different popular languages.

The fifth and sixth sections of the poem also emphasize positive elements of the workers' lives—especially their ability to store up experiences of oppression "Till life is turned / The other way!" (160). However, Livesay must not have been happy with the tone of these passages, since she added six stanzas to the conclusion of the poem some twenty years after its original publication.[28] Inserted before the fourth-to-last stanza, these verses do not alter the poem's final sentiment, but they do shift its reference points. While the original poem moved directly from "Add up hate / And let it mount" to the revolutionary optimism of "One step forward / Two steps back / Will soon be over," the post-1976 version includes the possibility that workers will wait out their lives in hunger, though not necessarily in hellish suffering:

> Into thy maw I commend my body
> But the soul shines without
> A child's hands as a leaf are tender
> And draw the poison out
>
> Green of new leaf shall deck my spirit
> Laughter's roots will spread:
> Though I am overalled and silent
> Boss, I'm far from dead! (159)

This considerably more temperate note introduces a vocabulary of "soul" and "spirit" that was, to say the least, not characteristic of Livesay's work in the 1930s, and the allegorizing of the factory/furnace as "thy maw" lessens the sense of political urgency. The factory becomes a symbol in these stanzas, not a site of immediate struggle and suffering. After 1976, it represents a barrier to the shining soul, although some revolutionary desire is still present, since some sort of "new leaf" is required to spread "laughter" throughout the day and night.

Inhering in these added verses, then, are some of the differences between the New and the Old Left; there is also a noticeable difference in voice. While the earlier voices—whether lyric, didactic, popular, descriptive, or folkloric—were all concerned with articulating widely held but not necessarily widely recognized states of mind, these later stanzas use personal experience as a corrective to public stereotypes: "Though I am overalled and silent / Boss, I'm far from dead!" While lines written in the 1930s assume the worker is alive and struggle to find words to express that fact publicly, these later stanzas insist on the priority of the worker's personal experience of him- or herself. This noticeable difference reveals an element common to all the 30s voices in the poem. Altogether, the juxtaposed, alternating voices form a public mosaic. The overall tendency is a multidirectional conversation among them, a public discourse of snippets whose patterns, rhythms, and repeated sounds reveal its import. This aesthetic continued to characterize documentary poetry for some time after the immediate situation in which it developed had faded away.

The Legacy of the Thirties: A Public Voice in Canada

As noted at the outset of this chapter, when the story of the documentary aesthetic of the 1930s is told in terms of the United States, it often ends with James Agee and Walker Evans's *Let Us Now Praise Famous Men,* and it generally concludes with the sense that the documentary project was an interesting failure. In Dorothy Livesay's case, however, the documentary aesthetic against which Agee and Evans worked was neither facile nor passive, since it involved an intricate series of negotiations among different voices. Livesay's work employs the mosaic of voices often associated with Canadian multiculturalism; an alternative to the U.S. "melting pot," the image of the mosaic takes the proximity of various and distinct cultures as an emblem of national identity. It is a vision of simultaneity rather than assimilation—of public dialogues rather than moral majorities.[29] As a mosaic of voices from different cultural locations, the documentary is, as Livesay claimed in her essay "The Documentary Poem: A Canadian Genre," emblematic of Canadian culture.

Speculation on national identity aside, though, adding Canadian culture to a North American literary history of the documentary makes it difficult to claim that the documentary ceased to be viable with the publication of Agee and Evans's text. In Livesay's career alone, rather than ceasing to be relevant, the documentary became an increasingly important form in the 1940s and 1950s. Livesay wrote a number of radio plays after World War II, not least of which was the work to which she refers repeatedly in her essay on the documentary: *Call My People Home.* This story of the internment of Japanese Canadians during World War II is notable for the variety of voices it employs; although the play does not strive for the insider's view of that culture that one finds in more recent works such as Joy Kogawa's *Obasan,* it does present an interesting moment of intercultural contact between Anglo- and Japanese Canadians.[30] Furthermore, the play offers a reasonably nuanced view of the spectrum of voices within a minority culture as well as insisting that this culture have a voice in the public culture.

Similarly, in other postwar documentary plays and reportage Livesay attempts to portray the variety of voices in Native, Métis, East Indian, German, African, and women's communities. As Lee Thompson has argued, this precocious interest in multiculturalism reflects not only Livesay's political motivations, but also the fact that she had found a medium adequate to her politics.[31] In particular, the opportunities provided by radio broadcasting affected Livesay's writing. Radio's emphasis on voice and song, of course, appealed to Livesay, as did the medium's fusion of an intimate, personal voice with a public forum. Furthermore, the federally funded stations on which most of her writing for radio was performed had some of their roots in cultural activism of the 1930s; prominent CCF-er and former editor of the *Canadian Forum,* Graham Spry, for example, played a key role in the early days of the CBC, and Livesay seems to have been friendly with a number of the CBC producers and managers. Their correspondence suggests an involvement in a common political subculture.[32] In short, the voice associated with Canadian public radio was continuous with the left-wing experiments in written documentary found in the culture of the 1930s. Both were interested in resisting the invasion of U.S. mass culture, and both functioned by way of a mosaic of interlocking voices.

Of course, as the CBC documentary aesthetic developed, its efforts to broadcast minority voices came to seem to some a form of elitism—and it reaped its share of criticism from those who argued that mass culture imported from the United States was the true public culture of Canada.[33] That is, the version of "the public" that came to replace "the masses" or "the people" in leftist cultural politics was also not a stable, or uncontested concept. But despite its difficulties, the public voice associated with documentary writing and, for some writers in Canada, with the promise of a national genre or national identity, placed writers associated with the cultural activism of the 1930s at the center of concerns that rose to prominence later in the century. Turning from the formal problem of the subject/object dilemma in documentary to the more broadly cultural problem of the role of minority voices in a multicultural society, writers such as Dorothy Livesay increasingly found ways to employ the political and cultural education begun in the 1930s in the postwar literary world.

Conclusion

REMEMBERING THE SUBURB OF DISSENT

In the poem that provides the epigraph for this study, W. H. Auden acts as an indigenous ethnographer of "the suburb of dissent."[1] He locates himself in left-wing culture, he narrates the cosmological origins of that culture, and he demonstrates some of its transnational features. In short, as a participant in the cultural politics of the 1930s, Auden provides invaluable observations.

His cultural history begins in a "golden" age:

> We, too, had known golden hours
> When body and soul were in tune,
> Had danced with our true loves
> By the light of a full moon . . .

In such lovely hours, the narrator proposes, the 30s generation built up a foundation of happiness. They experienced forms of delight, satiation, and pleasure that are now available only as a stereotyped memory. With the "tune/moon" rhyme, Auden reminds us how dated the Jazz Age crooners have come to seem; he spreads a glaze of irony over his nostalgia. This irony is necessary because the Depression made the era that preceded it seem a harmonious "golden" age, because it was accompanied by the proliferation of a compensatory popular culture and a cult of the good old days.

But, since Auden like Nathanael West is never comfortable for long in the company of sentimentality, he proceeds quickly to the next ideologeme—the ideologeme that situates his nostalgia more precisely in the social world: "We, too,"

> . . . sat with the wise and good
> As tongues grew witty and gay

> Over some noble dish
> Out of Escoffier.

Resting between dances, still employing the fairy tale vocabulary of nostalgia ("wise and good," "witty and gay"), these lines establish the aristocratic under-pinnings of the "golden" age. Culminating in the reference to August Escoffier, the renowned chef at London's exclusive Savoy Hotel whose cookbooks intro-duced French *haute cuisine* to Britain, these lines remind us of the trickle-down system of cultural distribution on which the "golden" age relied. We, too, the poem asserts at this point, enjoyed the pleasures of the aristocracy. It's not that we upper-crust poets were philistines incapable of appreciating the luscious grandeur of our environs; we

> Had felt the intrusive glory
> Which tears reserve apart,
> And would in the old grand manner
> Have sung from a resonant heart.

In fact, Auden implies a little defensively that he and his peers might have continued quite happily in "the old grand manner" of the troubadours, cele-brating their emotional upswings and the precious moments in which their upper-class "reserve" was broken, if something else had not happened. "But," he writes, in a single word that encapsulates an entire generational shift of temperament—that is to say, a shift of social and psychic relations,

> . . . pawed-at and gossiped-over
> By the promiscuous crowd,
> Concocted by editors
> Into spells to befuddle the crowd,
> All words like Peace and Love,
> All sane affirmative speech,
> Had been soiled, profaned, debased
> To a horrid mechanical screech.

These lines begin the definitive move away from the vaguely Edwardian setting of the first section of the poem and into "mechanical" civilization. And, here, the parallels to the North American left grow strongest. Although Auden's focus on nostalgia bears the traces of a specifically British wistfulness for a hierarchical social order (versus the U.S. sense of "the folk" as the bearers of the past), the suspicion we find here of the "crowd" and "editors" and "spells" marks one of the cultural reference points shared by literary leftists on both sides of the Atlantic.

With this formulation, in fact, Auden openly paraphrases Hemingway's famous assertion in *A Farewell to Arms* that capitalized abstract words such as Peace, Love, and Glory no longer have any significance. Opposing "all sane affirmative speech" to the "horrid mechanical screech" of the culture industry, Auden points to one of the sources of the tremendous cultural anxiety experienced by literary figures in the 1920s and 1930s. Although his view is close to Clement Greenberg, in that he too sees mass culture as kitsch, Auden identifies a major dilemma of 30s writers, like Dos Passos, who felt themselves to be in competition with the editors in charge of the machines of cultural production.

But, though sharing Dos Passos's concern, Auden found his own way to respond. For him,

> No civil style survived
> That pandemonium
> But the wry, the sotto-voce,
> Ironic and monochrome.

That is, Auden and his peers felt they had lost a "civil style" in which one could speak politely and publicly about political issues; they felt it was no longer possible to affirm their culture, and they had only the "monochrome" devices of post-Eliotic irony with which to condemn it. This cultural reference point, too, resembles those of the North American 1930s; as Dorothy Livesay noted, North American poets also set themselves in constant contest with the modernist writers of the 1920s, whom they saw as entirely too "sotto-voce," too isolated, negative, and uncivilized. Although, as I hope I have demonstrated in the preceding pages, the projects of the 1930s were not always naively sanguine about historical change, in comparison to the writers of the 1920s, they did have a more upbeat attitude overall. Although they, too, saw their culture disintegrating into a kind of "pandemonium," they were, like Auden, interested in finding "shelter / For joy or mere content," and they, too, found "little . . . left standing / But the suburb of dissent."

Finally, this phrase—"the suburb of dissent"—reveals a habit common to writers of the 1930s: the habit of imagining themselves to be inhabiting "islands" or "suburbs" or other enclosed, more or less claustrophobic spaces. If this note sounds more self-effacing and ironic in Auden's poem than in some of the writings of the 1930s I have examined, it is probably because in the atomic era of the 1950s the "shelter" provided by the "suburb of dissent" seemed considerably less secure. Auden's ethnography reminds us that the particularly 30s blend of revolutionary localism and nationalism hardly seemed adequate in the postwar world.

However, if we have learned anything from postmodernist anthropology, we have learned to think about ways that a stranger's approach to distant islands of culture is negotiated. We have learned to attend to the binocularity of vision produced by the ethnographer's relation to the indigenous ethnographer. We have learned that the indigenous informant usually has his or her own position and stake in the culture under investigation. In Auden's case, this means that it is vital that we understand how the perspective of 1950 pervades "We Too Had Known Golden Hours." In 1950, Auden was no longer the young Turk described in the poem; he was a U.S. citizen and a considerably more religious person. He was a popular lecturer and a renowned writer who could collaborate with artistic celebrities such as Igor Stravinsky. In this context, his reflections on the 1930s have something of the character of an apology. It is easy enough to imagine that "We Too" was written in response to some youngster's query about why Auden's generation was so angry and didn't they understand happiness or pleasure. To defend himself, Auden describes a spiral of options tried and discarded and explains that this spiral led inevitably to dissent; he presents his free choice as a matter of historical necessity. In a sense, this option, this insistence that there was no shelter other than the suburb of dissent, is only a notch more sophisticated than McCarthy's claim that Communists were "dupes"; Auden suggests that he and his peers simply and innocently sought a home. He implies that they were drawn to Communism only because they, naively, thought it would shelter them and their always quite different concerns. Furthermore, the rapidity with which he races through the options open to his younger self suggests that he is using a kind of shorthand— a shorthand that only works when its referents are recent enough to be familiar to the audience, but distant enough that we are supposed to recognize the standard criticisms of them all but immediately. In this way, Auden identifies himself as an early incarnation of the late modernist cultural critic, whose ironic bemusement insists on his distance both from the slightly tasteless (and ironically bourgeois) suburb of dissent and from the equally, dully earnest contemporaneous attack on that suburb.

It is not a political amnesia or a forgetting of one's participation in the leftist movements of the 1930s that we find in Auden's recollection. This, after all, is one of a great many pieces of midcentury writing devoted to the left movements. Rather, this kind of Cold War memory of the 1930s is characterized by a displacement—a rearranging of ideologemes that ultimately isolates the past from the present. Cold War memoirs of the 1930s, such as Malcolm Cowley's, William Phillips's, Alfred Kazin's, or those famously collected in *The God That Failed,* are frequently designed to underwrite the author's change of heart; they are de-conversion narratives that insist quite openly on discontinuity and historically determined breaks. Like later memoirists of the New Left, veterans of the 1930s narrated the shift from dissent to dissension, attributing the downward turn of the left movements to their factional implosion. Self-propelled, these movements can then be understood as closed, collapsed, complete.

By contrast, our 1990s view of the 1930s has stressed continuities. Especially apparent in long-distance retrospect are the ties that bound 30s leftist writers to their national tradition—often with what we might now consider an elitist or aristocratic version of that tradition. Similarly, once the terms in which we understand the culture industry have shifted from the purely negative, the attraction/repulsion that many 30s writers felt for mass culture is more apparent. They were fascinated by the transformation it was working on their society even while they sought space away from its invasive "screech." Also, the portability of the most prominent form of "dissent" to which 30s leftists turned in their search for something new and genuine—the proletarian novel—is now visible. While the mechanics of this form were associated most centrally with the discourse of class, they were also modified in representations of race and ethnicity—strongly influencing later developments of so-called minor literatures. Interestingly, this project is not described in Auden's poem, and this absence supports the conclusion that my consideration of Canadian materials has suggested. That is, it is clear that national situation inflects the position that leftist culture takes in different nations. Thus, from the perspective of the 1990s the cultural politics of the 1930s circulate through a double double bind. Beginning with the competing commitments to national and class cultures, they move into the territory between mass and minority cultures. Yet, the way in which these negotiations take place varies by nation, and so we return, on a second level of interpretation, to the question of relations between "major" and "minor" nations, such as the United States and Canada. From the vantage point of the 1990s, in other words, the important question about the 1930s is not only "when did they end?" but also "how have these practices continued to shape our culture?"

Of course, while the 1930s did not end in 1939 any more than the 1960s ended in 1969, they did *appear* to end for several reasons. The backlogs that developed in a Depression-era, and then a wartime, publishing industry meant that many texts clearly written in the ideological context of the 1930s were not published until after the decade had formally ended; Wright's *Native Son* or Garner's *Cabbagetown* might serve as examples. Similarly, wartime censorship drove many leftist parties underground or made opposition to practices in the liberal democracies politically unwise as well as personally dangerous.[2] And of course, Roosevelt's efforts in the New Deal to address many of the more pressing demands posed by activists made allies of some of those who had earlier been alienated from the government, much as wartime patriotism absorbed anti-fascist protest movements in Canada during the late 1930s.

In my view, we should regard these developments not as signs of the implosion of the 30s left but rather as signs of its transformation. By 1950, as Auden's career demonstrates, the ideological environment had changed substantially. Since the business of 30s leftists was not to propose the same theses infinitely but to act in and on their environment, they changed, too. Where the major factional division among leftist writers during the 1930s had been that between the defenders of proletarian culture (with its implicit thesis of the imminence of revolution) and proponents of the Popular Front (with its implicit defense of reform and mainstream aesthetics), the postwar period saw a different division. Modernist cultural critics, like Auden and the *Partisan Review* circle, acting as public intellectuals set themselves against a less prestigious set of middlebrow manipulators of mass culture; in the United States, we might take the writings of Howard Fast and Harvey Swados or the defensive political campaigns launched by Stevenson liberals as emblems of this latter project, while reminding ourselves of the Canadian left's preoccupation with the CBC and the potential for an engaged public sphere made available by the Massey Commission.[3] From the 1930s to the 1950s, the left's ideological focus shifted from "class" to "mass," with "nation" becoming increasingly uneven in its appeal. The nature of the massive explosion in the postwar culture industry worked to erode "nation" as a category of resistance, at the same time that the new forms of mass culture arguably began to feed the subterranean currents of what would become "the 1960s."

This shift in the ideological environment was prefigured in the practices of the 1930s, though it was also related to other shifts in economics, power, technology, the law, and so on that have been very briefly sketched at various points in *The Suburb of Dissent*. As we have seen, the economy of the 1930s and 1940s was saturated with a range of products resulting from the mass production of the combustion engine. At the same time, geopolitical relations were changing as the political empires of the British Commonwealth gave way to U.S. economic imperialism. Politics within nations were changing as the vocabulary of the universal franchise increasingly exposed its racial and ethnic limitations. Finally, culture itself was industrialized and widely commodified in the 1930s—thus altering the role it had earlier in the century as a separate sphere from which one could voice opposition to capitalism. In short, from the 1930s to the 1950s, the total set of relations among the elements of the social structure shifted. While the Depression remains an important example of the determining effect the economy can have under certain circumstances on other elements of a society, one of its unpredictable effects was a shift in the ideological environment toward a postwar suspicion of the very concepts of effect, structure, and determination.[4] The Depression of the 1930s stimulated an emphasis on culture and politics as sites of struggle that expanded exponentially in the postwar years, to the virtual exclusion of the economy as a site of officially recognized contest—at least in the United States.

Of course, the developments I have examined here can also be located at other sites. For instance, a project not limited to the English language or the decade of the 1930s might compare the specific subculture of the left internationally—looking at Henri Barbusse, George Orwell, Ernst Toller, and others. Or, one might contrast the role that leftist subculture played in Europe and North America to that in India, China, or Africa.[5] When cultural nationalism is part of a vital and often revolutionary, anti-colonial movement, the role that national culture plays in politics differs from the residual nationalisms of imperialist countries. No doubt international comparison would also focus on the difficulties in developing a program of proletarian culture in nations, such as India, where the relation of realist fiction to preexisting literary traditions is not organic, and it is likely that the ambivalence of many leftist writers toward mass culture would seem less elitist when its entanglement in a critique of imperialism was explored.

These new objects suggest themselves at this point in cultural history in part because of a second ideological shift, in which the partisanship of Cold War politics has given way to the different but still partisan quality of a more postmodern concern with mining the past. Rather than standing as a negative example of the pitfalls of political commitment, the 1930s can remind us to historicize our notions of opposition, protest, and dissent. By critically examining these older practices, we can approach a fuller understanding of the various roles literary intellectuals can and have played in promoting social change. Furthermore, with the 30s model of centralized, party-organized opposition before our eyes, we can see exactly how diffusely pervasive and commodified the sphere of culture has more recently become. This in turn may help us to assess the present more carefully in contrast to the quite different—and consequential—cultural politics of the past.

NOTES

Introduction

1 Simone de Beauvoir, *America Day by Day,* 41.

2 For a detailed discussion of *Partisan Review* and anti-Stalinism, see Alan Wald's *The New York Intellectuals.*

3 See Cathy N. Davidson's " 'Loose Change': Presidential Address to the American Studies Association, November 4, 1993," *American Quarterly* 46 (June 1994): 123–38.

4 For a discussion of variants on Marxism and Communism in the twentieth century, see Perry Anderson, *Considerations on Western Marxism.*

5 Aileen Kraditor discusses the attraction of communal life in *"Jimmy Higgins": The Mental World of the Rank-and-File Communist, 1930–1958.* Several of the essays in Ralph Bogardus's *Literature at the Barricades* discuss the impact that revelations of the role played by the Soviets during the Spanish civil war had on U.S. writers.

6 The first wave of participant-observers of the 1930s would include Alfred Kazin's *On Native Grounds* (1956), Malcolm Cowley's *The Dream of the Golden Mountains* (1980), William Phillips's *A Partisan View* (1983), and Philip Rahv's "Proletarian Literature: A Political Autopsy" in *Literature and Sixth Sense* (1969), 7–20. In the second wave, I place Walter Rideout, *The Radical Novel in the United States, 1900–1954* (1956), Daniel Aaron, *Writers on the Left* (1977), and sometimes James Gilbert, *Writers and Partisans* (1968). For multiculturalist scholarship on the 1930s, see Paula Rabinowitz, *Labor and Desire: Women's Revolutionary Fiction in the Depression Era;* Cary Nelson, *Repression and Recovery: Modern American Poetry and the Politics of Cultural Memory, 1910–1945;* Robbie Lieberman, *"My Song Is My Weapon": People's Songs, American Communism, and the Politics of Culture, 1930–1950;* James Murphy, *The Proletarian Moment: The Controversy over Leftism in Literature;* Paul Buhle, *Marxism in the United States;* Alan Wald, *The New York Intellectuals: The Rise and Decline of the Anti-Stalinist Left from the 1930s to the 1980s;* and Barbara Foley, *Radical Representations: Politics and Form in U.S. Proletarian Fiction, 1929–1941.*

7 However, one can argue over when the "modern" era and the global economy begin. For two influential views, see Immanuel Wallerstein, *The Modern World System,* and Ernest Mandel, *Late Capitalism.*

8 "Our Country and Our Culture," *Partisan Review* 19.3 (1952): 286–326. James Gilbert (*Writers and Partisans,* 221–33) describes the *Partisan Review* editors' rejection of middlebrow culture as a necessary corollary to their rejection of radical left culture. For the history of the development and diversification of suburbia, see Kenneth T. Jackson, *Crabgrass Frontier: The Suburbanization of the United States.*

9   Criticisms of the consensus school include Jeffrey Louis Decker, "Disassembling the Machine in the Garden: Anti-Humanism and the Critique of American Studies"; Michael Denning, " 'The Special American Conditions': Marxism and American Studies"; and Sacvan Bercovitch, "Investigations of an Americanist."

10 For instance, see the essays collected in *Cultures of United States Imperialism,* ed. Amy Kaplan and Donald E. Pease.

11 I am borrowing the term "New Americanist" from Donald Pease's introductions to special issues of *boundary 2* that featured revisionist scholarship in American Studies.

12 In *Americans in Canada: Migration and Settlement,* David D. Harvey demonstrates that crossing of the U.S./Canadian border is so frequent that U.S.–born Canadians make up the largest immigrant group in several western Canadian provinces. Elsewhere, Americans are generally the largest immigrant group, after the British. The number of Canadians entering the United States, in turn, is approximately triple that of Americans heading north.

13 Douglas Coupland, "Canada and the United States in the Year 2092," *New York Times* (Oct. 21, 1992): A23.

14 In the postnationalism issue of *boundary 2* (1992), Pease argues that New Americanists object to the normative subject presumed by nationalist fictions.

15 Denning, *The Cultural Front: The Laboring of American Culture in the Twentieth Century;* Isserman, *If I Had a Hammer: The Death of the Old Left and the Birth of the New Left.*

16 The intertwining of these narratives is well established by James N. Gregory in *American Exodus: The Dust Bowl Migration and Okie Culture in California,* chap. 1.

17 See Katie Louchheim, ed., *The Making of the New Deal: The Insiders Speak.*

18 Hugh MacLennan, "What It Was Like to Be in Your Twenties in the Thirties," in Michiel Horn, *The Dirty Thirties,* 720–25.

19 Raymond Williams, *Marxism and Literature,* 121–27.

1 Before F. O. Matthiessen: 30s Literary Histories and a Radical Concept of National Culture

1   Further references to this volume will appear in the text. For an account of the process by which *American Renaissance* became a foundational text, see Marc Dolan, "The 'Wholeness' of the Whale: Melville, Matthiessen, and the Semiotics of Critical Revisionism." Contributors to the debate over the significance of Matthiessen's treatment of Whitman and of homosexuality generally include David Bergman, "F. O. Matthiessen: The Critic as Homosexual."

2   Leo Marx, "Double Consciousness and the Cultural Politics of F. O. Matthiessen," 49. This view is also supported by Giles B. Gunn, *F. O. Matthiessen: The Critical Achievement.*

3   For criticisms of Matthiessen as originator of the canon, see Jane Tompkins, *Sensational Designs,* 227; for criticisms of humanism that implicate Matthiessen, see Jeffrey Louis Decker, "Disassembling the Machine in the Garden: Anti-Humanism

and the Critique of American Studies"; for antinationalist arguments, see Donald Pease, "New Americanists 2: National Identities, Postmodern Artifacts, and Post-national Narratives."

4 See Donald Pease, "*Moby Dick* and the Cold War," 127; and Jonathan Arac, "Authorizing an American Renaissance." For a classic articulation of consensus history, see Lionel Trilling, *The Liberal Imagination*. For further discussion of pre-consensus historians, see Richard Hofstadter, *The Progressive Historians: Turner, Beard, Parrington*, conclusion.

5 I am paraphrasing Paula Rabinowitz's critique of anti-reflectionism in *Labor and Desire*, 18–21.

6 For an analysis of Parrington's ambivalent relation to Marxism, see Hofstadter, 429–33.

7 Matthiessen, "The Great Tradition: A Counterstatement," in *The Responsibilities of the Critic: Essays and Reviews by F. O. Matthiessen*, 189–99.

8 James Murphy convincingly demonstrates that, contrary to the *Partisan Review* editors' desire to claim the position for themselves, the "anti-leftist" position was widely held during the 1930s (*The Proletarian Moment*, conclusion).

9 Cain, *F. O. Matthiessen and the Politics of Criticism*, 149.

10 See Gerald Graff, *Professing Literature: An Institutional History;* Andrew Ross, *No Respect: Intellectuals and Popular Culture;* Richard Ohmann, *Politics of Letters;* Peter Carafiol, *An American Ideal;* and Vincent Leitch, *American Literary Criticism from the 30's to the 80's*.

11 A list of new work on the 1930s would include James D. Bloom, *Left Letters: The Culture Wars of Mike Gold and Joseph Freeman;* Paul Buhle, *Marxism in the United States;* Michael Denning, *The Cultural Front: The Laboring of American Culture in the Twentieth Century;* Elizabeth Faue, *Community of Suffering and Struggle;* Robin D. G. Kelley, *Hammer and Hoe: Alabama Communists during the Great Depression;* Robbie Lieberman, *"My Song Is My Weapon": People's Songs, American Communism, and the Politics of Culture, 1930–1950;* Barbara Melosh, *Engendering Culture: Manhood and Womanhood in New Deal Public Art and Theatre;* James Murphy, *The Proletarian Moment;* Cary Nelson, *Repression and Recovery;* Paula Rabinowitz, *Labor and Desire;* and Alan Wald, *The New York Intellectuals*. Most of these works stress the creative or politically progressive aspects of 30s culture.

12 The publishing history of these studies also demonstrates their interwovenness. Peter J. Bellis in the *Dictionary of Literary Biography* (ed. Gregory S. Jay [Detroit: Gale Research Co., 1988], 63: 213) notes that Parrington's *Main Currents* was accepted by Harcourt, Brace on the recommendation of their reader, Van Wyck Brooks. The success of Parrington's work certainly paved the way for Calverton at Scribner's, Hicks at Macmillan, and Brooks at E. P. Dutton. Although Brooks and Smith do belong in this category, I do not discuss them as thoroughly as the others since Smith's work is properly metacritical while Brooks's is a narrower project. Further references to Hicks, Parrington, Brooks, and Calverton will appear in the text.

Gold's criticism has been reprinted in *Mike Gold: A Literary Anthology.* Samples of Wilson's criticism can be found in *A Literary Chronicle: 1920–1950.* Cowley's opinions can be found in his memoir, *The Dream of the Golden Mountains: Remembering the 1930's.*

13 The exceptionalist thesis was central to factional disputes in the Communist Party during the late 1920s—especially those centering around Jay Lovestone. The episode is described in Paul Buhle's *Marxism in the United States,* chap. 4. For an even more detailed account, see Theodore Draper, *American Communism and Soviet Russia,* chaps. 11–13, 18.

14 For a discussion of typical patterns of American exceptionalist thinking, see Michael Kammen, "The Problem of American Exceptionalism: A Reconsideration."

15 Williams's use of the terms dominant, residual, and emergent is clearly defined in *Marxism and Literature,* 121–28.

16 This is the definition of "modern tragic realism" that Erich Auerbach associates with Stendhal (*Mimesis* 408).

17 Harvey Teres, "Remaking Marxist Criticism: *Partisan Review*'s Eliotic Leftism, 1934–1936"; Robert F. Haugh, "Sentimentalism in the American Proletarian Novel," chap. 2; Adam Jacob Fischer, "Formula for Utopia: The American Proletarian Novel, 1930–1939," 10–14.

18 Many critics of the proletarian novel have charged that it is simply the expression of a wish-fulfillment fantasy, and some reviewers of literary histories identified the same tendency. See Leonard Wilcox, *V. F. Calverton: Radical in the American Grain,* 117–18. I am making the slightly different argument, however, that the dialectic between realism and wish-fulfillment is a central feature of both genres. I do not see that it is necessary to understand wish-fulfillment or "romance" as a betrayal of realism; it could just as easily be the logical counterpart and completion to an always already imaginary realism.

19 I am referring to this slogan in the spirit adopted by Warren Susman in his essay "History and the American Intellectual: The Uses of a Usable Past" in *Culture as History,* 7–26. Susman suggests that the most important aspect of the "usable past" thesis was not its unacceptably presentist bias, but rather its reflection of the attempt to "provide a new role for the intellectual as agent of discovery, critic of the old history, the old social order, and the old ideology and liaison to the new men of power bringing them a new history, a new ideology, new insights for the development of programs of action" (20).

20 Hofstadter (352–55) considers the rise of New Criticism as a primary factor in the decline of the reputation of the literary historians of the 1930s. The critical preference for form over content, in his view, was accompanied by a new anarchic individualism that made the 30s figures' interest in the proletariat seem outmoded, even genteel.

21 Matthiessen, "The Great Tradition," 192.

22 *The Dream of the Golden Mountains,* x.

23 For this distinction between a culture of consumption and a culture of political commitment, I am drawing, rather schematically, from Warren Susman's excellent essay "Culture and Commitment" in *Culture as History*, 150–83.

24 Charles C. Alexander, *Nationalism in American Thought, 1930–1945*.

25 See Granville Hicks, "Writers in the Thirties," in *As We Saw the Thirties*, ed. Rita James Simon, 76–101, for an account of Hicks's withdrawal from the Communist Party.

26 Hicks, review of *American Renaissance*, by F. O. Matthiessen, *New England Quarterly* 14 (1941): 556–66.

27 Hicks, review of *American Renaissance*, 562.

28 Most of my account of anti-fascist movements in the United States is drawn from Larry Ceplair's *Under the Shadow of War: Fascism, Anti-Fascism and Marxists, 1918–1939*, 181–201.

29 For an anecdotal account of this practice, see Max Schachtman, "Radicalism in the Thirties: A Trotskyist View," in Simon, *As We Saw the Thirties*, 8–45.

30 The classic articulation of the totalitarian thesis is Hannah Arendt's *The Origins of Totalitarianism*. For recent adaptation of this thesis, see Gerald Graff, "American Criticism Left and Right" in *Ideology and Classic American Literature*, ed. Sacvan Bercovitch and Myra Jehlen, 91–121.

31 Mies, *Patriarchy and Accumulation on a World Scale*, 36.

32 In Canada, cultural nationalism was most frequently expressed in periodical criticism and various booster projects. See John Herd Thompson with Allen Seager, *Canada 1922–1939: Decades of Discord*, chap. 8.

2 "All right we are two nations": Speed and the Stratification of Culture in *U.S.A.*

1 See Dee Garrison, *Mary Heaton Vorse: The Life of an American Insurgent*.

2 Joseph Nathan Kane, *Famous First Facts*, 59, 672.

3 I am summarizing here from the excellent chapter on the effects of technology on social life since the 1920s in Alan I. Marcus and Howard P. Segal's *Technology in America: A Brief History*, 257–311. Despite the rhetorical emphasis placed here on technology, I do not mean to imply that technology was solely responsible for these social changes. Since the scientific breakthroughs that led to the development of these technologies significantly predate the incorporation of those technologies into the society at large, one can conclude that the new technologies only altered U.S. society because they were accompanied by a number of shifts in economics, politics, and culture as well. Although a patent claim for an early motorcar was filed as early as 1879, for example, automobiles did not become common until the 1910s and 1920s, when they were produced using the techniques of mass production associated with Frederick Taylor and put into practice in the factories of Henry Ford. See Kane, *Famous First Facts*, 57.

4 In *Made in America: Science, Technology and American Modernist Poets*, Lisa M. Stein-

man argues that the influx of science and technology into American culture gave poets opportunities to borrow scientific authority and prestige for poetry. In "American Literary Culture and the Fatalistic View of Technology," Leo Marx describes a genealogy of pastoralist critiques of technology stretching from Thoreau and Whitman to William Carlos Williams and the Beat poets (in *The Pilot and the Passenger: Essays on Literature, Technology and Culture in the United States*, 179–207). Meanwhile, in *The Flying Machine and Modern Literature*, Lawrence Goldstein identifies a strain of Romantic zeal for technology.

5   In his chapter "The Dynamo and the Virgin" Adams recounts his sudden reconceptualization of history as a sequence of forces. *The Education of Henry Adams: An Autobiography* (Boston: Houghton Mifflin, 1918), 379–90.

6   Mumford, *Technics and Civilization;* Chase, *Men and Machines.*

7   Thorstein Veblen, "A Memorandum on a Practicable Soviet of Technicians," in *The Engineers and the Price System*, 168. Veblen was an important figure for leftists during the 1930s, as Kazin notes in *On Native Grounds*, 130–42.

8   For historical information on the Technocracy movement, see William Akin, *Technocracy and the American Dream.* The story of the impact engineering had on cultural institutions, such as the university, is told in David Noble's excellent *America by Design.*

9   Here, my argument differs from Joseph W. Slade's excellent essay "Hart Crane and John Dos Passos," which downplays Dos Passos's interest in Adams and, I think, overdraws his technophilia. In my view, one need not argue that Dos Passos was comfortable with the social effects of technology in order to pinpoint his dispute with his left-wing contemporaries. My reading is closer to Cecilia Tichi's, which sees Dos Passos as an engineer-novelist struggling with the machinic aspects of his own writing (*Shifting Gears: Technology and Culture in Modernist America*, 194–216).

10   "The Workman and His Tools," in *Occasions and Protests*, 9. Although this piece is dated 1936 in *Occasions and Protests*, it is an amalgamation of three earlier meditations on the role of the writer: the introduction to the Modern Library edition of *Three Soldiers* (1932); "The Writer as Technician," in *American Writers' Congress*, ed. Henry Hart (1935), 78–82; and "The Duty of the Writer," in *Writers in Freedom*, ed. B. Hermon Ould (London: Hutchinson, 1942), 24–26. The explicit political references in the essay change slightly with each revision, but the structure of the social analysis remains the same. I refer to the *Occasions and Protests* version of the piece as the 1964 version.

11   "The Workman and His Tools," 13. The phrase "of historical change" appears in the 1935 version of the piece, but not in the 1964 version.

12   See Paul Buhle, *Marxism in the United States*, 184–221.

13   See Hicks, *The Great Tradition;* Calverton, *The Liberation of American Literature;* Parrington, *Main Currents of American Thought.*

14   "The Workman and His Tools," 12.

15   The "Workman" essay is clearly designed to express Dos Passos's discomfort with

the Communists; the 1964 version includes the subtitle "On Being Invited to Join a Communists' Writers Union."

16 Dos Passos is quoted in Donald Pizer, "The Camera Eye in *U.S.A.:* The Sexual Center," 418. Two other critical essays that have been particularly interesting for this project argue that *U.S.A.* fails to complete its planned dialectical synthesis because (*a*) Dos Passos finally had a mechanistic theory of history, and (*b*) according to Dos Passos, the motion of America is for the most part Brownian, purposeless, and drifting, while synthetic, positive freedom is only achieved in the case of individuals who willfully determine their own purposes. See Barbara Foley, "The Treatment of Time in *The Big Money:* An Examination of Ideology and Literary Form," and Robert James Butler, "The American Quest for Pure Movement in Dos Passos's *U.S.A.*"

17 Whitman's influence on *U.S.A.* is discussed by Robert P. Weeks, "The Novel as Poem: Whitman's Legacy to Dos Passos."

18 *Leaves of Grass* (New York: Cornell University Press, 1973), 100.

19 *U.S.A.*, xix. All further references to *U.S.A.* will be included in the main body of the text.

20 In this respect, Dos Passos's project is not all that different from Matthiessen's in *American Renaissance*. Both writers construct intricate machines that operate by way of only partially authorized resonances between sections. This is quite different from the attempted master-narrative that both writers have been charged with attempting to write. See Marc Dolan's discussion of totality in "The 'Wholeness' of the Whale." Many critics of Dos Passos interpret this complex, outreaching structure as a form of totalizing and associate it with a masculinist pose. See especially Donald Pizer, "The Camera Eye in *U.S.A.*," 417–30.

21 Similar alterations of chronology and form are relevant to the study of oral history. Italian historian Alessandro Portelli, for example, argues that when Dos Passos and other writers visited the striking miners in Harlan County in 1932, they produced accounts of the strike that were dramatically at odds with those produced by the miners. In their efforts to construct a narrative that was reconcilable with their beliefs, the miners shrank and expanded time frames, omitted information and attributed causality to different factors than the intellectuals did. For further examples of the way one might interpret narrative time-frames, see "No Neutrals There: The Cultural Class Struggle in the Harlan Miners' Strike of 1931–32" and several of the other essays in Portelli, *The Death of Luigi Trastulli and Other Stories: Form and Meaning in Oral History.*

22 Marshall McLuhan, "John Dos Passos: Technique vs. Sensibility."

23 Jean-Paul Sartre describes this quality of Dos Passos's prose ("John Dos Passos and '1919' "). For Sartre, the requirement that one be one's own journalist is the sign of the special alienation provoked by American culture. I am suggesting quite the contrary—that Dos Passos undermines the importance of psychological alienation.

24 "The Treatment of Time," 456–58.

25 For a provocative discussion of the coterminous development of the techniques of

total war and the media, see Virilio, *Speed and Politics*. Although I find Virilio's arguments too exclusively centered on U.S. and French culture to represent geopolitical developments, his thesis that military strategy after World War II has increasingly centered on a war of perception seems, so to speak, right on target. For a remarkably lucid and concise summary of Virilio's argument, see McKenzie Wark, "The Logistics of Perception," *Meanjin* 49 (autumn 1990): 95–101.

26 Virilio, 96–118.

27 One could easily argue that the trajectory of Dos Passos's career reflects his progressive reification of the concepts of both liberty and history. In 1964, for example, he writes that history has become stiff and irreversible; see "A Protest Protested," in *Occasions and Protests*, 291–304.

3 A Confluence of Nationalisms: Hugh MacLennan's Early Writings

1   Information in this and the preceding paragraph is derived from John Robert Colombo, *1001 Questions about Canada*, 325–32.

2   See Stephen Leacock, *Canada: The Foundations of Its Future*, preface. For a young people's history, see Mary Graham Bonner, *Canada and Her Story*.

3   George W. Brown, *Building the Canadian Nation*, v. See also George M. Wrong, *The Canadians: The Story of a People*.

4   Wrong, 433.

5   Eric Hobsbawm, *Nations and Nationalism Since 1780: Programme, Myth, Reality*, 14–45.

6   W. H. New, *A History of Canadian Literature*, 137–50.

7   Dermot McCarthy, "Early Canadian Literary Histories and the Function of a Canon," 45.

8   See Bruce Nesbit's introduction to the New Canadian Library edition.

9   Birney's activities during the 1930s included organizing, as the letters in the Earle Birney Collection at the University of Toronto reveal.

10 George Woodcock, *Introducing Hugh MacLennan's* Barometer Rising, 66; Mari Reepre-Bordessa, *Hugh MacLennan's National Trilogy: Mapping a Canadian Identity (1940–1950)*, 15. See also essays collected in Paul Goetsch, ed., *Hugh MacLennan*.

11 Doris Sommer, *Foundational Fictions: The National Romances of Latin America*.

12 MacLennan, *Two Solitudes*, 9. Further references to this and other works by MacLennan will appear in the body of the text.

13 Elspeth Cameron, *Hugh MacLennan: A Writer's Life*, 1–24.

14 Figures on the percentage of the Canadian population of Scottish origin appear in W. Stanford Reid's essay "The Scot and Canadian Identity" in *The Scottish Tradition in Canada*, ed. W. Stanford Reid, 302–10.

15 Cameron, 32.

16 HM to DD, March 5, 1935; March 12, 1935; March 19, 1935; September 19, 1936. Container 6; files 1–8, Hugh MacLennan Collection, MacLennan Library, McGill University, Montreal, Quebec.

17   Benedict Anderson, *Imagined Communities: Reflections on the Origin and Spread of Nationalism.*

18   HM to DD, June 6, 1934; July 10, 1934; July 17, 1934; July 26, 1934.

19   Cameron, 78–79.

20   See September 13, 1935 letter to DD; and September 6, 1935.

21   Cameron, 90–93.

22   During the early 1930s, the activities of Maritime smugglers were a particularly sore point for American enforcers of Prohibition and thus often a point of pride for Canadians. In fact, the well-publicized sinking of the Canadian schooner *I'm Alone* by the U.S.S. *Dexter* off the Louisiana coast in 1929 seems to be a referent for MacLennan's scenes. See John H. Thompson, *The United States and Canada: Ambivalent Allies,* 108.

23   HM to DD, May 14, 1934.

24   For an exhaustively detailed reconstruction of the events of the Halifax explosion and its effects, see Janet F. Kitz, *Shattered City: The Halifax Explosion and the Road to Recovery.*

25   George Woodcock discusses MacLennan's interest in myth in *Introducing Hugh MacLennan's* Barometer Rising, 30ff.

26   Jane Spence Southron, "Catastrophe at Sea," *New York Times Book Review* (Oct. 5, 1941): 32; G. C. Andrew, "The Great Explosion," *Canadian Forum* (Dec. 1941): 282; EHW, review of *Barometer Rising, Queen's Quarterly* 48 (1941): 427–28; H. L. Stewart, review of *Barometer Rising, Dalhousie Review* 21 (1941): 512–13; Woodcock, *Introducing,* 54.

27   J. L. Granatstein and J. M. Hitsman, *Broken Promises: A History of Conscription in Canada,* 24–34.

28   Like most white Canadian radicals during the 1930s, MacLennan demonstrates almost no interest in the rights or conditions of Native Canadians. For a pointed reading of the dialectical relationship between this exclusion and a MacLennan-esque understanding of the land, see Scott Watson, "Race, Wilderness, Territory and the Origins of Modern Canadian Landscape Painting" in *canadas,* ed. Jordan Zinovich, 93–104.

29   The fascist sympathies and associations of leading Quebec separatists during the 1930s are well documented. For a discussion of these associations and the responses of left-wing observers, see Martin Robin, *Shades of Right: Nativist and Fascist Politics in Canada, 1920–1940,* 171–75, and Lita-Rose Betcherman, *The Swastika and the Maple Leaf: Fascist Movements in Canada in the Thirties.*

30   Maurice Cagnon, *The French Novel of Quebec,* 28. For an account of Ringuet's [Philippe Panneton's] career and the origins and reception of the novel, see Jean Panneton, *Ringuet.*

31   See C. P. Stacey, *A Very Double Life: The Private World of Mackenzie King.*

32   J. Russell Harper, *Painting in Canada: A History;* Dennis Reid, *Le Groupe des sept/The Group of Seven;* Harry Hunkin, *A Story of the Group of Seven;* Roald Nasgaard, *The Mystic*

North: Symbolist Landscape Painting in Northern Europe and North America, 1890-1940; Ruth Stephens Appelhof, ed., *The Expressionist Landscape: North American Modernist Painting, 1920-1947.*

33 MacDonald, *The Group of Seven,* 15.

34 Herman Boeschenstein, "Hugh MacLennan, A Canadian Novelist" in *Hugh MacLennan,* ed. Paul Goetsch, 35-57; Eleanor McNaught, review of *Two Solitudes, Canadian Forum* (May 1945): 46.

35 HM to DD, November 23, 1934.

36 Malcolm Cowley, "The Learned Poggius," *Southern Review* 9 (1973): 3-17.

4 Situating "the Worker": An Overview of Proletarian Fiction

1   See Ellen Schrecker, ed., *The Age of McCarthyism: A Brief History with Documents.*

2   For other interesting efforts to work through this opposition, see Wai-chee Dimock and Michael T. Gilmore, eds. *Rethinking Class: Literary Studies and Social Formations.*

3   Jameson, *Late Marxism, Adorno, or the Persistence of the Dialectic.*

4   "The Programme of the Communist International," in *A Handbook of Marxism,* 963–1042; the quotation is from p. 985, emphasis added. All further references to this work will appear in the text.

5   See James Murphy, *The Proletarian Moment,* chaps. 1 and 2.

6   See David McLellan, ed., *Marxism: Essential Writings.*

7   Edward W. Soja, *Postmodern Geographies: The Reassertion of Space in Critical Social Theory,* 76.

8   On Stalinist terror, see Geoffrey Hosking, *The First Socialist Society: A History of the Soviet Union from Within.* Peter N. Carroll's *The Odyssey of the Abraham Lincoln Brigade: Americans in the Spanish Civil War* is a valuable contribution to the literature on Spain.

9   Geoffrey Ponton, *The Soviet Era: Soviet Politics from Lenin to Yeltsin;* J. Arch Getty, *Origins of the Great Purges: The Soviet Communist Party Reconsidered, 1933-38.*

10 See Arendt, *The Origins of Totalitarianism;* Elisabeth Young-Bruehl, *Hannah Arendt: For Love of the World.*

11 Robert McElvaine, *The Great Depression: America, 1929-1941,* 51-94.

12 Katie Louchheim, ed., *The Making of the New Deal: The Insiders Speak.*

13 Alan Brinkley, *Voices of Protest: Huey Long, Father Coughlin and the Great Depression.*

14 Vivian Gornick, *The Romance of American Communism,* chap. 2. Of course, an exploration of the social life of the CPUSA, not the discourse surrounding it, would also need to take seriously the counter-narratives stressing a sense of betrayal and disaffiliation, such as Aileen Kraditor's *"Jimmy Higgins": The Mental World of the American Rank-and-File Communist, 1930-1958.*

15 Mike Gold, "Wilder: Prophet of the Genteel Christ," reprinted in *Proletarian Literature in the United States,* ed. Granville Hicks, 351.

16 See also Mike Gold, "Towards Proletarian Art," *Liberator* (Feb. 1921); "Go Left, Young Writers!" *New Masses* (Jan. 1929): 3-4.

17 "ART IS A WEAPON!" *New Masses* (Aug. 1931): 11–13. On Soviet aesthetics, see Katerina Clark, *The Soviet Novel: History as Ritual,* chap. 1.

18 See Alan Wald, "The Culture of 'Internal Colonialism': A Marxist Perspective," in *The Responsibility of Intellectuals,* 133–42.

19 Of course, we would do better to understand this view of the Soviet Union as a sign of American leftists' desires than as sociopolitical reality. See Régine Robin, *Socialist Realism: An Impossible Aesthetic;* Lynn Mally, *Culture of the Future;* and Samuel Farber, *Before Stalinism.*

20 John Scott Bowman, "The Proletarian Novel in America," 183–84.

21 Granville Hicks, "Revolution and the Novel," *New Masses* (April 10, April 17, May 15, 1934).

22 Kenneth Burke, "Revolutionary Symbolism in America," in Hart, *American Writers' Congress,* 87–94.

23 "Discussion and Proceedings," in *American Writers' Congress,* 167–70.

24 *American Writers' Congress* 165–67.

25 Cowley, "What the Revolutionary Movement Can Do for a Writer," 65; Le Sueur, "Proletarian Literature and the Middle West," 137. All in *American Writers' Congress.*

26 James Gilbert, *Writers and Partisans: A History of Literary Radicalism in America;* Alan Wald, *The New York Intellectuals: The Rise and Decline of the Anti-Stalinist Left from the 1930s to the 1980s.*

27 Rahv, "Proletarian Literature: A Political Autopsy," in *Literature and Sixth Sense,* 7–20.

28 David Madden, ed., *Proletarian Writers of the Thirties;* Maurice Isserman, *If I Had a Hammer: The Death of the Old Left and the Birth of the New Left.*

29 Susan Rubin Suleiman, *Authoritarian Fictions: The Ideological Novel as a Literary Genre.*

30 Murphy, *The Proletarian Moment;* Paula Rabinowitz, *Labor and Desire;* Cary Nelson, *Repression and Recovery.*

31 Gornick 19–20.

32 Cowley, *The Dream of the Golden Mountains,* 250–51.

33 See Suleiman, chap. 1; Clark, *The Soviet Novel,* appendix A; Adam Jacob Fischer, "Formula for Utopia: The American Proletarian Novel, 1930–1939."

34 See Walter Rideout, *The Radical Novel in the United States, 1900–1954;* Barbara Foley, *Radical Representations: Politics and Form in U.S. Proletarian Fiction, 1929–1941;* Rabinowitz, *Labor and Desire.*

35 Donato, *Christ in Concrete,* 122.

36 See Rabinowitz, *Labor and Desire,* chap. 1; Laura Hapke, *Daughters of the Depression: Women, Work, and Fiction in the American 1930s.*

37 Guthrie, *Bound for Glory,* 319.

38 Michael Denning, *The Cultural Front,* chaps. 5 and 6.

39 Rabinowitz, *Labor and Desire,* chap. 2.

40 Daniel Aaron, introduction to *The Disinherited.*

42 For detailed description of the way that middlebrow reformers introduced Old English ballads and crafts into Appalachia, see David Whisnant, *All That Is Native and Fine: The Politics of Culture in an American Region,* chap. 1.

43 Whisnant, chap. 3.

44 See Joseph R. Urgo, "Proletarian Literature and Feminism: The Gastonia Novels and Feminist Protest."

45 Hapke, *Daughters,* chap. 4.

46 Alan Wald, "The Subaltern Speaks."

47 *Babouk,* 168.

48 Foley argues for the use of narratologically precise descriptions of these didactic redundancies in *Radical Representations,* chap. 7.

49 Robin, *Socialist Realism,* chap. 1.

50 Rabinowitz, "Ending Difference/Different Endings: Class, Closure, and Collectivity in Women's Proletarian Fiction"; Foley, "Women and the Left in the 1930s."

51 Rabinowitz, *Labor and Desire,* 145–50.

52 Elinor Langer, *Josephine Herbst: The Story She Could Never Tell,* 260–63.

53 George Bisztray, *Marxist Models of Literary Realism.*

54 *Rope of Gold,* 429.

55 D. A. Miller, *Narrative and Its Discontents,* afterword.

56 Robert Stone, quoted in Ian Jack's editorial, *Granta* (summer 1996): 13.

5 Spatial Phobias in *Native Son:* Richard Wright's Revisions of the Proletarian Novel

1 *American Hunger,* 64. Further references to this work will appear in the text.

2 Keneth Kinnamon remarks that "Wright's effort in [*Native Son*] is to reconcile his sense of black life with the intellectual clarity and the possibility of social action provided by Communism, to interpret each group to the other" in his introduction to *New Essays on* Native Son, 3; in the same volume, John M. Reilly argues that Wright rewrote the "social novel as a black text" ("Giving Bigger a Voice: The Politics of Narrative in *Native Son,*" 41). Barbara Foley also sees *Native Son* as a performative dialogue in "The Politics of Poetics: Ideology and Narrative Form in *An American Tragedy* and *Native Son*"; and Martin Kilson argues Wright adopted the strategy of the "Marginal Man" in "Politics and Identity among Black Intellectuals." My argument differs from these in more specifically focusing on how Wright used this dialogue to reformulate the proletarian novel.

3 For example, Walter Rideout uses Wright to demonstrate Communism's lack of appeal for African Americans and incorrectly cites 1938 as the date of Wright's split from the Communist Party (*Radical Novel in the United States, 1900–1954,* 194). Daniel Aaron mentions Wright only in passing in *Writers on the Left.* Similarly, studies of African American intellectual life from the same period regularly qualify their praise of Wright with the mention of his "overreliance on the Communist ideology with which he encumbered his powerful indictment of society." See Margaret Just Butcher, *The Negro in American Culture,* 178; Harold Cruse, *The Crisis of the Negro Intellectual,* 182; S. P. Fullinwider, *The Mind and Mood of Black America: Twentieth-Century Thought,* 191. This tendency to neglect Wright is somewhat ameliorated by

Barbara Foley's fuller treatment of him in her 1993 *Radical Representations;* see also Paul Gilroy's extensive discussion of Wright's later work in *The Black Atlantic.*

4   James Baldwin, "Many Thousands Gone," in *Notes of a Native Son,* 33.

5   "Many Thousands Gone," 32; "Everybody's Protest Novel," *Notes of a Native Son,* 18.

6   The complex nature of Baldwin and Wright's personal relationship—in which Baldwin responded to Wright much as an angry son would—is discussed at length in Fred L. Stanley's "Richard Wright and James Baldwin," in Hakutani, *Critical Essays on Richard Wright,* 91–106.

7   Jane Tompkins's critique in *Sensational Designs* of the modernist, masculinist standards that condemn Stowe's novel to the margins of literary history has, of course, been a major factor in this shift in the critical climate.

8   Robin D. G. Kelley, " 'Comrades, Praise Gawd for Lenin and Them!': Ideology and Culture among Black Communists in Alabama, 1930–1935."

9   See Robin D. G. Kelley, *Hammer and Hoe: Alabama Communists during the Great Depression;* Mark Naison, *Communism in Harlem during the Depression.*

10 Richard Wright, "A Blueprint for Negro Writing," *New Challenge* 2 (fall 1937): 53–65. Further references will appear in the text.

11 Allyn Keith, "A Note on Negro Nationalism," and Eugene C. Holmes, "Problems Facing the Negro Writer Today," *New Challenge* 2 (fall 1937): 65–69; 69–75.

12 Further references to *Twelve Million Black Voices* will appear in the text.

13 Houston Baker Jr., "Richard Wright and the Dynamics of Place in Afro-American Literature" in Kinnamon, ed., *New Essays on* Native Son, 85–116. Elements of this thesis also appear in Houston Baker Jr., "Racial Wisdom and Richard Wright's *Native Son,*" in Hakutani, ed., *Critical Essays on Richard Wright,* 66–81.

14 Baker, "Richard Wright and the Dynamics of Place," 108.

15 See Jack B. Moore, "The Voice in *Twelve Million Black Voices.*"

16 In the Foreword (6), Wright cites E. Franklin Frazier's *The Negro Family in the United States;* Charles W. Taussig's *Rum, Romance and Rebellion;* Arthur Raper and Ira De A. Reid's *Sharecroppers All;* Elizabeth Lawson's *History of the American Negro People, 1619–1918;* Louis Wirth's "Urbanism as a Way of Life"; and Horace R. Cayton and George S. Mitchell's *Black Workers and the New Unions.*

17 Richard Wright, "How 'Bigger' Was Born," in *Native Son,* xx. Further references to this essay and to *Native Son* will appear in the text.

18 Ross Pudaloff, "Celebrity as Identity: Richard Wright, *Native Son,* and Mass Culture."

19 See Lynda Hungerford, "Dialect Representation in *Native Son.*"

20 Kelley, " 'Comrades,' " 74.

21 Burton Rascoe, "Negro Novel and White Reviewers," *American Mercury* 50 (May 1940): 113–16; for discussion of Wright's didacticism, see, e.g., Edward Margolies, "*Native Son* and Three Kinds of Revolution."

22 Margolies, 44.

23 Dorothy S. Redden demonstrates that Wright opposes liberal guilt theory and emotionalism in "Richard Wright and *Native Son:* Not Guilty."

24 Margolies, 44.

25 Laura E. Tanner, "The Narrative Presence in *Native Son.*"

26 Here, I am in agreement with Robert James Butler, who in "The Function of Violence in Richard Wright's *Native Son*" argues that Bessie represents a naturalist tendency in the text, while Mary represents romance. Butler argues that Bigger murders each woman because each represents a side of his own person that he can no longer face; thus, death and violence generally in *Native Son* are symbolic displacements of a self-hatred that is really, latently, hatred of the system that helped to shape oneself.

27 My approach on this subject differs from that of Barry Gross, who, following Harold Cruse, sees Wright's novel as a gesture of defiance against the "intellectual overlordship" of Jews in the Communist Party (" 'Intellectual Overlordship': Blacks, Jews and *Native Son*").

28 Richard Wright, "I Bite the Hand that Feeds Me," *Atlantic Monthly* (June 1940): 826–28.

29 Thomas King, "Godzilla and the Post-Colonial."

30 See photo credits, *Twelve Million Black Voices*, 149–52.

6 Evading the Garrison: Class and Ethnicity in Canadian Regional Fiction

1   Ruth McKinzie, "Proletarian Literature in Canada," *Dalhousie Review* (April 1939): 39–64.

2   Robert L. McDougall, "The Dodo and the Cruising Auk: Class in Canadian Literature"; Robin Mathews, *Canadian Identity: Major Forces Shaping the Life of a People.*

3   Northrop Frye, "Conclusion to *A Literary History of Canada,*" reprinted in *The Bush Garden: Essays on the Canadian Imagination*, 225.

4   Frye, 236.

5   Donald Avery, *"Dangerous Foreigners": European Immigrant Workers and Labour Radicals in Canada, 1896–1932*, introduction.

6   William Repka and Kathleen M. Repka, *Dangerous Patriots: Canada's Unknown Prisoners of War.*

7   Michiel Horn, *The League for Social Reconstruction.*

8   Earle Birney, "Short Story Contest—A Report," *Canadian Forum* (June 1937): 96–97.

9   Dick Harrison, "Fiction of the 1930s," in *The Dirty Thirties in Prairie Canada*, ed. D. Francis and H. Ganzevoort, 82.

10 On race-based discrimination in Canada, see Narindar Singh, *Canadian Sikhs: History, Religion and Culture of Sikhs in North America*; Robin W. Winks, *The Blacks in Canada: A History.*

11 See William Petersen, "Concepts of Ethnicity," in William Petersen, Michael Novak, and Philip Gleason, eds., *Concepts of Ethnicity*, 1–27.

12 Criticisms of leftist parties' assimilative tendencies include John Kolasky, *The Shattered Illusion: The History of Ukrainian Pro-Communist Organizations in Canada.*

13 Brian Young and John A. Dickinson, *A Short History of Quebec: A Socio-Economic Perspective,* chaps. 6 and 7.

14 The literature of this community was written in several languages as well; see Irving Massey, *Identity and Community: Reflections on English, Yiddish, and French Literature in Canada.*

15 Irving Layton, with David O'Rourke, *Waiting for the Messiah: A Memoir.*

16 The relationship between Quebecois separatism and anti-Semitism has remained quite controversial. See Esther Delisle, *The Traitor and the Jew: Anti-Semitism and Extremist Right-Wing Nationalism in Quebec from 1929 to 1939.*

17 Avery, 116–17.

18 H. Blair Neatby, *The Politics of Chaos,* 117–18.

19 Louis Fournier, *FLQ: The Anatomy of an Underground Movement.*

20 Antonio Gramsci, *The Modern Prince and Other Writings.*

21 See Ben-Zion Shek, *Social Realism in the French-Canadian Novel.*

22 Maurice Cagnon, *The French Novel of Quebec,* 110.

23 Richard H. Condon, "Bayonets at the North Bridge: The Lewiston-Auburn Shoe Strike, 1937," *Maine Historical Society Quarterly* 12 (1981): 75–98.

24 *Les demi-civilisées* 203, 237. Further references to this and the other novels discussed below appear in the text. The translation changes the image somewhat; in the original, Harvey describes Quebec society as a triangle, lacking the fourth leg—an active intelligentsia—to make it a more stable rectangle. See the critical edition by Guildo Rousseau, 248.

25 See essays in *Art et combat;* also *La correspondance étrangère de Jean-Charles Harvey,* 32, 50.

26 Glen Shortliffe, introduction to *The Town Below* (translated by Samuel Putnam), v–xii. Quotations below follow this translation; references appear in the text.

27 Pauline Greenhill argues in *Ethnicity in the Mainstream: Three Studies of English Canadian Culture in Ontario* (introduction) that evasion of their ethnicity has been a mainstay of English Canadian cultural power.

28 Neatby, chap. 8.

29 Breton, Isajiw, Kalbach, Reitz, *Ethnic Identity and Equality.*

30 Kolasky, 10.

31 See Paul Buhle, *Marxism in the United States,* chap. 4.

32 Brian Osborne, "'Non-Preferred' People: Inter-war Ukrainian Immigration to Canada," in *Canada's Ukrainians: Negotiating an Identity,* ed. Lubonyr Luciuk and Stella Hryniuk, 81–102.

33 According to the *Historical Atlas of Canada,* the percentage of the population on relief was as high as 40 percent in Ontario, Quebec, and Saskatchewan (ed. Donald Kerr and Deryck W. Holdsworth), 3: plate 41.

34 C. B. Macpherson, *Democracy in Alberta: Social Credit and the Party System;* Michael B. Stein, *Dynamics of Right-Wing Protest.*

35 Gerald Friesen, *The Canadian Prairies,* chap. 15.

36   Orest Subtelny, *Ukrainians in North America: An Illustrated History,* 123. See also Avery, 13.

37   Carmela Patrias gives an excellent analysis of the way that this polarization was produced in the experience of immigration in *Patriots and Proletarians: Politicizing Hungarian Immigrants in Interwar Canada,* introduction.

38   R. Douglas Francis, *Images of the West: Responses to the Canadian Prairies,* chap. 5.

39   Douglas Spettigue, *Frederick Philip Grove.*

40   See *New Yorker* (Dec. 16, 1939): 101–2; *New York Times Book Review* (Dec. 10, 1939): 7; Margaret Wallace, "Labor on the March," *Saturday Review of Literature* (Dec. 16, 1939): 7; Eleanor Godfrey, review of *Waste Heritage, Canadian Forum* (Feb. 1940): 364–65.

41   Marco Carynnyk, "Swallowing Stalinism: Pro-Communist Ukrainian Canadians and the Soviet Ukraine in the 1930s," in Luciuk and Hryniuk, eds., *Canada's Ukrainians,* 187–205.

42   Foucault is cited in Walter Benn Michaels, *The Gold Standard and the Logic of Naturalism,* 187.

7   Provincial Avant-gardes: Confronting Mass Culture in U.S. and Canadian Literary Periodicals of the 1930s

1   Robert Forsythe, "Hollywood — or Gorky," in New Masses: *An Anthology of the Rebel Thirties,* ed. Joseph North, 210–11. For a more complete analysis of leftist intellectuals' views on mass culture, see Paul R. Gorman, *Left Intellectuals and Popular Culture in Twentieth-Century America.*

2   Clement Greenberg, "Avant-garde and Kitsch," *Partisan Review* 6 (1939): 34–49. Greenberg's essay is usually understood as an argument for a self-supporting avant-garde. My reading is closer to T. J. Clark's in "Clement Greenberg's Theory of Art."

3   While the hostility of 30s leftists to mass culture can be overstated, it is certainly the case that as segments of the 30s left drifted further towards the anti-Stalinism of the postwar period, their discomfort with popular culture increased. See Andrew Ross, *No Respect: Intellectuals and Popular Culture,* chap. 1.

4   Reprinted in the 1976 *New Provinces,* ed. Michael Gnarowski, xxvii–xxxii. Although Smith's preface was not printed with the first edition of the anthology, it shares its basic terms with the considerably shorter and more politic piece written by F. R. Scott. Further references to Smith's preface will appear in the text.

5   Joyce Wayne and Stuart MacKinnon describe the controversy surrounding *A Book of Canadian Poetry* in "Dorothy Livesay: A Literary Life on the Left," in *A Public and Private Voice: Essays on the Life and Work of Dorothy Livesay,* ed. Lindsay Dorsey et al., 37–38.

6   Warren Susman, "Culture and Civilization in the Nineteen-Twenties," in *Culture as History: The Transformation of American Society in the Twentieth Century,* 105–21.

7   See Robert Weaver, "Books," in *Mass Media in Canada,* ed. John A. Irving, 31–50; and

in the same volume, Arnold Edinborough, "The Press," 15–28. More recent studies agree with this assessment; see Fraser Sutherland's *The Monthly Epic: A History of Canadian Magazines, 1789–1989.* For discussion of the U.S. publishing industry in the 1930s, see Alice G. Marquis, *Hopes and Ashes: The Birth of Modern Times, 1929–1939;* and Theodore Peterson, *Magazines in the Twentieth Century.*

8 See Isaiah Litvak and Christopher Maule, *Cultural Sovereignty: The* Time *and* Reader's Digest *Case in Canada,* 23–26.

9 Dos Passos contributed the "near-beer" anecdote to a *Modern Quarterly* survey entitled "Whither the American Writer" (summer 1932): 11–12. Cited in Townsend Ludington's exhaustive biography, *John Dos Passos: A Twentieth-Century Odyssey,* 313.

10 Jack Conroy recounts the many difficulties he and Nelson Algren encountered in their many years of publishing little magazines in Chicago in the introduction to *Writers in Revolt: The* Anvil *Anthology,* ed. Jack Conroy and Curt Johnson, ix–xxi.

11 Judy Kutulas, *The Long War: The Intellectual People's Front and Anti-Stalinism, 1930–1940,* 126–31.

12 For example, Walter Rideout charges that Gold retained editorship of *New Masses* "with the result that the literary contents often seemed artistically crude and the circulation remained numerically unimpressive" (*The Radical Novel in the United States,* 149). James D. Bloom evaluates Gold's influence on the literary scene of the 1930s more positively (*Left Letters: The Culture Wars of Mike Gold and Joseph Freeman*).

13 *N. W. Ayer Directory of Newspapers and Periodicals* (Philadelphia: Ayer, 1930–39).

14 Peterson, *Magazines in the Twentieth Century,* chap. 13.

15 Henry Siedel Canby, "The Threatening Thirties," *Saturday Review of Literature* (May 22, 1937): 3–4, 14; Alan Calmer, "Portrait of the Artist as a Proletarian," *Saturday Review of Literature* (July 31, 1937): 3–4, 14; Robert Briffault, "The Left Turn in Literature," *Scribner's* (Aug. 1932): 88–90; R. W. Steadman, "A Critique of Proletarian Literature: An Objective Appraisal of Recent Radical Writing in America," *North American Review* 247 (March 1939): 142–52; Harold Strauss, "Realism in the Proletarian Novel," *Yale Review* 28 (Dec. 1938): 360–74; Sidney Hook, "Socialism at the Crossroads," *Saturday Review* (July 21, 1934): 1.

16 Frederick J. Hoffman et al., *The Little Magazine: A History and a Bibliography,* 159.

17 Charles Yale Harrison, "A Child Is Born," *New Masses* (July 30, 1930): 8; John Dos Passos, "1919 Two Portraits," *New Masses* (Nov. 1931): 6–9; Edward Newhouse, "New York to New Orleans," *New Masses* (Jan. 1931): 13–14; Whittaker Chambers, "Can You Make Out Their Voices," *New Masses* (March 1931): 7+; Mary Guimes Lear, "Bessie: A Garment Strike Story," *New Masses* (March 1931): 17–18; Maria Teresa Leon, "Acorns," *New Masses* (April 1935): 16–17.

18 Leane Zugsmith, "Room in the World," in *Writing Red: An Anthology of American Women Writers, 1930–1940,* ed. Charlotte Nekola and Paula Rabinowitz, 46–51.

19 Robert F. Haugh makes this argument about the whole genre in "Sentimentalism in the American Proletarian Novel."

20 For commentary of this type from 60s and 50s-era anti-Stalinists, see, respectively, Todd Gitlin, *The Whole World Is Watching: Mass Media in the Making and Unmaking of the New Left;* Leslie Fiedler, *What Was Literature? Class Culture and Mass Society.*

21 See Isidor Schneider, "Theodore Roosevelt Hyman," *Partisan Review* (April–May 1934): 12–16; Ben Field, "The Sheep Dip," *Partisan Review* (Feb.–March 1934): 24–31; Sender Garlin, "Queen City of the Adirondacks," *Partisan Review* (April–May 1934): 27–32; John Wexley, "Southern Highway 51," *Partisan Review* (June–July 1934): 11–14.

22 Barney Conal, "Notes on a Character," *Partisan Review* (June–July 1934): 46–51.

23 James T. Farrell, "Studs Lonigan," *Partisan Review* (Feb.–March 1934): 16–23; James T. Farrell, "Guillotine Party," *Partisan Review* (Oct.–Nov. 1935): 44–50; Edward New-house, "Bum's Rush in Manhattan," *Partisan Review* (June–July 1934): 32–39; Nelson Algren, "Storm in Texas," *Partisan Review* (Sept.–Oct. 1934): 26–29; Nelson Algren, "A Place to Lie Down," *Partisan Review* (Jan.–Feb. 1935): 3–9.

24 James T. Farrell, "A Jazz-Age Clerk," *New Frontier* (July 1936): 9–11. Although this story appeared in a Canadian magazine, it closely resembles the Farrell stories printed in *Partisan Review.*

25 William Stott offers a typical critique of leftist documentary in his *Documentary Expression and Thirties America.* Stott charges that written forms of radical documentary, such as reportage, were primitive, emotional, distorted, reductive and fanatical (189).

26 Meridel Le Sueur, "I Was Marching," *New Masses* (Sept. 18, 1934): 16–18.

27 Harrison George, "They Killed My Son," *New Masses* (March 24, 1936): 15–16; Tom Johnson, "I Handed Out Relief," *New Masses* (March 5, 1935): 10–12; Joseph Kalar, "My Uncle Was a Miner," *New Masses* (April 1931): 12–13; Myra Page, "On the Picket Line," *New Masses* (July 1931): 5–6; Ella Ford, "We Are Mill People," *New Masses* (Aug. 1929): 3–5.

28 Josephine Herbst's reports on Cuba appear in the March and April 1935 issues of *New Masses;* Smedley's reports from China and the Far East appear in 1930 and 1931 issues of *New Masses* and the *New Republic;* Vorse covered textiles and steel for the *New Republic* and *New Masses* throughout the decade.

29 Tillie Lerner, "The Strike," *Partisan Review* (Sept. and Oct. 1934): 3–9.

30 Georg Lukács argues that reportage is based on an exaggerated rejection of psychologism in the bourgeois novel, and that reportage will therefore remain within the constraints of psychologism; see "Reportage or Portrayal?" in *Essays on Realism,* 45–75. Lukács's views were not unknown in the United States in the 1930s, since the editors of *Partisan Review* published an abridged version of another essay of his on a similar theme, "Propaganda or Partisanship?" (April–May 1939): 36–46.

31 For discussion of the gendering of mass culture, see Charlotte Nekola, "Worlds Unseen: Political Women Journalists and the 1930s," in Nekola and Rabinowitz, *Writing Red,* 189–97; and Andreas Huyssens's "Mass Culture as a Woman: Modernism's Other."

32 For a very well researched account of the origins of the CCF and of the role of intel-

lectuals in the party, see Michiel Horn, *The League for Social Reconstruction: Intellectual Origins of the Democratic Left in Canada, 1930–42.*

33 Maria Tippett, *Making Culture: English-Canadian Institutions and the Arts before the Massey Commission;* Paul Litt, *The Muses, the Masses and the Massey Commission.*

34 Large-scale Canadian counter-espionage did not begin until World War II, and even in the 1950s, the Canadian government tended to take a reactive rather than proactive role in persecuting Communists. See J. L. Granatstein and David Stafford, *Spy Wars: Espionage and Canada from Gouzenko to Glasnost,* v–xii.

35 See Kenneth McNaught, "Socialism and the Canadian Political Tradition."

36 The CCF, for example, had strong bases of support on the prairies, while Communist organizers had important drives from Vancouver to Prince Edward Island. For discussions of some of the controversies this widely spread support engendered, see Horn, *League for Social Reconstruction,* and Irving Abella, *Nationalism, Communism, and Canadian Labour: The CIO, the Communist Party, and the Canadian Congress of Labour, 1935–1956.*

37 In the first issue of *Masses,* L. F. Edwards wrote that the writers in the Canadian Authors Association "seem totally unaware of the obligation to endeavor to express the feelings and thoughts of their countrymen" ("Authorship and Canadiana," 1 [April, 1932]: n.p.). Editors of *New Frontier* were out "to acquaint the Canadian public with the work of those writers and artists who are expressing a positive reaction to the social scene" (April 1936: 3). Nationalism was a very complicated issue for leftists in the 1930s; in labor struggles, especially, contradictions between supporting local resistance to U.S. imperialism sometimes conflicted with desire for unionization. For two differing assessments of the results in union organizing, see Abella, *Nationalism,* and Desmond Morton, *Working People,* chaps. 14 and 15. For discussion of the left-wing debates on Canadian nationalism, see Robin Mathews, *Canadian Identity: Major Forces Shaping the Life of a People.*

38 Ken Norris, *The Little Magazine in Canada, 1925–1980: Its Role in the Development of Modernism and Post-Modernism in Canadian Poetry,* chap. 3.

39 Sutherland notes the correspondences between *Canadian Forum* and *New Frontier* in particular (*The Monthly Epic* 128).

40 Ralph Bates, "Death in the Olive Field," *New Frontier* (Sept. 1937): 7–9; Valentine Ackland, "Federico: A True Story," *New Frontier* (Oct. 1937): 9–10; Jean Watts, "Spain Is Different," *New Frontier* (June 1936): 12–14; Bernard Rawlinson, "Cornwall—Diary of a Strike," *New Frontier* (Oct. 1936): 15–18, 23; William E. Kon, "Boom Town into Company Town," *New Frontier* (Nov. 1936): 6–9; Ted Allan, "Guilty! Mr. Croll: A Story of Hawkesbury," *New Frontier* (Jan. 1937): 7–8.

41 Dorothy Livesay, "Corbin—A Company Town Fights for Its Life," in *Right Hand, Left Hand* 202–8; originally published in *New Frontier* (1936).

42 *Canadian Forum* sketches of working-class labor and social practices include B. Gluckman, "Juggernaut" (Oct. 1932): 19–20; M.D., "Mrs. Bancroft" (Dec. 1932): 95–99; Andrew Cowan, "Hangover" (Feb. 1933): 177–78; Florence Rhein, "Beauty Parlour"

(Nov. 1934): 64–66; John Lawn, "Advent" (Dec. 1935): 397–99; Luella Bruce Creighton, "The Cornfield" (June 1937): 97–99; Guy Mason, "Sea Piece" (Sept. 1937): 206–7; Matt Armstrong, "Rooster Which Walked in a Circle" (April 1937): 23–24; Eleanor Godfrey, "The Samaritans" (Dec. 1939): 290–91. *Masses* pieces include Maurice Zigler, "Four Carts a Bread" (April 1932); A. Poole, "Fish" (July–Aug. 1932); George Winslade, "Rainbow Chasing" (July–Aug. 1932); Dan Faro, "Colonist Freight" (Nov. 1932); Robert Hall, "Breadline" (Dec. 1932); H. Francis, "Freedom of Contract" (March–April 1933). *New Frontier* pieces include Jean Barton, "Janet McCrostie" (May 1936): 13–15; Jack Parr [Dyson Carter], "Rush This One Maxer" (Sept. 1936): 16–18; Jack Parr [Dyson Carter], "The Boss the Mockingbird" (Feb. 1937): 19–22; J. K. Thomas, "Production" (July–Aug. 1937); Jack Parr [Dyson Carter], "Exit R.N." (Oct. 1937): 18–20.

43 Dyson Carter, "East Nine," in *Voices of Discord,* ed. Donna Phillips, 68–86; originally published in *New Frontier* (June 1936).

44 Carter's "short stories are well known to readers of *New Frontier,* many of whom have written to us to ask for more of them," his editors wrote (Feb. 1937: 1). John Ravenhill, "When I'm a Man" (Nov. 1932): 58–60; Harold Strong, "Lots More of Something Else" (June 1933): 336–38; Marcus Adenay, "The Dress" (March 1931): 216–18; Mary Quayle Innis, "The Party" (June 1931): 334–36; Yvonne Firkins, "The Enchanted" (Dec. 1937): 315–16. All in *Canadian Forum.*

45 Mary Quayle Innis, "Holiday," *Canadian Forum* (Jan. 1932): 140–42.

46 Margaret Prang, "Some Opinions of Political Radicalism in Canada between the Two World Wars," 30. Other work on the *Forum* also stresses its conservative critical tastes; Ann Stephenson Cowan, "*The Canadian Forum, 1920–1950.*"

47 "A Criticism," *New Frontier* (April 1936): 24.

48 Leon Edel, "The Eternal Footman Snickers," *Canadian Forum* (Dec. 1930): 96–98; Robert Greer Allen, "The Rest Is Silence," *Canadian Forum* (Jan. 1940): 325–26; Marion Nelson, "What's Wrong with Us, Webb?" *New Frontier* (June 1937): 8–12.

49 Political explanations of national differences between the United States and Canada include McNaught, "Socialism," Mathews, *Canadian Identity,* and Tippett, *Making Culture;* ethical explanations appear in T.D. Maclulich, *Between Europe and America: The Canadian Tradition in Fiction,* 100, and Horn, *League for Social Reconstruction.* Other factors are discussed in Paul Rutherford, *The Making of the Canadian Media;* Marshall McLuhan, "Canada: The Borderline Case"; John A. Irving, "The Development of Communications in Canada," in *Mass Media in Canada,* 3–12.

50 Margaret Atwood, *Survival.*

51 Atwood, 242.

52 Livesay expresses her irritation in her correspondence with Atwood. Folder 55, box 46, Dorothy Livesay Collection, Special Collections and Archives, University of Manitoba, Winnipeg.

53 See Peter Dale Scott, "The Difference Perspective Makes: Literary Studies in Canada and the United States."

8 Proletarians Who Resemble Horatio Alger:
Parody in Nathanael West's *A Cool Million*

1   The argument that the definitive feature of the avant-garde is a critique of the institutions of art is Peter Bürger's, in *Theory of the Avant-garde*.

2   Leslie Fiedler, *Love and Death in the American Novel*, 485–86.

3   For example, in "Challenging Mass Culture: American Writers and Literary Authority, 1880–1940," Thomas Strychacz argues that West appropriates the narrative disorder of Hollywood (chap. 5); although Strychacz does not explicitly counterpose West to American leftists, both Dieter Schulz and Rita Barnard prefer to place West in the context of the Frankfurt School critique of the culture industry rather than in an American context. See Barnard, "The Great Depression and the Culture of Abundance: Literature and Mass Culture in the 1930s," chap. 3; Dieter Schulz, "Nathanael West's *A Cool Million* and the Myth of Success."

4   West's biographer Jay Martin mentions that "West satirized the political success fictions of the proletarian novels; for these, as much as Alger's books, were wooden contests of vice and virtue" (*Nathanael West: The Art of His Life*, 256).

5   Nathanael West and Boris Ingster, *A Cool Million: A Screen Story* (cited in Martin, 218–19).

6   Gary Scharnhorst and Jack Bales have described the transformation of Alger's reputation both in the afterword to their biography (*The Lost Life of Horatio Alger, Jr.*, 148–56) and in their extensive bibliography of Alger works and criticism.

7   Barnard, chap. 3.

8   Susman, "Culture and Commitment," in *Culture as History: The Transformation of American Society in the Twentieth Century*, 150–83.

9   The publication of a hoax biography in 1928 (Herbert R. Mayes, *Alger: A Biography without a Hero*) encouraged these twentieth-century misrepresentations of Alger. See discussion of the Mayes biography in Scharnhorst and Bales, *Lost Life*, ix–xxii.

10   *Two Novels by Nathanael West*, 148. *A Cool Million* was originally published in 1934. All further references to this novel will appear in the text.

11   For further elaboration of the concept of the ideologeme, see Fredric Jameson, *The Political Unconscious*, 76, 87–88, 115–19.

12   Martin, 353.

13   Michael Moon, " 'The Gentle Boy from the Dangerous Classes': Pederasty, Domesticity, and Capitalism in Horatio Alger," 90.

14   Carol Nackenoff notes the nostalgic elements of Alger's critique of capitalism ("Of Factories and Failures: Exploring the Invisible Factory Gates of Horatio Alger, Jr."). One could also suggest that the "gentle boy" image is necessarily nostalgic; see Hawthorne's story of this name; Hawthorne also deploys Alger's major tropes (the beautiful, though poor, boy who is befriended by an older man in a story that affirms the values of a petit-bourgeois family of men, at the expense of women). *Twice-Told Tales* (New York: Airmont, 1965), 43–66. Hawthorne's story shifts these issues from

the mid–nineteenth century that Alger idealizes into an equally romantic view of colonial America.

15   Kenneth Burke, "Revolutionary Symbolism in America," in *American Writers' Congress*, ed. Henry Hart, 87–94.

16   "Wilder: Prophet of the Genteel Christ," in *Years of Protest: A Collection of American Writings of the 1930s*, ed. Jack Salzman, 233–38. See also the excellent summaries of Gold's positions offered in Paula Rabinowitz, *Labor and Desire*, 21–33, and James Murphy, *The Proletarian Moment*, 64–69.

17   V. L. Parrington, *Main Currents of American Thought*, 3: 86; Granville Hicks, *The Great Tradition*, 30; V. F. Calverton, *The Liberation of American Literature*, 276.

18   Gary Scharnhorst, "From Rags to Patches, or *A Cool Million* as Alter-Alger," 65. Ironically, the passage is borrowed from Alger, so it also encodes Alger's parody of the pretentious radicalism of the national poet.

19   Gold, *Jews without Money*, 224. Subsequent references appear in the text.

20   David H. Richter, "The Reader as Ironic Victim."

21   Scharnhorst, "From Rags to Patches," 65.

22   Moon, "Gentle Boy," 97.

23   Rabinowitz, *Labor and Desire*, 50–52, 97–136.

24   Rabinowitz, *Labor and Desire*, 99–100.

25   Apparently West based his description on an actual turn-of-the-century brothel in Chicago that used this name and concept. Charlie Chaplin mentions the House of All Nations in *My Autobiography* (New York: Penguin, 1964): 126–27.

26   West's supposed anti-Semitism is discussed in Stacey Olster, "The 'Other' in Nathanael West's Fiction: Jewish Rejection or Jewish Projection."

27   "[T]his marriage of convenience often enough turns into the crassest prostitution— sometimes on both sides, but much more generally on the part of the wife, who differs from the ordinary courtesan only in that she does not hire out her body, like the wage-worker, on piecework, but sells it into slavery once for all." Friedrich Engels, "Excerpt from *The Origin of Family, Private Property and the State*," in *The Marx-Engels Reader*, ed. Robert C. Tucker, 742.

28   David Whisnant explains the invention of Appalachia as a site of authenticity in *All That Is Native and Fine: The Politics of Culture in an American Region*. For more general discussion of the history of folklore studies see Simon J. Bronner, *American Folklore Studies: An Intellectual History*. For discussions of the leftist folk aesthetic in music, see Robbie Lieberman, *"My Song Is My Weapon": People's Songs, American Communism, and the Politics of Culture, 1930–1950* and R. Serge Denisoff, *Great Day Coming: Folk Music and the American Left*.

29   For an explication of these theses, see Robert Wexelblatt, "Nathanael West, Paul Valéry, and the Detonated Society."

30   On the proletarian novel as formula, see, for example, Adam Jacob Fischer, "Formula for Utopia: The American Proletarian Novel, 1930–1939." On Alger as a formula, see

Daniel T. Rodgers, *The Work Ethic in Industrial America, 1850–1920* (Chicago: University of Chicago Press, 1978), 140–42 (cited in Scharnhorst and Bales, *Bibliography,* 99).

31 Moon, "Gentle Boy," 100–105.

32 Walter Rideout, *The Radical Novel in the United States, 1900–1954,* 246–54.

9 The Emergence of Public Culture:
Dorothy Livesay's Documentary Poems

1 Kazin, *On Native Grounds,* 387; Stott, *Documentary Expression and Thirties America,* x.

2 This is Shirley Neuman's argument in "After Modernism: English-Canadian Poetry Since 1960."

3 Dorothy Livesay, *Right Hand, Left Hand,* 153.

4 For further information on radical poets in the United States, see Alan Wald, *The Revolutionary Imagination;* Cary Nelson, *Repression and Recovery;* Jack Salzman, ed., *Social Poetry of the 30s.* A list of radical poets in Canada during the 1930s would also be fairly extensive—including Livesay's friend Leo Kennedy, and some writers she would have considered political adversaries at the time, such as F. R. Scott, E. J. Pratt, A. M. Klein, Earle Birney, and A. J. M. Smith. Michael Gnarowski draws attention to the influence of the Auden group on Scott and Smith's 1936 anthology *New Provinces* in his introduction to that volume. Eliot's influence on Livesay has been noticed by critics such as W. E. Collin in "Canadian Writers of Today: Dorothy Livesay," *Canadian Forum* 12 (1932): 137–40. While studying at the Sorbonne in the early 1930s, Livesay wrote a thesis on Eliot and the Sitwells.

5 See *A Private and Public Voice: Essays on the Life and Work of Dorothy Livesay,* ed. Lindsay Dorney et al.

6 Livesay gives several conflicting versions of this episode, but the conflict of race and love and nationality is always central. See also "The Times Were Different," in *Right Hand, Left Hand,* 132–50; *The Self-Completing Tree: A Memoir, 1909–1963,* 144–51.

7 Lee Thompson (*Dorothy Livesay,* 16) emphasizes the importance of song and dance—and by extension, music—in Livesay's work.

8 Dorothy Livesay, "The Documentary Poem: A Canadian Genre," 269.

9 This description annoyed Livesay, because it meant Atwood was ignoring the role of intermediary categories such as nation, region, and gender in her work. See correspondence between the two in folder 55, box 46, Dorothy Livesay Collection, Special Collections and Archives, University of Manitoba, Winnipeg.

10 Reprinted in *Right Hand, Left Hand,* 177–82. Subsequent references appear in the text.

11 Stott, *Documentary Expression,* 145–51.

12 Peter Stevens, "Out of the Silence and across the Distance: The Poetry of Dorothy Livesay."

13 Folder 5, box 80, Livesay Collection.

14 See Sharon Cameron's discussion of this lyric tendency in *Lyric Time: Dickinson and the Limits of Genre,* 1-26.

15 In *Right Hand, Left Hand,* 250-55.

16 Reprinted in *Right Hand, Left Hand,* 259-62.

17 Box 86, folder 9, Livesay Collection. This poem was also published in *Canadian Forum* in June 1945.

18 Box 80, folder 4, Livesay Collection.

19 F. W. Watt in Carl F. Klinck's *Literary History of Canada,* 472. These poems have also been called "tedious or sententious" by Tom Marshall, "Major Canadian Poets III, The Modernists," *Canadian Forum* (Jan.-Feb. 1979): 13-17; "somewhat cold and intellectual" by R. E. Rashley in *Poetry in Canada: the First Three Steps,* 132; and "ludicrous" and "bathetic" by Beverly Mitchell in " 'How Silence Sings' in the Poetry of Dorothy Livesay, 1926-1973," *Dalhousie Review* 54 (autumn 1974): 510-28.

20 Cooley, *The Vernacular Muse,* 237.

21 Cooley, 247.

22 *Right Hand, Left Hand,* 154. Subsequent references to this poem will appear in the text.

23 On Eisenstein and Vertov, see James Goodwin, *Eisenstein, Cinema and History,* 53-56.

24 I am following the section divisions in *Right Hand, Left Hand.* When originally published, there was no division between the first and second stanzas.

25 DL to Paul Denham, June 20, 1980. Box 51, folder 37, Livesay Collection.

26 *Right Hand, Left Hand,* 99.

27 "Night and Day" in *103 Lyrics of Cole Porter,* sel. Fred Lounsberry (New York: Random House, 1954), 176-77.

28 I have not been able to date these stanzas precisely, but they appear in the 1976 *Right Hand, Left Hand* version, and not in the 1957 *Selected Poems,* so I assume that they were written—or considered part of the poem—in the 1960s.

29 The mosaic metaphor has a long history. It must have had currency in the 1930s, since a major academic study by John Murray Gibbon entitled *Canadian Mosaic: The Making of a Northern Nation* came out in 1938. I have also found references to a 1926 study by Kate Foster entitled *Our Canadian Mosaic,* so it is likely that Livesay would have been aware of this metaphor.

30 Paul Gilroy offers an incisive critique of making ethnic absolutism, or "insiderism," a criterion for cultural achievement in *The Black Atlantic,* chap. 1. Following from Gilroy's interest in hybridity, we might find figures like Livesay more important than they have previously seemed.

31 Lee Thompson, "A Coat of Many Cultures: The Poetry of Dorothy Livesay."

32 Maria Tippett grants oppositional groups a significant role in the development of a public culture in her *Making Culture: English-Canadian Institutions and the Arts before the Massey Commission,* 27-33. Paul Litt argues that liberals' desire for political control over the CBC and the National Film Board were crucial factors in the development of those agencies' missions; see his *The Muses, the Masses and the Massey*

Commission. The parallels between the CBC and the role that state-funded documentary film played in Great Britain are striking; see Ian Aitken, *Film and Reform: John Grierson and the Documentary Film Movement.* H. F. Tiessen and P. Tiessen discuss this link in "Dorothy Livesay's Louis Riel: The Unpublished Radio Plays."

33 The problem of minority culture versus mass culture receives some treatment in Bruce Raymond, "Radio," in *Mass Media in Canada,* ed. John Irving, 89–118. See also, Litt, *The Muses,* chap. 2.

Conclusion: Remembering the Suburb of Dissent

1 W. H. Auden, "We Too Had Known Golden Hours" in *Collected Poems,* ed. Edward Mendelson (London: Faber & Faber, 1976), 471.

2 Maurice Isserman, *Which Side Were You On? The American Communist Party During the Second World War.*

3 Paul Litt, *The Muses, the Masses and the Massey Commission;* Howard Fast, *Being Red;* Richard H. Pells, *The Liberal Mind in a Conservative Age: American Intellectuals in the 1940s and 1950s.*

4 See Fredric Jameson, "The Cultural Logic of Late Capitalism," in *Postmodernism, or The Cultural Logic of Late Capitalism,* 1–54.

5 Much of the groundwork for transnational study of the left, that is, works that analyze movements within particular countries, is already available. For instance, David Holm, *Art and Ideology in Revolutionary China* (New York: Oxford, 1991); Sharyn Pearce, "The Proletarianization of the Novel: The Cult of the Worker in Australian and American Fiction of the Depression," *Southerly* 48 (June 1988): 187–200; H. Gustav Klaus, ed., *The Socialist Novel in Britain* (New York: St. Martins, 1982); Sudhi Pradhan, ed., *Marxist Cultural Movement in India: Chronicles and Documents, 1936–1947* (Calcutta, 1979); and many more.

SELECTED BIBLIOGRAPHY

Manuscript Collections

Earle Birney Collection. Thomas Fisher Rare Book Library, University of Toronto, Toronto, Ontario.

Kenney Collection. Thomas Fisher Rare Book Library, University of Toronto, Toronto, Ontario.

Dorothy Livesay Collection. Special Collections and Archives, University of Manitoba, Winnipeg, Manitoba.

Hugh MacLennan Collection. MacLennan Library, McGill University, Montreal, Quebec.

J. S. Woodsworth Collection. Thomas Fisher Rare Book Library, University of Toronto, Toronto, Ontario.

Periodicals Consulted

American Mercury
Anvil
Canada Forward
Canadian Forum
Masses
Modern Monthly/Quarterly
Nation
New Challenge
New Commonwealth
New Frontier
New Masses
New Republic
Partisan Review
Saturday Review of Literature
Scribner's

Selected 30s Literature

Allan, Ted. *This Time a Better Earth*. New York: Morrow, 1940.
Anderson, Edward. *Hungry Men*. 1935. New York: Penguin, 1988.
Baird, Irene. *Waste Heritage*. 1939. Toronto: Macmillan, 1974.
Bell, Thomas. *All Brides Are Beautiful*. Boston: Little Brown, 1936.
Birney, Earle. *Down the Long Table*. Toronto: McClelland & Stewart, 1955.
Bisno, Beatrice. *Tomorrow's Bread*. New York: Liveright, 1938.
Bontemps, Arna. *Black Thunder*. New York: Macmillan, 1936.

Brody, Catharine. *Cash Item.* New York: Longman, 1933.

———. *Nobody Starves.* New York: Longman, 1932.

Brooker, Bertram. *Think of the Earth.* Toronto: Thomas Nelson, n.d.

Burke, Fielding [Dargan, Olive Tilford]. *Call Home the Heart.* 1932. New York: Feminist Press, 1983.

———. *A Stone Came Rolling.* New York: Longman, 1935.

Callaghan, Morley. *Such Is My Beloved.* Toronto: McClelland & Stewart, 1933.

———. *They Shall Inherit the Earth.* Toronto: McClelland & Stewart, 1934.

Conroy, Jack. *The Disinherited.* New York: Covici, 1933.

Cunningham, William. *The Green Corn Rebellion.* New York: Vanguard, 1935.

Dahlberg, Edward. *Bottom Dogs.* London: Putnam, 1929.

———. *From Flushing to Calvary.* New York: Crowell, 1976.

———. *Those Who Perish.* New York: John Day, 1934.

Donato, Pietro di. *Christ in Concrete.* Chicago: Esquire, 1937.

Dos Passos, John. *U.S.A.* 1936. New York: Signet, 1979.

Endore, Guy. *Babouk.* 1934. New York: Monthly Review, 1991.

Farrell, James T. *Studs Lonigan, A Trilogy.* New York: Vanguard, 1935.

Garner, Hugh. *Cabbagetown.* 1950. Reprinted in *Hugh Garner Omnibus.* Toronto: McGraw-Hill, 1978.

Gilfillan, Lauren. *I Went to Pit College.* New York: Macmillan, 1934.

Gold, Michael. *Jews without Money.* New York: Liveright, 1930.

Graham, Gwethalyn. *Earth and High Heaven.* New York: Lippincott, 1944.

———. *Swiss Sonata.* London: Jonathan Cape, 1938.

Gregory, Claudius. *Forgotten Men.* Hamilton: Davis-Lisson, 1933.

Grove, Frederick Philip. *Fruits of the Earth.* London: J. M. Dent, 1933.

———. *Master of the Mill.* Toronto: Macmillan, 1944.

———. *Two Generations.* Toronto: Ryerson, 1939.

Harrison, Charles Yale. *Generals Die in Bed.* New York: Morrow, 1928.

———. *Meet Me on the Barricades.* New York: Scribner's, 1938.

Harvey, Jean-Charles. *Les demi-civilisées.* 1934. Ed. Guildo Rousseau. Montreal: University Press de Montreal, 1988.

Herbst, Josephine. *Rope of Gold.* New York: Harcourt Brace, 1939.

Kromer, Tom. *Waiting for Nothing.* New York: Hill & Wang, 1935.

Lemelin, Roger. *Au pied de la pente douce.* 1944. Trans. by Samuel Putnam as *The Town Below.* 1948. Toronto: McClelland & Stewart, 1961.

Livesay, Dorothy. *Day and Night.* Toronto: Ryerson, 1944.

Lumpkin, Grace. *To Make My Bread.* New York: Macauley, 1932.

———. *The Wedding.* 1939. Carbondale: Southern Illinois University Press, 1976.

MacLennan, Hugh. *Barometer Rising.* 1941. Toronto: McClelland & Stewart, 1989.

———. *Two Solitudes.* Toronto: Popular Library, 1945.

Marlyn, John. *Under the Ribs of Death.* Toronto: McClelland & Stewart, 1957.

McKay, Claude. *Banana Bottom.* New York: Harper & Row, 1933.

McKenney, Ruth. *Industrial Valley.* New York: Harcourt, 1939.

Page, Myra. *Gathering Storm.* New York: International, 1932.

Ringuet [Philippe Panneton]. *Trente Arpentes/Thirty Acres.* 1938. Toronto: McClelland & Stewart, 1989.

Ross, Sinclair. *As for Me and My House.* Toronto: Reynal & Hitchcock, 1941.

Roth, Henry. *Call It Sleep.* 1934. New York: Avon 1962.

Slesinger, Tess. *The Unpossessed.* 1934. New York: Feminist Press, 1984.

Smedley, Agnes. *Daughter of Earth.* 1927/29. New Brunswick: Feminist Press, 1973.

Trumbo, Dalton. *Johnny Got His Gun.* 1939. New York: Bantam, 1982.

Vorse, Mary Heaton. *Strike!* New York: Vanguard, 1930.

Weatherwax, Clara. *Marching! Marching!* New York: John Day, 1935.

West, Nathanael. Miss Lonelyhearts & The Day of the Locust. 1933; 1939. New York: New Directions, 1962.

———. *Two Novels by Nathanael West:* The Dream Life of Balso Snell *and* A Cool Million. 1931; 1934. New York: Farrar, Strauss, 1988.

Wilhelm, Gale. *We Too Are Drifting.* New York: Random, 1935.

Wright, Richard. *Native Son.* 1940. New York: Harper, 1968.

Zugsmith, Leane. *The Reckoning.* New York: Harrison Smith & Robert Haas, 1934.

Selected 30s Nonfiction

Brooks, Van Wyck. *The Flowering of New England.* New York: Dutton, 1937.

Calverton, V. F. *The Liberation of American Literature.* New York: Scribner's, 1932.

Chase, Stuart. *Men and Machines.* New York: Macmillan, 1929.

Conroy, Jack, and Curt Johnson, eds. *Writers in Revolt: The* Anvil *Anthology.* New York: Lawrence Hill, 1974.

Gnarowski, Michael, ed. *New Provinces.* Toronto: University of Toronto Press, 1976.

Gold, Mike. *The Hollow Men.* New York: International Publishers, 1941.

———. *Mike Gold: A Literary Anthology.* Ed. Michael Folsom. New York: International Publishers, 1972.

A Handbook of Marxism. London: Gallancz, 1935.

Hart, Henry, ed. *American Writers' Congress.* New York: International Publishers, 1935.

Harvey, Jean-Charles. *Art et combat.* Montreal: ACF, n.d.

———. *La correspondance étrangère de Jean-Charles Harvey.* Ed. Sylvianne Savard Boulanger. Sherbrooke: Éditions Naaman, 1984.

Hicks, Granville. *The Great Tradition.* New York: Macmillan, 1933.

———, ed. *Proletarian Literature in the United States.* New York: International Publishers, 1935.

Kazin, Alfred. *On Native Grounds.* 1942. New York: Doubleday, 1956.

Le Sueur, Meridel. *Harvest Song: Collected Essays and Stories.* Albuquerque: West End Press, 1977.

———. *Ripening: Selected Work, 1927–1980.* Ed. Elaine Hedges. Old Westbury, NY: Feminist Press, 1982.

Livesay, Dorothy. *Right Hand, Left Hand.* Erin: Press Porcepic, 1977.

MacLennan, Hugh. *Scotchman's Return.* New York: Scribner's, 1960.

Matthiessen, F. O. *American Renaissance: Art and Expression in the Age of Emerson and Whitman.* New York: Oxford University Press, 1941.

————. *The Responsibilities of the Critic: Essays and Reviews by F. O. Matthiessen.* Sel. John Kackliffe. New York: Oxford University Press, 1982.

Mumford, Lewis. *Technics and Civilization.* New York: Harcourt Brace, 1934.

Parrington, V. L. *Main Currents in American Thought.* New York: Harcourt Brace, 1927-30.

Rourke, Constance. *American Humor: A Study of the National Character.* 1931. New York: Harcourt Brace, 1959.

Smith, Bernard. *Forces in American Criticism: A Study in the History of American Literary Thought.* New York: Harcourt Brace, 1939.

Wilson, Edmund. *A Literary Chronicle: 1920-1950.* New York: Doubleday, 1952.

Wright, Richard. *Twelve Million Black Voices.* 1941. New York: Arno, 1969.

Wrong, George M. *The Canadians: The Story of a People.* Toronto: Macmillan, 1938.

Selected Memoirs

Beauvoir, Simone de. *America Day by Day.* Trans. Patrick Dudley. New York: Grove, 1953.

Cowley, Malcolm. *The Dream of the Golden Mountains: Remembering the 1930's.* New York: Viking, 1980.

Crossman, R. H. S., ed. *The God That Failed.* New York: Harper, 1949.

Dos Passos, John. *The Best Times: An Informal Memoir.* New York: New American Library, 1966.

————. *Occasions and Protests.* Chicago: H. Regnery, 1964.

Freeman, Joseph. *American Testament.* New York: Farrar & Rinehart, 1936.

Guthrie, Woody. *Bound for Glory.* New York: Dutton, 1943.

Kazin, Alfred. *Starting Out in the Thirties.* New York: Vintage, 1962.

Layton, Irving, with David O'Rourke. *Waiting for the Messiah: A Memoir.* Toronto: McClelland & Stewart, 1985.

Livesay, Dorothy. *The Self-Completing Tree: A Memoir, 1909-1963.* Vancouver: Douglas & MacIntyre, 1991.

Phillips, William. *A Partisan View.* New York: Stein & Day, 1983.

Ryan, Toby. *Stage Left.* Toronto: CTR, 1981.

Simon, Rita James, ed. *As We Saw the Thirties.* Chicago: University of Illinois Press, 1967.

Wright, Richard. *American Hunger.* New York: Harper & Row, 1977.

Secondary Sources

Aaron, Daniel. *Writers on the Left.* New York: Oxford University Press, 1977.

Abella, Irving. *Nationalism, Communism, and Canadian Labour: The CIO, the Communist Party, and the Canadian Congress of Labour, 1935-1956.* Toronto: University of Toronto Press, 1973.

Aitken, Ian. *Film and Reform: John Grierson and the Documentary Film Movement.* New York: Routledge, 1990.

Akin, William. *Technocracy and the American Dream.* Berkeley: University of California Press, 1977.

Alexander, Charles C. *Nationalism in American Thought, 1930-1945.* Chicago: Rand McNally, 1969.

Anderson, Benedict. *Imagined Communities: Reflections on the Origin and Spread of Nationalism.* New York: Verso, 1991.

Anderson, Perry. *Considerations on Western Marxism.* New York: New Left Books, 1976.

Appelhof, Ruth Stephens, ed. *The Expressionist Landscape: North American Modernist Painting, 1920–1947.* Birmingham: Birmingham Museum of Art, 1988.

Arac, Jonathan. "Authorizing an American Renaissance." *The American Renaissance Reconsidered.* Ed. Walter Benn Michaels. Baltimore: Johns Hopkins University Press, 1985. 90–112.

Arendt, Hannah. *The Origins of Totalitarianism.* New York: Harcourt, Brace, 1951.

Atwood, Margaret. *Survival.* Toronto: Anansi, 1972.

Auerbach, Erich. *Mimesis.* Princeton: Princeton University Press, 1953.

Avery, Donald. *"Dangerous Foreigners": European Immigrant Workers and Labour Radicals in Canada, 1896–1932.* Toronto: McClelland & Stewart, 1979.

Baldwin, James. *Notes of a Native Son.* Boston: Beacon, 1955.

Barnard, Rita. "The Great Depression and the Culture of Abundance: Literature and Mass Culture in the 1930s." Ph.D. diss., Duke University, 1989.

Beach, Joseph Warren. *American Fiction, 1920–1940.* 1941. New York: Atheneum, 1972.

Bercovitch, Sacvan. "Investigations of an Americanist." *Journal of American History.* 78 (1991): 972–87.

Bercovitch, Sacvan, and Myra Jehlen, eds. *Ideology and Classic American Literature.* New York: Cambridge University Press, 1986.

Bergman, David. "F. O. Matthiessen: The Critic as Homosexual." *Raritan* 7.4 (1990): 62–82.

Betcherman, Lita-Rose. *The Swastika and the Maple Leaf: Fascist Movements in Canada in the Thirties.* Toronto: Fitzhenry & Whiteside, 1975.

Bhabha, Homi, ed. *Nations and Narration.* New York: Routledge, 1990.

Bisztray, George. *Marxist Models of Literary Realism.* New York: Columbia University Press, 1978.

Bloom, Harold, ed. *Bigger Thomas.* New York: Chelsea, 1990.

Bloom, James D. *Left Letters: The Culture Wars of Mike Gold and Joseph Freeman.* New York: Columbia University Press, 1992.

Bogardus, Ralph, ed. *Literature at the Barricades.* Tuscaloosa: University of Alabama Press, 1982.

Bone, Robert A. *The Negro Novel in America.* New Haven: Yale University Press, 1965.

Bonner, Mary Graham. *Canada and Her Story.* New York: Knopf, 1942.

Bothwell, Robert. *A Short History of Ontario.* Edmonton: Hurtig, 1986.

Bowman, John Scott. "The Proletarian Novel in America." Ph.D. diss., Pennsylvania State University, 1939.

Breton, Raymond et al. *Ethnic Identity and Equality: Varieties of Experience in a Canadian City.* Toronto: University of Toronto Press, 1990.

Brinkley, Alan. *Voices of Protest: Huey Long, Father Coughlin and the Great Depression.* New York: Vintage, 1982.

Bronner, Simon J. *American Folklore Studies: An Intellectual History.* Lawrence: University of Kansas Press, 1986.

Brown, George W. *Building the Canadian Nation.* Toronto: Dent, 1942.

Buhle, Paul. *Marxism in the United States: Remapping the History of the American Left.* New York: Verso, 1987.

Bürger, Peter. *Theory of the Avant-Garde.* Trans. Michael Shaw. Minneapolis: University of Minnesota Press, 1984.

Butcher, Margaret Just. *The Negro in American Culture.* New York: Knopf, 1956.

Butler, Robert James. "The American Quest for Pure Movement in Dos Passos's *U.S.A.*" *Twentieth-Century Literature* 30 (spring 1984): 80–99.

———. "The Function of Violence in Richard Wright's *Native Son.*" *Black American Literature Forum* 20 (1986): 9–26.

Cagnon, Maurice. *The French Novel of Quebec.* Boston: Twayne, 1986.

Cain, William E. *F. O. Matthiessen and the Politics of Criticism.* Madison: University of Wisconsin Press, 1988.

Cameron, Elspeth. *Hugh MacLennan: A Writer's Life.* Toronto: University of Toronto Press, 1981.

Cameron, Sharon. *Lyric Time: Dickinson and the Limits of Genre.* Baltimore: Johns Hopkins University Press, 1979.

Cappon, Paul, ed. *In Our Own House: Social Perspectives in Canadian Literature.* Toronto: McClelland & Stewart, 1978.

Carafiol, Peter. *An American Ideal.* New York: Oxford University Press, 1991.

Carroll, Peter N. *The Odyssey of the Abraham Lincoln Brigade: Americans in the Spanish Civil War.* Stanford: Stanford University Press, 1994.

Ceplair, Larry. *Under the Shadow of War: Fascism, Anti-Fascism and Marxists, 1918–1939.* New York: Columbia University Press, 1987.

Clark, Katerina. *The Soviet Novel: History as Ritual.* Chicago: University of Chicago Press, 1981.

Clark, T. J. "Clement Greenberg's Theory of Art." *Critical Inquiry* 9 (1982): 139–56.

Clifford, James. "Traveling Cultures." *Cultural Studies.* Ed. Lawrence Grossberg et al. New York: Routledge, 1992. 96–116.

Cohen, Robert. *When the Old Left Was Young: Student Radicals and America's First Mass Student Movement, 1929–1941.* New York: Oxford University Press, 1993.

Colombo, John Robert. *1001 Questions about Canada.* Toronto: Doubleday, 1986.

Conway, Jill Ker. *The Road from Coorain.* New York: Knopf, 1989.

Cooley, Dennis. *The Vernacular Muse.* Canada: Turnstone, 1987.

Cowan, Ann Stephenson. "*The Canadian Forum,* 1920–1950." Ph.D. diss., Carleton University, 1974.

Cruse, Harold. *The Crisis of the Negro Intellectual.* New York: Morrow, 1967.

Davey, Frank. *Post-National Arguments: The Politics of the Anglophone-Canadian Novel Since 1967.* Toronto: University of Toronto Press, 1993.

Decker, Jeffrey Louis. "Disassembling the Machine in the Garden: Anti-Humanism and the Critique of American Studies." *New Literary History* 23 (spring 1992): 281–306.

Delisle, Esther. *The Traitor and the Jew: Anti-Semitism and Extremist Right-Wing Nationalism in Quebec from 1929 to 1939.* Trans. Madeleine Hébert. Montreal: Robert Davies, 1993.

Denisoff, R. Serge. *Great Day Coming: Folk Music and the American Left.* Chicago: University of Illinois Press, 1971.

Denning, Michael. *The Cultural Front: The Laboring of American Culture in the Twentieth Century.* New York: Verso, 1996.

———. *Mechanic Accents: Dime Novels and Working-Class Culture in America.* New York: Verso, 1987.

———. " 'The Special American Conditions': Marxism and American Studies." *American Quarterly* 38 (1986): 356–80.

Dimock, Wai-chee, and Michael T. Gilmore, ed. *Rethinking Class: Literary Studies and Social Formations.* New York: Columbia University Press, 1994.

Dolan, Marc. "The 'Wholeness' of the Whale: Melville, Matthiessen, and the Semiotics of Critical Revisionism." *Arizona Quarterly* 48.3 (1992): 27–58.

Dorsey, Lindsay, et al., eds. *A Public and Private Voice: Essays on the Life and Work of Dorothy Livesay.* Waterloo, ON: University of Waterloo Press, 1986.

Draper, Theodore. *American Communism and Soviet Russia.* New York: Vintage, 1960.

Fabre, Michel. *The Unfinished Quest of Richard Wright.* New York: Morrow, 1973.

Farber, Samuel. *Before Stalinism.* New York: Verso, 1990.

Faue, Elizabeth. *Community of Suffering and Struggle.* Chapel Hill: University of North Carolina Press, 1991.

Fiedler, Leslie. *Love and Death in the American Novel.* New York: Stein & Day, 1966.

———. *What Was Literature? Class Culture and Mass Society.* New York: Touchstone, 1982.

Fischer, Adam Jacob. "Formula for Utopia: The American Proletarian Novel, 1930–1939." Ph.D. diss., University of Massachusetts, 1973.

Fogel, Stanley. *A Tale of Two Countries: Contemporary Fiction in English Canada and the United States.* Toronto: ECW, 1984.

Foley, Barbara. "The Politics of Poetics: Ideology and Narrative Form in *An American Tragedy.*" *Narrative Poetics: Innovations, Limits, Challenges.* Ed. James Phelan. Columbus: Ohio State University Press, 1987. 55–67.

———. *Radical Representations: Politics and Form in U.S. Proletarian Fiction, 1929–1941.* Durham, NC: Duke University Press, 1993.

———. "The Treatment of Time in *The Big Money:* An Examination of Ideology and Literary Form." *Modern Fiction Studies* 26 (autumn 1980): 447–69.

———. "Women and the Left in the 1930s." *American Literary History* 2.1 (spring 1990): 150–69.

Fournier, Louis. *FLQ: The Anatomy of an Underground Movement.* Toronto: NC, 1984.

Francis, D., and H. Ganzevoort, eds. *The Dirty Thirties in Prairie Canada.* Vancouver: Tantalus, 1980.

Francis, R. Douglas. *Images of the West: Responses to the Canadian Prairies.* Saskatoon: Western Producer Prairie Books, 1989.

Friesen, Gerald. *The Canadian Prairies.* Lincoln: University of Nebraska Press, 1984.

Frye, Northrop. *The Bush Garden: Essays on the Canadian Imagination.* Toronto: Anansi, 1971.

Fullinwider, S. P. *The Mind and Mood of Black America: Twentieth-Century Thought.* Homewood, IL: Dorsey, 1969.

Gallagher, Tag. *John Ford: The Man and His Films.* Berkeley: University of California Press, 1986.

Garrison, Dee. *Mary Heaton Vorse: The Life of an American Insurgent.* Philadelphia: Temple University Press, 1989.

Getty, J. Arch. *Origins of the Great Purges: The Soviet Communist Party Reconsidered, 1933–38.* New York: Cambridge University Press, 1985.

Gibbon, John Murray. *Canadian Mosaic: The Making of a Northern Nation.* Toronto: McClelland & Stewart, 1938.

Gilbert, James. *Writers and Partisans: A History of Literary Radicalism in America.* New York: Columbia University Press, 1968.

Gilroy, Paul. *The Black Atlantic.* Cambridge: Harvard University Press, 1994.

Gitlin, Todd. *The Whole World Is Watching: Mass Media in the Making and Unmaking of the New Left.* Berkeley: University of California Press, 1980.

Goetsch, Paul, ed. *Hugh MacLennan.* Toronto: McGraw-Hill, 1973.

Goldstein, Lawrence. *The Flying Machine and Modern Literature.* Bloomington: Indiana University Press, 1986.

Goodwin, James. *Eisenstein, Cinema and History.* Urbana: University of Illinois Press, 1993.

Gorman, Paul R. *Left Intellectuals and Popular Culture in Twentieth-Century America.* Chapel Hill: University of North Carolina Press, 1996.

Gornick, Vivian. *The Romance of American Communism.* New York: Basic, 1977.

Graff, Gerald. *Professing Literature: An Institutional History.* Chicago: University of Chicago Press, 1987.

Gramsci, Antonio. *The Modern Prince and Other Writings.* New York: International Publishers, 1957.

Granatstein, J. L., and J. M. Hitsman. *Broken Promises: A History of Conscription in Canada.* Toronto: Oxford University Press, 1977.

Granatstein, J. L., and David Stafford. *Spy Wars: Espionage and Canada from Gouzenko to Glasnost.* Toronto: Key Porter, 1990.

Gregory, James N. *American Exodus: The Dust Bowl Migration and Okie Culture in California.* New York: Oxford University Press, 1989.

Greenhill, Pauline. *Ethnicity in the Mainstream: Three Studies of English Canadian Culture in Ontario.* Montreal: McGill-Queens University Press, 1994.

Gross, Barry. "'Intellectual Overlordship': Blacks, Jews and *Native Son.*" *Journal of Ethnic Studies* 5 (1977): 51–59.

Gunn, Giles B. *F. O. Matthiessen: The Critical Achievement.* Seattle: University of Washington Press, 1975.

Hakutani, Yoshinobu, ed. *Critical Essays on Richard Wright.* Boston: G. K. Hall, 1982.

Hampton, Wayne. *Guerilla Minstrels: John Lennon, Joe Hill, Woody Guthrie, Bob Dylan.* Knoxville: University of Tennessee Press, 1986.

Hapke, Laura. *Daughters of the Depression: Women, Work, and Fiction in the American 1930s.* Athens: University of Georgia Press, 1996.

Harper, J. Russell. *Painting in Canada: A History.* Toronto: University of Toronto Press, 1966.

Harvey, David D. *Americans in Canada: Migration and Settlement.* Lewiston, NY: E. Mellen Press, 1991.

Haugh, Robert F. "Sentimentalism in the American Proletarian Novel." Ph.D. diss., University of Michigan, 1947.

Hobsbawm, Eric. *Nations and Nationalism Since 1789: Programme, Myth, Reality.* New York: Cambridge University Press, 1990.

Hoffman, Frederick J., et al. *The Little Magazine: A History and a Bibliography.* Princeton: Princeton University Press, 1946.

Hofstadter, Richard. *The Progressive Historians: Turner, Beard, Parrington.* New York: Knopf, 1968.

Horn, Michiel. *The Dirty Thirties: Canadians in the Great Depression.* Toronto: Copp Clark, 1972.

———. *The League for Social Reconstruction: Intellectual Origins of the Democratic Left in Canada, 1930-42.* Toronto: University of Toronto Press, 1980.

Hosking, Geoffrey. *The First Socialist Society: A History of the Soviet Union from Within.* Cambridge: Harvard University Press, 1990.

Hungerford, Lynda. "Dialect Representation in *Native Son.*" *Language and Style* 20 (1987): 3-15.

Hunkin, Harry. *A Story of the Group of Seven.* Toronto: McGraw-Hill, 1976.

Huyssen, Andreas. "Mass Culture as Woman: Modernism's Other." *Studies in Entertainment: Critical Approaches to Mass Culture.* Ed. Tania Modeleski. Bloomington: Indiana University Press, 1986. 188-207.

Hyman, Roger Leslie. "Wasted Heritage and *Waste Heritage.*" *Journal of Canadian Studies* 17 (1982): 74-87.

Hynes, Samuel. *The Auden Generation: Literature and Politics in England in the 1930s.* Toronto: Bodley Head, 1976.

Irving, John, ed. *Mass Media in Canada.* Toronto: Ryerson, 1962.

Isserman, Maurice. *If I Had a Hammer: The Death of the Old Left and the Birth of the New Left.* New York: Basic, 1987.

———. *Which Side Were You On? The American Communist Party During the Second World War.* Middletown, CT: Wesleyan University Press, 1982.

Jackson, Kenneth T. *Crabgrass Frontier: The Suburbanization of the United States.* New York: Oxford University Press, 1985.

James, C. Vaughn. *Soviet Socialist Realism: Origins and Theory.* New York: St. Martin's, 1973.

Jameson, Fredric. *Late Marxism: Adorno, or the Persistence of the Dialectic.* New York: Verso, 1990.

———. *The Political Unconscious.* Ithaca: Cornell University Press, 1981.

———. *Postmodernism, or, The Cultural Logic of Late Capitalism.* Durham, NC: Duke University Press, 1991.

Kammen, Michael. "The Problem of American Exceptionalism: A Reconsideration." *American Quarterly* 45 (March 1993): 1-43.

Kane, Joseph. *Famous First Facts: A Record of First Happenings, Discoveries, and Inventions in American History.* New York: H. M. Wilson, 1981.

Kaplan, Amy, and Donald E. Pease, eds. *Cultures of United States Imperialism.* Durham, NC: Duke University Press, 1994.

Kelley, Robin D. G. " 'Comrades, Praise Gawd for Lenin and Them!': Ideology and Culture among Black Communists in Alabama, 1930-1935." *Science and Society* 52 (1988): 59-82.

————. *Hammer and Hoe: Alabama Communists during the Great Depression.* Chapel Hill: University of North Carolina Press, 1990.

Kerr, Donald, and Deryck W. Holdsworth, eds. *Historical Atlas of Canada.* Toronto: University of Toronto Press, 1990.

Kilson, Martin. "Politics and Identity among Black Intellectuals." *Dissent* 28 (1981): 339–49.

King, Thomas. "Godzilla and the Post-Colonial." *World Literature Written in English* 39 (1990): 10–16.

Kinnamon, Keneth, ed. *New Essays on* Native Son. New York: Cambridge University Press, 1990.

Kitz, Janet F. *Shattered City: The Halifax Explosion and the Road to Recovery.* Halifax: Nimbus, 1989.

Klinck, Carl F., ed. *Literary History of Canada.* Toronto: University of Toronto Press, 1965.

Kolasky, John. *The Shattered Illusion: The History of Ukrainian Pro-Communist Organizations in Canada.* Toronto: Peter Martin, 1979.

Kraditor, Aileen. *"Jimmy Higgins": The Mental World of the Rank-and-File Communist, 1930–1958.* New York: Greenwood, 1988.

Kutulas, Judy. *The Long War: The Intellectual People's Front and Anti-Stalinism, 1930–1940.* Durham, NC: Duke University Press, 1996.

Langer, Elinor. *Josephine Herbst: The Story She Could Never Tell.* New York: Warner, 1983.

Leacock, Stephen. *Canada: The Foundations of Its Future.* Montreal: Gazette, 1941.

Lecker, Robin, ed. *Canadian Canons: Essays in Literary Value.* Toronto: University of Toronto Press, 1991.

Leitch, Vincent. *American Literary Criticism from the 30's to the 80's.* New York: Columbia University Press, 1988.

Lentricchia, Frank. *Criticism and Social Change.* Chicago: University of Chicago Press, 1983.

Lieberman, Robbie. *"My Song Is My Weapon": People's Songs, American Communism, and the Politics of Culture, 1930–1950.* Chicago: University of Illinois Press, 1989.

Light, James F. "Varieties of Satire in the Art of Nathanael West." *Modern Critical Views: Nathanael West.* Ed. Harold Bloom. New York: Chelsea House, 1986. 129–44.

Litt, Paul. *The Muses, the Masses and the Massey Commission.* Toronto: University of Toronto Press, 1992.

Litvak, Isaiah, and Christopher Maule. *Cultural Sovereignty: The* Time *and* Reader's Digest *Case in Canada.* New York: Praeger, 1974.

Litz, Gordon A., ed. *Modern American Fiction: Essays in Criticism.* New York: Oxford University Press, 1963.

Livesay, Dorothy. "The Documentary Poem: A Canadian Genre." In *Contexts of Canadian Criticism.* Ed. Eli Mandel. Chicago: University of Chicago Press, 1971. 267–82.

Long, Robert Emmett. *Nathanael West.* New York: Frederick Unger, 1985.

Long, Terry. *Granville Hicks.* Boston: Twayne, 1981.

Louchheim, Katie, ed. *The Making of the New Deal: The Insiders Speak.* Cambridge: Harvard University Press, 1983.

Luciuk, Lubonyr, and Stella Hryniuk, eds. *Canada's Ukrainians: Negotiating an Identity.* Toronto: University of Toronto Press, 1991.

Ludington, Townsend. *John Dos Passos: A Twentieth-Century Odyssey.* New York: Dutton, 1980.

Lukács, Georg. *Essays on Realism.* Ed. David Fernbach. Cambridge: MIT Press, 1980.

MacDonald, Thoreau. *The Group of Seven.* Toronto: Ryerson, 1944.

Maclulich, T. D. *Between Europe and America: The Canadian Tradition in Fiction.* Toronto: ECW, 1988.

———. *Hugh MacLennan.* Boston: Twayne, 1983.

Macpherson, C. B. *Democracy in Alberta: Social Credit and the Party System.* Toronto: University of Toronto Press, 1962.

Madden, David, ed. *Proletarian Writers of the Thirties.* Carbondale: Southern Illinois University Press, 1968.

Mally, Lynn. *Culture of the Future.* Berkeley: University of California Press, 1990.

Mandel, Eli, ed. *Contexts in Canadian Criticism.* Chicago: University of Chicago Press, 1971.

Mandel, Ernest. *Late Capitalism.* New York: Verso, 1975.

Marcus, Alan I., and Howard P. Segal. *Technology in America: A Brief History.* New York: Harcourt Brace, 1989.

Marcuse, Herbert. *The Aesthetic Dimension.* Boston: Beacon, 1977.

———. *Soviet Marxism.* New York: Vintage, 1961.

Margolies, Edward. "*Native Son* and Three Kinds of Revolution." *Bigger Thomas.* Ed. Harold Bloom. New York: Chelsea, 1990. 43–53.

Marquis, Alice G. *Hopes and Ashes: The Birth of Modern Times, 1929–1939.* New York: Free Press, 1986.

Martin, Jay. *Nathanael West: The Art of His Life.* New York: Farrar, Straus & Giroux, 1970.

Marx, Leo. "Double Consciousness and the Cultural Politics of F. O. Matthiessen." *Monthly Review* 39 (1983): 34–56.

———. *The Pilot and the Passenger: Essays on Literature, Technology and Culture in the United States.* New York: Oxford University Press, 1988.

Massey, Irving. *Identity and Community: Reflections on English, Yiddish, and French Literature in Canada.* Detroit: Wayne State University Press, 1994.

Mathews, Robin. *Canadian Identity: Major Forces Shaping the Life of a People.* Ottawa: Steel Rail, 1988.

Mayes, Herbert. *Alger: A Biography without a Hero.* New York: Macy-Masius, 1928.

McCarthy, Dermot. "Early Canadian Literary Histories and the Function of a Canon." *Canadian Canons: Essays in Literary Value.* Ed. Robin Lecker. Toronto: University of Toronto Press, 1991. 30–45.

McDougall, Robert L. "The Dodo and the Cruising Auk: Class in Canadian Literature." *Canadian Literature* (1963): 6–20.

McElvaine, Robert. *The Great Depression: America, 1929–1941.* New York: New York Times Books, 1984. Rev. 1993.

McLellan, David, ed. *Marxism: Essential Writings.* New York: Oxford University Press, 1988.

McLuhan, Marshall. "Canada: The Borderline Case." *The Canadian Imagination: Dimensions of a Literary Culture.* Ed. David Staines. Cambridge: Harvard University Press, 1977. 226–48.

————. "John Dos Passos: Technique vs. Sensibility." *Modern American Fiction: Essays in Criticism.* Ed. A. Walton Litz. New York: Oxford University Press, 1963. 138–49.

McNaught, Kenneth. *The Penguin History of Canada.* New York: Penguin, 1988.

————. "Socialism and the Canadian Political Tradition." *On F. R. Scott: Essays on His Contributions to Law, Literature, and Politics.* Ed. Sandra Djwa and R. St. J. MacDonald. Montreal: McGill-Queen's University Press, 1983. 89–102.

Melosh, Barbara. *Engendering Culture: Manhood and Womanhood in New Deal Public Art and Theatre.* Washington: Smithsonian, 1991.

Michaels, Walter Benn. *The Gold Standard and the Logic of Naturalism.* Berkeley: University of California Press, 1987.

————, ed. *The American Renaissance Reconsidered.* Baltimore: Johns Hopkins University Press, 1985.

Mies, Maria. *Patriarchy and Accumulation on a World Scale.* London: Zed, 1986.

Miller, D. A. *Narrative and Its Discontents.* Princeton: Princeton University Press, 1981.

Miller, Eugene. *Voice of a Native Son: The Poetics of Richard Wright.* Jackson: University of Mississippi Press, 1990.

Moon, Michael. " 'The Gentle Boy from the Dangerous Classes': Pederasty, Domesticity, and Capitalism in Horatio Alger." *Representations* 19 (1987): 87–110.

Moore, Jack B. "The Voice in *Twelve Million Black Voices." Mississippi Quarterly* 42 (1989): 415–24.

Morton, Desmond. *Working People.* Toronto: Summerhill, 1990.

Murphy, James. *The Proletarian Moment: The Controversy over Leftism in Literature.* Chicago: University of Illinois Press, 1991.

Nackenoff, Carol. "Of Factories and Failures: Exploring the Invisible Factory Gates of Horatio Alger, Jr." *Journal of Popular Culture* 25.4 (1992): 63–80.

Naison, Mark. *Communism in Harlem during the Depression.* Urbana: University of Illinois Press, 1983.

Nasgaard, Roald. *The Mystic North: Symbolist Landscape Painting in Northern Europe and North America, 1890–1940.* Toronto: University of Toronto Press, 1984.

Neatby, H. Blair. *The Politics of Chaos.* Toronto: Macmillan, 1972.

Nekola, Charlotte, and Paul Rabinowitz, eds. *Writing Red: An Anthology of American Women Writers, 1930–1940.* New York: Feminist Press, 1987.

Nelson, Cary. *Repression and Recovery: Modern American Poetry and the Politics of Cultural Memory, 1910–1945.* Madison: University of Wisconsin Press, 1989.

Neuman, Shirley. "After Modernism: English-Canadian Poetry Since 1960." *Studies on Canadian Literature: Introductory and Critical Essays.* Ed. Arnold E. Davidson. New York: MLA, 1990. 54–73.

New, W. H. *A History of Canadian Literature.* London: Macmillan, 1986.

Noble, David. *America by Design.* New York: Knopf, 1977.

Norris, Ken. *The Little Magazine in Canada, 1925–1980: Its Role in the Development of Modernism and Post-Modernism in Canadian Poetry.* Toronto: ECW, 1984.

North, Joseph, ed. New Masses: *An Anthology of the Rebel Thirties.* New York: International Publishers, 1969.

Ohmann, Richard. *Politics of Letters.* Middletown, CT: Wesleyan University Press, 1987.

Olssen, Andrée L'evesque. "The Canadian Left in Quebec During the Great Depression:

The Communist Party of Canada and the CCF in Quebec, 1929–1939." Ph.D. diss., Duke University, 1972.

Olster, Stacey. "The 'Other' in Nathanael West's Fiction: Jewish Rejection or Jewish Projection." *MELUS* 15.4 (1988): 51–65.

Panneton, Jean. *Ringuet.* Ottawa: Éditions Fides, 1970.

Patrias, Carmela. *Patriots and Proletarians: Politicizing Hungarian Immigrants in Interwar Canada.* Montreal: McGill-Queen's University Press, 1994.

Pease, Donald. "*Moby Dick* and the Cold War." *The American Renaissance Reconsidered.* Ed. Walter Benn Michaels. Baltimore: Johns Hopkins University Press, 1985. 113–155.

———. "New Americanists: Revisionist Interventions into the Canon." *boundary 2* 17 (1990): 1–37.

———. "New Americanists 2: National Identities, Postmodern Artifacts, and Postnational Narratives." *boundary 2* 19 (1992): 1–13.

Pells, Richard H. *The Liberal Mind in a Conservative Age: American Intellectuals in the 1940s and 1950s.* Middletown, CT: Wesleyan University Press, 1989.

Peterson, Theodore. *Magazines in the Twentieth Century.* Urbana: University of Illinois Press, 1956.

Petersen, William, Michael Novak, and Philip Gleason, eds. *Concepts of Ethnicity.* Cambridge: Harvard University Press, 1982.

Phillips, Donna, ed. *Voices of Discord.* Toronto: New Hogtown, 1979.

Pizer, Donald. "The Camera Eye in *U.S.A.:* The Sexual Center." *Modern Fiction Studies* 26 (autumn 1980): 417–30.

Ponton, Geoffrey. *The Soviet Era: Soviet Politics from Lenin to Yeltsin.* Cambridge: Blackwell, 1994.

Portelli, Alessandro. *The Death of Luigi Trastulli and Other Stories: Form and Meaning in Oral History.* Albany: State University of New York Press, 1991.

Prang, Margaret. "Some Opinions of Political Radicalism in Canada between the Two World Wars." Ph.D. diss., University of Toronto, 1953.

Pratt, Mary Louise. *Imperial Eyes: Travel Writing and Transculturation.* New York: Routledge, 1992.

Pudaloff, Ross. "Celebrity as Identity: Richard Wright, *Native Son,* and Mass Culture." *Studies in American Fiction* 11 (1983): 3–18.

Rabinowitz, Paula. "Ending Difference/Different Endings: Class, Closure, and Collectivity in Women's Proletarian Fiction." *Genders* 8 (summer 1990): 62–77.

———. *Labor and Desire: Women's Revolutionary Fiction in Depression America.* Chapel Hill: University of North Carolina Press, 1991.

Radway, Janice. "The Scandal of the Middlebrow: The Book-of-the-Month Club, Class Fracture, and Cultural Authority." *South Atlantic Quarterly* 89 (fall 1990): 703–36.

Rahv, Philip. *Literature and Sixth Sense.* New York: Houghton Mifflin, 1969.

Rashley, R. E. *Poetry in Canada: The First Three Steps.* Toronto: Ryerson, 1958.

Redden, Dorothy S. "Richard Wright and *Native Son:* Not Guilty." *Bigger Thomas.* Ed. Harold Bloom. New York: Chelsea, 1990. 73–82.

Reepre-Bordessa, Mari. *Hugh MacLennan's National Trilogy: Mapping a Canadian Identity (1940–1950).* Helsinki: Academia Scientiarium Femmica, 1990.

Reid, Dennis. *Le Groupe des sept/The Group of Seven.* Ottawa: National Gallery of Art, 1970.

Reid, Randall. *The Fiction of Nathanael West: No Redeemer, No Promised Land.* Chicago: University of Chicago Press, 1967.

Reid, W. Stanford, ed. *The Scottish Tradition in Canada.* Toronto: McClelland & Stewart, 1976.

Reilly, John M. "Giving Bigger a Voice: The Politics of Narrative in *Native Son.*" *New Essays on* Native Son. Ed. Keneth Kinnamon. New York: Cambridge University Press, 1990. 35–62.

Repka, William, and Kathleen M. Repka. *Dangerous Patriots: Canada's Unknown Prisoners of War.* Vancouver: New Star, 1982.

Richter, David H. "The Reader as Ironic Victim." *Novel* 14 (1981): 135–51.

Rideout, Walter. *The Radical Novel in the United States, 1900–1954.* Cambridge: Harvard University Press, 1956.

Robin, Martin. *Shades of Right: Nativist and Fascist Politics in Canada, 1920–1940.* Toronto: University of Toronto Press, 1992.

Robin, Régine. *Socialist Realism: An Impossible Aesthetic.* Trans. Catherine Porter. Stanford: Stanford University Press, 1992.

Ross, Andrew. *No Respect: Intellectuals and Popular Culture.* New York: Routledge, 1989.

Rostovtzeff, Mikhail. *The Social and Economic History of the Roman Empire.* Trans. P. M. Fraser. 1926. London: Oxford University Press, 1963.

Rubin, Joan Shelley. *The Making of Middlebrow Culture.* Chapel Hill: University of North Carolina Press, 1992.

Rutherford, Paul. *The Making of the Canadian Media.* Toronto: McGraw-Hill, Ryerson, 1978.

Salzman, Jack, ed. *Social Poetry of the Thirties.* New York: B. Franklin, 1978.

———, ed. *Years of Protest: A Collection of American Writings of the 1930s.* New York: Pegasus, 1967.

Sanders, David, ed. *The Merrill Studies in* U.S.A. Columbus, OH: Merrill, 1972.

Sartre, Jean-Paul. "John Dos Passos and '1919.'" *Merrill Studies in* U.S.A. Ed. David Sanders. Columbus, OH: Merrill, 1972. 30–37.

Scharnhorst, Gary. "From Rags to Patches, or *A Cool Million* as Alter-Alger." *Ball State University Forum* 21 (autumn 1980): 58–65.

Scharnhorst, Gary, and Jack Bales. *Horatio Alger, Jr.: An Annotated Bibliography of Comment and Criticism.* Metuchen: Scarecrow, 1981.

———. *The Lost Life of Horatio Alger, Jr.* Bloomington: Indiana University Press, 1985.

Schrecker, Ellen, ed. *The Age of McCarthyism: A Brief History with Documents.* Boston: Bedford, 1994.

Schulz, Dieter. "Nathanael West's *A Cool Million* and the Myth of Success." *Studien zur englishchen und amerikanischen Prosa nach dem ersten Weltkrieg.* Darmstadt: Buchgesellschaft, 1986. 164–75.

Schwartz, Lawrence. *Marxism and Culture: The CPUSA and Aesthetics in the 1930s.* Port Washington, NY: Kennikat, 1980.

Scott, Peter Dale. "The Difference Perspective Makes: Literary Studies in Canada and the United States." *Essays on Canadian Writing* 49 (fall 1991): 1–60.

Shek, Ben-Zion. *Social Realism in the French-Canadian Novel.* Montreal: Harvest, 1977.

Singh, Narindar. *Canadian Sikhs: History, Religion and Culture of Sikhs in North America.* Ottawa: Canadian Sikh's Studies, 1994.

Slade, Joseph W. "Hart Crane and John Dos Passos." *American Literature and Science.* Ed. Robert J. Scholnick. Lexington: University of Kentucky Press, 1992. 172–93.

Soja, Edward W. *Postmodern Geographies: The Reassertion of Space in Critical Social Thought.* New York: Verso, 1989.

Sommer, Doris. *Foundational Fictions: The National Romances of Latin America.* Berkeley: University of California Press, 1991.

Spettigue, Douglas. *Frederick Philip Grove.* Toronto: Copp Clark, 1969.

Stacey, C. P. *A Very Double Life: The Private World of Mackenzie King.* Toronto: Macmillan, 1976.

Stafford, David. *Spy Wars: Espionage and Canada from Gouzenko to Glasnost.* Toronto: Key Porter, 1990.

Stein, Michael B. *Dynamics of Right-Wing Protest.* Toronto: University of Toronto Press, 1973.

Steinman, Lisa M. *Made in America: Science, Technology and American Modernist Poets.* New Haven: Yale University Press, 1987.

Stevens, Peter. "The Development of Canadian Poetry between the Wars and Its Reflection of Social Awareness." Ph.D. diss., University of Saskatchewan, 1969.

———. "Out of the Silence and across the Distance: The Poetry of Dorothy Livesay," *Queen's Quarterly* 78 (1971): 579–91.

Stott, William. *Documentary Expression and Thirties America.* New York: Oxford University Press, 1973.

Strychacz, Thomas. "Challenging Mass Culture: American Writers and Literary Authority, 1880–1940." Ph.D. diss., Princeton University, 1986.

Subtelny, Orest. *Ukrainians in North America: An Illustrated History.* Toronto: University of Toronto Press, 1991.

Suleiman, Susan. *Authoritarian Fictions: The Ideological Novel as a Literary Genre.* New York: Columbia University Press, 1983.

Susman, Warren. *Culture as History: The Transformation of American Society in the Twentieth Century.* New York: Pantheon, 1984.

Sutherland, Fraser. *The Monthly Epic: A History of Canadian Magazines, 1789–1989.* Markham, ON: Fitzhenry & Whiteside, 1989.

Tanner, Laura E. "The Narrative Presence in *Native Son.*" *Bigger Thomas.* Ed. Harold Bloom. New York: Chelsea, 1990. 127–42.

Teres, Harvey. "Remaking Marxist Criticism: *Partisan Review*'s Eliotic Leftism, 1934–1936." *American Literature* 64 (1992): 127–54.

Thompson, J. Lee. "A Coat of Many Cultures: The Poetry of Dorothy Livesay." *Journal of Popular Culture* 15 (1981): 53–61.

———. *Dorothy Livesay.* Boston: Twayne, 1987.

———. "Emphatically Middling: A Critical Examination of Canadian Poetry in the Great Depression." Ph.D. diss., Queen's University, 1975.

Thompson, John H. *The United States and Canada: Ambivalent Allies.* Athens: University of Georgia Press, 1994.

Thompson, John Herd, with Allen Seager. *Canada 1922–1939: Decades of Discord.* Toronto: McClelland & Stewart, 1985.

Tichi, Cecilia. *Shifting Gears: Technology and Culture in Modernist America.* Chapel Hill: University of North Carolina Press, 1987.

Tiessen, H. F., and P. Tiessen. "Dorothy Livesay's Louis Riel: The Unpublished Radio Plays." Department of English Research Paper Series No. 87104. Wilfrid Laurier University. n.d.

Tippett, Maria. *Making Culture: English-Canadian Institutions and the Arts before the Massey Commission.* Toronto: University of Toronto Press, 1990.

Tompkins, Jane. *Sensational Designs: The Cultural Work of American Fiction, 1790–1860.* New York: Oxford University Press, 1985.

Trilling, Lionel. *The Liberal Imagination.* Garden City, NY: Doubleday, 1953.

Tucker, Robert C., ed. *The Marx-Engels Reader.* New York: Norton, 1978.

Urgo, Joseph R. "Proletarian Literature and Feminism: The Gastonia Novels and Feminist Protest." *Minnesota Review* 24 (spring 1985): 64–84.

Virilio, Paul. *Speed and Politics.* 1977. New York: semiotext(e), 1986.

Wald, Alan. *The New York Intellectuals: The Rise and Decline of the Anti-Stalinist Left from the 1930s to the 1980s.* Chapel Hill: University of North Carolina Press, 1989.

———. *The Responsibility of Intellectuals: Selected Essays on Marxist Traditions in Cultural Commitment.* New Jersey: Humanities, 1992.

———. *The Revolutionary Imagination: The Poetry and Politics of John Wheelwright and Sherry Mangan.* Chapel Hill: University of North Carolina Press, 1983.

———. "The Subaltern Speaks." *Monthly Review* 43.11 (1992): 17–29.

Wallerstein, Immanuel. *The Modern World System.* New York: Academic, 1974.

Weeks, Robert P. "The Novel as Poem: Whitman's Legacy to Dos Passos." *Modern Fiction Studies* 26 (1976): 431–46.

Whisnant, David. *All That Is Native and Fine: The Politics of Culture in an American Region.* Chapel Hill: University of North Carolina Press, 1983.

Wilcox, Leonard. *V. F. Calverton: Radical in the American Grain.* Philadelphia: Temple University Press, 1992.

Williams, Raymond. *Marxism and Literature.* New York: Oxford University Press, 1977.

Wilson, Edmund. *O, Canada: An American's Notes on Canadian Culture.* New York: Farrar, Straus & Giroux, 1964.

Winks, Robin W. *The Blacks in Canada: A History.* New Haven: Yale University Press, 1971.

Woodcock, George. *Introducing Hugh MacLennan's* Barometer Rising. Toronto: ECW, 1989.

Young, Brian, and John A. Dickinson. *A Short History of Quebec: A Socio-Economic Perspective.* Toronto: Copp Clark, 1988.

Young-Bruehl, Elizabeth. *Hannah Arendt: For Love of the World.* New Haven: Yale University Press, 1982.

Zinovich, Jordan, ed. *canadas.* New York: semiotext(e), 1994.

INDEX

Caren Irr is Assistant Professor of English and American Studies at
Pennsylvania State University.

Library of Congress Cataloging-in-Publication Data
Irr, Caren.
The suburb of dissent : cultural politics in the United States and
Canada during the 1930s / by Caren Irr.
p.   cm. — (New Americanists)
Includes bibliographical references and index.
ISBN 0-8223-2176-9 (alk. paper). — ISBN 0-8223-2192-0 (pbk. : alk.
paper)
1. American literature—20th century—History and criticism.
2. Communism and literature—United States—History—20th
century.   3. Culture—Political aspects—United States—History—
20th century.   4. Culture—Political aspects—Canada—History—
20th century.   5. Canadian literature—20th century—History and
criticism.   6. Communism and literature—Canada—History—20th
century.   7. United States—Intellectual life—20th century.
8. Canada—Intellectual life—20th century.   9. Working class in
literature.   I. Title.   II. Series.
PS228.C6I77   1998
810.9'358—DC21   97-42958